The Noiseless Tenor

The Noiseless Tenor

The Bicycle in Literature

Edited and with introductions by James E. Starrs

Illustrations by Kevin Schaeffer

New York ● Cornwall Books ● London

Cornwall Books
4 Cornwall Drive
East Brunswick, New Jersey 08816

Cornwall Books
27 Chancery Lane
London WC2A 1NS, England

Cornwall Books
Toronto M5E 1A7, Canada

Library of Congress Cataloging in Publication Data
Main entry under title:

The Noiseless tenor.

   Bibliography: p.
   1. Cycling—Literary collections.   2. Literature,
Modern.   I. Starrs, James E.
PN6071.C95N6   1982   808.8'0356   81-67758
ISBN 0-8453-4736-5   AACR2

Printed in the United States of America

To the Starrs family bicyclists: From Nicky to Siobhán

Contents

Part V: Not Just Ordinary Humor

Part VI: Bang of the Last Lap Bell

Part VII: No Flying Creature

Foreword
by William Saroyan

The bicycle is the noblest invention of mankind.

Who says so? I say so, and my saying so is serious, silly, and final, for that is the law of sayings. Somebody says something, and the saying is passed from person to person like a dollar from hand to hand or a woman from man to man, as the famous song goes.

Sayings have always been preposterous and, if not irrelevant, certainly useless: A rolling stone gathers no moss. (Anonymous.) Roll out the barrel, we'll have a barrel of fun. Who said that? Also Anonymous, or at any rate Anonymous enough, for the writer of the words to that famous beer-drinking song surely heard somebody say the saying. When the roll is called up yonder. Well, that's another order of roll entirely, but the irrelevance of the saying shares with the other rolls their deepest and best connection to the human experience.

I love the bicycle. I always have. I can think of no sincere, decent human being, male or female, young or old, saintly or sinful, who can resist the bicycle.

Captain Boyle asked his pal, Joxer, in that sweet play of Dublin early in this century: "What is the moon? What is the stars?" Any question that is so wildly, so innocently, so rhetorically pert is more meaningful than any answer, or any attempt at an answer. But of course 88 billion light-years of answers in books and talk have accumulated every day among the living in the form of *attempted* answers. And of course every answer is mistaken, if now and then nicely so, as for instance when the singer says he knows Jesus loves him because the Bible tells him so. The fact is, before the Bible told him so, or told him *anything*, he had experienced the unstoppable light and warmth of the sun telling him so.

When the Englishman Stuart Leslie, the songwriter, gone to Alabama, also early in the century, rejoices that *he knows* black Lily of Laguna loves him, he is loudly asked by the world, by skeptics, by science, by allegory: How do you know? And instantly replies: Because she says so.

What is the bicycle? Well, like coins of money (but perhaps unlike paper of money, which connects essentially to conspiracy—to defraud the working class, if you will not mind too much, and there is *that* class, and the majority of the people of the world

11

belong to it) like coins of money, the bicycle is something to every person. Something *else*, that is. To me it is, for starters, movement, music, departure, arrival, design, poetry, art, health, fun. But most of all, it is this incredible machine that involves two wheels, a pipe frame, handlebars, seat, hangar (if that's the spelling of the word), pedals, and chain. You get on this simple machine, you hold the handlebars, you press down on the pedals with your feet, and you *go*. That's what you do, and to a boy of eight or nine, going is the thing, going is *living*. It is experience, art, observation. It is even religion, even if you are an atheist or think you are. As for myself, I have never had any impulse to confine myself to any such theory of disbelief. I am a believer, and my faith is enlarged by the awesome reality of the bicycle, and by the meaning of ownership and usage of the contraption, or marvel. The bicycle has a fork to hold the front wheel, and I like *that* fact, too.

My brother Henry and I had one bike between us in Fresno at 2226 San Benito Street in 1919. We got into a dispute about its ownership and proper usage. Suddenly, in the tradition of brothers, Henry picked up the notched metal wheel upon which the chain works, and with all his might directed it at my head. The wheel had been thrown with such force that it stuck in the barn wall beside which we had been taking the bike apart for an hour or more. I did not believe that, as in pistol dueling of yore among gentlemen, he *deliberately* chose to miss my head. He threw to strike it. This realization drove me out of my head, although the head was unharmed. Henry noticed the madness, and bolted around the house.

Our mother, Takoohi, heard me shout, You tried to kill me, Henry, so I'm going to kill *you*.

She came out of the house, grabbed me, and thereby permitted Henry to hurry a mile and a half to the Public Library.

He came home about three hours later, by which time I had decided that he had thrown the weapon to miss.

If he hadn't, I wouldn't be writing this homage both to the bicycle, and to Henry, a good brother, who ever afterwards restricted his outrage to polite, reasonable talk.

Good boy, as his father, Armenak, informed him when he rode his tricycle at the age of four to fetch nails from a barrel around our house in Campbell, near San Jose, where a few years later Armenak died. As a poet and a Presbyterian preacher, without a pulpit, *he* also rode a bike, but solely for transportation, for didn't he go, at the age of thirty-six, straight out of himself? Had he loitered on his bike he would surely have escaped some of the anxieties that ruptured his appendix and brought on the peritonitis that burned him in the manner of hell-fire itself, compelling him to cry out, Takoohi, for the love of God, let me drink water. He drank his fill, even though the doctor had suggested that perhaps it might be best if he drank none at all. But by then it was too late, and Takoohi thought she saw him on the Celestial Bicycle, trying to escape from the Devil, while his real bicycle rested against the apricot tree in our backyard. (July 1911, not exactly recent, but recent enough for me not to have forgotten the telling of the tale.)

Mohammed was called the Messenger, and as I have always associated that designation with *telegraph* messengers, I have put Mohammed on a bicycle, as I myself had been for three years at the Postal Telegraph Office in Fresno, from 1921 through 1924, at which time I moved along into vineyard work, at slightly better pay—thirty cents an hour. I pruned vines with Japanese and Mexican vineyard workers, and I plowed vines and irrigated them. Whenever heavy rain prevented us from earning three dollars from dark of morning to dark of evening, I rode the wheel to an old bookshop on Mariposa Street where for a nickel I could buy many kinds of magnificent magazines. One of them was called the *Dial*, and it contained, for instance, *The Oral History of the World* by Joe Gould. Another was called *Broom*, published in 1922. It was full of all manner of new writing by all kinds of new writers, including Sherwood Anderson and the young fellow he was encouraging, William Faulkner.

Sprocket? Is that the word for the metal wheel that Henry threw at my head? Cain didn't kill Abel with a bicycle sprocket, but perhaps only because at that time the bicycle had not come to the human race. Stones had always been around, however, so poor Cain killed his brother with one of them. That which Henry did, but didn't *quite* do, so to put it, made real for me the story of Cain and Abel, which I had heard at the First Armenian Presbyterian Sunday School in the class of my father's kid brother, Mihran, surely one of many unassuming saints of the human race. Mihran never knew he was a saint, of course. Thus, his modesty was no virtue; it was a simple fact of being.

Aha, I thought when the flying sprocket missed my head, this is how it happens between brothers. And of course there are brothers *and* brothers, apart from the simple truth that all men are brothers, persecuted and penitent down the ages for their terrible but finally innocent crimes.

Mohammed was a walking Messenger. When the Moslems first saw Christian missionaries mounted upon bicycles, they stoned the gentle souls, for the contraption seemed to have come from the Devil.

Takoohi herself let me know that Turks and Kurds, our neighbors in Bitlis at the turn of the century (everything is at the turn of the century forever, isn't it?), our good friends, all of us sharing our languages and cuisine and customs, the Turks and Kurds threw stones at the missionaries, chased after them, shouting wildly, knocked them off their wheels, and beat them.

Now, what does this mean, this apparently automatic, impulsive, helpless, early resentment of the bicycle? Why wasn't the connection between a man and a bicycle pleasing to all tribes and branches of the human family? I am not thinking of the earliest bicycles, with enormous front wheels and tiny back wheels, and the rider perched away up there at the top. I am thinking of the simple, beautiful, balanced, practical, sensible bicycle we all know. The earliest bicycles were very nearly night-marish. It would be easy to understand the simultaneous disbelief and anger about its intrusion into the business of going for all of us—by foot, whether by two-footed man, or four-footed animal.

Ali, on the other hand, having appropriated the Messenger's holy name as his own first name, Muhammad Ali, that is, one of the human marvels of our age, Muhammad

Ali—spell it as you choose, it is the sound of it that we are concerned about—goes by airplane in his large pieces of going, as we all do, and walks in his smallest pieces of going.

"What is the moon? What is the stars?" We ask, and we listen to replies, but in the end we accept that which seems to our simple souls, our simple minds, our simple unaccountableness, the simple truth: *we don't know.*

Putting a walking man on the moon only compels one or another of us to write a play about this equivalent of early bicycle riding, now out into the universe, the bicycle being logically pushed ahead into the rocket, but without handlebars and seat and openness.

Lord God, the riders to the moon are prisoners of the mystery of exploding molecules, and endless locked-in systems that refuse to yield further information.

But it *was* really so. Several Americans walked on the moon. Only it wasn't really the moon at all. They landed on television, on processes of light, cameras, film, making the present instantly the past, and history.

The whole human race walked on photography, which only seemed to be the moon. It was not *altogether* unlike riding a bike to an old bookshop for some bargains in magazines. Just a little more difficult to put to use, that's all.

I own three wheels: a three-speed Raleigh, a one-speed Japanese bike called Jet Wind, and an Italian foldable bike, which can be taken in the trunk of a car to the country, for riding where a car cannot go.

I ride the Japanese wheel pretty much every day. It is a beautiful bike. It cost twenty-eight dollars about fourteen years ago, at a White Front store. I assembled it, after which Vartan Avakian, about seventy-eight these days, of the famous Avakian Brothers of Fresno, at The Broadway Cyclery, about four years later assembled the whole bike all over again, without in any way taking from the bike its connection to me, which every bike soon acquires.

What is the moon? Never mind. What is the bicycle? Well, my bike is himself (myself). I am still the Messenger in *The Human Comedy.*

Preface

Bicyclists merit the best. And why not? Bicycling is one of the most favored forms of physical exercise, second only to swimming. The bicycle provides an exemplary means of transportation, unequaled in its efficiency and its conservation of costly and unrenewable fuel. Bicycle racing, in all its forms, is a premier spectator sport for millions throughout the world. Society is singularly in debt to the bicycle, since bicycle mechanics developed the airplane as well as the automobile. And many of the world's most renowned authors have written literature about the bicycle, often of the highest caliber and in the most exalted terms. This book is the proof of this last proposition.

This anthology is more than just confirmation of the role of the bicycle as a theme in the creation of outstanding literature. It is also a collection of very readable and entertaining prose and poetry. This vintage yield of some complete and some excerpted literary works is intended for the enjoyment of the bicyclist and nonbicyclist alike.

The idea for this collection originated from my rueful recognition that there is little or no literature to delight and to relax the touring bicyclist during his or her "off-saddle" hours. Aleksandr I. Solzhenitsyn's *The Gulag Archipelago*, for example, is a superb book by a famed author, but it is hardly suitable for the after-hours reading of most touring bicyclists. It is just too hefty in weight and content for the needs of the bicyclist while on the trail. Or so I discovered in 1974, to my regret, when I carried this book by bicycle from my home in the suburbs of Washington, D.C., to the exposition in Spokane, Washington.

Serious and even ponderous texts may have a place on a bicycle tour if the book is integral to the purpose of the trip. T. E. Lawrence, better known as Lawrence of Arabia, is reported to have carried a volume of Eugène Viollet-le-Duc's now ten volume work on French architecture from the eleventh to the sixteenth century entitled *Dictionnaire raisonné de l'architecture française du onzième au seizième siècle* as he toured France by bicycle in 1906. But his tour was hardly a pleasure jaunt. On the contrary, he was bicycling to prove a scholarly point to which Viollet-le-Duc's volume was more germane. But few of us are patterned after Lawrence of Arabia. His tour was the rare exception rather than the prevailing custom, where research works are definitely déclassé as traveling companions.

Nor is Eugene Sloane's *The Complete Book of Bicycling* any improvement as recommended reading for the touring bicyclist. During my resting hours, whether bicycle camping or moteling, I am not particulary relaxed or renewed by intricate disquisitions on the art of lacing a wheel, whether two-cross or more.

Nor does the touring bicyclist want to read a catalog of helpful hints to assist him or her in catching the prevailing westerly, which is, after all, a little like seeking the Holy Grail. Guidebooks and repair manuals are for the preparatory stages of planning a tour, not for the tour itself.

Indeed, tour books are like cookbooks, to be used when in doubt. They serve a limited purpose, and their utility must be judged in that light. But this book is of an entirely different character. It caters, very simply, to the pleasure principle, according to which the reader demands entertainment. The journeyman bicyclist, it is to be hoped, will welcome it as giving him or her the opportunity to enjoy the bicycle in literature as well as on the road.

But this book is self-evidently more than just a pleasure trove of reading materials. It also serves a didactic purpose, which should, alas, not be necessary. This anthology should once and for all time put to rout the nonsense heard near and far, in private and governmental circles, that the bicycle is no more than a toy for recreational purposes. This collection, if nothing else, should persuasively establish the respectability of the bicycle as a moving force in literature as in life. It should accord a deserved dignity to the bicycle, as the bicycle has in its turn enhanced the literature of the world.

A glance at the chapter headings and the authors represented in them will reveal the extraordinary versatility of the bicycle in quickening the literary impulse. Moreover, the selections span the years from the inception of the bicycle in the 1800s to the present, proving that the bicycle is no transient phenomenon in the world of literature. Indeed, this admixture of authors from this country and afar convincingly attests to the universal as well as the timeless appeal of the bicycle.

If this selection is to be faulted, it is because the authors represented are preponderantly from countries other than the United States. In fact, the bicycle would seem to be more of a leitmotif for Irish authors than for others, that is if Shaw, Beckett, and Murdoch, Irishers by birth, can be included in the tally of Irish authors. Such a literary preoccupation with the bicycle is understandable if the streets of Dublin are truly "aswarm with bicycles" as J. P. Donleavy tells us in his latest novel. One step beyond is Stephen Jones, who in his superb Flann O'Brien reader propounds the novel view that there is a literary phenomenon in Ireland known as the "bike novelist." The Irish even dignify historic occasions by their appearance at them on bicycles. Tim Severin writes in *The Brendan Voyage* that "there were many who came on bicycles" to Brandon creek in Dingle to bid him farewell as he embarked on his trans-Atlantic voyage in a curragh to duplicate the sixth-century crossing that Saint Brendan was reputed to have navigated.

The total absorption of the bicycle into every phase of the life of the citizens of foreign countries readily explains its frequent usage in the literature there. In this country, the bicycle lags sadly behind the automobile and the motorcycle as such a vital force.

It is not necessary to be a committed bicyclist to note the prevalence of the bicycle abroad for any and all uses of the populace, which is in sharp contrast to its displacement by the automobile in this country. Paul Theroux's very undiarylike Baedeker of a very unorthodox train ride from England through Asia and return in *The Great Railway Bazaar* proves this point, quite by accident, I am sure. Theroux did not write his book to elevate or even to feature the bicycle. But his acute sense of observation found it everywhere he went.

He spied the "Swiss cycling in kerchiefs," conveying a calendar-scene effect "that you admire for a moment before feeling an urge to move on to a new month." He reports witnessing Yugoslavian farmers "wobbling on bicycles loaded with hay bales." To us, a most acrobatic and highly unnecessary feat, outside the circus.

Also in Yugoslavia, he was privy to a drama enacted outside Nis, in which the omnipresent bicycle played but a token role.

> At a road near the track a crowd of people fought to look at a horse, still in its traces and hitched to an overloaded wagon, lying dead on its side in a mud puddle in which the wagon was obviously stuck. I imagined its heart had burst when it tried to free the wagon. And it had just happened: children were calling to their friends, a man was dropping his bike and running back for a look, and farther along a man pissing against a fence was straining to see the horse. The scene was composed like a Flemish painting in which the pissing man was a vivid detail. The train, the window frame holding the scene for moments, made it a picture. The man at the fence flicks the last droplets from his penis and, tucking it in his baggy pants, begins to sprint; the picture is complete.[1]

In Burma, bicyclists pedaled along country roads bordered by giant peepul trees. And in Vietnam, Theroux himself took to the saddle. The sight of others powering their bicycles must have been too much to resist.

A journey by train is a voyeur's paradise. It opens windows on sights that might not otherwise have been seen. Theroux's trip was a constant reminder that the world is a train passenger's oyster, indeed to be viewed at leisure. "V" had the same experience in Nabokov's *The Real Life of Sebastian Knight* as he traveled by rail in his quest for the missing details in the life of his supposed brother, Sebastian. At one point in his journey, "[a] road drew out and glided for a minute along the train, and just before it turned away a man on a bicycle wobbled among snow and slush and puddles. Where was he going? Who was he? Nobody will ever know."[2] For all we are told, "V" could have been describing his own plight as much as that of the stranger on a bicycle.

By all reports, the People's Republic of China is the world's premier bicycling haven. What cars are to the West, bicycles are to China: both a means of transport and a status symbol. In China, the bicycle is a force that affects marital customs as much as it marks a person's stratum in society. As sinologist Dr. Ryckmans puts it:

> In rural areas, many girls ask boyfriends to guarantee them the "three things that go round" (san chuan: a watch, a bicycle, and a sewing machine) before agreeing to marry them. In the cities, from heavy utility bicycles made in Shenyang to the light Shanghai bicycles, luxury and prestige machines named Swallows, the wide range of models can help you place their owners nearly as exactly as you can European carowners, Mini or Jaguar.[3]

More recently, Chalmers M. Roberts, former diplomatic correspondent for the *Washington Post,* has visited and reported his assessment of life in the People's Republic of China. The wave of bicycles he saw there impressed him both for its magnitude and for the cavalier attitude of the bicyclists toward the dangers of daytime and nighttime riding. Headlights, and I suppose taillights as well, were simply non-existent on bicycles. And what with trucks and buses driving at night with "dims," the lightless bicyclists were courting disaster on the roads. Our Consumer Product Safety Commission would be in a purple frenzy if such a situation existed in the United States.

When, on rare moments, the bicycle assumes the ascendancy on the roads of the Western world, bicyclists display an air of hauteur that is dangerous to their survival in the contest between the bicycle and the automobile. Roger Vailland, in his novel *The Law,* which dissects rural life according to the caste system in the south of Italy, has an agronomist from the north lament that

> driving along the roads of the South, he must have been obliged time after time to jam on the brakes to avoid a cyclist who had suddenly turned to his left. Yes. What did the cyclist do? He held out his arm and immediately turned to the left, even if there was a car right behind him doing a hundred miles an hour. Why? Because it was his right. He had held out his arm, as the law demanded; so he had the right to turn. He did not stop to ask himself whether the driver of the car right behind him would be able to brake in time. That was up to the driver. As for himself, since he had the right to turn, it was a matter of honour for him to turn, even if it cost him his life. If he gave way to the driver when the law gave him precedence over the driver, when he had the right of way, he would lose his honour, which meant more to him than life.[4]

In deference to the variety of reading tastes alive in all of us, this collection is arranged into distinct chapters in which subjects as diverse as the literature of romance and that of humor are compiled. It is to be observed, though, that my classification scheme is not flawless and is occasionally quite arbitrary. For example, the selections by Iris Murdoch and R. K. Narayan in the section entitled "Head over Wheels in Love," although properly situated back to back, might just as well have been included in "Not Just Ordinary Humor"—as you will see for yourself. I offer no excuse or explanation for this classification, except to say that editors are much like symphonic conductors. They are constantly called upon to make hard choices in their cutting and pasting for the purpose of developing a well-orchestrated entity.

Another aspect of an editor's freedom must also be mentioned. The titles to excerpted selections are entirely of my own design. They seemed suitable to flag the particular presence that attracted me to these passages. A conscious effort went into the phrasing of the titles to key the selections to the entire work from which they were abstracted. If, however, the original work is represented in toto, then the title for the work as it originally appeared was retained.

A word is in order in explanation of the title chosen for this anthology. The source and import of this title are of much more than historical interest. "The noiseless tenor" is a phrase that appears in Thomas Gray's celebrated "Elegy Written in a Country

Churchyard." This poem, first printed in 1751, has been termed "the best-known poem in the English language." The full context in which these words appear in Gray's poem provides a clue to their significance as a title for this work:

> Far from the madding crowd's ignoble strife,
> Their sober wishes never learn'd to stray;
> Along the cool sequester'd vale of life
> They kept the noiseless tenor of their way.[5]

The personal pronoun in this quatrain refers to the simple folk who lived their unexceptional lives, neither in splendor nor in shame. Indeed, the dignified iambic pentameter of the entire poem sounds the praises of the common man. The moving melancholy of the poem's lines manifests the might of death as the great leveler. Rich and poor alike are in its swath.

As Gray's poem focuses on the unheralded lives of the Everymen of society, this book speaks of the proletariat of wheels. The bicycle is the common man among vehicles, for which an ode, not an elegy, is in order.

For present purposes, the words *noiseless tenor* suggest the subdued whirring of the bicycle in contrast to the noisome clamor of other more modern forms of vehicular conveyance, whose din derives from the action of the internal combustion engine. The word *noiseless* was carefully chosen by Gray; it was substituted for the word *silent* in an earlier draft of the poem. The term is a particularly apt modifier in the title to this volume, too, for it has a power that *silent* lacks, and it sets the bicycle apart from the ceaseless clamor of modern society.

In addition, the bicycle's purpose and direction in conveying more than human beings and their baggage is the focus of the title. It is intended to suggest that, if the bicycle could speak, it would have much to say, presented ever so quietly and unobtrusively. The selections in this volume speak of and for the mute wheels of the bicycle.

As a matter of history, too, these words from Gray's "Elegy" are completely fitting as the title to this work. A stained-glass window at the church of Saint Giles at Stoke Poges, Buckinghamshire, England, whose graveyard is memorialized in the "Elegy," shows a person astride what might well be one of the earliest and most rudimentary depictions on record of a bicycle. The window is said to date from somewhere between the late sixteenth century to the middle of the seventeenth century.

The origins of this stained-glass window have been the topic of some debate, but none more mirthful than Robert Benchley's assertion that

the man [on the bicycle] looks quite a lot like me, except for a full beard and a more nervous expression around the eyes. The name underneath the figure is in Gothic letters and very difficult to make out, but it certainly begins with a "Ben" and the rest seems to be something of a compromise between "wgaalle" and "chhaalle."

Now, my people originally came from Wales (which, in itself, would account for the spelling), and, for a man with a contraption like the one in the picture, a spin from Wales to Buckinghamshire would have been mere child's play. As I figure it out, this man Benwgaalle or Benchhaalle built his bicycle, took along some lunch, and pushed himself along to Stoke Poges, at which place he became a sort of local hero, like Lindbergh at Le Bourget, and a stained-glass window was made in his honor. I rather imagine that he stayed in Stoke Poges all the rest of his life, as he probably was pretty lame.[6]

In a more sober vein, although the portrayal in the Stoke Poges church window looks vaguely like a bicycle, it could have been only a surveyor's device to measure distances, a commonplace contrivance in those days.[7] If the nature of this window is in some doubt, it has been said, with considerable authority, that the bicycle was known, in nearly all its essential modern components, as early as 1493. A recently discovered drawing on the reverse side of one of the glued pages in Leonardo da Vinci's *Codex Atlanticus* pictures a bicycle, including pedals, crank, chain, and a toothed cog on the rear wheel. All it lacks to be ready for riding is a maneuverable front wheel, a diamond frame for strength and stability, and rounded rather than square teeth on the cog.[8]

It has long been recognized that da Vinci had worked, as appears in the drawings in his *Codex Madrid I*, on a chain-and-toothed-wheel mechanism that coincides exactly with that found in his *Codex Atlanticus*. It is not, therefore, inconceivable that the craftsman of the Stoke Poges window would have hit upon a bicycle design even more rudimentary than that in da Vinci's collection.

In his recent volume of short stories, David Davenport delights us with the accolade that Salai might have uttered upon perceiving that his master, da Vinci, had invented, at least on paper, a bicycle.

Light with extravagance and precision, mirror of itself *atomo per atomo* from its dash against the abruptness of matter to the jelly of the eye, swarmed from high windows onto the two-wheeled balancing machine. The rider would grasp horns set on the fork in which the front wheel was fixed and thus guide himself with nervous and accurate meticulousness. Suddenly he saw the Sforze going into battle on it, a phalanx of these *due ruote* bearing lancers at full tilt.[9]

To which da Vinci might have replied: it will move, it will sweep "like the wind, like Ezekiel's angel, like the horses of Ancona."

It will early be noted by the reader that some of the selections are prefaced and even interrupted by the explanatory comments of the editor. These editorial incursions are in some cases elaborate, in others minimal, and in still others nonexistent. The intention of these comments and summaries is simply to add a dimension of continuity and lucidity to works that were sometimes gravely excised or truncated by the compiler. The object was to preserve the essence of the work, while emphasizing its thematic reliance on the bicycle. On other occasions, the editor was content to let the reader enjoy an unannotated version of the selection, where considerations of space and content made that feasible.

In initiating the research for this bicycling Chautauqua, it never dawned on me that suitable materials would be found in such galactic profusion. But the search was not always easy or even successful. Many false starts and futile promises were made, often involving enjoyable but unusable literary references.

A long-distance telephone call set me to rereading Agatha Christie's tour de force *The Murder of Roger Ackroyd*. Ackroyd was said to be a builder of wheels. He was. Wagon wheels, not bicycle wheels. And did not the child buyer, in John Hersey's novel of that name, arrive in town on a bicycle? No, it was—happily, for the child buyer was not exactly the type whom one would entrust with baby-sitting chores—a motorcycle. The longest and most exhausting was my scanning—certainly not reading—the two volumes of the collected short stories of O. Henry. The bicycle was remarkable by its absence.

And what is one to make of E. B. White's collection of stories bearing the tempting and curious title *Quo Vadimus? Or the Case for the Bicycle*. Upon close inspection, the book is not in the slightest of or about the bicycle. A little tomfoolery, Mr. White?

Indisputedly, my compilation is not so thorough as to lay claim to being exhaustive. Many works of literature have assuredly been omitted wholly by the accident of my not having run them down. My apologies for these exclusions, but the time did come in my research when I felt I had enough literary works of substantial merit to justify going to press. Later editions, if any, can fill the gaps.

Other materials were purposely omitted, some because of my decision that only good tales deserved inclusion. A good tale I define as did Helen McGill in Christopher Morley's *Parnassus on Wheels:*

> A good book ought to have something simple about it. And, like Eve, it ought to come from somewhere near the third rib: there ought to be a heart beating in it. A story that's all forehead doesn't amount to much. [10]

Unfortunately, even some stories qualifying as good reading were dropped either because this anthology had to be kept within manageable limits or because the necessary copyright releases could not be obtained or the cost of those permissions was well beyond this book's budget. In some cases, materials that just did not and could not, by any stretching, be wormed into any chapter were most unwillingly excluded. One of these was the short story "The Bicycle Key" by Thomas M. Cockrell, a story that brings the impersonal inhumanity of the Vietnam War home to a noncombatant brother and sister whose bicycle key locks them, for a moment, in its terror.

Most distasteful of all was my reluctant decision to eliminate an originally planned chapter on the poetry of the bicycle. Not doggerel, mind, but poetry! W. H. Auden's "Miss Gee" with her "back-pedal brake" and George Oppen's love for his "light and miraculous" bicycle and John Betjeman's "keen ecclesiologist" who was "broad before and broad behind," as well as David Shapiro's "talented bicycle rider" who "flew out of the winter for a sad party" and Jerzy Harasymowicz's bicycle transfigured to a mountain goat must be found not here but elsewhere, possibly gathered with George Kendrick's *Bicycle Tyre in a Tall Tree*. It is not that I, like William Empson's Johnson, "could see no bicycle would go." It was simply a question of basic economics. Poetry costs too dearly to be anthologized in a book already suffering from other copyright-cost overruns.

Certain observations concerning trends among these selections are sufficiently intriguing to be briefly noted. A significant number of the selections were drawn from well-known authors' first works. Aldous Huxley's *Crome Yellow* is one illustration. Nabokov's *Mary* is another. Many of the authors were journalists turned authors or authors while journalists. Ernest Hemingway, Flann O'Brien, Stephen Crane, and Jimmy Breslin are in this category. Further, the bicycle, except in mystery stories, rarely appears clothed with a malevolent function. When it is not a beneficent instrumentality, it is neutral rather than the agency of evil deeds.

No one needs to be reminded that writers speak of what they know and that the best writers seem to speak of what they know best. In the preparation of this book, it became a repetitious refrain to find autobiographical incidents involving the bicycle transferred bodily into an author's fictional works. Nabokov's youthful romance became the focus of Ganin's most coveted remembrance in *Mary*. Hemingway bicycled in Europe with F. Scott Fitzgerald and composed some of his best literature while watching the six-day bike races. It was inevitable that *The Sun Also Rises* would be influenced by this background. Alfred Jarry went from a bicycle faddist to a bicycle fanatic to an author who could see the Crucifixion as an uphill bicycle race. William Saroyan was a bicycle messenger for Western Union. *The Human Comedy* shows the influence of the experiences of those early years. Again and again the autobiographical theme reverberates throughout the writings in this collection.

In acquiring the raw materials for this book, many items were discovered that had no direct bearing on its subject matter, but that reaffirmed the pervasive influence of the bicycle in the arts. My files are crammed with clippings from comic strips and cartoons that feature the bicycle. The bicycle has played its part in contemporary music from the vocal music of Jethro Tull and the rock group Queen to the instrumental music of Leo Kottke ("Busted Bicycle"). Even in the more formal circles of the opera, the bicycle is seen on stage in the opera *Fedora* by Umberto Giordano. This opera is notable, moreover, since its first performance marked the debut of a twenty-three-year-old tenor by the name of Enrico Caruso.

Elsewhere in the fine arts, we find two watercolors by the artist of the American West, Charles M. Russell, which, taken together, portray the mischievous tale of a bicycling dandy who, having encountered three cowboys on horseback, is somehow tricked into mounting one of their horses while one of the cowboys is pictured as ready to spur his horse into excited action with a surprise slap on its rump. In a more somber mood, Russell's 1899 pencil sketch *The Last of His Race* depicts the tragedy of the new devouring the old in an era of industrialization. Another American artist, watercolorist Andrew Wyeth, features the bicycle and a bicyclist in his *Portrait of Young America*, festooned as if they were charting the carefree, open-roads course of a Jack Kerouac.

Toulouse-Lautrec is well known as a designer of posters with a bicycling motif. And Winslow Homer's wood engraving entitled *The New Year—1869* features a kindly and kingly youth pumping a bicycle. Even Picasso was touched by the bicycle, to the extent of sculpting an expertly crafted *Bull's Head* out of the handlebars and seat of a bicycle. Marcel Duchamp's *Bicycle Wheel* is a recognized exemplar of the "ready-made" school of sculpture.

No book would be worth its printer's ink without the invaluable assistance of other

The Last of His Race by Charles M. Russell (1899)

persons. This book is no exception, except that assistance was received from count-less persons. The kindness of various bicycling magazines, such as *Bicycling*, *Bike World*, the *L.A.W. Bulletin*, the *Pedal Patter*, and *Cycle Touring*, in publishing my author's query for information was of inestimable value in my research. The letters I received in reply to those solicitations were so numerous and so eminently helpful as to cause me to forsake the Library of Congress's main reading room for more fruitful pursuits elsewhere. I acknowledge the aid of those correspondents with a brace of warmth.

Others were helpful just by lending me an attentive and perceptive ear, as did then law student Carl Fink, or by aiding me to corral the books and other materials I wished to research, as did Mrs. Martha McClellan, then of the George Washington University's Law Library staff.

This compilation has been very much a family affair. My three brothers-in-law, Tom, Frank, and Rod Smyth, teachers all, constantly brought very relevant source materials to my attention out of devotion, I am sure, less to the bicycle than to literature and to me. They also read and forthrightly commented upon rough drafts.

The encouragement they extended to me at every turning sustained and bolstered my enthusiasm for this enterprise. No one could have married into a more loving, unselfish, and well-read family.

But most importantly and most unreservedly, I wish to commend my children, particularly Jim and Mary Alice, and my wife for the timely and unstinting assistance they have voluntarily given me at every asking in this task of compilation. My daughter, Monica, has been most gracious in providing me with two drawings and poem for this book, all of which show distinct talent. Working with my family was so pleasurable and rewarding for me that the completion of this anthology creates a void in my life that not even a long-distance bicycle tour could fill. I am also indebted to my daughter-in-law, Lori, for her keen editorial labors.

And, of course, my gratitude goes out to my doughty friend, my steadfast Rocinante, my bicycle, which was not only my inspiration for this volume but my support in its development. What was said of Raman in *The Painter of Signs* could, in truth, be said of me.

While bicycling, his mind attained a certain passivity, and ideas bubbled up, lingered a while, burst and vanished.[11]

I would add: only to return again and again.

Acknowledgments

Part I

SPRING IN WASHINGTON by Louis J. Halle, Jr. (Atheneum, 1963). Copyright © 1947, 1957 by Louis J. Halle, Jr. Reprinted by permission of Louis J. Halle, Jr.

"Four-in-Hand Forsyte" is reprinted by permission of Charles Scribner's Sons from ON FORSYTE 'CHANGE by John Galsworthy. Copyright 1930 Charles Scribner's Sons.

HOVEL IN THE HILLS by Elizabeth West reprinted by permission of Faber and Faber Ltd.

THE BICYCLE RIDER IN BEVERLY HILLS by William Saroyan, published by Ballantine Books, Inc., is reprinted by permission of William Saroyan. Copyright 1952 by William Saroyan.

"Wheels on Parnassus" from the book THE ROMANY STAIN by Christopher Morley. Copyright 1926, renewed 1954 by Christopher Morley. Reprinted by permission of J. B. Lippincott Company.

For permission to reprint "The Bicycle," from POEMS by James Reaney, copyright 1972 by James Reaney, New Press (1972), Toronto, Canada, thanks are due to the author, the publisher, and Sybil Hutchinson, literary agent.

For permission to use the illustration accompanying James Reaney's poem "The Bicycle" gratitude is expressed to McGraw-Hill Ryerson Limited.

THE MAN WHO LOVED BICYCLES by Daniel Behrman (Harper's Magazine Press, 1973). Copyright © 1973 by Daniel Behrman. Reprinted by the courtesy of Daniel Behrman.

Poem by A. L. Anderson beginning "In older times . . ." appearing in *Wisconsin Then and Now* reprinted by permission of the State Historical Society of Wisconsin.

"My Best Friend" by Henry Miller reprinted from MY BIKE & OTHER FRIENDS by Henry Miller (Capra Press, 1978). Copyright © 1978 by Henry Miller. By permission of Capra Press.

"Different Bicycles" by Dorothy Baruch from FAVORITE POEMS, OLD AND NEW, edited by Helen Ferris, published by Doubleday & Company, Inc. Reprinted by permission of Doubleday & Company, Inc.

The extract from John Betjeman's poem "The Commander" is used with the permission of John Murray (Publishers) Ltd and Houghton Mifflin Co.

Part II

Part III

Part IV

Part V

Part VI

Part VII

The Noiseless Tenor

Part I
A Bicycling Calliope

Introduction

Many are the warm and glowing words that have been written in praise of the bicycle. The selections in this chapter, both long and short, may not constitute a full-scale ode to the bicycle, but they are singularly respectful and even reverent to it for the enriched dimensions it has impressed on the life of its riders.

Christopher Bellman, one of the principals in Iris Murdoch's *The Red and the Green*, summed up the innate simplicity of the bicycle very neatly and tidily. As he put it:

> The bicycle is the most civilized conveyance known to man. Other forms of transport grow daily more nightmarish. Only the bicycle remains pure in heart.[1]

The civilizing aspects of the bicycle often come into sharper focus when viewed from places quite remote from the hurly-burly of the technological age. The Wests, Elizabeth and Alan, capitalized on this opportunity during their self-inflicted exile to the outback of Wales, where they lived a Spartan existence in a cottage they named Hafod. Alan West is reported by his wife, Elizabeth, in her book *Hovel in the Hills*, to be unflinching in his conviction that

> the bicycle is mechanical perfection. When man invented the bicycle he reached the peak of his attainments. Here was a machine of precision and balance for the convenience of man. And (unlike subsequent inventions for man's convenience) the more he used it, the fitter his body became. Here, for once, was a product of man's brain that was entirely beneficial to those who used it, and of no harm or irritation to others. Progress should have stopped when man invented the bicycle.[2]

The bicycle can and does foster outbursts of emotional frenzy among its adherents. It is "the realization of a dream as old as mankind," according to Irish playwright Stewart Parker in his successful play *Spokesong, or, The Common Wheel*. At another point, he tells us that "You can't despair for the human race when you see somebody riding a bicycle." And again, "the bicycle was the last advance in technology that everybody understands. Anybody who can ride one can understand how it works." Unlike the automobile, "a bicycle hides nothing and threatens nothing. It is what it does, its form is its function."

The bicycle is not always so plainly lauded. Sometimes, it is the instrument by

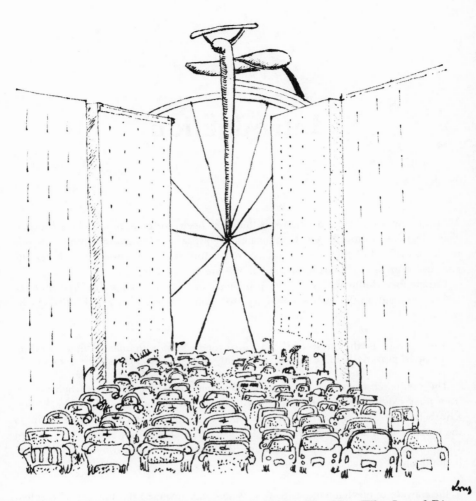

"The bicycle is a vehicle for revolution." (From *The Man Who Loved Bicycles* by Daniel Behrman)

which other virtues are extolled. The Good Samaritan in James Joyce's short story "Grace," who breaks through a crowd of gawkers to wash the blood from Kernan's mouth and to revive him with a gulp of brandy, is described as "a young man in a cycling suit." He is distinctive both for his attire and for the unsolicited aid he gives to Kernan, who lost more than his silk hat when he missed his footing and tumbled down the stairs.

A childhood without a bicycle is a sailboat becalmed. A bicycle has the grace and style to give a billowing gaiety and a transcendent innocence to the fragile moments of childhood. In later years, those moments may be recalled for refuge, however evanescent, from the fits and frights of life.

Thérèse Desqueroux, in François Mauriac's novel *Thérèse*, recaptured such memories of childhood's airy abandon as she returned in trepidation to her husband, Bernard. Thérèse had just been acquitted of charges that she had attempted to murder Bernard with poison. Although in fact guilty of the crime, she is not free, but the uncertainty of her reception by Bernard at their estate at Argelouse deeply troubles her. As her carriage approaches Argelouse and her tension heightens, Thérèse sees roadside signs of the happy and carefree days of her youth.

At a turn in the road she recognized a farm where the low outbuildings looked like sleeping, crouching animals. It was here that, in the old days, Anne (Anne de la Trave, Thérèse's close friend) had always been frightened of a dog which had a way of jumping out at her bicycle wheel. A little farther on a slight dip in the ground was screened by alders. No matter how hot the day, a tremulous breath of coolness had always touched their faces as they passed it. . . . A child on a bicycle, her teeth gleaming beneath a sun hat—the sound of a bicycle bell—a voice crying "Look! I've taken my hands off!" . . . In those muddled memories was summed up all to which Thérèse could cling.[3]

Both in poetry and in prose, but most, it seems, in poetry, memories of events captured while bicycling are susceptible to an uncanny total recall. John Betjeman has rhymed of "The Commander," with whom

> I remembered our shared delight in architecture and nature
>> As bicycling we went
> By saffron-spotted palings to crumbling box-paved churches
>> Down hazel lanes in Kent.[4]

On other occasions, even for the most tawdry and crass reasons, the bicycle may serve very pragmatic purposes. It, for example, saves carfare. Hans Schnier, the clown, in Heinrich Böll's book of that name, grasped this utilitarian view of the bicycle in his most down and almost out financial situation:

all I had left was one mark, with no prospect of being able to earn much more in the near future. . . . The only thing I could really sell would be the bike, but if I decided to do the cheap music halls the bike would come in very handy and would save me taxi and train fares.[5]

This same cost-benefit analysis moved Jack London's Martin Eden, one of the author's least compelling heroes, to eschew the leisure of a train for the rigors of a 140-mile bicycle ride. To Martin Eden, money was more valuable than time or creature comforts. Of course,

> it would have been easier to go on the train, but the round trip was two dollars and a half, and he (Martin Eden) was intent on saving money.[6]

More frequently, the bicycle is admired for its ability to inspirit a ride by adding a fresh color and a vision-expanding character to the experiences of daily life. Simone de Beauvoir, in her partial autobiography *La Force de l'age*, recounts her experiences and sensations during a bicycle journey with Jean-Paul Sartre through France during the Second World War. She reflects upon the joys of bicycling and contrasts them with the ennui of walking.

> Sartre much preferred riding a bicycle to walking. The monotony of walking bored him, while the intensity of effort and the rhythm of a bicycle journey varied constantly. He would amuse himself by sprinting on the hills. I would become winded and fall behind him. On level stretches, he pedaled with such indifference that on two or three occasions he landed in the ditch. "I was thinking of other things," he would say. Both of us loved the freedom of downhill runs. The scenery flew by more quickly than when we were on foot. Like him, I was quite willing to swap my old passion for walking for this new pleasure.[7]

The cathartic function of bicycling has been noted time and again in literature. More than any other emotion, melancholy is incompatible with bicycling. A bicycle ride is a flight from sadness. It is a release from despair and a resurgence of hope. Belacqua, Beckett's anti-hero in *More Pricks Than Kicks*, instinctively appreciated this purgative aspect of bicycling when he

> came to where the bicycle lay in the grass. It was a fine light machine, with red tires and wooden rims. He ran down the margin to the road and it bounded alongside under his hand. He mounted and they flew down the hill and round the corner till they came at length to the stile that led into the field where the church was. The machine was a treat to ride, on his right hand the sea was foaming among the rocks, the sands ahead were another yellow again, beyond them in the distance the cottages of Rush were bright white, Belacqua's sadness fell from him like a shift. He carried the bicycle into the field and laid it down on the grass.[8]

Charles Lumley, in John Wain's *Born in Captivity*, suffers a huge identity crisis. That was ill-omened enough until he eyes Veronica and is hopelessly smitten by her. But she does not reciprocate his distant ogling. The doldrums summon him. So

> He had acquired a rust-eaten bicycle, and increasingly took to pedalling into the countryside to dull his pain with the monotonous grind at the worn-out pedals and the peacefully bitter silence of the fields and woods. Heedless of route or destination, he would turn his handlebars at random; when night fell he lit his lamps and

mournfully pushed on. It was a powerful drug, and he turned eagerly to it whenever his daily toil allowed.[9]

Bicycling can be an airy time when troubles evaporate and temptations are purged. Peter Sears found bicycling to be an ideal and the only "Place for Four-letter Words":

> I had it all wrong from the start
> about four-letter words. I thought
> they were big words with four letters.
>
> Sure, I thought about being wrong.
> I kept it quiet, cobweb quiet,
> like our house, even our garage.
>
> All but the shed where I kept
> my bike. I looked for a place
> to hear these words, all of them
>
> Before someone tried to tell me
> where this one belonged and that
> one didn't. Leaning streamlined
>
> Over the handlebars, I heard them
> in the tire's lick and spin. Faster,
> tearing all out down a hill, hunched
>
> Under the wind, blinking at the rain,
> I yelled every four-letter word I knew,
> yelled them until they were as real
>
> As the hill, yelled them until I
> broke them in my throat and they were
> just words spinning in the spokes.[10]

Environmentalists, as naturalists are casually called today, have spoken eloquently of the bicycle's place in the renaissance of enthusiasm for nature. Henry Beetle Hough, one of the high priests of Martha's Vineyard, has asserted that

> The bicycle makes summer a roomier and more intimate apartment of the year. The world nowadays is too big anyway, and most of us want to bring it closer, and personalize it. We want space about us, but space of our own, not the vastness of doubt. Talk too of rugged individualism—the bicycle gives you individualism which is not only rugged but smooth and purring underneath, as witness the sound of rubber tires on damp streets. You discover things on a wheel that escape you in a car, and you get around so much faster than you can walk that you feel pretty fine about it.[11]

Such musings, in harmony as they are with the ambience of Martha's Vineyard, are unexpected in the habitats of megalopolis man. Yet Louis J. Halle, Jr., in his *Spring in Washington*, could bear most sensitive witness to the renewal of spring in our nation's capital. His nature-watching journeys by bicycle about town and into the suburban countryside moved him to say that

Bicycling . . . is the nearest approximation I know to the flight of birds. The airplane simply carries a man on its back like an obedient Pegasus; it gives him no wings of his own. There are movements on a bicycle corresponding to almost all the variations in the flight of the larger birds. Plunging free downhill is like a hawk stooping. On the level stretches you may pedal with a steady rhythm like a heron flapping; or you may, like an accipitrine hawk, alternate rapid pedaling with gliding. If you want to test the force and direction of the wind, there is no better way than to circle, banked inward, like a turkey vulture. When you have the wind against you, headway is best made by yawing or wavering, like a crow flying upwind. I have climbed a steep hill by circling or spiraling, rising each time on the upturn with the momentum of the downturn, like any soaring bird. I have shot in and out through stalled traffic like a goshawk through the woods. The best way to ride, especially downhill, is with both hands in your pockets and leaning backwards. This is not so hard as it looks; like a bird, you control your direction perfectly by unconscious shifts in your balance. Especially on the long downslopes, this is to know the freedom of the wind. The air rushing past your ears reminds you that the birds must be partially deafened by their own speed.[12]

Hemingway took a very earthy approach to the learning ways that the bicycle instigates. In his view, you tend to recall what you most arduously work to achieve. In that way,

It is by riding a bicycle that you learn the contours of a country best, since you have to sweat up the hills and coast down them.
Thus you remember them as they actually are, while in a motor car only a high hill impresses you, and you have no such accurate remembrance of country you have driven through as you gain by riding a bicycle.[13]

Another author, Alain Fournier, who in 1928 wrote that masterpiece of realistic fiction about life in rural France, where he was reared, entitled *The Wanderer*, saw none of the exertion in bicycling which Hemingway perceived. To Fournier, bicycling was just pure joy. The ride, to him, is redolent of an incomparably exuberant and stimulating excitement, even the initial ride.

I had never been for a really long ride on a bicycle. This was my first. . . . A bicycle is fairly good fun for any ordinary fellow: what should it not mean to a poor chap like me, who, only a short time back, dragged his leg wretchedly along, sweating after a mile or two? To sweep down hills and plunge into the valley hollows; to cover as on wings the far stretches of the road ahead and to find them in bloom at your approach; to pass through a village in a moment, and to take it all with you in one glance . . . in dreams only, till then, had I known such a delightful, such an easy way of getting about. I tackled even the hills with zest.[14]

Death and the bicycle would seem, at first blush, to be poles apart. Death is final, painful, and inscrutable, whereas to straddle a bicycle is to begin anew, to cast out stale melancholy and to see clearly now. Death may have no master, but the bicycle is, most emphatically, not its slave. Leo Tolstoy and Henry Adams both came to this understanding, upon suffering the tragedy of death within their immediate families.

Tolstoy, at sixty-seven, was stricken by the death of his most beloved son

Vanichka, who, at seven years of age, had died on February 23, 1895. Tolstoy's personal diary reveals his anguish and his agony. He searched everywhere for an explanation and for relief until

> one month after Vanichka's death, Leo Tolstoy, aged sixty-seven, took his first bicycle lesson. His brand-new machine was a present from the Moscow Society of Velocipede-Lovers. An instructor came to teach him, free of charge, how to keep his balance. What could Sonya be thinking, on March 28, 1895, as she watched her husband pedaling awkwardly along the snow-edged garden paths? She was probably shocked to see him enjoying a new sport so soon after their bereavement. Was it callousness, selfishness or the reaction of a prodigiously vital organism against the creeping fear of doom? She envied and hated him for being so strong. That evening, Tolstoy's entry in his diary consisted of the three ritual initials— "i.I.l." (if I live)—and nothing else.[15]

Unlike Leo Tolstoy, Henry Adams locked his bereavement upon the death of his wife in the privacy of his heart. True, he did commission Augustus Saint-Gaudens to sculpt an enigmatic but sepulchral bronze figure at his wife's grave in Washington, D.C.'s Rock Creek Cemetery, which instantly became something of a tourist attraction. But his famed autobiography barely mentions his wife's death, never referring to her by name. Saint-Gaudens sculpture occupies a single page of desultory commentary, but we are never informed that it commemorates his wife.

That Adams grieved was nonetheless plain. After describing himself, always in the third person, as being "landed, lost, and forgotten, in the center of this vast plain of self-content," his words convey a mood bordering on total despondency. "Nothing new was to be done or learned," he bemoans.

Still, a glint of hope remained. As Adams recounted it,

> At past fifty, Adams solemnly and painfully learned to ride the bicycle. Nothing else occurred to him as a means of new life. Nothing else offered itself, however carefully he sought.[16]

The greatest praise the bicycle could receive is found in the lives of those who have never replaced it by a reliance upon the automobile. Edmund Wilson is representative of this unique class of persons for even at the age of sixty, he had not learned to drive a car. As a nineteenth-century man who lived well into the twentieth century, he would write that he had not "progressed further than the bicycle" and that he rather disliked the automobile as a means of travel. That seemed not to trouble him for, at another place, he wrote, in lofty terms, of

> cutting across from Rumson to Oceanic on my bicycle, a little dim-eyed, plunging in a dream through the clear medium of air, rich autumnal shade from the wall of undergrowth and trees of some estate beside the road and the deep golden stripes of autumn sun.[17]

Persons and places often assume an enhanced, a charming and even a picturesque quality when captured in association with the bicycle. In *Glory* Nabokov, whose masterful verbal imagery could give the drab toad class, animately portrays Archibald Moore, the Russian scholar at Cambridge, as "pale and dark-haired, with a pince-nez on his thin nose . . . riding by, sitting perfectly upright, on a bicycle with high handlebars." Moore's bicycling was fiction, but that of James Murray, father of the *Oxford English Dictionary*, was fact. An impressive and conspicuous figure at all times, Murray was even more so on his bicycle. In February 1913, a journalist painted the scene in Oxford as one of

> a day of bitter cold and splendid sunshine when Winter stood with naked sword in the streets of Oxford. . . . Age kept the hearth. Down the Banbury road came a picturesque exception, an almost prophetic figure, his long white beard shaking like snowflakes in the wind. His seventy-sixth winter, and he cycles still![18]

Cambridge, like Oxford, is a college town. Bicycles are necessary trappings there. Nabokov, in explaining why, gives us colorful impressions of Cambridge which cannot be divorced from the place of the bicycle in its life.

> The lecture halls were scattered about the whole town. If one lecture immediately followed another but was given in a different hall, you had to hop on your bicycle, or else scuttle along back alleys and cross the echoing stone of courts. Limpid chimes called back and forth from tower to tower; the din of motors, the crepitation of wheels, and the tinkle of bicycle bells filled the narrow streets. During the lecture the glittering swarm of bicycles clustered at the gates, awaiting their owners. The black-gowned lecturer would mount the platform and with a thump put his tasseled square cap on the lectern.[19]

In the late 1900s, during the triumphal days of bicycling, poets and others of the literary fraternity championed the bicycle in phrases that became more and more mellifluous as time went on. It was clear from these writings that bicycling had the power to transport its riders to empyrean heights of boundless ecstasy. One writer described his delight in bicycling with proselytizing zeal as follows:

> Good-morning, fellow Wheelmen; here's a warm, fraternal hand,
> As with a rush of victory we sweep across the land!
> If some may be dissatisfied to view the way we ride
> We only wish their majesties could wander by our side!
>   For we are good philanthropists—
>   Unqualified philanthropists—
> And would not have *our* happiness to any one denied.
> We claim a great utility that daily must increase;
> We claim for inactivity a bright and grand release;
> A constant mental, physical, and moral help we fell,
> Which makes us turn enthusiasts, and bless the silent wheel![20]

Dithyrambs on this order were spun off on a global scale during the years of the fin de siècle. In France in 1898, Maurice Leblanc, creator of the romantic and roguish gentleman-burglar Arsène Lupin, had Pascal Fauvières, the protagonist in his *Wings to Fly*, apostrophize the bicycle as no longer just a thing, Madeleine. It is no longer a beast of steel . . . no . . . it is a friend. Destiny has accorded man this new friend. . . . It is a faithful and powerful ally against one's worst enemies. It is stronger than anxiety, stronger than sadness. It has all the power of hope. . . . Sweet friend, Sweet little friend! When I think of the last years, the years of slumber, torpor and constraint! It has lifted me from the shadows and guided me toward truth.[21]

Bicycling has had its detractors too, many of whom were among the literati. Their barbs were just as pointed as the praises of its supporters were lofty. John Ruskin is reputed to have decried the bicycle and to have been willing

to spend all [his] best "bad language" in reprobation of bi-, tri-, and 4, 5, 6 or 7 cycles, and every other contrivance and invention for superseding human feet on God's ground.[22]

More recently, Max Beerbohm has scorned the "bikish chaos" of "Fashion's foible" which "gratifies that instinct which is common to all stupid people, the instinct to potter with machinery."[23] But alas poor Max, his ridicule knew no bounds. Motorcars, the "flying machine," the concertina, and even stilts were in its path. He offended all, save possibly equestrians, whose vote would amount to less than a fox's start toward general public approval of his views.

The following selections are paeans, some simple, some lofty, but all singing the praises of the bicycle.

1

Daniel Behrman

Dreams to Spin By

From *The Man Who Loved Bicycles*

It is true that I dream. I have been too long in Lanloup (France) where there are still sorcerers around, although, so I was told in the village graveyard, they do not practice any more. Perhaps the retired sorcerers have been casting a few spells over me just as the retired seamen cast a few nets from the little boats they sail out of Brehec on a calm sunny day. We need spells and mystery in our lives, the modern city drives them away and replaces them with drugs and neuroses. Just as the automobile allows us to travel without moving our muscles, drugs let us dream without moving our minds. . . .

I wonder where Merlin spends his summers. I suspect he comes to Paris as an Augustan. That may be why I can dream in the Paris of August. I coast hands off down Rue d'Assas on a Sunday morning, the first batch of newly made air comes fresh to me through the grille of the Luxembourg Gardens. The Seine sparkles like all the seas I have ever known, the sky over the Left Bank is as washed and clear as it is over the English Channel between Saint-Brieuc and Jersey. I dream of a Paris year of twelve Augusts.

I dream of the day when we will travel once more on the little wooden passenger coaches that were turned into sheds and summer houses when the branch line closed down at Brehec. I do not know who will be driving the train, perhaps it will be the man who ran a switch engine I once saw outside the old roundhouse at Nogent-sur-Marne that is now dust. From the track, I admired his engine; from the cab, he admired my racing bike. He told me that he came to work himself on a racing bike all the way from Livry-Gargan. Perhaps it was from Brooklyn Heights, it could have been from Dragør (Denmark). I am not sure. I saw him only once. All I can remember is that he invited

From Daniel Behrman, *The Man Who Loved Bicycles* (New York: Harper's Magazine Press, 1973), pp. 129–30.

me to come aboard his little steam engine for a fireside chat. Its copper pipes gleamed, he opened the firebox door, threw in a shovelful of coal and closed it, all in the same dancing movement.

Then we talked about bicycles.

2

James Reaney

"The Bicycle"

Halfway between childhood & manhood,
  More than a hoop but never a car,
The bicycle talks gravel and rain pavement
  On the highway where the dead frogs are.

Like sharkfish the cars blur by,
  Filled with the two-backed beast
One dreams of, yet knows not the word for,
  The accumulating sexual yeast.

Past the house where the bees winter,
  I climb on the stairs of my pedals
To school murmuring irregular verbs
  Past the lion with legs like a table's.

Autumn blows the windfalls down
  With a twilight horn of dead leaves.
I pick them up in the fence of November
  And burrs on my sweater sleeves.

Where a secret robin is wintering
  By the lake in the fir grove dark
Through the fresh new snow we stumble
  That Winter has whistled sharp.

The March wind blows me ruts over,
  Puddles past, under red maple buds,

From James Reaney, *Twelve Letters to a Small Town* (Toronto: The Ryerson Press, 1962), pp. 31–32.

Over culvert of streamling, under
   White clouds and beside bluebirds.

Fireflies tell their blinking player
   Piano hesitant tales
Down at the bridge through the´swamp
   Where the ogre clips his rusty nails.

Between the highschool & the farmhouse
   In the country and the town
It was a world of love and of feeling
   Continually floating down.

On a soul whose only knowledge
   Was that everything was something,
This was like that, that was like this—
   In short, everything was
The bicycle of which I sing.

                                       (1962)

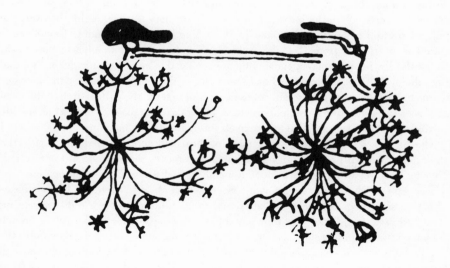

3

Christopher Morley

"Wheels on Parnassus"

From *The Romany Stain*

The bicycle, the bicycle surely, should always be the vehicle of novelists and poets. How pleasant if one could prove that a decline in literary delicacy followed the disappearance of the bike from American roads. After eleven years without one, here I am in a country where the bicycle abounds. My memory returns to old Shotover, the tall green curio I bought in England in 1910. She had a queer double frame, much stared at by rustics from Basel to Auld Reekie, from the Cotswolds to the Wash. Delightful British pushbikes, some of them even used to have multiple gears. Not that I am disloyal to the automobile. For I know the peculiar thrill of motor cars, how one learns to love the steady drumming of their faithful organs, the gallant arch of the hood as it goes questing, like a sentient creature, along dazzling roads. Yet in a car you are carried; on a bike you go. You are yourself integral with the machine.

The bicycle is to me a kind of symbol of those old careless days long ago. How cheering to find still posted, on country inns in France, the emblem of the Cyclists' Touring Club, of which one was once a member, and whose little identification card was accepted (Oh, simple days!) as a passport. One always sought out the hostelries with that sign, because they were supposed to give the members a reduced rate for "bed and breakfast." And how they hated to do it. One wonders if the young French person on that Rhine steamer remembers herself of the three eccentric youths with the C.T.C. badges. She was a damsel of rather free manners, just the kind of person Jean Jacques was always encountering on his travels. The C.T.C. emblems roused her curiosity, and she asked what they were. "Mademoiselle," replied one of the trio, "it is the Club Terrestre de la Chasteté."

And speaking of the C.T.C., has everyone forgotten the jolly old L.A.W.—the

From Christopher Morley, *The Romany Stain* (New York: Doubleday, Page & Co., 1926), pp. 35–39.

League of American Wheelmen? That too had its literary flavours, for was not Mr. S. S. McClure editor of its magazine?

It is when you come back to bicycling, after long dispractice, that you realize how exquisite a physical art it is. Once more that strong tightness of the thigh muscles, once more the hot sun on the shoulder blades, the odd shift in bodily *tenue* when you have to push on foot up a long hill (comparable to the flatness of walking after skating, or that uneasiness in a ship in still harbour after days at sea). As you spin down aisles of hedgeway you can ponder the daintily equilibrated poise that makes those two wheels your obedient Siamese twins. I read once of a savage chief in Africa who was given an old bicycle and a top hat, in exchange for a caravan of ivory, I suppose. He traversed the sunbaked paths near his village riding the one and wearing the other, hallooing with innocent glee. I can understand his feelings. If one wears a hat at all while biking it might as well be the silk cylinder of fashion, to express a sense of psychic and carnal welfare. In a recent play, "Roger Bloomer," one of the characters remarked, "I wear a silk hat as a charm against passion." The bicycle also is an amulet against various disorders. To see before one a forked or meandering road, a wedge-towered Norman church in the valley, to explore the fragrance of lanes like green tunnels, to hear the whispering hum beneath you and the rasp of scythes in a hayfield, all this might well be homoeopathic against passion, for it is a passion itself.

But these letters are adjured to have some bearing on literary matters. So let's take this turning on the left (which leads across links toward the sea) and sit on the dunes to think out our rearward idea. A warm southwest gale is creaming the surf on to the beach; the sandy turf, sheep-cropped, is speckled with small pink and yellow flowers.

An odd feeling comes sometimes to a writer who has long carried in the knapsack of the mind some notion that he wants to put in ink. It is a sensation I can only describe as Getting Ready to Write. Those phantoms of imagination, so long halted frozen in mid-gesture, begin to show marks of animation. In my particular case, it is now four and half years that I have seen them sitting in their absurd unchanged attitudes. No wonder they are stiff: one of them (what a dear she is!) told me her foot had gone to sleep. They are sitting round a table; it is a birthday party. You would think that the cake must be very stale by this time, the little red candles guttered out. But no: I can see them burning steadily, the bright untrembling candles of a dream. Even in the puppet postures where I left them I can see those phantoms strangely show an air of expectation. Something must be done about it.

In these moods bicycling seems perfectly the right employ. It is all very well to say to yourself that you are not thinking as you wheel serenely along; but you *are*, and that sure uncertainty of the cyclist's balance, that unconsciously watchful suspension (solid on earth yet so breezily flitting) seems to symbolize the task itself. The wheel slidders in a rut or on a slope of gravel: at once, by instinct, you redress your perpendicular. So, in the continual joy and disgust of the writer's work, he dare not abandon that difficult trained alertness. How much of the plain horror and stupidity is he to admit into his picture? how many of the grossly significant minutiae can he pause to include? how often shall he make a resolute fling to convey that incomparable energy of life that should be the artist's goal above all? These are the airy tinkerings of his doubt; and as he passes from windy hill-top to green creeks and grazings some-times the bicycle sets him free. He sees it all afresh; nothing, nothing has ever been written yet: the entire white paper of the world is clean for his special portrait of all hunger, all joy, and all vexation. In the sunny market-place, sitting on a warm stone under the statue of the *poilu*, he feels that noble thrill of living and being surrounded by similar life. Even ants in an ant-hill feel it too, I dare say.

Blundering with a foreign language there sometimes comes a moment when you find, astonished, that you have talked for a few sentences fluently and without con-scious choice. Just so, in unexpected purities of feeling, you are aware that for an instant you might almost have stammered a phrase or two of the strangest foreign tongue, the universal cryptograms of beauty that legislatures are too busy to hear. This was the language, for instance, that Llewelyn Powys glimpsed between the lines when he read Matthew Arnold in the wilderness of Africa. He tells about it in his glorious "Black Laughter," a book richly written, with the savour of an old, old speech; one of those rarest of books, a book written not in dialect but in English sound and sparkling from the ancient cellars of the language.

So you climb on your bicycle again, renewing in your nostrils the summer sweetness of this divine and anxious land, and swim off with the Southwest at your back. What a book it would be if one could truly write just a straight record of one human farce. What an audacious book, with the title "For I So Loved the World."

4
Stijn Streuvels

Memories of a Naming Day

From *Memories*

*Then, it was "an ever-saddled horse which eats nothing." Today, it is simply a bicycle.
In between, it was variously styled a velocipede, a draisienne, a penny farthing, a high
wheeler, an ordinary, a kangaroo, a cycle, or a wheel, among others.*

*This nominative confusion is still with us. Call a bicycle a bike and watch the
motorcyclists' heads snap to attention. A bicyclist is not a cyclist, either. Otherwise how
explain that Frank Rooney's short story "Cyclists' Raid," which became the Marlon
Brando movie* The Wild Ones, *was all motorcycles and not a bicycle. Bicyclists be
grateful!*

*The only prudent course is to call this two-wheeled vehicle a bicycle, or so it would
seem. At least, its pronunciation is not disputed. Early difficulties over whether it was to
be a bi-sick-le or a bi-sigh-cle have been resolved. Joyce's bi-sex-ycle is but a distinctively Joycean evolution. So, a bicycle is a safe bet for a name, or is it?*

> When I ride my bicycle
> I pedal and pedal
> Knees up, knees down.
> Knees up, knees down.
>
> But when the boy next door
> Rides his,
> It's whizz—
> A chuck A chuck—

From Stijn Streuvels, *Volledige Werken, Deel 9: Herinnerringen*, trans. Bart Van't Riet ('t Leieschip
Kortryk), pp. 71–78.

And away
He's gone
With his
Knees steady—straight
In one place . . .
Because—
　　His bicycle has
　　A motor fastened on.[1]

Stijn Streuvels, the pseudonym for the Flemish author Frank Lateur, lived long enough (1871–1969) to see the bicycle named, unnamed, and renamed. Its appeal to him was instant and lasting, for it harmonized with his devotion to nature in its every detail, which he expressed so compellingly in his masterpiece The Flax Field *(1907). Streuvels was essentially a man of the soil whose prose works portrayed the Flemish countryside and its inhabitants impressionistically. His preoccupation was with the influence of environment upon a man's destiny. He enjoyed a considerable reputation in Flanders, Belgium, and Holland. Others of his works translated into English are* Working People *(1927) and* The Path of Life *(1915). These excerpts are a first translation into English from volume 9, entitled* Memories, *of his* Collected Works.

Yesterday, once again, after a mild summer rain, I was sitting in my vineyard distractedly watching a swarm of mosquitoes dancing on a sunbeam. The mosquitoes were so quick and nimble. They dashed around each other, gliding so effortlessly that, for them, there might not have been a law of gravity. It was as if the air itself gave them buoyancy. The little sunbeam, viewed through the fresh foliage and the unstirred air, seemed to be a place of supreme bliss, a heaven, for these little creatures, who were voluptuously enjoying the delights of motion.

We, poor mortals, can experience such ecstasy only in the mind. We can only observe the blue sky with a sigh of regret for that which is denied to us. We are full of longing because we feel the same impulse as the mosquitoes in ourselves. We realize the basic truth that motion is life, that the delight of motion is its rhythm and that in rhythm is happiness.

Notice with what pleasure the swallow skims through the air—an artist of flight—all space is his own. He possesses infinity. He bathes in the light as if it were his source of life.

Notice how the fish courses smoothly through the water and how he turns, dives, rises or stays in the same place, without effort.

For these blithe creatures, motion is a delight. They find happiness in their own nature. Their agility is their life.

But the paltry earthworm is not so endowed. Every moment for him is an effort. Happiness for him is found in resting, stretched out in a horizontal position. And like a fallen angel who once knew divine happiness, the earthworm feels the desire in his blood to join in the intoxicating game of flying and movement. He feels a passion to move through space, to go forward with furious speed, up and down hill, to swallow distances and to travel to places beyond belief. Yet, those with awkward limbs were given by God an intelligence and common sense to find ways to compensate for the limitations of their nature.

Shortly after his creation man must have realized that his ability to move was inferior to that of other creatures subordinate to him. He must have noticed that a horse could run faster than he could and so he thought of jumping on it and riding along. When he first looked at the birds in the air, man must have thought what it would be like to fasten wings to his shoulders.

Unfortunately that is as far as it went. Other and more serious matters kept mankind busy. His thirst for power busied him in a thousand different ways. Meanwhile, he continued to walk over the ground, without appreciating that wheels could improve on that, that instruments of iron and steel could help him to move over the surface of the earth.

The sunbeam is gone now and the mosquitoes too. The moon shines through the tops of the trees and the leaves are weighted in shadows. All movement has ceased and all is quiet, completely quiet.

As I lie there thinking, I imagine the joys of motion. At one moment, I sense the pleasures of the heaving and the rising of a small boat. At another, I toboggan away into the distance. I glide through space unsupported and I frolic there and sprawl and float like a fish in the water. On my own power I rise from the earth and I belong to the atmosphere. My happiness is not complete, for some consciousness remains that I delude myself because I feel my body lying down, very softly, but still lying, in the grass, under the trees.

Yet life is becoming more and more pleasant on earth. Only when mankind sought to improve his fate, to make his life more comfortable, did new pleasures come into his life. People are now able to travel on water and on land, and even in the air. We don't have to do everything on foot anymore and sport has become synonymous with pleasure. . . .

Bicycle, motorcycle, automobile, aeroplane, etc. These are the names of the machines that are to bring us new convenience. However long it took and however difficult it was to invent these machines and to get them working, to name them is proving even more difficult. The name iself is not so difficult—it is easy enough to find a name, but people won't accept just any word. The problem is, rather, to find a "living" word, a name that fits, a word which makes you feel, as if at the touch of a magic wand, that the machine could never have had any other name and that the word will live as long as the machine does.

Words have to be allowed to grow, they cannot be fabricated—that is the issue here.

I think of our Flemish word "rijwiel" for "bicycle." Has any machine ever become so popular, so widespread in so short a time, and have we ever had more difficulty in finding a name for it? The new vehicle was like a revelation, everyone wondered how something so simple could have remained unknown for so long, why it had taken so long to discover it. Each nation gave it a name of its own in their own language. The French had little trouble with this and, as always when they have to name something new, they took a piece of Greek and a piece of Latin and stuck them together, giving us the "vélocipède."

For everyday use, however, this name proved too long and too cumbersome for something so speedy, and they shortened it to "vélo." We Flemings, however, who seldom take the trouble to invent a new word and prefer to borrow from our neighbors, but then try to find some kind of related concept in the foreign word, changed it into "vlosse-peerd" (literally: "floss-horse" or "floss-machine"). The authorities, however, produced "rijwiel," "schrijwiel," "trapwiel," "wielpeerd" and finally "fiets," which in Holland at least proved to be the "living word." The English went about the task in their customary rational manner and came up with "bicycle," "wheel," or simply "cycle," which became the real name, the true name. The practical Germans started with "Fahrrad" and ended with "Rad."

The search is still on for what to call the self-propelled automobile. It has finally become just "auto."

We are still witnessing the development of flying machines and at the same time the development of the name to be given to them. It is too early yet to say which of the terms "aeroplane," "monoplane" and "biplane," "aerostat," "aeronautics" and "aviation" will survive.

It is curious that, if in any event we are going to give the known object a foreign name, it always has to be the French, with their clumsy, borrowed terms, who are the ones who win out in the end. Why shouldn't we borrow a word from another foreign language if, for example, that word sounds better and seems more appropriate, as when the inspired d'Annunzio invented the name "velivolo" for his Italian compatriots practicing the sport of gliding.

I don't know what the name was for the two-wheeled contraption that I first saw someone ride in my village, but I remember perfectly well what it looked like and how it was ridden.

It was in the good old simple days, when every village still had its "characters," unknown geniuses who lived the life of an ordinary villager in the guise of a baker, blacksmith or carpenter, accepted their lack of recognition and endeavored as best they could to maintain their name and reputation as "half-touched."

In our village, Benignus Kamslager was an "Übermensch" (character) of this category.

They called him "the Inventor." I was still only a lad then and didn't understand much of what went on, so that I can only speak of the "impression" Benignus made on us. It was a kind of fear mixed with admiration. He was a quiet man, a carpenter by trade, but his workshop was full of dark corners crammed with mystery and strange tools. He was friendly with Levinus, the local blacksmith, and the two of them worked together on their "inventions."

And so it happened one day. We kids had noticed nothing of the preparations, but there we all were that afternoon, together with everyone else in the village, when Benignus, the blacksmith and the smith's apprentices came out with something strange, the likes of which we had never seen before. One gigantic wheel with thin spokes radiating out from an axle like the beams of light radiating from a star, with a narrow rim round the outside; a bent piece of metal connected this big wheel with a tiny lower wheel, holding it between its two arms as in a pair of pincers. We suspected that something strange and miraculous was going to happen and we waited with bated breath. The show began almost immediately. Two of the blacksmith's helpers held the contraption upright; Levinus and the third apprentice hoisted Benignus up and placed him above the giant wheel, where he sat on a kind of saddle and had a metal bar to hold on to and two stirrups to put his feet in.

We had no idea yet of what was going to happen and couldn't imagine how Benignus would ever manage to keep his balance without assistance. But he suddenly yelled, "Let go!" and the apprentices jumped out of the way. Benignus began moving his feet like a weaver on the treadles of his loom. Nobody had expected this. Like a real-life miracle, the "inventor" moved forward atop his wheel. Shouts and yells filled the air. A whole gang of us ran after the magician; we screamed and waved our arms but, suddenly, in the midst of the general rejoicing, before anyone had seen it coming, there was a thud and the carpenter hit the cobbles while his contraption landed on top of him! We felt we had just witnessed a disaster. Then Klette, our hero's wife, shot through the crowd. She had a furious look on her face and she shouted something like: "You village idiot!" She added other recriminations, and all the bystanders burst out laughing. The experiment was finished for today, and the spectacle ended in general ridicule. Nobody believed any longer in the practicality of the invention, and the "inventor" himself was once more the laughing stock of the village.

But Benignus began again the next day, and the days after that. He rode his contraption, he fell off again, picked himself up and began afresh, nothing daunted. We got used to cramming the food into our mouths and running to the square to watch the spectacle of the "iron horse."

Levinus tried it in turn, and so did the smith's apprentices. One thing I know for sure, however, is that not one of them ever got farther than the village square. One time the wheel was badly cracked and it was taken to the workshop and left there with many other "inventions" in a corner of that storehouse of mysteries.

This was the first instance of the sport of bicycling that we saw in our village. Much later, when a real bicyclist appeared all of a sudden riding along the street on his camel-like "tricycle" and disappeared again without falling, we realized that such a thing was indeed possible. But for a long time afterwards there was genuine excitement whenever anyone spotted a "vlosse-peerd." I was too young at the time to plumb Benignus' feelings about these "bicycle machines" that worked better than his own; but I suspect that he must have regarded himself as a misunderstood genius—just like all other "inventors"—and maybe he got his own back by letting his wife know: "There, you see, I wasn't so stupid after all!"

5

Henry Miller

"My Best Friend"

From *My Bike & Other Friends*

Believe it or not, it was my bike. This one I had bought at Madison Square Garden, at the end of a six-day race. It had been made in Chemnitz, Bohemia and the six-day rider who owned it was a German, I believe. What distinguished it from other racing bikes was that the upper bar slanted down towards the handle bars.

I had two other bikes of American manufacture. These I would lend my friends when in need. But the one from the Garden no one but myself rode. It was like a pet. And why not? Did it not see me through all my times of trouble and despair?

Yes, I was in the throes of love, a first love, than which nothing is more disastrous, as a rule. My friends had become disgusted with me; they were deserting me, or *vice versa*, one by one. I was desolate and alone. Whether my parents knew of my sad plight I don't recall, but I am sure they knew that *something* was bothering me. That "something" was a beautiful young woman named Una Gifford, whom I had met during my high school days.

As I have told elsewhere, we were such naive creatures that perhaps we kissed two or three times—at a party, for example, never elsewhere. Though we both had telephones, we never telephoned one another. Why? I ask myself. (Because it would have been too bold perhaps.) We did write each other, but our letters were far apart. I remember how each day when I came home I turned first to the mantelpiece, where letters were kept, and it was almost always a blank absence that greeted me.

It was a period when I spent most of my days job-hunting (presumably). Actually, I went to a movie or the burlesk, (if I could afford it). Suddenly I stopped doing this, *and* did nothing. Nothing but ride the bike. Often I was in the saddle, so to speak, from morning till evening. I rode everywhere and usually at a good clip. Some days, I

From Henry Miller, "My Best Friend," in *My Bike & Other Friends* (Santa Barbara, Calif.: Capra Press, 1978), pp. 105–10.

encountered some of the six-day riders at the fountain in Prospect Park. They would permit me to set the pace for them along the smooth path that led from the Park to Coney Island.

I would visit old haunts, such as Bensonhurst, Ulmer Park, Sheepshead Bay and Coney Island. And always, no matter how diverse the scenery, I am thinking of *her*. Why doesn't she write me? When will the next party be? Etc., etc. I never had obscene thoughts about her, never dreamt of fucking her some day or even feeling her twat. No, she was like the princess in the fairy tale—untouchable even in dream.

Nor did it ever occur to me to ride to Greenspoint, where she lived, and ride up and down her street in the hope of catching a glance of her. Instead I rode to the faraway places, scenes associated with my childhood—and happy days.

I thought of those idyllic days ruefully, with a heavy heart. Where were they now, these dear pals of my early youth? Were they going through the same anguish as I—or were some of them married already perhaps?

Sometimes, after having finished a good book, I would think of nothing but the characters in that book. The characters I speculated about most were usually out of Dostoievsky's novels, particularly *The Idiot, The Brothers Karamazov* and *The Possessed*. Indeed they were no longer characters from a book, but living creatures, people who haunted my reveries and dream life. Thus, thinking of some absurd individual like Smerdyakov I would suddenly burst out laughing, only to quickly check myself and veer my thoughts toward her. It was impossible to rid my mind of her. I was obsessed, fascinated, bereaved. If by some great chance I may have run into her I would doubtless have been tongue-tied.

Oh yes, once in a blue moon I would receive a letter from her, usually from some summer resort where she was spending her vacation. It would always be a short letter, couched in conventional language—and, to my mind, completely devoid of feeling. And my reply would pretty much match her letter despite the fact that my heart was breaking.

Heart break! There was a subject I gave myself to totally. Did other people my age suffer the same pangs? Was first love always as painful, awkward and barren as this? Was I perhaps a special case, a "romantic" of the first water? The answers to these self-addressed queries were generally written in my friend's faces. The moment I mentioned her name a look of total uninterest would emanate from them. "Still thinking about her?" "Haven't you had enough already?" And so on. Implicit in their reactions was—how stupid can a guy become? And over a girl, no less.

As we spun along (me and my double) I went over these fundamental facts backwards and forwards. It was like studying a theorem in algebra. And never once did I run into a compassionate soul! I became so desolate that I took to calling my bike my friend. I carried on silent conversations with it. And of course I paid it the best attention. Which meant that everytime I returned home I stood the bike upside down, searched for a clean rag and polished the hubs and the spokes. Then I cleaned the chain, and greased it afresh. That operation left ugly stains on the stone in the walkway. My Mother would complain, beg me to put a newspaper under my wheel before starting to clean it. Sometimes she would get so incensed that she would say to me, in full sarcasm, "I'm surprised you don't take that thing to bed with you!" And I would retort—"I would if I had a decent room and a big enough bed."

That was another grievance I had to put up with—no room of my own. I slept in a narrow hall bedroom, decorated only by a shade to keep out the early morning light. If I read a book it was at the dining room table. I never used the parlor except to listen to phonograph records. It was when listening to some of my favorite records (in the gloomy parlor) that I would go through the greatest anguish about her. Each record I put on the machine only deepened my sorrow. The individual who moved me the most—from ecstasy to absolute despair—was the Jewish Cantor Sirota. Next to him came Amato, the baritone at the Metropolitan Opera. And after these came Caruso and John McCormack, the beloved Irish tenor.

I took care of my wheel as one would look after a Rolls Royce. If it needed repairs I always brought it to the same shop on Myrtle Avenue run by a Negro named Ed Perry. He handled the bike with kid gloves, you might say. He would always see to it that neither front nor back wheel wobbled. Often he would do a job for me without pay, because, as he put it, he never saw a man so in love with his bike as I was.

There were streets I avoided and streets I favored. In some streets the setting or the architecture actually gave me a lift. There were sedate streets and run-down ones, streets full of charm and others horrendously dull. (Didn't Whitman say somewhere, "Architecture is what you do to it when you look at it"?) As a dromomaniac I was able to carry on an elaborate interior dialogue and at the same time be aware of the stage setting through which I was moving. Riding the bike was a little different; I had to watch my p's and q's or take a bad spill.

About this time the champion sprinter was Frank Kramer, whom of course I idolized. Once I managed to stay right behind him during one of his practice spins from Prospect Park to Coney Island. I remember him slapping me on the back when I caught up with him and, as he slapped my back, said, "Good work, young feller— keep it up!" That day was a red letter day in my life. For once I forgot about Una Gifford and gave myself up to dreams of riding in Madison Square Garden some day, along with Walter Rutt, Eddie Root, Oscar Egg and the other celebrities of the track.

After a time, habituated to spending so many hours a day on my bike, I became less and less interested in my friends. My wheel had now become my one and only friend. I could rely on it, which is more than I could say about my buddies. It's too bad no one ever photographed me with my "friend." I would give anything now to know what we looked like.

Years later in Paris, I got myself another bike, but this one was an everyday sort, with brakes. To slow up demanded an effort on the part of one's legs. I could have had hand brakes put on my handle bars but that would have made me feel like a sissy. It was dangerous and thrilling to race through the city streets at top speed. Fortunately the automobile was not then much in evidence. What one really had to watch out for were youngsters playing in the middle of the street.

Mothers would warn their children to be careful, to keep their eyes open for that crazy young man who loves to speed through the streets. In other words I soon became a terror in the neighborhood.

I was both a terror and a delight. The kids were all begging their parents to get them a bike like mine.

How long can the heart ache without bursting? I have no idea. I only know that I put in a grueling period courting a girl *in absentia*. Even on my 21st birthday—a great event in my life—I sat some distance apart from her, too timid to open my mouth and tell her of my love. The last time I saw her was shortly after, when I plucked up the courage to ring her doorbell and tell her I was leaving for Juneau, Alaska, to become a placer miner.

It was almost harder to separate from my wheel from Chemnitz, Bohemia. I must have given it to one of my cronies, but to whom, I no longer remember.

It should be borne in mind that, although my heart was breaking, I could still enjoy a good laugh. When I had the dough, I would often take in a vaudeville show at the Palace or spend the afternoon at the Houston Street Burlesk or some other burlesk house. The comedians from these shows were later to become figures in radio and television. In other words, I could literally laugh on the wrong side of my face. It was this ability to laugh in spite of everything that saved me. I had already known that famous line from Rabelais—"For all your ills I give you laughter." I can say from personal experience that it is a piece of the highest wisdom. There is so precious little of it today—it's no wonder the drug pushers and psychoanalysts are in the saddle.

6

William Saroyan

Selections from Saroyan

From *The Bicycle Rider in Beverly Hills*

William Saroyan, Pulitzer Prize winner and author of The Human Comedy, *among many other works, was, in his youth, a Western Union messenger. His experiences as he bicycled his messages of gladness or of gloom became the focus of* The Human Comedy. *His grateful appreciation to the bicycle for all that it imparted to his life pervades his* Bicycle Rider in Beverly Hills, *from which the ensuing series of excerpts is taken.*

Saroyan's frequent use of the bicycle as a dominant element in his works, both long and short, compels the conclusion that he, like no other author, has been touched by the movement, the grace, and the mystique of the bicycle. As he said of Dewey in "The Coldest Winter since 1854," it could also be said of him—he must have done "some mighty ornamental riding" and then "with elegance and daring."

It is Saroyan's particular strength that, as Flann O'Brien put it, he can take the ordinary and infuse it with "meaning and sentiment."

The Rhyme and Rhythm of It All

Before I was sixteen I had many bicycles. I have no idea what became of them. I remember, though, that I rode them so hard they were always breaking down. The spokes of the wheels were always getting loose so that the wheels became crooked. The chains were always breaking. I bore down on the handlebars with so much force

From William Saroyan, *The Bicycle Rider in Beverly Hills* (New York: Ballantine Books, 1952), pp. 8–10, 16–17, 22–23.

in sprinting, in speeding, in making quick getaways, that the handlebars were always getting loose and I was always tightening them. But the thing about my bicycles that I want to remember is the way I rode them, what I thought while I rode them, and the music that came to me.

First of all, my bikes were always rebuilt second-hand bikes. They were lean, hard, tough, swift, and designed for usage. I rode them with speed and style. I found out a great deal about style from riding them. Style in writing, I mean. Style in everything. I did not ride for pleasure. I rode to get somewhere, and I don't mean from the house on San Benito Avenue in Fresno to the Public Library there. I mean I rode to get somewhere *myself*. I did not loaf on my bike. I sometimes rested on it after a hard day's riding, on my way home to supper and sleep, sliding off the seat a little to the left, pedaling with the left leg, resting the other on the saddle, and letting the bike weave right and left easily as I moved forward. The style I learned was this: I learned to go and make it fast. I learned to know at one and the same time how my bike was going, how it was holding up, where I was, where I would soon be, and where in all probability I would finally be.

In the end I always went home to supper and sleep.

A man learns style from everything, but I learned mine from things on which I moved, and as writing is a thing which moves I think I was lucky to learn as I did.

A bike can be an important appurtenance of an important ritual. Moving the legs evenly and steadily soon brings home to the bike-rider a valuable knowledge of pace and rhythm, and a sensible respect for timing and the meeting of a schedule.

Out of rhythm come many things, perhaps all things. The physical action compels action of another order—action of mind, memory, imagination, dream, hope, order, and so on. The physical action also establishes a deep respect for grace, seemliness, effectiveness, power with ease, naturalness, and so on. The action of the imagination brings home to the bicycle-rider the limitlessness of the potential in all things. He finds out that there are many excellent ways in which to ride a bike effectively, and this acquaintanceship with the ways and the comparing of them gives him an awareness of a parallel potential in all other actions. Out of the action of the imagination comes also music and memory.

In the early days of the search I heard many great symphonies which no composer ever put to paper and no orchestra ever peformed. This is understandable, I hope. As the saying is, they came to me. I was born restless and was forever eager to be going. There never seemed to be enough of going for me. I wanted to get out to more and more. This might have worn me out, but what it actually did was refresh and strengthen me. Wanting to go and not being able to do so might have given me another order of strength, but the order that I received was to *want* to go and to go. To want to search and to do so.

On the way I found out all the things without which I could never be the writer I am. I was not yet sixteen when I understood a great deal, from having ridden bicycles for so long, about style, speed, grace, purpose, value, form, integrity, health, humor, music, breathing, and finally and perhaps best of the relationship between the beginning and the end.

The Singing Wheel

As I rode my bike, music began to *happen* to me. Insofar as I am able to describe it it was orchestral music. The piano was often involved, but on the whole the music was that of a large orchestra which had become a single instrument. The music had magnificent form, great accumulative power, and passion of a high order—the passion, that is, of control, restraint, and denial—the human conditions out of which we know collective passion is most apt to reach an individual body and soul. Even though I alone knew about this music, I cherished it deeply and took great pride in it.

I both listened to the music and made it, or at any rate so it seemed. It was certainly happening to me, and it was happening as I performed other, less magnificent, work— as I delivered or picked up telegrams. The adventure of the music was always great, but in a quiet way. While the music was happening I kept wondering how it would fulfill itself, how it would round out its form and be finished. The music, I think it is quite understandable, tended to end when a bike ride ended, but this was not always so. Frequently one work, in one key of music or one dimension of memory or inner experience, would endure an entire work day and then carry itself over into evening, night, and sleep. In the morning, though, it would be gone and forgotten. It would be forgotten, that is, in its details, but not in its quality. If I took to the music actively and began to whistle as well as listen to it, this did not stop the orchestra. But when the bike ride ended and it was time for me to go among people to deliver or pick up a telegram, the orchestral portion of the music would fall away from inner hearing, no doubt because now the external hearing was involved with other sounds, but the whistling would continue while I was among the people, in a business office, or in a grape packing house, or in the telegraph office itself. This whistling bothered some people. The wife of the manager of the telegraph office once complained about it to her husband who took me aside and with some awkwardness asked me not to whistle while I was in the telegraph office. I was astonished by this request for two reasons: first, because I couldn't imagine anybody resenting it. But genius is often deeply resented by small souls, so that if the world were a reasonable place all geniuses would be despised outcasts and eccentrics.

I was not always lucky in what I heard. It was not always an orchestra at work on a grand symphony. It was frequently a song, and quite strangely it would be a song which was not whole, which never in fact became whole. It would be a fragment of a song, certainly insofar as the words were concerned. And here perhaps lies the clue to the failure of this form to fulfill itself—its involvement in words. For words are inadequate instruments of communication, or of the making of wholeness. Sounds and rhythms and measures must apparently see themselves through to ends, but words must be *driven* to their ends, and that is the difficulty and majesty of writing. All the same I was lucky enough. At a time when the air of the world still had purity I heard great music which no one else heard.

A Past Recollection Refreshed

My son wanted a bicycle, I bought him one, he rode it a month, and then he wanted a bigger one. His own bicycle was too big for him, but it was not the biggest bicycle built, and he wanted the biggest. I told him he would not be able to ride the big bicycle. He said he would. I knew he wouldn't, but I also knew it was necessary and important for him to believe that he would. I spoke to the bicycle man about the matter while my son listened. The man said my son would not be able to ride the bicycle. It was altogether too big for him. My son told the bicycle man that he *would* be able to ride it. I asked the man how much of the sixty dollars I had paid for my son's bicycle he would be able to allow me in a trade-in for the big bicycle. He said he would not be able to allow me anything for it, but that he would try to sell the bicycle for me. He believed he might be able to get thirty dollars for it. I took my boy and his bike home. I told him his bike was a fine one. I told him he rode it well, which was the truth. These things meant nothing to him. He wanted the big bike. I discussed the matter with his mother and we had an argument, and I became angry at my son, at his mother, and at myself. The boy wept. I went out of the house to a small bar and sat there an hour, drinking and thinking. I had shouted at my son that I would not buy him the big bike, I would never again buy him anything, because he did not appreciate anything I bought him. Early the next morning I went to the bicycle shop and bought the big bike, a Raleigh, manufactured in England. I took it home and showed it to my son. I let him get up on the seat and try to ride, and sure enough, my son rode the bike, just as he had said he would, but he did not ride it well. I told him it was my bike but that it was also his bike, and that he and I would go for rides in Beverly Hills together, beginning that May evening when I got home after work. I put the bike in the garage of the house on North Rodeo and locked it. That evening after work my son and I got on our bikes and rode up Benedict Canyon until we came to the top of a hill there. Then we rode down the hill together.

Riding a bicycle in Beverly Hills with my son made me remember the bicycle-rider I was years ago in Fresno, and it made me want to keep a record of what I remember, which is this book.

7

W. Somerset Maugham

The Transports of Bicycling

From *Cakes and Ale*

Bicycling through the rural countryside of England in and about Blackstable, Kent, as described by W. Somerset Maugham in Cakes and Ale, *could just as easily recall a similar experience in this country or elsewhere. Indeed, the feeling is so universal that the imagery of Maugham's narrator, Willie Ashenden, could summon up identical emotions today, yesterday or whenever.*

Ashenden recollects the days when, some thirty years before, he had bicycled for pleasure and in search of brass rubbings in the company of the famed novelist Edward Driffield and his first wife, Rosie. This book, Cakes and Ale, *has not received the critical acclaim of its author's* Of Human Bondage, *but Maugham considered it to be the one he liked best. And the resemblance of Edward Driffield to Thomas Hardy, also a bicyclist, is so intriguingly close, in spite of the author's disclaimers, that it has been the source of some study and much speculation.*

But though I couldn't remember that Driffield had ever said anything significant during those long rides of ours, I had a very acute recollection of the *feel* of them. Blackstable was peculiar in this, that though it was on the sea, with a long shingly beach and marshland at the back, you had only to go about half a mile inland to come

From W. Somerset Maugham, *Cakes and Ale* (New York: Random House, 1950), pp. 133–34.

into the most rural country in Kent. Winding roads that ran between the great fat green fields and clumps of huge elms, substantial and with a homely stateliness like good old Kentish farmers' wives, high-coloured and robust, who had grown portly on good butter and homemade bread and cream and fresh eggs. And sometimes the road was only a lane, with thick hawthorn hedges, and the green elms overhung it on either side so that when you looked up there was only a strip of blue sky between. And as you rode along in the warm, keen air you had a sensation that the world was standing still and life would last for ever. Although you were pedalling with such energy you had a delicious feeling of laziness. You were quite happy when no one spoke, and if one of the party from sheer high spirits suddenly put on speed and shot ahead it was a joke that everyone laughed at and for a few minutes you pedalled as hard as you could. And we chaffed one another innocently and giggled at our own humour. Now and then one would pass cottages with little gardens in front of them and in the gardens were hollyhocks and tiger lilies; and a little way from the road were farmhouses, with their spacious barns and oasthouses; and one would pass through hopfields with the ripening hops hanging in garlands. The public houses were friendly and informal, hardly more important than cottages, and on the porches often honeysickle would be growing. The names they bore were usual and familiar: the Jolly Sailor, the Merry Ploughman, the Crown and Anchor, the Red Lion. . . .

8

Frederic Remington

The Bicycle Goes to War

From "The Colonel of the First Cycle Infantry"

Frederic Remington, best known as America's artist of the West, was also an author. His writings were often simply the backdrop for his sketches, which was apparently the case in the following selection from his short story "The Colonel of the First Cycle Infantry." How else can one explain the writing of an ill-disguised panegyric on behalf of the bicycle by the man who memorialized the horse in the settlement of the American West?

In this excerpt Colonel Pedal, the aptly named commander of the First Cycle Infantry, explains to Ladigo, a colonel of the cavalry, the merits of the bicycle in executing quick and silent wartime raids. Remington's prescience was uncanny. He did not live to know of Japanese General Yamashita's "clever use of the bicycle" in transporting men and supplies through the jungle to force the British evacuation of Singapore in 1942. Indeed, at the same time as the Japanese had mobilized the bicycle for assault purposes, on the European front some Dutch resistance fighters were bicycling "with foolhardy courage" during saturation air raids while others "cycled all over the area, delivering forged food ration cards to Dutchmen hiding out from the Germans."[1]

Nor could Remington have foreseen that the Viet Minh during their war with the French in Indochina would cause the fall of Dien Bien Phu in 1954 largely because "the bicycle proved itself superior to every other means of supply and transport."[2] Remington would not have known, as J. G. Farrell relates in his historical novel The Siege of Krishnapur, *that the British defenders of Krishnapur during the Sepoy uprising of 1857 would bring the bicycle (really the Draisienne) "out of oblivion . . . as the very design required for [a] new system of defence"[3]—a defense that broke the Sepoy attack. The bicycle, as a support vehicle, was significant in another famed British defense, this*

From Frederic Remington, "The Colonel of the First Cycle Infantry," *Harper's Weekly*, May 18, 1895.

"I began the retreat as I intended." (From "The Colonel of the First Cycle Infantry" by Frederic Remington)

time of Mafeking during the Anglo-Boer War of 1899. While Colonel Robert S. S. Baden-Powell stoutly repulsed the Boer attack for 217 days from October 12, 1899, to May 17, 1900, his communications system throughout the widespread Mafeking compound was kept intact by the intrepid assistance of young bicyclists who carried the messages which informed and alerted the defenders.

Even in the Vietnam War, so recently ended, bicycles specially designed to "haul 500 pounds of supplies," more than even an elephant could carry through the jungle, poured down the Ho Chi Minh Trail to the dismay and frustration of the South Vietnamese and their American allies, who could find no effective means to plug the dike. "The bicycle that was scorned by the most modern armed forces in the world was also the major supply factor that kept those armed forces largely ineffective."[4]

"Now, Colonel, do you consider that you can move your men successfully in a hilly or mountainous country?" inquired Ladigo.

"In all candor, no—not to good advantage. I can march up a hill as fast as infantry, and go down at limited-express speed; but I really want a rather flat country, with lots of roads. I am not particular as to the quality of the roads, so there are enough of them. I can move through snow which has been tracked down by teams; I can fly on the ice; and when it is muddy there is always an inch or so beside the road which is not muddy, and that is enough for me. A favorable place for a bicycle is along a railroad track—going in the center or at one side. When suddenly attacked, my men can get out of the road like a covey of quail, and a bicycle can be trundled across the worst possible country as fast as a man can travel; for, you see, all the weight of the man's gun and pack are on the wheel, which runs without any appreciable resistance, and all bikemen know how to throw a bicycle over a fence with ease, and my average march is eighty miles a day. Ladigo, remember—eighty miles a day! No kind of roads, no conditions of weather, or anything but superior force, can stop my command for an instant, sir."

And the Colonel of Cavalry rose and added, "Colonel Pedal, will you have a drink with me?"

9

Flann O'Brien

All Those Endearing Charms

From *The Third Policeman*

The bicycle as a sex symbol? Hardly! But it has come perilously close.

The bicycle has served as a suggestively amorous device in Nabokov's Lolita *where, after having tweaked Humbert Humbert's memory of the hotel where he "raped" her, "with a yelp of amorous vernal laughter she [Lolita] slapped the glossy bole and tore uphill, to the end of the street, and then rode back, feet at rest on stopped pedals, posture relaxed, one hand dreaming in her print-flowered lap."[1] At an earlier point in their fevered romance, Humbert is almost overcome by the contagion of youth and movement. In his treasured memory, he sees his little Lo, his most cherished nymphet*

spinning up and down Thayer Street on her beautiful young bicycle: rising on the pedals to work on them lustily, then sinking back in languid posture while the speed wore itself off; and then she would stop at our mailbox and, still astride, would flip through a magazine she found there, and put it back, and press her tongue to one side of her upperlip and push off with her foot, and again sprint through pale shade and sun.[2]

To the Irish, the bicycle can be a subject of merriment, as Flann O'Brien has handily established in The Third Policeman *and* The Dalkey Archive. *But it can also be the object of quite lavish and sexually symbolic praise by them, as Flann O'Brien proved again in the following excerpts from* The Third Policeman.

In this work, the protagonist and narrator is under a loose sort of imprisonment in a

From Flann O'Brien, *The Third Policeman* (New York: Walker and Company, 1967), pp. 167–71, 173–74.

rural Irish police barracks while awaiting his execution for the robbery and killing of old Phillip Mathers. His warders are Sergeant Pluck and Policeman MacCruiskeen. During the momentary absence of both, the narrator awakens to discover that Sergeant Pluck's bicycle is involved in some strange bedevilment.

I arose and stretched my legs up and down the floor. From my chair by the fire I had noticed idly that the front wheel of a bicycle was protruding into view in the passage leading to the rear of the barrack. It was not until I sat down again on the chair after exercising for a quarter of an hour that I found myself staring at this wheel in some surprise. I could have sworn it had moved out farther in the interval because three-quarters of it was now visible whereas I could not see the hub the last time. Possibly it was an illusion due to an altered position between my two sittings but this was quite unlikely because the chair was small and would not permit of much variation of seat if there was any question of studying comfort. My surprise began to mount to astonishment.

I was on my feet again at once and had reached the passage in four long steps. A cry of amazement—now almost a habit with me—escaped from my lips as I looked around. MacCruiskeen in his haste had left the door of the cell wide open with the ring of keys hanging idly in the lock. In the back of the small cell was a collection of paint-cans, old ledgers, punctured bicycle tubes, tyre repair outfits and a mass of peculiar brass and leather articles not unlike ornamental horse harness but clearly intended for some whole different office. The front of the cell was where my attention was. Leaning half-way across the lintel was the Sergeant's bicycle. Clearly it could not have been put there by MacCruiskeen because he had returned instantly from the cell with his can of paint and his forgotten keys were proof that he had not gone back there before he rode away. During my absence in my sleep it is unlikely that any intruder would have come in merely to move the bicycle half-way out of where it was. On the other hand I could not help recalling what the Sergeant had told me about his fears for his bicycle and his decision to keep it in solitary confinement. If there is good reason for locking a bicycle in a cell like a dangerous criminal, I reflected, it is fair enough to think that it will try to escape if given the opportunity. I did not quite believe this and I thought it was better to stop thinking about the mystery before I was compelled to believe it because if a man is alone in a house with a bicycle which he thinks is edging its way along a wall he will run away from it in fright; and I was by now so occupied with the thought of my escape that I could not afford to be frightened of anything which could assist me.

The bicycle itself seemed to have some peculiar quality of shape or personality which gave it distinction and importance far beyond that usually possessed by such machines. It was extremely well-kept with a pleasing lustre on its dark-green bars and oil-bath and a clean sparkle on the rustless spokes and rims. Resting before me like a tame domestic pony, it seemed unduly small and low in relation to the Sergeant yet when I measured its height against myself I found it was bigger than any other bicycle that I knew. This was possibly due to the perfect proportion of its parts which combined merely to create a thing of surpassing grace and elegance, transcending all standards of size and reality and existing only in the absolute validity of its own unexceptionable dimensions. Notwithstanding the sturdy cross-bar it seemed ineffably female and fastidious, posing there like a mannequin rather than leaning idly like a loafer against the wall, and resting on its prim flawless tyres with irreproachable precision, two tiny points of clean contact with the level floor. I passed my hand with unintended tenderness—sensuously, indeed—across the saddle. Inexplicably it reminded me of a human face, not by any simple resemblance of shape or feature but by some association of textures, some incomprehensible familiarity at the fingertips. The leather was dark with maturity, hard with a noble hardness and scored with all the sharp lines and fine wrinkles which the years with their tribulations had carved into my own countenance. It was a gentle saddle yet calm and courageous, unembittered by its confinement and bearing no mark upon it save that of honourable suffering and honest duty. I knew that I liked this bicycle more than I had ever liked any other bicycle, better even than I had liked some people with two legs. I liked her unassuming competence, her docility, the simple dignity of her quiet way. She now seemed to rest beneath my friendly eyes like a tame fowl which will crouch submissively, awaiting with out-hunched wings the caressing hand. Her saddle seemed to spread invitingly into the most enchanting of all seats while her two handlebars, floating finely with the wild grace of alighting wings, beckoned to me to lend my mastery for free and joyful journeyings, the lightest of light running in the company of the swift groundwinds to safe havens far away, the whir of the true front wheel in my ear as it spun perfectly beneath my clear eye and the strong fine back wheel with unadmired industry raising gentle dust on the dry roads. How desirable her seat was, how charming the invitation of her slim encircling handle-arms, how unaccountably competent and reassuring her pump resting warmly against her rear thigh!

With a start I realised that I had been communing with this strange companion and—not only that—conspiring with her. Both of us were afraid of the same Sergeant, both were awaiting the punishments he would bring with him on his return, both were thinking that this was the last chance to escape beyond his reach; and both knew that the hope of each lay in the other, that we would not succeed unless we went together, assisting each other with sympathy and quiet love.

*   *   *

In the next moment I was fumbling for the barrack latch with the Sergeant's willing bicycle in my care. We had travelled the passage and crossed the kitchen with the grace of ballet dancers, silent, swift and faultless in our movements, united in the acuteness of our conspiracy. In the country which awaited us outside we stood for a moment undecided, looking into the lowering night and inspecting the dull sameness of the gloom. It was to the left the Sergeant had gone with MacCruiskeen, to that quarter the next world lay and it was leftwards that all my troubles were. I led the bicycle to the middle of the road, turned her wheel resolutely to the right and swung myself into the centre of her saddle as she moved away eagerly under me in her own time.

How can I convey the perfection of my comfort on the bicycle, the completeness of my union with her, the sweet responses she gave me at every particle of her frame? I felt that I had known her for many years and that she had known me and that we understood each other utterly. She moved beneath me with agile sympathy in a swift, airy stride, finding smooth ways among the stony tracks, swaying and bending skilfully to match my changing attitudes, even accommodating her left pedal patiently to the awkward working of my wooden leg. I sighed and settled forward on her handlebars, counting with a happy heart the trees which stood remotely on the dark roadside, each telling me that I was further and further from the Sergeant.

I seemed to cut an unerring course between two sharp shafts of wind which whistled coldly past each ear, fanning my short side hairs. Other winds were moving about in the stillness of the evening, loitering in the trees and moving leaves and grasses to show that the green world was still present in the dark. Water by the roadside, always over-shouted in the roistering day, now performed audibly in its hidings. Flying beetles came against me in their broad loops and circles, whirling blindly against my chest; overhead geese and heavy birds were calling in the middle of a journey. Aloft in the sky I could see the dim tracery of the stars struggling out here and there between the clouds. And all the time she was under me in a flawless racing onwards, touching the road with the lightest touches, surefooted, straight and faultless, each of her metal bars like spear-shafts superbly cast by angels.

10

John Galsworthy

Pedaling the Suffrage

From "Four-in-Hand Forsyte"

"Few articles ever used by man (or woman) have ever created so great a revolution in social conditions"[1] as has the bicycle. The bicycle's role in the early suffragette movement was crucial. With the advent of the safety bicycle and the drop frame, women in large numbers took to the wheel. To increase their comfort and safety, the long and cumbersome skirts they had routinely worn had to be altered. Bloomers, designed much earlier by Mrs. Amelia Bloomer, were the ideal dress to complement a women's cycling costume. Then too pedal pushers also came into vogue. As a result, "[t]he bicycle makers . . . accomplished more for [women's] dress reform in two years than the preachers of that cult [had] accomplished since clothes began to be the fashion."[2] These "bifurcated garments" soon became the order of the day for bicycling women.

Once women went out riding they soon went alone or with a man—unchaperoned. The bicycle built for two was not expandable to include a chaperone. And chaperones, who were usually elderly ladies, were not inclined to blaze new trails for themselves, even on safety bicycles. The new freedom this afforded women led one poet to proclaim

> In olden times the woman rode
>   As fitted one of subject mind:
> Her lord and master sat before,
>   She on a pillion sat behind.
>
> But now upon her flying wheel
>   She holds her independent way,
> And when she rides a race with man,
>   'Tis even chance she wins the day.[3]

From John Galsworthy, "Four-in-hand Forsyte," in *On Forsyte 'Change* (New York: Charles Scribner's Sons, 1930), pp. 203–12.

Once women were accepted as bicyclists, other avenues to full-fledged independence opened to them. As Roger Vailland put it in his post–World War II fictional study of the life-ways in the rural Italian town of Manacore,

Then a few girls had appeared, the same brave band of girls who, in the chaos of the immediate post-war years, had dared to go about on bicycles, despite the abuse of the old women and stones of the *guaglioni,* incited by the priest, and who had forced Manacore to accept their use of the bicycle, despite the obscenities shouted at them by the men of the town, who compared the cycle saddle with other pointed objects and cycles in general with everything else which could be straddled, despite another schoolmaster, who was a Red but who said it was necessary to seize

power first and *then* change standards of behaviour, who maintained that women's claims to ride bicycles, like Klara Zetkin's claim to free love, formed part of the bourgeois demands condemned by Lenin in a famous letter. These same girls, having conquered the bicycle, then braved the beach, in the same swimming costumes they still wore today, extending over the shoulders and descending to half-way down the thigh, with a brassiere underneath and skirt covering the stomach and thighs. The first two seasons, their brothers protected them, standing guard up on the road, their hands in their pockets, wrapped round grafting knives, while the girls bathed or lay in the sun, glorious in defiance, drunk with audacity.[1]

The bicycle did not have the staying power to carry women's liberation to its fruition. Nor did it make its inroads unimpeded by harsh insults and strident criticism. To some

it was horrid to see "unchaperoned women . . . blithely riding along lonely lanes . . . a
prey to any passing tramp, desperate with hunger and naturally vicious. Their limbs
. . . on display for the world to leer at. Petticoats fluttering brazenly . . . sleeves drawn
back, bosoms unlaced. . . . Now you see what . . . bicycles have brought us to—
licentiousness and depravity."⁵ Although these brickbats were hurled by the Trick Cy-
clist in Stewart Parker's play Spokesong, or, The Common Wheel, *they could just as*
well have been the words of Swithin Forsyte in the following selection from John
Galsworthy's Forsyte Saga.

Such historians as record the tides of social manners and morals, have neglected
the bicycle. Yet would it be difficult to deny that this 'invention of the devil,' as
Swithin Forsyte always called it because 'a penny-farthing' had startled his greys at
Brighton in 1874—has been responsible for more movement in manners and morals
than anything since Charles the Second. At its bone-shaking inception innocent,
because of its extraordinary discomfort, in its 'penny-farthing' stage harmless, because only dangerous to the lives and limbs of the male sex, it began to be a dissolvent
of the most powerful type when accessible to the fair in its present form. Under its
influence, wholly or in part, have wilted chaperons, long and narrow skirts, tight
corsets, hair that would come down, black stockings, thick ankles, large hats, prudery
and fear of the dark; under its influence, wholly or in part, have bloomed week-ends,
strong nerves, strong legs, strong language, knickers, knowledge of make and shape,
knowledge of woods and pastures, equality of sex, good digestion and professional
occupation—in four words, the emancipation of woman. But to Swithin, and possibly
for that reason, it remained what it had been in the beginning, an invention of the
devil. For, apart from that upset to his greys, having lived his first sixteen years with
'Prinny' in the offing, and formed himself under Lord Melbourne, the Cider Cellars
and the Pavilion at Brighton, he remained to the end in taste and deportment a Buck
of the Regency, unable to divest himself of a love for waistcoats and jewellery, or the
conviction that women were perquisites to whom elegance and—ah—charm were of
the first necessity.

These are the considerations which must be borne in mind when we come to the
recital of an episode current on Forsyte 'Change in the year 1890.

Swithin had spent the early months at Brighton and was undoubtedly feeling his
liver by April. The last three years had tried him severely and for some time past he
had parted with his phaeton, confining his carriage exercise to a double brougham, in
which, drawn by his greys, he passed every afternoon up and down the front from the
end of Hove to the beginning of Kemptown. What he thought of during these excursions has never been disclosed. Possibly of nothing. And why not? For so entirely
lonely an old man, provocation towards thought was conspicuous by its absence; and
though there was always himself to think about, a man cannot for ever be bothered by

that. The return to his hotel would be achieved by four o'clock. He would be assisted to alight by his valet, and would walk into the hotel unaided, Alphonse following with the specially strong air-cushion on which he always sat, and his knee rug of a Highland plaid. In the hall Swithin would stand for perhaps a minute, settling his chin more firmly, rounding his heavy eyelids more carefully over his gouty eyes. He would then hold out his gold-headed malacca cane to be taken from him, and slightly spread his hands, gloved in bright wash-leather, to indicate that his coat, blue, lined with squirrel and collared with astrakhan, should be removed. This having been done and his gloves and black felt hat with somewhat square top taken off, he would touch the tuft on his lower lip, as if to assure himself that its distinction was still with him.

At this hour he was used to take a certain seat in a certain draughtless corner and smoke half a cigar before ascending in the lift to the sitting-room of his suite. He sat there so motionless and was known to be so deaf, that no one spoke to him; but it seemed to him that in this way he saw more life and maintained the outlived reputation of 'Four-in-Hand' Forsyte. Wedged forward by cushions, as though still in his brougham, with his thick legs slightly apart, he would apply the cigar to his ear; having heard it carefully in its defence, he would hold it a minute between puffy thumb and puffier forefinger of that yellowish-white which betokens the gouty subject, then place it in his mouth and wait for it to be lighted. With chest pouted, under a black satin stock and diamond pin, so that he appeared to be of one thickness from neck down, he would sit, contemplating that which was not yet called the Lounge from under drooped puffy lids, as might some Buddah from the corner of a temple. His square old face, perfectly pale, of one long withdrawn from privilege of open air, would be held so still that people would glance at it as they might have at a clock. The little white moustaches and tuft on the lower lip, the tufts above the eyes, and hair still stylish on the forehead, accentuated perhaps its resemblance to a dial. Once in a way someone whose father or uncle had known him in old days, would halt in passing, as though about to set his watch by him and say: "How d'you do, Mr. Forsyte?" Then would an expression as of a cat purring spread on Swithin's face, and he would murmur in a voice fat and distinguished: "Ah! How de do? Haven't seen your father lately." And as the father was almost always dead, this would end the conversation. But Swithin would sit the squarer because he had been spoken to.

When his cigar was about half smoked a change would come. The hand holding it would loll over the arm of the chair, trembling a little. The chin would slip slowly down between the wide apart point of the stiff white collar; the puffy rounding of the eyelids would become complete; a slight twitching would possess the lips, a faint steady puffing take its place—Swithin would be asleep. And those who passed would look at him with cold amusement, a kind of impatience, possibly a touch of compassion, for, on these occasions, as if mindful of past glories, Swithin did not snore. And then, of course, would come the moment of awakening. The chin would jerk up, the lips part, all breath would seem to be expelled from him in a long sigh; the eyes coming ungummed would emit a glassy stare; the tongue would move over the roof of the mouth and the lips; and an expression as of a cross baby would appear on the old face. Pettishly he would raise the half-smoked cigar, look at it as if it owed him something which it was not going to pay, and let it slip between finger and thumb into a spittoon. Then he would sit the same, yet not the same, waiting for some servant to come near enough for him to say: "Hi! Tell my valet to come, will you?" and when Alphonse appeared: "Oh! There you are! I nodded off. I'll go up now."

Assisted from the chair, he would stand fully a minute feeling giddy, then square but bearing heavily on the cane and one leg, would move towards the lift, followed by Alphonse and the special cushions. And someone perhaps would mutter as he passed: "There goes old Forsyte. Funny old boy, isn't he?"

But such was not the order of events on that particular April afternoon reported on Forsyte 'Change. For when, divested of hat and overcoat, he was about to walk to his accustomed corner, he was observed to raise his cane with the words: "Here! There's a lady sitting in my chair!"

A figure, indeed, in rather a short skirt, occupied that sacred spot.

"I'll go up!" said Swithin, pettishly. But as he moved, she rose and came towards him.

"God bless me!" said Swithin, for he had recognised his niece Euphemia.

Now the youngest child of his brother Nicholas was in some respects Swithin's pet aversion. She was, in his view, too thin, and always saying the wrong thing; besides, she squeaked. He had not seen her since, to his discomfort, he had sat next her at the concert of Francie's fourpenny foreigner.

"How are you, Uncle? I thought I *must* look you up, while I was down."

"I've got gout," said Swithin. "How's your father?"

"Oh! just as usual. He says he's bad, but he isn't." And she squeaked slightly.

Swithin fixed her with his stare. Upset already by her occupation of his chair, he was on the point of saying: 'Your father's worth twenty of you,' but, remembering in time the exigencies of deportment, he murmured more gallantly: "Where have you sprung from?"

"My bicycle."

"What!" said Swithin. "You ride one of those things!"

Again Euphemia squeaked.

"Oh! Uncle! One of those things!"

"Well," said Swithin, "what else are they—invention of the devil. Have some tea?"

"Thank you, Uncle, but you must be tired after your drive."

"Tired! Why should I be tired? Waiter! Bring some tea over there—to my chair."

Having thus conveyed to her the *faux pas* she had committed by sitting in his chair, he motioned her towards it and followed.

On reaching the chair there was an ominous moment.

"Sit down," said Swithin.

For a moment Euphemia hovered on its edge, then with a slight squeak said: "But it's your chair, Uncle."

"Alphonse," said Swithin, "bring another."

When the other chair had been brought, the cushions placed for Swithin in his own, and they were seated, Euphemia said:

"Didn't you know that women were beginning to ride bicycles, Uncle?"

The hairs on Swithin's underlip stood out.

"Women," he said. "You may well say women. Fancy a lady riding a thing like that!"

Euphemia squeaked more notably.

"But, Uncle, why *like that?*"

"With a leg on each side, disturbing the traffic," and glancing at Euphemia's skirt, he added: "Showing their legs."

Euphemia gave way to silent laughter.

"Oh! Uncle," she said, at last, in a strangled voice, "you'll kill me!"

But at this moment came tea.

"Help yourself," said Swithin, shortly; "I don't drink it." And, taking from the waiter a light for his cigar, he sat staring with pale eyes at his niece. Not till after her second cup did she break that silence.

"Uncle Swithin, do tell me why they called you 'Four-in-Hand Forsyte,' I've always wanted to know."

Swithin's stare grew rounder.

"Why shouldn't they?"

"'Four-in-hand'; but you never drove more than a pair, did you?"

Swithin preened his neck. "Certainly not! It was just a compliment to my—er—style."

"Style!" repeated Euphemia. "Oh, Uncle!" and she grew so crimson that he thought she had swallowed a crumb.

Then slowly but surely it dawned on him that he was the cause of her emotion. Into his cheeks a faint pink crept; something moved in his throat, something that might choke him if he were not careful. He did not stir.

Euphemia rose.

"I *must* be going, Uncle. I *have* enjoyed seeing you, you're looking so well. Don't get up, please, and thank you ever so for the tea." She bent above him, pecked at his forehead, and showing her legs, walked towards the door. Her face was still very red and as she went, Swithin seemed to hear her squeak.

He stayed unmoving for a second, then struggled to get up. He had no stick to help him, no time to give to the process, and he struggled. He got on his feet, stood a moment to recover, and then, without his cane, walked, he knew not how, to the window of the hall that looked out on to the parade. There she was—that niece of his, that squeaker, mounting her bicycle, moving it, mounting it, riding it away. Into the traffic she went, pedalling, showing her ankles; not an ounce of grace, of elegance, of anything! There she went! And Swithin stood, drumming a puffy forefinger against the pane, as if denouncing what he saw. Style! Style! She—she had been laughing at him. Not a doubt of it! If he *had* only driven a pair, it had been the finest in the kingdom! He stood with that distressing pink still staining the pallor of his cheeks—ruffled to the bottom of his soul. Was he conscious of the full sting in his niece's laughter? Conscious of how the soubriquet 'Four-in-hand Forsyte' epitomised the feeling Society had ever held of him; the feeling that with his craving for distinction he had puffed himself out into the double of what he really was? Was he conscious of that grievous sneer? Only, perhaps, sub-conscious, but it was enough; a crabbed wrath possessed him to the soles of the patent leather boots still worn, in public, on his painful feet.

So she rode one of 'those things,' and laughed at him, did she? He would show her. He left the window and went to the writing table. And there, his eyes round and yellow, his hand trembling, he took paper and began to write. In a shaky travesty of what had once been almost copperplate, he traced these lines:

"This is a codicil to the last Will of me Swithin Forsyte. To mark my disapproval of the manners and habits of my niece Euphemia, the daughter of my brother Nicholas Forsyte and Elizabeth his wife, I hereby revoke the bequest of the share of my property left to her in my said Will. I leave her nothing whatever."

He paused and read it through. That would teach her! Faithful to the ladies, the half of his property he had left to his three sisters in equal shares; the other half to his eight nieces in equal shares. Well, there would only be seven now! And he sounded the bell.

"Boy, fetch my valet and tell the hall porter to come here."

When they arrived he was adding the words: "Signed in the presence of—"

"Here!" he said. "This is a codicil to my Will. I want you to witness it. Write your names and occupations here."

When they had done so, and he had blotted the whole, he addressed an envelope, wrote:

"Dear James,

"This is a codicil. Put it with my Will, and let me know you've had it.

"Your affectionate brother,

"SWITHIN FORSYTE."

and sealed the envelope with the 'pheasant proper' obtained from the College of Arms in 1850 at some expense.

"Take that," he said to Alphonse, "and post it. Here, help me back to my chair."

When he settled in again, and Alphonse had gone, his eyes moved restlessly.

Style! His old cronies—all gone! No one came in here now who had known him in the palmy days of style! Days when there was elegance. Bicycles, forsooth! Well, that young lady had had an expensive ride, an expensive laugh. Cost her a matter of six or seven thousand pounds. They laughed best who laughed last! And with the feeling that he had struck a blow for elegance, for manners, for—for style, Swithin regained his pallor, his eyes grew less yellow, his eyelids rounder over them, and the expression in those eyes became almost wistful. This damned East wind—if he didn't take care he'd have no appetite for dinner.

Four-in-hand Forsyte! Why not—why not? He could have driven four-in-hand if he'd liked, any day. Four-in-ha—! His chin dropped slightly. Four-in—! His eyes closed; his lips puffed; he slept, his hand still resting on his cane.

Into the hall strolled two young men on a week-end from town. Hatted, high-collared, with their canes swinging, they passed not far from Swithin's chair.

"Look at that old buck," said one in a low voice. And they halted, staring at him sideways.

"Hallo! It's old Uncle Swithin, Giles."

"By George! So it is. I say, Jesse, look at his rings, and his pin, and the shine on his hair and his boots. Fancy the old josser keeping it up like that!"

"By jove! Hope *I'll* never be old. Come on Giles!"

"Stout old boy!"

And 'the Dromios,' as they were called, swung on, their lean hungry faces bravely held above their collars.

But the old pale lips of Swithin, between the little white moustaches and the little white tuft, puffed and filled, puffed and filled. He had not heard.

Part II

Bicycling into the Orbicular Millennium

Introduction

In the beginning, there was doubt. It never occurred to me in planning this volume that the bicycle would have been featured in so many and such important fictional works of the absurd or fantastic mode.

Indeed, the fear existed that the bicycle, if it were to be found in such literature, would be debased into a perfidious plaything of malign deviltry or an instrument for the commission of lurid crimes with exaggerated malice aforethought. And that expectation was quite understandable.

After all, was not Miss Gulch in *The Wizard of Oz* a heartless termagant who tried to take Dorothy's dog Toto away in the basket on her bicycle? And was not Miss Gulch later transformed into the Wicked Witch of the West and her bicycle into the witch's broom? But Miss Gulch, it appears, was only the inspired creation of a Hollywood scriptwriter. Nowhere is any such person found in L. Frank Baum's text from which the movie version was adapted.

As this chapter developed, however, the stories depicted the bicycle as less absurd or fantastic than the people who sought to maneuver it. Save for *The Voyeur* by Alain Robbe-Grillet, the proper interpretation of which is an enigma wrapped in a conundrum, the bicycle was found to be the source of surprise endings of jolly impact, as in *A Connecticut Yankee in King Arthur's Court,* or just plain spoofing, as in Flann O'Brien or the absurd representation of absurd people doing absurd things in a never-never-land atmosphere as in Samuel Beckett's *Molloy*. But the bicycle, happily, was generally not the terror of the midway or anything so demoralizing.

Various considerations beyond my control forced me to exclude two very workman-like short stories of the fantasy genre. One, by Ray Bradbury, is entitled "The Great Collision of Monday Last." Another, by Avram Davidson, is called "Or All the Seas with Oysters." If the materials in this book please, then these stories will add to the sum of your pleasure—at a later time. Along with these, I would recommend the book for young adults *I Am the Cheese* by Robert Cormier. Its timely and original design is engrossing for persons of all ages. "The Bicycle Chain," another omission from this anthology, is a short story by Yuri Olesha that, although delightful, defies more precise categorization.

In my bones, I feel certain that other fictional works on the order of these, whether included or not, exist someplace out there, as yet undiscovered by me. H. P. Love-

**"There is no reason why a man on a smooth road should lose his balance on a
bicycle; but he could." (From *Perelandra* by C. S. Lewis)**

craft is known to have bicycled about Nantucket Island in 1934, for, in a letter, he
wrote of his journey that it was

> the first time in twenty years I had been on a wheel. Riding proved just as easy and
> familiar as if I had last dismounted only the day before—and it brought back my
> lost youth so vividly that I felt as if I ought to hurry home for the opening of Hope St.
> High School! I wish it were not conspicuous for sedate old gents to ride a bike in
> Providence![1]

Unfortunately, his literature does not seem to reflect his enthusiasm for the bicycle.

J. R. R. Tolkien, author of *The Lord of the Rings*, is described as having bicycled
through Oxford "with his long black robe flapping in the breeze." And yet the bicycle
has not been a central character in his works. But there was more than an ample
supply of selections in the literature to take up the slack.

Of these, *Rendezvous with Rama* by Arthur C. Clarke (author of *2001: A Space
Odyssey*) depicts a space exploration by Dragonfly, a sky-bike weighing "only twenty
kilograms" that could be pedaled through space "at a steady twenty kilometers an
hour." Tragically, Dragonfly, described as "a soap bubble . . . wrapped around a
delicate tracery of aerofoil sections," is destroyed by an electric wind on its maiden
voyage. As a consequence it loses its chance to race in the Lunar Olympics and to
play more than a fleeting role in the plot. Arthur Clarke's sky-bike is Larry Niven's

flycycle in *Ringworld*. They are of a piece, fantastically futuristic versions of a bicycle.

Futuristic visions of bicyclelike conveyances are not unique to the current "sci fi" era. In earlier times, even before the advent of the bicycle, there were creative persons who attempted to put a rudimentary form of self-propelled cycle into actual operation—sometimes avoiding disaster by a hair. Sir Richard Lovell Edgeworth, developer of a form of telegraphic communication, was of such an inventive bent. As he recalled his cycling experiment in his early-nineteenth-century memoirs:

> During my residence at Hare Hatch, another wager was proposed by me among our acquaintance, the purport of which was that I undertook to find a man, who should, with the assistance of machinery, walk faster than any other person that could be produced. The machinery which I intended to employ was a huge hollow wheel made very light, within side of which, in a barrel of six feet diameter, a man should walk. Whilst he stepped thirty inches, the circumference of the large wheel, or rather wheels, would revolve five feet on the ground; and as the machine was to roll on planks, and on a plane somewhat inclined, when once the *vis inertiae* of the machine should be overcome, it would carry on the man within it, as fast as he could possibly walk. I had provided means of regulating the motion, so that the wheel should not run away with its master. I had the wheel made, and when it was so nearly completed as to require but a few hours' work to finish it, I went to London for Lord Effingham, to whom I had promised, that he should be present at the first experiment made with it. But the bulk and extraordinary appearance of my machine had attracted the notice of the country neighbourhood; and taking advantage of my absence, some idle curious persons went to the carpenter I employed, who lived on Hare Hatch common. From him they obtained the great wheel, which had been left by me in his care. It was not finished. I had not yet furnished it with the means of stopping or moderating its motion. A young lad got into it, his companions launched it on a path which led gently down hill towards a very steep chalk-pit. This pit was at such a distance, as to be out of their thoughts, when they set the wheel in motion. On it ran. The lad withinside plied his legs with all his might. The spectators, who at first stood still to behold the operation, were soon alarmed by the shouts of their companion, who perceived his danger. The vehicle became quite ungovernable, the velocity increased as it ran down hill. Fortunately the boy contrived to jump from his rolling prison before it reached the chalk-pit; but the wheel went on with such velocity, as to outstrip its pursuers, and, rolling over the edge of the precipice, it was dashed to pieces.[2]

Even in today's real world of space exploration there are respected scientists who would opt for a modified bicycle for, say, lunar travel. M.I.T.'s David Gordon Wilson is one of those who believe that the virtual lack of atmosphere in the lunar environment makes it ideal for astronaut-powered bicycle-type vehicles. Bieriot, the French airplane pioneer, surely would have agreed with Wilson, for he "drifted across the English channel in 1909 in a (plane) that looked like a bicycle with fins."[3] And in 1979 Bryan Allen, bringing fact to fantasy, furiously pumped the bicycle pedals of his seventy-seven-pound makeshift airplane, the *Gossamer Albatross*, successfully across the English Channel.

The literature of the absurd and the fantastic is not so far removed from reality that it could exclude or has excluded the bicycle.

1

Mark Twain

Not a Spoke Too Soon

From *A Connecticut Yankee in King Arthur's Court*

Mark Twain's fable A Connecticut Yankee in King Arthur's Court *was not an unlikely place to find a bicycle reference and, indeed, to find the bicycle marvelously exploited for comically fantastic purposes.*

According to Twain's tale, a Yankee, born in Hartford, Connecticut, whose father was a blacksmith and whose uncle was a "horse-doctor," finds himself transported from nineteenth-century America to sixth-century Arthurian England after being hit on the head by a crowbar during a fight. The Yankee is immediately collared by a knight who claims him as his property. He is about to be executed, according to the custom of the times, when his knowledge that a solar eclipse is in the offing enables him to predict it, to parade his prevision as magic, and to secure his release. The Yankee performs so many and such varied feats of seeming magic that he is dubbed "Sir Boss" and becomes confidant and minister to King Arthur. At the same time, however, he attracts the emnity of Merlin, a magician who had dominated that market before Sir Boss's arrival.

In the course of the tale, Sir Boss adopts as his aide-de-camp one Clarence, whom he instructs in the technological wizardry of the nineteenth century, which he had learned as foreman of an arms factory and as a consummate nineteenth-century technocrat. The Yankee establishes a telegraph and a railroad and, in general, reproduces the industrial revolution in sixth-century England.

A major concern in Sir Boss's transformation of sixth-century England is to politicize it by introducing a hitherto unknown egalitarianism between the kingly types and the general populace. As part of this plan, Sir Boss convinces King Arthur to travel incognito with him throughout his kingdom, learning the ways of the masses and perceiving

From Mark Twain, *A Connecticut Yankee in King Arthur's Court* (New York: Charles L. Webster, 1889), pp. 487–91.

SIR GALAHAD TAKES A HEADER.

their plight. But, after many adventures, the king and Sir Boss are sold as slaves for lack of proof that they are freemen. Sir Boss, in true Houdini fashion, escapes from his bonds in order to telegraph Clarence for assistance. He does so and is rearrested and sentenced to die with the other slaves who had rebelled and killed their master when he gave them a drubbing, and then some, upon his learning of the escape of Sir Boss, his most valuable slave.

The scene is now set for the hangings to begin. Sir Boss all but despairs of being rescued, for it would take nothing short of a miracle for Sir Launcelot and his troops to arrive from Camelot on time.

Nearing four in the afternoon. The scene was just outside the walls of London. A cool, comfortable, superb day, with a brilliant sun; the kind of day to make one want to live not die. The multitude was prodigious and far-reaching; and yet we fifteen poor devils hadn't a friend in it. There was something painful in that thought, look at it how you might. There we sat, on our tall scaffold, the butt of the hate and mockery of all those enemies. We were being made a holiday spectacle. They had built a sort of grand-stand for the nobility and gentry, and these were there in full force, with their ladies. We recognized a good many of them.

The crowd got a brief and unexpected dash of diversion out of the king. The moment we were freed of our bonds he sprang up, in his fantastic rags, with face bruised out of all recognition, and proclaimed himself Arthur, King of Britain, and denounced the awful penalties of treason upon every soul there present if a hair of his sacred head were touched. It startled and surprised him to hear them break into a vast roar of laughter. It wounded his dignity, and he locked himself up in silence, then, although the crowd begged him to go on, and tried to provoke him to it by catcalls, jeers, and shouts of:

"Let him speak! The king! The king! his humble subjects hunger and thirst for words of wisdom out of the mouth of their master his Serene and Sacred Raggedness!"

But it went for nothing. He put on all his majesty and sat under this rain of contempt and insult unmoved. He certainly was great in his way. Absently, I had taken off my white bandage and wound it about my right arm. When the crowd noticed this, they began upon me. They said:

"Doubtless this sailor-man is his minister—observe his costly badge of office!"

I let them go until they got tired, and then I said:

"Yes, I am his minister, The Boss; and to-morrow you will hear that from Camelot which—"

I got no further. They drowned me out with joyous derision. But presently there was silence; for the sheriffs of London, in their official robes, with their subordinates, began to make a stir which indicated that business was about to begin. In the hush which followed, our crime was recited, the death-warrant read, then everybody uncovered while a priest uttered a prayer.

Then a slave was blindfolded; the hangman unslung his rope. There lay the smooth

KNIGHTS PRACTICING ON THE QUIET.

road below us, we upon one side of it, the banked multitude walling its other side—a good clear road, and kept free by the police—how good it would be to see my five hundred horsemen come tearing down it! But no, it was out of the possibilities. I followed its receding thread out into the distance—not a horseman on it, or sign of one.

There was a jerk, and the slave hung dangling; dangling and hideously squirming, for his limbs were not tied.

A second rope was unslung, in a moment another slave was dangling.

In a minute a third slave was struggling in the air. It was dreadful. I turned away my head a moment, and when I turned back I missed the king! They were blindfolding him! I was paralyzed; I couldn't move. I was choking, my tongue was petrified. They finished blindfolding him, they led him under the rope. I couldn't shake off that clinging impotence. But when I saw them put the noose around his neck, then everything let go in me and I made a spring to the rescue—and as I made it I shot one more glance abroad—by George! here they came, a-tilting!—five hundred mailed and belted knights on bicycles!

The grandest sight that ever was seen. Lord, how the plumes streamed, how the sun flamed and flashed from the endless procession of webby wheels!

I waved my right arm as Launcelot swept in—he recognized my rag—I tore away noose and bandage, and shouted:

"On your knees, every rascal of you, and salute the king! Who fails shall sup in hell to-night!"

I always used that high style when I'm climaxing an effect. Well, it was noble to see Launcelot and the boys swarm up onto that scaffold and heave sheriffs and such overboard. And it was fine to see that astonished multitude go down on their knees and beg their lives of the king they had just been deriding and insulting. And as he stood apart there, receiving this homage in rags, I thought to myself, well, really there *is* something peculiarly grand about the gait and bearing of the king, after all.

I was immensely satisfied. Take the whole situation all around, it was one of the gaudiest effects I ever instigated.

And presently up comes Clarence, his own self! and winks, and says, very modernly:

"Good deal of a surprise, wasn't it? I knew you'd like it. I've had the boys practising this a long time, privately; and just hungry for a chance to show off."

2

Alfred Jarry

Pass the E.R.G., Please!

From *The Supermale*

This excerpt from Alfred Jarry's The Supermale *does not fit altogether comfortably into any single chapter in this book. This selection, like Jarry himself, defies precise classification.*

I have chosen to place this very imaginary description of a most extraordinary bicycle race by a five-man bicycle against an express train over a distance of ten thousand miles in this chapter because it is so obviously beyond the pale of any recognizable bicycle race.

Yet, in the real world of the bicycle, strange occurrences, bordering on the fantastic, have been reported. A bicyclist is said to have "coasted down the steps of the Capitol in Washington, D. C., in fifteen seconds flat," landing with body intact in a heap among broken spokes and bent rims.

On another occasion, echoing The Supermale:

One cyclist challenged a speeding express train. Cycle and iron horse raced side by side, the engine on the tracks and the cycle on the path alongside. With his head down and pumping for all he was worth, the cycler could not see that the path ended as the tracks crossed a bridge. Bicycle and rider shot off the bank, sailing thirty feet into the mud flats below. If there was a cycling saint in heaven he was on the job that day, because the bicyclist regained conciousness after half an hour and struggled out of the muck with nothing worse than a broken collarbone and two sprained ankles. He had apparently landed as he had taken off—pedaling like a fiend.[1]

This excerpt from The Supermale *could, of course, have found a ready niche in the*

*chapter on bicycle racing, but Jarry is already represented there by another selection of
the same equally mystifying and outrageous character as that which appears here.*

*Some would find in Jarry's bicycle-racing episode traces of the black humor for which
he is renowned. Such a discovery might justify its inclusion in the chapter on the
literature of humor. But Jarry is best known as the author of the play* Ubu Roi, *which
has given him first claim to be the father of the "Theater of the Absurd." In the last
analysis, I have asserted my editor's prerogative to settle any doubt as to the category in
which this selection is most appropriate.*

*Alfred Jarry's short (he died in 1907 at the age of thirty-four) and troubled life has
left us with the image of a man of brilliant literary creativity, both propelled and
hindered by his personal idiosyncrasies and dissipations. He was a devotee first of
absinthe and later of ether. He was an "ardent cyclist" who, Barbara Wright tells us in
the introduction to her translation of* The Supermale, *purchased a "Clement luxe"
bicycle in 1896, "the latest, fastest and most elegant model." The influence of the
bicycle on Jarry's literary offerings was quite pervasive. He even proposed a new calendar, the "Almanache du Père Ubu," which commenced, naturally enough, with Jarry's
birth on September 8, 1873, and includes the feast of Andre Marcueil, the "ascete
cycliste" of* The Supermale, *as the second day of the year of "Pedale."*

*A reading of Alfred Jarry is not for the timid or the conventional. The symbolism of
his work mystifies, when it does not also startle.*

In The Supermale *the hero, Andrew Marcueil, seeks to prove his unlimited potential,
which presumably is shared by other similar supermales. The medium for his proof is a
record-breaking orgy of lovemaking with Ellen Elson, during which eighty-two separate
acts of sexual intercourse are climaxed over a twenty-four-hour period by Marcueil,
disguised as an Indian. Not inappropriately, it is Ellen Elson's father who is the
inventor of the Perpetual Motion Food, a potion with a strychnine-and-alcohol base,
which the bicycle racers in* The Supermale *consume to give them the energy to perform
feats that today E. R. G. (electrolyte replacement with glucose) is said to facilitate.*

*As a modest warm-up for Marcueil's prodigious sexual feat, Jarry describes a ten-
thousand-mile bicycle race in which Marcueil, in mufti as the Road hog, bests both the
five-man bicycle and an express train in the five-day race, all without the benefit of
William Elson's Perpetual Motion Food. Surely bigger and more torrid accomplish-
ments are in the offing for Andre Marcueil, first bicyclist par excellence as the Road hog
and later sensualist nonpareil as the Indian.*

We shall take our account of this race, known as the Perpetual Motion Food Race,
or the Ten-Thousand-Mile Race, from one of the members of the five-man bicycle
team, Ted Oxborrow, as reported by and published in the *New York Herald:*

Lying horizontally on the five-man bicycle—standard 1920 racing model, no handle bars, fifteen-millimeter tires, development 57.34 meters—our faces lower than
our saddles, sheltered behind masks from wind and dust, our ten legs jointed on either

side by aluminum rods, we started off down the interminable, 10,000-mile-long track that had been prepared alongside the lines of the great express. At first we were towed by a bullet-shaped car at the provisional speed of 120 kilometers per hour.

We were strapped tightly to the machine, so that we didn't fall off, in this order: at the back, myself—Ted Oxborrow; in front of me, Jewey Jacobs, George Webb, Sammy White—a Negro—and Bill Gilbey, the leader of our team, whom we jokingly called Corporal Gilbey because he was in charge of four men. I don't count a dwarf, Bob Rumble, tossing in a trailer behind us, whose counterweight served to increase or decrease the traction of our rear wheel.

At regular intervals Corporal Gilbey passed to us over his shoulder the small, colorless, crumbly, and bitter-tasting cubes of Perpetual Motion Food that were our only nourishment for nearly five days. He took them five at a time from a small platform behind the starting car. Beneath this platform glowed the white dial of the speedometer, and underneath the dial a revolving drum was suspended, to cushion any shocks to the front wheel of our machine.

When night began to fall, this drum, unseen by the people on the train, was connected to the wheels of the starting car so as to revolve in the opposite direction to them. Corporal Gilbey had us pull forward so that our front wheel rested against the drum; they locked together like gears, and we were towed, effortlessly and fraudulently, during the first hours of the night.

Sheltered behind the starting car, there was of course not a breath of air. On our right the locomotive, looking like a big, good-natured animal, seemed to be grazing in the same part of our visual "field," neither advancing nor receding. Its only apparent motion was a slight trembling of its flank—where, apparently, the drive shaft was oscillating. In front it had a cowcatcher whose bars, which looked like prison bars or the grille on a water mill, could be counted. It was all rather like a peaceful scene by a river—the silent flow of the smooth track being the river itself, and the regular bubbling of the great beast seeming like the sound of a waterfall. . . .

Sammy White was humming, in time with the strokes of our legs, the little nursery rhyme: Twinkle, twinkle, little star . . .

And, in the solitude of the night, the falsetto voice of Bob Rumble, who was feeble-minded, yelped behind us:

"Something's following us!"

Nothing, either living or mechanical, however, could have followed us at that speed, and besides, the people on the train were able to keep an eye on the level, empty track behind Bob Rumble. It is true that it was impossible to see the last few yards of the track behind the cars, for they only had lateral openings, and we riders could not look behind us. But it would have been most unlikely that anyone could have been traveling on that bumpy track. The dwarf must have been expressing his pride at having his puerile self towed behind us.

When the second day dawned, a strident and snoring sound, an immense vibration in which we seemed to be bathed, nearly drew the blood from my ears. I heard that the last, bullet-shaped car had been "turned loose," and then replaced by a trumpet-shaped flying machine. It was revolving on its own axis, corkscrewing through the air just above the ground in front of us, while a furious wind was sucking us toward its funnel. The silken thread of the speedometer was still quivering regularly, tracing a vertical blue spindle against Corporal Gilbey's cheek, and I read on its ivory dial, as had been predicted for that time, the number of kilometers per hour: 250. . . .

It was now broad daylight, and I could not doubt what I saw: all that I could glimpse of the car was hidden by red roses; enormous, full-blown, and as fresh as if they had just been picked. Their perfume spread through the stillness of the air behind the shelter of the windshield.

When the girl lowered the window, part of the curtain of flowers was torn, but they did not fall immediately: for several seconds they traveled through space at the same speed as the machines; then the largest one, caught by a sudden gust, was swallowed up inside the car.

It seemed to me that Miss Elson uttered a cry and raised her hand to her breast, and then I saw her no more all that day. The roses gradually shed their petals, owing to the vibration, and flew off, singly or by threes and fours; the varnished wood of the sleeping car reappeared, immaculate, reflecting more clearly than any mirror the ugly profile of Bob Rumble.

The following day the rosy inflorescence was renewed. I wondered whether I was going mad, and Miss Elson's anxious face thenceforth never left the window.

But a more serious incident engaged my attention.

On that morning of the third day a terrible thing occurred; terrible, especially, because it could have cost us the race. Jewey Jacobs, in the seat immediately in front of me, his knees a yard away from my knees, connected by the aluminum rods—Jewey Jacobs, who had been working with fantastic vigor from the very start, so much so that the strength of his pedaling could have thrust our machine forward faster than our schedule permitted, so that I had on several occasions had to pedal against him—Jewey Jacobs suddenly seemed to take a perverse pleasure in straightening his legs in return, pushing my knees up disagreeably against my chin, and forcing me to get down to some serious leg-work.

Neither Corporal Gilbey nor, behind him, Sammy White nor George Webb were able to turn around in their masks and harnesses to see what had got into Jewey Jacobs, but I could bend over sufficiently to catch a glimpse of his right leg; his foot was still thrust into the leather toe-clip and was still moving regularly up and down, but the ankle seemed to have become numb and the ankle-play had ceased. Moreover, and perhaps this is too much of a technicality, I had not taken sufficient notice of a peculiar odor, which I had attributed to his black jersey shorts where, like the rest of us, he satisfied both his needs into some fuller's earth. But a sudden idea made me shudder, and I looked again at the heavy, marble ankle which was within a yard of my leg, and linked to it, and I breathed in the cadaverous odor of an incomprehensibly rapid decomposition.

Half a yard off to my right, another sort of change struck me: instead of the middle of the tender, I saw opposite me the second door of the first car.

"We're seizing up!" cried George Webb at that instant.

"We're seizing up!" repeated Sammy White and George Webb; and, as a mental shock weakens the limbs more than physical fatigue, the last door of the second car appeared by my shoulder, the last flowering door of the second and last car. The voices of Arthur Gough and his crew rose in a cheer.

"Jewey Jacobs is dead," I cried, woefully, with all my strength.

The third and second team members roared into their masks, up to Bill Gilbey: "Jewey Jacobs is dead!"

The sound whirled in the rushing air as far as the sides of the trumpet-shaped flying machine, which repeated three times—for it was enormous enough for two echoes to resound along its length—which repeated from the heights of the heavens onto the fabulous track behind us, like a summons to the Last Judgment:

"Jewey Jacobs is dead! Dead! Dead!"

"Oh! He's dead, is he? I don't give a damn," said Corporal Gilbey. "Stand by: keep Jacobs going!"

It was a tedious task, such as I hope never to see again in any race. The man was kicking backward, counterpedaling, seizing up. It is extraordinary how this term, which is applied to the friction of machines, was marvelously applicable to the corpse. And it went on doing what it had to do, right under my nose, into its fuller's earth. Ten times we were tempted to unscrew the rods that bound our five pairs of legs together—counting the dead man's. But he was harnessed, padlocked, weighted, packaged, and sealed into his seat—and then . . . he would have been a . . . dead weight (I can't help the pun) and to win this difficult race we couldn't do with a dead weight.

Corporal Gilbey was a practical man, just as William Elson and Arthur Gough too were practical gentlemen, and Corporal Gilbey ordered us to do what they themselves would have ordered. Jewey Jacobs was under contract to be fourth man in the great and honorable Peretual Motion Food Race; he had signed a paper that would have set him back twenty-five thousand dollars for nonperformance, payable on his future races. If he were dead, he could no longer race, and would be unable to pay. So he had to race, then, alive or dead. One can sleep on a bike, so one should be able to die on a bike with no more trouble. And besides, this was called the perpetual motion race!

William Elson explained to us later that the stiffness of a corpse, which he called rigor mortis, I believe, means absolutely nothing, and can be overcome by the slightest effort. As for the sudden putrefaction, he himself admitted that he did not know its cause. Perhaps, he said, it was due to the secretion of an extraordinary abundance of muscular toxins.

Soon Jewey Jacobs began to pedal, with a bad grace at first, and we couldn't see whether he was making any grimaces, as his face was still in his mask. We encouraged him with friendly insults of the sort that our grandfathers used to shout at Terront, during the first Paris-Brest race: "Get going, you pig!" Little by little he entered into the swing of it, his legs caught up with ours, the ankle-play returned, and finally he started pedaling madly.

"He's acting as a flywheel," said the corporal. "He's steadying, and I think he's about to race."

Indeed, not only did he catch up with us, he increased his speed beyond ours, and

Jacobs' death-sprint was a sprint the like of which the living cannot conceive. So much so that the last car, which had disappeared during the time it took us to train the deceased, grew larger and larger, and resumed its normal place, which it never should have left, with the middle of the tender half a yard off my right shoulder. All this did not take place, naturally enough, without our cheers being raised, thundered into our four masks:

"Hip, hip, hurray for Jewey Jacobs!"

And the flying trumpet echoed throughout the skies:

"Hip, hip, hurray for Jewey Jacobs!"

I had lost sight of the locomotive and its two cars while we were teaching the dead to live; when he was able to get along by himself I saw the rear of the last car growing bigger as though it were coming back to hear the latest news. It was no doubt a hallucination—the distorted reflection of the five-man machine in the mahogany of the great sleeping car, more limpid than a mirror—but I saw what looked like a hunchbacked human being—hunchbacked or bearing some enormous burden—pedaling along behind the train. His legs were moving at exactly the same speed as ours.

Instantly, the vision disappeared, hidden by the back corner of the car, which we had already passed. I thought it very comical to hear the ridiculous Bob Rumble, panic-stricken and jumping from side to side of his wicker seat like a monkey in a cage, yapping as before:

"There's something pedaling, there's something following us!"

The education of Jewey Jacobs had taken us a whole day. . . .

The night of the fourth day was falling. . . .

As the darkness came on I cast one last glance at the speedometer, which I would not be seeing again before the dawn. As I looked, the silken thread, writhing and trembling at the edge of the speedometer frame, flared up in the form of a bright blue spinkle, and suddenly all was dark.

Then, as though under a shower of meteorites, blows rained down upon us, blows both hard and soft, sharp, feathery, bleeding, howling, and lugubrious, caught in our speeding path like flies, and our machine swerved and bumped against the still seemingly motionless locomotive. They remained in contact for the space of a few yards, though the mechanical movements of our legs did not stop.

"Nothing," said the corporal. "Birds."

We were no longer sheltered behind the tow cars, and it is remarkable that no such accident had befallen us earlier, as soon as the flying funnel was released.

At that moment, without even a word from the corporal, the midget, Bob Rumble, crawled toward me on his tow rod, to bring all his weight to bear on the rear wheel and so increase its traction. This maneuver informed me that our speed was still increasing.

I heard the chatter of his teeth, and realized that Bob Rumble had only come closer to escape what he called the "something following us."

Behind my back, and a little to the left, he lit an acetylene lamp which oddly cast, in front of us and somewhat to our right (the locomotive now being on our left), the fivefold shadow of our team on the white track.

In the cheerful light, the dwarf was no longer complaining. And we kept pace with our shadow.

I no longer had any idea how fast we were going. I tried to catch a few snatches of the silly little songs Sammy White was humming to himself to keep his pedaling in time. Just before the speedometer needle had gone up in flames he had been jabbering the refrain, like a burst of hail, of his final sprint, so well-known from his record-breaking mile and half-mile races on the hairpin tracks of Massachusetts: Poor Papa paid Peter's potatoes!

Beyond that he would have had to improvise, but his legs were going too quickly for his brain.

Thought, at least Sammy White's, is not so rapid as they say, and I can't see it going on exhibition on any track. . . .

Immersed in these thoughts or this reverie, I did not notice that the vibrations caused by our speed had put out the lamp, and yet the same odd outline, still visible because the track was very white and the night quite clear, was "leading the pack" fifty yards in front!

It could not have been projected by the locomotive's headlamps: the very kerosene from both lamps had long since gone to add more heat to the darkening boiler.

Still, there is no such thing as a ghost—then what could this shadow be?

Corporal Gilbey hadn't noticed that our lamp had gone out, otherwise he would have sharply reprimanded Bob Rumble. Jovial and practical as ever, he encouraged us with his catcalls:

"Come on, boys, let's catch up with it! It can't hold out for long! We're gaining on it. It's running out of oil; that's no shadow, it's a turnspit!"

In the vast silence of the night, we hurried even more.

Suddenly . . . I heard . . . I thought I heard something like the chirping of a bird, but it had a singularly metallic tone.

I was not mistaken: there was a noise, somewhere in front, a clanking noise. . . .

I was sure of what was causing it, and I wanted to cry out, to call the corporal, but I was too terrified by my discovery.

The shadow was creaking like an old weathercock!

There was no longer any doubt about the only really extraordinary occurrence of the race: the appearance of the *Road hog*.

And yet I shall never believe that anyone, man or devil, could have followed—and passed—us during the Ten Thousand Miles!

Especially considering the way he was gotten up! This is what must have happened: the Road hog, who had let us catch up with him, naturally, and was keeping to the left, almost in front of the locomotive; the Road hog, coming up at the very instant when the shadow disappeared, and merging for a second with it, crossed the track in front of our machine with incredible awkwardness but with providential luck, both for him and for us. On his apocalyptic machine, he went veering into the first rail. . . . You would have thought, my goodness, from the amount of zigzagging he was doing, that he hadn't ridden a bicycle for more than three hours in his life. He crossed the first rail at right angles, at the risk of his life, and he looked quite desperate, as if he knew he would never cross the second. Hypnotized by the functioning of his handle bars, his eyes on his front wheel, he did not appear to realize that he was carrying out his imbecilic little maneuvers in front of a great express train that was booming down on him at more than three hundred kilometers an hour. He seemed suddenly struck with some extremely prudent and ingenious idea, swerved sharply to the right, and took off down the gravel straight in front of him, fleeing before the locomotive. At precisely that instant the front of the machine caught up with his rear wheel.

During that second when he was about to be crushed to pulp, everything about his comical silhouette, down to the details of the spokes in his bicycle wheels, remained photographically imprinted on my retinas. Then I closed my eyes, not wishing to count his ten thousand fragments. . . .

Surprised to hear the regular clicking, as well as the grating sound of the worn bearings, a good half-minute after what I had supposed must be the catastrophe, I opened my eyes again and couldn't believe them—I couldn't even believe that they were open. The Road hog was still gliding along on our left, on the track! The locomotive was up against him and he seemed in no way inconvenienced by it. Then I saw the explanation of this marvel: the wretched fellow was no doubt unaware of the arrival of the great train behind him, otherwise he would not have shown such perfect composure. The locomotive had bumped into his bicycle and was now pushing it by the rear mudguard! As for the chain—for of course the ridiculous and senseless character would not have been able to move his legs at such a speed—the chain had been snapped in two by the impact, and the Road hog was pedaling joyfully in space—needlessly, moreover, since the elimination of all transmission constituted for him an excellent and uncontrolled "free wheeling"—congratulating himself on his performance which he attributed, no doubt, to his natural capacities!

The light of an apotheosis appeared on the horizon, and the Road hog was the first to appear in its aureole. It was the illumination of the terminal point of the Ten Thousand Miles!

I had the impression that a nightmare was ending. . . .

There was a movement on the platform of the locomotive, as though some momentous event were about to take place. Arthur Gough gently pushed back Miss Elson, who was leaning forward to watch, with love, it seemed, the unknown racer. The engineer seemed to be conferring with Mr. Elson in sharp tones, apparently trying to exact some exorbitant concession from him. The old man's beseeching voice reached me:

"You're not going to give it to the locomotive to drink? It would hurt it! It's not a human creature! You're not going to kill this animal!"

After a few rapid and unintelligible phrases:

"Then let me make the sacrifice myself! Let me only be separated from it at the last instant!"

The white-bearded chemist raised a phial in his hands with infinite precaution. It contained, I have since learned, an admirable rum that could have been his ancestor, and that he had been saving to drink alone; he poured this ultimate fuel into the locomotive's boiler. . . . The alcohol was no doubt too admirable: the machine went psshhh . . . and went out.

So it was that the Perpetual Motion Food's five-man cycle won the Ten-Thousand-Mile Race; but neither Corporal Gilbey nor Sammy White nor George Webb nor Bob Rumble nor, I think, Jewey Jacobs in the other world nor I, Ted Oxborrow, who sign this report for all of them, will ever be able to console ourselves for finding, when we arrived at the finish post—where no one was waiting for us, since no one had foreseen so prompt an arrival—this post crowned with red roses, the same haunting red roses that had blazed the trail during the entire race. . . .

No one has been able to tell us what became of the fantastic racer.

3

Flann O'Brien

The Lilt of a Bicycle by Bogside

From *The Third Policeman*

Flann O'Brien had the consummate talent to beguile his readers into a numinous world where fact loiters while fantasy leaps. His works have the warmth of a hearthside on a blustery Irish evening. The humor, although typically Irish, can be enjoyed by all and sundry for it speaks in the universal language of gentle mirth.

Flann O'Brien's world was a place where pins with invisible shafts could exist side by side with boxes that fit into boxes that fit into boxes that fit into boxes ad aeternam. Bicycles can move on their own volition, while elevators traverse the territory between the heavens and the earth. Nothing was beyond his imagining and anything was worth our enjoying.

"Writing is like fishing," Rudyard Kipling said, "you cast your hook in the stream— that's the story part; but to catch anything you must bait the hook; you must bait your hook with words, gaudy words."[1] And that is just what Flann O'Brien has done, for he can be prodigal in his use of just the right words.

It is a heady delight to read any of the witty fables of Flann O'Brien. Anyone who would think otherwise must be a "gawm," as the Irish would say. If you would mix fantasy with your guffaws, then the reading of the excerpts that follow will be but a prelude to your immersing yourself in the entire book, which is to be recommended. Both bicyclists and lovers of a yarn spung by a bog to be enjoyed in the warmth of a pub will be enthralled by its airy lyricism.

From Flann O'Brien, *The Third Policeman* (Walker and Company, 1967), pp. 54–63, 76–82. Copyright © 1967 by Evelyn Nolan.

Not unexpectedly, "Flann O'Brien" is a pseudonym for Brian O'Nolan, an Irish journalist whose major work At Swim-Two-Birds *(1939) was published when the author was twenty-eight years old, but which the author in later years would deprecate as "juvenile blather." Among his other novels are* The Hard Life *(1961) and* The Dalkey Archive *(1964).*

The Third Policeman, *written in 1940, but first published posthumously in 1967, is of the life-after-death variety, but the reader is not informed of this fact until the end of the novel. It is the narrator who is dead, although neither he nor the reader learns of this until near the end of the tale when the reader, at least, is made privy to the secret.*

The narrator has died before he can enjoy the profits from his killing old Phillip Mathers. He doesn't realize it but John Divney, his quondam friend and coconspirator in the killing of Mathers, has blown him to bits rather than share the treasures in Mathers's little black box. The only consequence of this explosion, as far as the narrator is aware, is that he has lost his identity, or at least, he is an amnesiac as to it. Otherwise, he finds himself tracking the black box with a single-minded, almost maniacal, determination.

The scheme the narrator devises to locate the black box is as ingenious as it is impossible to accomplish. He will go to the nearest police barracks where he will enlist their aid in finding his American gold watch, which he will claim to have been stolen when encased in a little black box. The police will find the black box, and he will be the beneficiary of their detective labors, or so, in his fantasy, he believes.

The narrator finds the police barracks with the aid of Martin Finnucane, a scoundrel with a wooden leg, whom he meets along the highway. Finnucane, at first, prepares to kill the narrator, but, upon learning that they both sport wooden legs, he spares him and directs him to the police barracks.

At the barracks, the narrator first meets Sergeant Pluck, who, being obsessed with bicycle-mania, naturally inquires:

"Is it about a bicycle?" he asked.

His expression when I encountered it was unexpectedly reassuring. His face was gross and far from beautiful but he had modified and assembled his various unpleasant features in some skilful way so that they expressed to me good nature, politeness and infinite patience. In the front of his peaked official cap was an important-looking badge and over it in golden letters was the word SERGEANT. It was Sergeant Pluck himself.

"No," I answered, stretching forth my hand to lean with it against the counter. The Sergeant looked at me incredulously.

"Are you sure?" he asked.

"Certain."

"Not about a motor-cycle?"

"No."

"One with overhead valves and a dynamo for light? Or with racing handle-bars?"

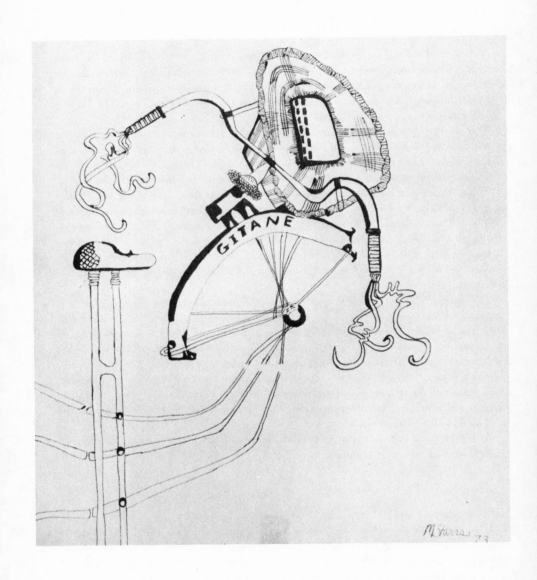

"No."

"In that circumstantial eventuality there can be no question of a motor-bicycle," he said. He looked surprised and puzzled and leaned sideways on the counter on the prop of his left elbow, putting the knuckles of his right hand between his yellow teeth and raising three enormous wrinkles of perplexity on his forehead. I decided now that he was a simple man and that I would have no difficulty in dealing with him exactly as I desired and finding out from him what had happened to the black box. I did not understand clearly the reason for his questions about bicycles but I made up my mind to answer everything carefully, to bide my time and to be cunning in all my dealings with him. He moved away abstractedly, came back and handed me a bundle of differently-coloured papers which looked like application forms for bull-licences and dog-licences and the like.

"It would be no harm if you filled up these forms," he said. "Tell me," he continued, "would it be true that you are an itinerant dentist and that you came on a tricycle?"

"It would not," I replied.

"On a patent tandem?"

"No."

"Dentists are an unpredictable coterie of people," he said. "Do you tell me it was a velocipede or a penny-farthing?"

"I do not," I said evenly. He gave me a long searching look as if to see whether I was serious in what I was saying, again wrinkling up his brow. . . .

At this stage there were footsteps at the door and in marched a heavy policeman carrying a small constabulary lamp. He had a dark Jewish face and hooky nose and masses of black curly hair. He was blue-jowled and black-jowled and looked as if he shaved twice a day. He had white enamelled teeth which came, I had no doubt, from Manchester, two rows of them arranged in the interior of his mouth and when he smiled it was a fine sight to see, like delph on a neat country dresser. He was heavy-fleshed and gross in body like the Sergeant but his face looked far more intelligent. It was unexpectedly lean and the eyes in it were penetrating and observant. If his face alone were in question he would look more like a poet than a policeman but the rest of his body looked anything but poetical.

"Policeman MacCruiskeen," said Sergeant Pluck.

Policeman MacCruiskeen put the lamp on the table, shook hands with me and gave me the time of day with great gravity. His voice was high, almost feminine, and he spoke with a delicate careful intonation. Then he put the little lamp on the counter and surveyed the two of us.

"Is it about a bicycle?" he asked.

"Not that," said the Sergeant. "This is a private visitor who says he did not arrive in the townland upon a bicycle. He has no personal name at all. His dadda is in far Amurikey.". . .

The Sergeant gave me a keen look which felt almost hot from being on the fire previously.

"The first beginnings of wisdom," he said, "is to ask questions but never to answer any. *You* get wisdom from asking and *I* from not answering. Would you believe that there is a great increase in crime in this locality? Last year we had sixty-nine cases of no lights and four stolen. This year we have eighty-two cases of no lights, thirteen cases of riding on the footpath and four stolen. There was one case of wanton damage to a three-speed gear, there is sure to be a claim at the next Court and the area of charge will be the parish. Before the year is out there is certain to be a pump stolen, a very depraved and despicable manifestation of criminality and a blot on the county."

"Indeed," I said.

"Five years ago we had a case of loose handlebars. Now there is a rarity for you. It took the three of us a week to frame the charge."

"Loose handlebars," I muttered. I could not clearly see the reason for such talk about bicycles.

"And then there is the question of bad brakes. The country is honeycombed with bad brakes, half of the accidents are due to it, it runs in families."

I thought it would be better to try to change the conversation from bicycles.

"You told me what the first rule of wisdom is," I said. "What is the second rule?"

"That can be answered," he said. "There are five in all. Always ask any questions that are to be asked and never answer any. Turn everything you hear to your own advantage. Always carry a repair outfit. Take left turns as much as possible. Never apply your front brake first."

"These are interesting rules," I said dryly.

"If you follow them," said the Sergeant, "you will save your soul and you will never get a fall on a slippy road."

"I would be obliged to you," I said, "if you would explain to me which of these rules covers the difficulty I have come here today to put before you."

"This is not today, this is yesterday," he said, "but which of the difficulties is it? What is the *crux rei*?"

Yesterday? I decided without any hesitation that it was a waste of time trying to understand the half of what he said. I persevered with my inquiry.

"I came here to inform you officially about the theft of my American gold watch."

He looked at me through an atmosphere of great surprise and incredulity and raised his eyebrows almost to his hair.

"That is an astonishing statement," he said at last.

"Why?"

"Why should anybody steal a watch when they can steal a bicycle?"

Hark to his cold inexorable logic.

"Search me," I said.

"Who ever heard of a man riding a watch down the road or bringing a sack of turf up to his house on the crossbar of a watch?"

"I did not say the thief wanted my watch to ride it," I expostulated. "Very likely he had a bicycle of his own and that is how he got away quietly in the middle of the night."

"Never in my puff did I hear of any man stealing anything but a bicycle when he was in his sane senses," said the Sergeant, "—except pumps and clips and lamps and the like of that. Surely you are not going to tell me at my time of life that the world is changing?". . .

Some time later Sergeant Pluck expounds on his "Atomic Theory," which, in the author's later work, The Dalkey Archive, *he has a Sergeant Fottrell recite and describe as the "Mollycule Theory." The theories are the same in point as well as largely in the words the author chooses to express them. Since the Sergeant Fottrell version as explicated to Mick Shaughnessay in the* The Dalkey Archive *is, in my view, the more polished and enjoyable of the two, it is included here:*

From *The Dalkey Archive*

The sergeant beckoned the waitress, ordered a barley wine for himself and a small bottle of "that" for his friend. Then he leaned forward confidentially.

—Did you ever discover or hear tell of mollycules? he asked.

—I did of course.

—Would it surprise or collapse you to know that the Mollycule Theory is at work in the parish of Dalkey?

—Well . . . yes and no.

—It is doing terrible destruction, he continued, the half of the people is suffering from it, it is worse than the smallpox.

—Could it not be taken in hand by the Dispensary Doctor or the National Teachers, or do you think it is a matter for the head of the family?

—The lock, stock and barrel of it all, he replied almost fiercely, is the County Council.

—It seems a complicated thing all right.

The sergeant drank delicately, deep in thought.

—Michael Gilhaney, a man I know, he said finally, is an example of a man that is nearly banjaxed from the operation of the Mollycule Theory. Would it astonish you ominously to hear that he is in danger of being a bicycle?

Mick shook his head in polite incomprehension.

—He is nearly sixty years of age by plain computation, the Sergeant said, and if he is itself, he has spent no less than thirty-five years riding his bicycle over the rocky roadsteads up and down the pertimious hills and into the deep ditches when the road goes astray in the strain of the winter. He is always going to a particular destination or other on his bicycle at every hour of the day or coming back from there at every other hour. If it wasn't that his bicycle was stolen every Monday he would be sure to be more than halfway now.

From Flann O'Brien, *The Dalkey Archive* (New York: Viking Penguin, 1977), pp. 86–93.

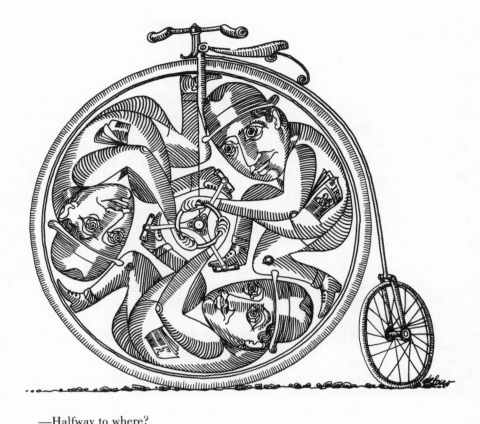

—Halfway to where?

—Halfway to being a bloody bicycle himself.

Had Sergeant Fottrell for once betrayed himself into drunken rambling? His fancies were usually amusing but not so good when they were meaningless. When Mick said something of the kind the Sergeant stared at him impatiently.

—Did you ever study the Mollycule Theory when you were a lad? he asked. Mick said no, not in any detail.

—That is a very serious defalcation and an abstruse exacerbation, he said severely, but I'll tell you the size of it. Everything is composed of small mollycules of itself and they are flying around in concentric circles and arcs and segments and innumerable various other routes too numerous to mention collectively, never standing still or resting but spinning away and darting hither and thither and back again, all the time on the go. Do you follow me intelligently? Mollycules?

—I think I do.

—They are as lively as twenty punky leprahauns doing a jig on the top of a flat tombstone. Now take a sheep. What is a sheep only millions of little bits of sheepness whirling around doing intricate convulsions inside the baste. What else is it but that?

—That would be bound to make the sheep dizzy, Mick observed, especially if the whirling was going on inside the head as well.

The sergeant gave him a look which no doubt he himself would describe as one of non-possum and noli-me-tangere.

—That's a most foolhardy remark, he said sharply, because the nerve-strings and the sheep's head itself are whirling into the same bargain and you can cancel out one whirl against the other and there you are—like simplifying a division sum when you have fives above and below the bar.

—To say the truth I did not think of that.

—Mollycules is a very intricate theorem and can be worked out with algebra but you would want to take it by degrees with rulers and cosines and familiar other instruments and then at the wind-up not believe what you had proved at all. If that happened you would have to go back over it till you got a place where you could believe your own facts and figures as exactly delineated from Hall and Knight's Algebra and then go on again from that particular place till you had the whole pancake properly believed and not have bits of it half-believed or a doubt in your head hurting you like when you lose the stud of your shirt in the middle of the bed.

—Very true, Mick decided to say.

—If you hit a rock hard enough and often enough with an iron hammer, some mollycules of the rock will go into the hammer and contrariwise likewise.

—That is well-known, he agreed.

—The gross and net result of it is that people who spend most of their natural lives riding iron bicycles over the rocky roadsteads of the parish get their personalities mixed up with the personalities of their bicycles as a result of the interchanging of the mollycules of each of them, and you would be surprised at the number of people in country parts who are nearly half people and half bicycles.

Mick made a little gasp of astonishment that made a sound like the air coming from a bad puncture.

—Good Lord, I suppose you're right.

—And you would be unutterably flibbergasted if you knew the number of stout bicycles that partake serenely of humanity.

Here the sergeant produced his pipe, a thing he did very rarely in public, and in silence commenced the laborious business of filling and ramming it from his battered tin of very dark tobacco. Mick began to muse and think of country places he had known in his younger days. He thought of one place he had been fond of.

Brown bogs and black bogs were neatly arranged on each side of the road with rectangular boxes carved out of them here and there, each with a filling of yellow-brown brown-yellow water. Far away near the sky tiny people were stooped at their turf-work, cutting out precisely-shaped sods with their patent spades and building them into a tall memorial the height of a horse and cart. Sounds came from them, delivered to his ears without charge by the west wind, sounds of laughing and whistling and bits of verses from the old bog-songs. Nearer, a house stood attended by three trees and surrounded by the happiness of a coterie of fowls, all of them picking and rooting and disputating loudly in the unrelenting manufacture of their eggs. The house was quiet in itself and silent but a canopy of lazy smoke had been erected over the chimney to indicate that people were within engaged on tasks. Ahead of him went the road, running swiftly across the flat land and pausing slightly to climb slowly up a hill that was waiting for it in a place where there was tall grass, grey boulders and rank stunted trees. The whole overhead was occupied by the sky, translucent, impenetrable, ineffable and incomparable, with a fine island of cloud anchored in the calm two yards to the right of Mr. Jarvis's outhouse.

The scene was real and incontrovertible but at variance with the talk of the sergeant. Was it not monstrous to allege that the little people winning turf far away were partly bicycles? He took a sideways view of him. He had now compacted his turf-like tobacco and produced a box of matches.

—Are you sure about the humanity of bicycles? Mick inquired of him. Does it not go against the doctrine of original sin? Or is the Molecule Theory as dangerous as you say?

The sergeant was drawing fiercely at the pipe as his match spluttered.

—It is between twice and three times as dangerous as it might be, he replied gloomily. Early in the morning I often think it is four times and, for goodness sake, if you lived here for a few days and gave full and free rein to your observation and inspection, you would know how certain the sureness of the certainty is.

—Policeman Pluck did not look like a bicycle, Mick said. He had no back wheel on him and hadn't so much as a bell on his right thumb.

The sergeant looked at him with some commiseration.

—You cannot expect him to grow handlebars out of his neck but I have seen him attempt things more acutely indescribable than that. Did you ever notice the queer behaviour of bicycles in the country, or the more-manbicycles?

—I did not.

—It's an indigenous catastrophe. When a man lets things go too far, you will not see much because he spends a lot of time leaning with one elbow on walls or standing propped up by one foot at the path. Such a man is a futile phenomenon of great charm and intensity and a very dangerous article.

—Dangerous to other people, you mean?

—Dangerous to himself and everybody. I once knew a man named Doyle. He was thirty-one per cent.

—Well, that's not too serious.

The sergeant was puffing industriously, his pipe now in fine order.

—Maybe. You can thank me. There were three Doyle brothers in the house and they were too contemptuously poor to have a bicycle apiece. Some people never know how fortunate they are when they are poorer than each other. But bedamn but one of the brothers won a prize of ten pounds in *John Bull*. When I got precise wind of this tiding I knew I would have to take quick steps unless there was to be two new bicycles in the family, because you will understand that I can steal only a limited number of bicycles in a month. Luckily I knew the postman well and I gave him a talking-to to divert the cheque to myself. The postman! Ah, great, sweet, brown stirabout!

Recollection of this public servant seemed to move the sergeant to sad sardonic chuckles, with intricate gesturings of his red hands.

—The postman? Mick asked.

—Seventy-two per cent, he said quietly.

—Great Lord!

—A round of twenty-nine miles on the bicycle every single day for forty years, hail, rain or snowballs. There was very little hope of getting his number down below fifty again. I got him to cash the cheque in a private suboffice and we split the money in the public interest paternalistically.

Funny thing, Mick did not feel that the sergeant had been dishonest; he had been sentimental, rather, and the state of the postman meant that no moral issue was involved.

He asked the sergeant how the bicycle, for its part, would behave from day to day in a situation like this.

—The behaviour of a bicycle with a very high content of homo sapiens, he explained, is very cunning and entirely remarkable. You never see them moving by themselves but you meet them in the least accountable of places unexpectedly. Did you ever see a bicycle leaning against the dresser in a warm kitchen when it is pouring outside?

—I did.

—Not very far from the fire?

—Yes.

—Near enough to the family to hear the conversation?

—I suppose so.

—Not a thousand miles from where they keep the eatables?

—I did not notice that. Good Lord, you do not mean to say that these bicycles *eat food?*

—They were never seen doing it, nobody ever caught them with a mouthful of seedy cake. All I know is that food disappears.

—What!

—It is not the first time I have noticed crumbs at the front wheels of some of those gentlemen.

Rather feebly Mick gestured to the waitress and ordered another drink. The Sergeant was in deadly earnest, no doubt about that. And this was the man Mick had decided to call in to help him in resolving the great St. Augustine enigma. He felt strangely depressed.

—Nobody takes any notice, the Sergeant said softly. Tom thinks that Pat is responsible for the missing grubsteaks, and Pat thinks that Tom is instrumental. Very few of the people guess what is going on in such a fearsomely infractional house. There are other things, too . . . but it's better not to talk of them.

—Oh come now, Sergeant. What sort of other things?

—Well, a man riding a lady's bicycle. It's the height of sulphurous immorality, the P.P. would be within his rights in forbidding such a low character put as much as his nose inside the church.

—Yes . . . such conduct is unseemly.

—God help the nation that weakens on such matters. You would have bicycles demanding votes, and they would look for seats on the County Council to make the roads far worse than they are for their own ulterior motivation. But against that and on the other hand, a good bicycle is a great companion, a friend, there is great charm about it.

—All the same, I doubt if I'll ever again get up on that bicycle of mine you have in the station out in Dalkey.

The sergeant shook his head genially.

—Ah now, a little of it is a good thing, it makes you hardy and puts iron into you.

4

Alain Robbe-Grillet

A Murderer to Watch

From *The Voyeur*

Last Year at Marienbad is probably the novel for which Alain Robbe-Grillet is most renowned. And that notoriety is attributable, in large part, to the movie of the same name, adapted from his novel.

Robbe-Grillet was something of a literary sensation in France after the publication in 1955 of his second novel, Le Voyeur. *It was awarded the important Prix de Critiques, and with it Robbe-Grillet became recognized as a leader of the "school" of the new novel in France.*

Interpreting the works of Robbe-Grillet is as hazardous as climbing Annapurna. To some, he reflects a surrealistic view of the world. To others, he captures the one-dimensional technique of the cinema, neither seeking depth nor claiming resonance. On the one hand, his characters are flat and underdeveloped. On the other hand, his plot races from place to place and person to person as if in headlong flight from simplicity and instant comprehension.

Even the title to The Voyeur *has been a steady subject of dispute and some dismay. Does it have the obvious sexual intimations that voyeurism has come to bear, or does it simply suggest that observation bulks large in the tale, as we find in the case of Julian Marek, a youthful islander, who follows Mathias the protagonist, with accusing eyes and stealthy pace? Or is the title simply an economic ploy to sell the novel? The jacket for the Grove Press paperback edition capitalizes on the erotic with its portrayal of a young girl dishabille, whereas its hardbound edition pictures the far less sensuous image of a seagull wheeling through the air.*

On one level, The Voyeur *is a straightforward tale of a watch salesman, Mathias, come upon hard times, who returns to the island of his birth in the expectation of*

From Alain Robbe-Grillet, *The Voyeur* (New York: Grove Press, 1958), pp. 131–37.

canvassing it by bicycle in an attempt to sell eighty-nine watches to its two thousand inhabitants. The profits from these sales will tide him over until better days return.

Like most avid bicyclists, Mathias is a visionary. But, unlike the run-of-the-mill bicyclist, Mathias has an accessible island where bicycles rule as a means of transportation. In the real world, the Fire Islands and the Mackinac Islands, where bicycles call the tune and automobiles pay the piper, are as rare as a broken spoke on the side of the rear wheel opposite the freewheel.

Mathias is not literature's only journeyman peddler. John McPhee, author and staff writer for the New Yorker, *has written in* The Crofter and The Laird *of another island, Colonsay by name, located in the open Atlantic, twenty-five miles west of the Scottish mainland. This island is peopled by one hundred thirty-eight persons (in 1970, that is) and is marked by sixteen hundred place names—a happy and remarkable disproportion. It is like the towns in the Idaho mountains where the population is lower than the elevation—a fact that ever moved my friend, Jim Phillips, to remark that he always felt most welcome in such places.*

Like Mathias's mythical island, Colonsay has need of its itinerant salesman, who boasts of a bicycle to boost his sales. As McPhee, with engaging charm, puts it:

> The itinerant peddler . . . visits the island several times a year, and spends four days riding his rounds. As saddlebags, he carries a thickly packed leatherboard suitcase and a bundle of goods rolled in a small tarpaulin. His bicycle looks like a thin mule. He has a plaid cap, an old tweed jacket. He wears high-topped shoes, and to protect his legs from the bicycle chain he has wrapped them in the way that soldiers wrapped their legs during the First World War. He is old enough to remember that, and perhaps to have done it. Margaret greets him with the news that he is going to sell her nothing, but she allows him to unstrap his suitcase and his canvas bundle, and to unpack them in her kitchen. She sits in a chair; he kneels on the floor—John Karem, peddler, versus Margaret MacMillan MacArthur McNeill. He shows her a cardigan. "It's lovely," she says. "What else have you got?" He shows her lumberjackets, shirts, lacy nylon nightgowns, and Shetland-wool pullovers for fifty shillings apiece. "They're lovely," she says. "What else have you got?"
>
> These itinerant peddlers used to go from house to house telling stories—part Homer, part drummer. They told tales of mermaids, fairies, seal women, and the warriors of the clans.[1]

Mathias, on the contrary, is no Homeric figure. Nor is he at all identifiable with the gay traveling troubadours of medieval times. He is, as Robbe-Grillet has explained, a "character who does not coincide with himself." Which is to say that he is in a constant state of inner and outward turmoil and confusion.

From the very outset, Mathias's venture is somber and ill fated. As the book opens, the ferry transporting him to the island is about to dock. Mathias retrieves a vagrant string, secretes it in his pocket, and is watched furtively by a girl of seven or so. He disembarks, rents a bicycle, and sets out to sell his watches throughout the rural parts of the four-mile-long island. As the story progresses, we realize that Mathias is acting out a fantasy of his own creation. He has six hours and fifteen minutes from ferry arrival to ferry departure to sell eighty-nine watches to the two thousand inhabitants of this sparsely settled island. The task, an impossible one at its inception, becomes more impossible as

Mathias consumes his valuable time in fruitless and even inapposite efforts to sell his watches.

The mathematical improbability of Mathias's assignment is evidence of a mental instability that becomes more manifest when a thirteen-year-old shepherdess, Jacqueline Leduc, is found floating in the sea, naked and apparently murdered. Mathias's actions and ruminations point to his complicity in this murder. Indeed, his visions of giants strangling virgins and his preoccupation with a certain Violet who enticingly slips in and out of the plot prepare us to denounce him as a sexually motivated psychopathic murderer.

The bicycle is a uniquely appropriate device in the development of the plot since it assumes the figure-of-eight form. Other objects and images appear in the same form. Cigarette smoke curls in a form of eight; the doors of the houses on the island bear the imprint of the figure eight, as in eyeglasses. Mathias uses a string coiled in a figure eight to bind his victim. Even seagulls, omnipresent throughout, course through the air, making swoops and swirls in figure eights.

Mathias's hesitancy, indecisiveness, and other-worldliness may best be illustrated in his madcap dash for the ferry that would seem to be a necessary haven for one who is likely to be seen as Jacqueline's murderer. And yet we are left with the nagging suspicion that the race was as much a pointless fraud as the murder itself might have been, if it occurred at all. Which is to say: feigned fact is frail fantasy.

Leaping onto the seat without bothering to fasten the suitcase to the luggage rack, he began pedaling as hard as he could, holding the handlebars with one hand and the imitation-leather handle of his suitcase in the other.

Luckily the road from here on was in slightly better condition. After the first village on the north coast, it became quite good in fact. The road now led to the fort and then the town. The wind was once again behind him—or almost.

He rode on at a steady speed, although conscious of a slight nervousness.

The houses were becoming a little more numerous—and less poverty-stricken—but whether it was because the salesman presented his wares too hurriedly, or simply did not permit his customers the minimum amount of time indispensable to country people's decisions, Mathias did not make as many sales as he had anticipated.

He made the first scheduled side-trip—a very short one—at the old Roman tower near the village of Saint-Sauveur. He was cordially received but managed to sell only one watch—and from the cheapest series.

When he looked at his watch again, it was already ten minutes to four.

He calculated rapidly that at most a mile and a quarter separated him from the little triangular square where he would leave the bicycle at the cafe-tobacco shop-garage. Without side-trips, it would take him about ten minutes to get there, including the short walk from the tobacco shop to the boat and the thirty seconds he needed to pay the garageman.

He had just under a quarter of an hour until then. The salesman would have time enough to try his luck at a few last doors.

Rushing on as if he were being pursued, running, bounding, throwing himself about—but without wasting his strength in gesticulations—he persisted until the last possible moment.

Leaving matters somewhat up to chance, as soon as a house along the road seemed to look rather prosperous, or less ramshackle, or newer, he jumped off the bicycle and raced to the door, suitcase in hand.

Once. . . . Twice. . . . Three times. . . .

When he found a window open on the ground floor, he spoke from outside, ready to show his merchandise from where he stood. Otherwise he walked into the kitchen without even knocking. Sometimes he economized on words and gestures—excessively, even.

As a matter of fact, all of these attempts were useless. He was going too fast: he was taken for a madman.

At five after four he caught sight of the fort. Now he would have to get back to town without stopping again. There were only three hundred yards or so to travel uphill, then the slope down to the harbor. He wanted to go faster still.

The bicycle chain began to make an unpleasant sound—as if it were rubbing sideways against the sprocket-wheel. Mathias pedaled vigorously.

But the grinding noise grew more pronounced so rapidly that he decided to get off and examine the transmission. He set his suitcase down on the ground and crouched over the machine.

There was no time to study the phenomenon in detail. He confined himself to pushing the sprocket-wheel back toward the frame—dirtying his fingers as little as possible—and started off again. The abnormal friction seemed to grow worse.

He got off again at once and twisted the axle of the sprocket-wheel in the opposite direction.

As soon as he was back on the seat again he realized that matters were going from bad to worse. He was making no progress at all: the machinery was almost completely jammed. Trying another remedy, he manipulated the gearshift—once, twice, three times—pedaling at the same time. As soon as it reached its maximum gear expansion, the chain sprang away from the sprocket-wheel.

He got off the bicycle, set down the suitcase, and lay the machine on its side in the road. It was eight minutes after four. This time, while adjusting the chain in place on the little toothed wheel, he covered himself with grease. He was sweating.

Without wiping his hands he seized his suitcase, mounted the bicycle again, and tried to pedal. The chain sprang away from the sprocket-wheel.

He put it back a second time, then a third. He tried it on all three gear-wheels, without managing to make it hold on any: it came off at the first revolution. Giving up, he continued on foot, half-running, half-walking, holding the suitcase in his left hand and with his right pushing the bicycle. An essential piece of the machinery must have been broken during the jolting on the bad road from Horses Point.

Mathias had just begun walking down the slope to town when he suddenly realized he might be able to coast down without using the pedals. He got back on the bicycle and impelled himself forward with a vigorous kick. For balance he pressed the hand carrying the suitcase against the left grip of the handlebars.

Now he had to be careful not to disturb the chain which he had put back around the sprocket-wheel—therefore he must not move his feet, or he would make it spring off again and tangle with the rear-wheel spokes. In order to fasten the chain more firmly to the sprocket-wheel, since it no longer had to revolve, the salesman thought of attaching it with a piece of cord he had picked up that morning; he began looking for the cord in the pockets of his duffle coat. But not finding it in either one, he remembered. . . . He remembered that he no longer had it.

Furthermore, he had arrived without mishap at the level section of the road just before the fork; he was forced to stop in order to avoid a little girl who was heedlessly crossing just in front of him. In order to gain momentum he unthinkingly gave the pedals a turn . . . then several more. The bicycle was working perfectly. The peculiar noise had entirely disappeared.

At the other end of the town he heard the little steamer's whistle: once, twice, three times.

He entered the square, the town hall on his left. The whistle blew again, shrill and prolonged.

On the movie bulletin-board, the advertisement had been changed. He leaned the bicycle against it and dashed into the case-tobacco shop. No one was there: no customer in the room, no proprietor behind the counter. He called. No one answered.

Outside there was no one either, no one in sight. Mathias remembered that the man had returned his security. The sum amounted to . . .

The ship's whistle blew a long blast—in a slightly lower tone.

The salesman jumped onto the bicycle. He would leave it at the end of the quay—would hand it to someone—with the amount he owed for its rental. But even pedaling as hard as he could along the uneven cobbles, he managed to remember that the garageman had still not told him the terms. At first it had only been a question of the two-hundred-crowns security, which obviously bore no relation to the value of the bicycle nor to the cost of a half-day's rental.

Mathias decided not to try riding along the pier, for it was encumbered with a great many baskets and hampers. There was not a single stroller on this part of the quay to take the money, so he abandoned the bicycle against the parapet and immediately ran toward the steamer. In a few seconds he had reached the landing slip, where a little crowd of about ten people was standing. The gangplank had been pulled up. The steamer was slowly pulling away from the embankment.

The tide was high now. The water covered a good part of the inclined plane—half of it, perhaps—or two-thirds. The seaweed on the bottom could no longer be seen, nor the tufts of greenish moss which made the lower stones so slippery.

Mathias looked at the narrow strip of water almost imperceptibly widening between the ship's side and the oblique edge of the landing slip. He could not jump across it, not so much because of the distance—which was still very slight—but because of the dangers of landing on the gunwale or in the midst of the passengers and their baggage on the stern deck. The downward slope along which he would have to run to gain momentum increased the difficulty still further, as did the heavy shoes and the duffle coat he was wearing, not to mention the suitcase he was carrying.

He looked at the half-turned backs of the people staying behind, their faces in profile, their stares motionless and parallel—meeting identical stares from the ship. Standing against an iron pillar that supported the deck above, a child of seven or eight was gravely staring at him with large calm eyes. He wondered why she was looking at him that way, but then something—a silhouette—came between him and the image— a sailor on board whom the salesman thought he recognized. He ran forward three steps toward the end of the pier and shouted: "Hey there!"

The sailor did not hear him over the noise of the engines. On the pier Mathias' immediate neighbors turned toward him—then others farther away, by degrees.

The passengers, noticing the general movement of heads on the pier, also looked in his direction—as if in astonishment. The sailor raised his eyes and caught sight of Mathias, who waved his arms in his direction and cried again: "Hey there!"

"Hey!" answered the sailor waving his arms in farewell. The little girl next to him had not moved, but the maneuver executed by the ship changed the direction of her gaze: now she would be looking at the top of the pier, above the landing slip, where another group of people was standing on the narrow passageway that led to the beacon light. These too were now facing Mathias. All of them had the same strained, frozen expression as before.

Without addressing anyone in particular, Mathias said: "I didn't miss it by much."

5

Samuel Beckett

Things Are Not What They Seem

From *Molloy*

In the works of Samuel Beckett, bicyclists often perform prodigious, outlandish, and even jocose feats. In "The Calmative," for example, the narrator records that

I only saw one cyclist! He was going the same way as I was. All were going the same way as I was, vehicles too, I have only just realized it. He was pedalling slowly in the middle of the street, reading a newspaper which he held with both hands spread open before his eyes. Every now and then he rang his bell without interrupting his reading. I watched him recede till he was no more than a dot on the horizon.[1]

In the same vein, the reader is treated, in Molloy, *to a number of illustrations of the circuslike capabilities of bicyclists and their curious attachment to their machines. In the first part of the plot, Molloy is about to set off on his journey to visit his mother, to settle his grievance with her.*

So I got up, adjusted my crutches and went down to the road, where I found my bicycle (I didn't know I had one) in the same place I must have left it. Which enables me to remark that, crippled though I was, I was no mean cyclist, at that period. This is how I went about it. I fastened my crutches to the cross-bar, one on either side, I propped the foot of my stiff leg (I forget which, now they're both stiff) on the projecting

From Samuel Beckett, *Molloy* (New York: Grove Press, 1965), pp. 15–16, 155–57.

"A lamplighter flew by on his bike, tilting with his pole at the standards, jousting a little yellow light into the evening." (From *More Pricks than Kicks* by Samuel Beckett)

front axle, and I pedalled with the other. It was a chainless bicycle, with a free-wheel, if such a bicycle exists. Dear bicycle, I shall not call you bike, you were green, like so many of your generation, I don't know why. It is a pleasure to meet it again. To describe it at length would be a pleasure. It had a little red horn instead of the bell fashionable in your days. To blow this horn was for me a real pleasure, almost a vice. I will go further and declare that if I were obliged to record, in a roll of honour, those activities which in the course of my interminable existence have given me only a mild pain in the balls, the blowing of a rubber horn—toot!—would figure among the first. And when I had to part from my bicycle I took off the horn and kept it about me. I believe I have it still, somewhere, and if I blow it no more it is because it has gone dumb. Even motor-cars have no horns nowadays, as I understand the thing, or rarely. When I see one, through the lowered window of a stationary car, I often stop and blow it. This should all be re-written in the pluperfect. What a rest to speak of bicycles and horns.

In the second part of the novel, we find Jacques Moran, who may or may not be a
personality distinct from the Molloy of the first part, en route on foot from his home in
Turdy to Molloy country to answer the Molloy question. He is accompanied by his son,
also named Jacques. Moran, worried lest the lameness which is taking hold of his leg
will frustrate his journey, sends Jacques to the town of Hole to buy a second hand bicycle
"by preference." Jacques leaves with four pounds ten shillings with strict instructions to
buy a new bicycle only if a second hand one is not available. Moran awaits the return of
his son for three days.

About five o'clock I ate my last tin of sardines and a few biscuits, with a good appetite. This left me with only a few apples and a few biscuits. But about seven o'clock my son arrived. The sun was low in the west. I must have dozed a moment, for I did not see him coming, a speck on the horizon, then rapidly bigger and bigger, as I had foreseen. But he was already between me and the camp, making for the latter, when I saw him. A wave of irritation broke over me, I jumped to my feet and began to vociferate, brandishing my umbrella. He turned and I beckoned him to join me, waving the umbrella as if I wanted to hook something with the handle. I thought for a moment he was going to defy me and continue on his way to the camp, to where the camp had been rather, for it was there no more. But finally he came towards me. He was pushing a bicycle which, when he had joined me, he let fall with a gesture signifying he could bear no more. Pick it up, I said, till I look at it. I had to admit it must once have been quite a good bicycle. I would gladly describe it, I would gladly write four thousand words on it alone. And you call that a bicycle? I said. Only half expecting him to answer me I continued to inspect it. But there was something so strange in his silence that I looked up at him. His eyes were starting out of his head. What's the matter, I said, is my fly open? He let go the bicycle again. Pick it up, I said. He picked it up. What happened to you? he said. I had a fall, I said. A fall? he said. Yes, a fall, I cried, did you never have a fall? I tried to remember the name of the plant that springs from the ejaculations of the hanged and shrieks when plucked. How much did you give for it? I said. Four pounds, he said. Four pounds! I cried. If he had said two pounds or even thirty shillings I should have cried. Two pounds! or, Thirty shillings! the same. They asked four pounds five, he said. Have you the receipt? I said. He did not know what a receipt was. I described one. The money I spent on my son's education and he did not know what a simple receipt was. But I think he knew as well as I. For when I said to him, Now tell me what a receipt is, he told me very prettily. I really did not care in the least whether he had been fooled into paying for the bicycle three or four times what it was worth or whether on the other hand he had appropriated the best part of the purchase money for his own use. The loss would not be mine. Give me the ten shillings, I said. I spent them, he said. Enough, enough. He began explaining that the first day the shops had been closed, that the second—I said. Enough, enough. I looked at the carrier. It was the best thing about that bicycle. It and the pump. Does it go by any chance? I said. I had a puncture two miles from Hole, he said. I walked the rest of the way. I looked at his shoes. Pump it up, I said. I held the bicycle, I forget which wheel it was. As soon as two things are nearly identical I am lost. The dirty little twister was letting the air escape between the valve and the connexion which he had purposely not screwed tight. Hold the bicycle, I said, and give me the pump. The tyre was soon hard, I looked at my son. He began to protest. I soon put a stop to that. Five minutes later I felt the tyre. It was as hard as ever. I cursed him. He took a bar of chocolate from his pocket and offered it to me. I took it. But instead of eating it, as I longed to, and although I have a horror of waste, I cast it from me, after a moment's hesitation, which I trust my son did not notice. Enough. We went down to the road. It was more like a path. I tried to sit down on the carrier. The foot of my stiff leg tried to sink into the ground, into the grave. I propped myself up on one of the bags. Keep her steady, I said. I was still too low. I added the other. Its bulges dug into my buttocks. The more things resist me the more rabid I get. With time, and nothing but my teeth and nails, I would rage up from the bowels of the earth to its crust, knowing full well I had nothing to gain. And when I had no more teeth, no more nails, I would dig through the rock with my bones. Here then in a few words is the solution I arrived at. First the bags, then my son's raincoat folded in four, all lashed to the carrier and the saddle with my son's bits of string. As for the umbrella, I hooked it round my neck, so as to have both hands free to hold on to my son by the waist, under the armpits rather, for by this time my seat was higher than his. Pedal, I said. He made a despairing effort, I can well believe it. We fell. I felt a sharp pain in my shin. I was all tangled up in the back wheel. Help! I cried. My son helped me up. My stocking was torn and my leg bleeding. Happily it was the sick leg. What would I have done, with both legs out of action? I would have found a way. It was even perhaps a blessing in disguise, I was thinking of phlebotomy of course. Are you all right? I said. Yes, he said. He would be. With my umbrella I caught him a smart blow on the hamstrings, gleaming between the leg of his shorts and his stocking. He cried out. Do you want to kill us? I said. I'm not strong enough, he said, I'm not strong enough. The bicycle was all right apparently, the back wheel slightly buckled perhaps. I at once saw the error I had made. It was to have settled down in my seat, with my feet clear of the ground, before we moved off. I reflected. We'll try again, I said. I can't, he said. Don't try me too far, I said. He straddled the frame. Start off gently when I tell you, I said. I got up again behind and settled down in my seat, with my feet clear of the ground. Good. Wait till I tell you, I said. I let myself slide to one side till the foot of my good leg touched the ground. The only weight now on the back wheel was that of my sick leg, cocked up rigid at an excruciating angle. I dug my fingers into my son's jacket. Go easy, I said. The wheels began to turn. I followed, half dragged, half hopping. I trembled for my testicles which swing a little low. Faster! I cried. He bore down on the pedals. I bounded up to my place. The bicycle swayed, righted itself, gained speed. Bravo! I cried, beside myself with joy. Hurrah! cried my son. How I loathe that exclamation! I can hardly set it down. He was as pleased as I, I do believe. His heart was beating under my hand and yet my hand was far from his heart. Happily it was downhill. Happily I had mended my hat, or the wind would have blown it away. Happily the weather was fine and I no longer alone. Happily, happily.

6

Bruno Schulz

Signs and Wonders in the Heavens

From *The Street of Crocodiles*

Quite possibly Bruno Schulz was a bicyclist. But we may never be certain, for little is known of his life and career. Yet how else could he have envisioned bicycles and their riders wheeling across the starry skies? Only a bicyclist seeking liberation from the boredom of counting milepost markers would be likely to look to the skies for diversion. And who else would find the stars assembled in configurations depicting manned and moving bicycles? The fact in this fantasy is that, in November 1977, a bicyclist touring through Colorado wrote Bicycling *magazine that he had seen a "biker constellation" which he continues to see "every clear night." Bruno Schulz, as you will see, would have been most gratified.*

Reading The Street of Crocodiles *by Bruno Schulz is like listening to the music of Gustav Mahler. Neither is a fully satisfying experience, for the prize in each is far greater than the audience can reach and, what is worse, so tantalizingly mystic.*

However, unlike Mahler's, Bruno Schulz's life and works are not well known. The records reveal that he was born in Poland in 1892 in the Galician city of Drogobych. Drogobych was his home, indeed his cloister, until he was killed in its streets in 1942 by a roving contingent of SS men. And it is Drogobych that we find lionized, transformed, and metamorphosed in The Street of Crocodiles.

Aside from the book's being a pastiche of life in the Drogobych of Schulz's imagination, it is also a kind of family outing to which no one but a family member would wish an invitation. Schulz's father is the cynosure of most attention, being patriarch and all that conveys. He is seen as a sick and even demented former proprietor of a dry goods

From Bruno Schulz, *The Street of Crocodiles* (New York: Penguin Books, 1977), pp. 152–56.

store who is obsessed by everything from cockroaches, to electricity, to tailor's dummies,
to his overflowing filing cabinets. Schulz's sister Adela, his brother and uncles, and even
a wastrel puppy adopted into the family all play roles, to a greater or lesser degree.

But it is not the story line or the characters that make the reading of this book an
entrancing experience. It is, on the contrary, the wondrously imaginative verbal creativ-
ity of Schulz. His imagery literally leaps out at you as you read its pages. He is a
conjurer of language whose landscape is verbal and whose illumination is exploding
images. His prose has been rightly appraised as "a running flame of amazing imagery."

Witness, for example, his description of a fragment of a garden in a tawdry suburban
area of Drogobych:

> Overlooked by the light of day, weeds and wild flowers of all kinds luxuriated
> quietly, glad of the interval for dreams beyond the margin of time on the borders of
> an endless day. An enormous sunflower, lifted on a powerful stem and suffering
> from hypertrophy, clad in the yellow mourning of the last sorrowful days of its life,
> bent under the weight of its monstrous girth. But the naive, suburban bluebells and
> unpretentious dimity flowers stood helpless in their starched pink and white shifts,
> indifferent to the sunflower's tragedy.[1]

The excerpt that follows is a segment of the book's concluding chapter, entitled "The
Comet." The earlier parts of this chapter depict the glorious transformation of
Drogobych from the cruelty of winter to the sweet meats of spring. Spring fosters a
reckless inventiveness in Schulz's father that had long lain dormant. He establishes a
home laboratory for experimentation with electrical circuitry. And poor but willing
Uncle Edward gains a new vision as his test animal but loses his life in the bargain.
With man and nature burgeoning bounteously, Schulz joins the two in a fabled
apotheosis of the bicycle.

One day my brother, on his return from school, brought the improbable and yet true
news of the imminent end of the world. We asked him to repeat it, thinking that we
had misheard. We hadn't. This is what that incredible, that completely baffling piece
of news was: unready and unfinished, just as it was, at a random point in time and
space, without closing its accounts, without having reached any goal, in mid-sentence
as it were, without a period or exclamation mark, without a last judgment or God's
Wrath—in an atmosphere of friendly understanding, loyally, by mutual agreement
and in accordance with rules observed by both parties—the world was to be hit on the
head, simply and irrevocably. No, it was not to be an eschatological, tragic finale as
forecast long ago by the prophets, nor the last act of the Divine Comedy. No. It was to
be a trick cyclist's, a prestidigitator's end of the world, splendidly hocus-pocus and
bogus-experimental—accompanied by the plaudits of all the spirits of Progress. There
was almost no one to whom the idea would not appeal. The frightened, the protesters,
were immediately hushed up. Why did not they understand that this was a simply
incredible chance, the most progressive, freethinking end of the world imaginable, in

line with the spirit of the times, an honorable end, a credit to the Supreme Wisdom? People discussed it with enthusiasm, drew pictures "ad oculos" on pages torn from pocket notebooks, provided irrefutable proofs, knocking their opponents and the skeptics out of the ring. In illustrated journals whole-page pictures began to appear, drawings of the anticipated catastrophe with effective staging. These usually represented panic-stricken populous cities under a night sky resplendent with lights and astronomical phenomena. One saw already the astonishing action of the distant comet, whose parabolic summit remained in the sky in immobile flight, still pointing toward the earth, and approaching it at a speed of many miles per second. As in a circus farce, hats and bowlers rose into the air, hair stood on an end, umbrellas opened by themselves, and bald patches were disclosed under escaping wigs—and above it all there spread a black enormous sky, shimmering with the simultaneous alert of all the stars.

Something festive had entered our lives, an eager enthusiasm. An importance permeated our gestures and swelled our chests with cosmic sighs. The earthly globe seethed at night with a solemn uproar from the unanimous ectasy of thousands. The nights were black and vast. The nebulae of stars around the earth became more numerous and denser. In the dark interplanetary spaces these stars appeared in different positions, strewing the dust of meteors from abyss to abyss. Lost in the infinite, we had almost forsaken the earthly globe under our feet; we were disoriented, losing our bearings; we hung head-down like antipodes over the upturned zenith and wandered over the starry heaps, moving a wetted finger across maps of the sky, from star to star. Thus we meandered in extended, disorderly, single file, scattering in all directions on the rungs of the infinite ladders of the night—emigrants from the abandoned globe, plundering the immense antheap of stars. The last barriers fell, the cyclists rode into stellar space, rearing on their vehicles, and were perpetuated in an immobile flight in the interplanetary vacuum, which revealed ever new constellations. Thus circling on an endless track, they marked the paths of a sleepless cosmography, while in reality, black as soot, they succumbed to a planetary lethargy, as if they had put their heads into the fireplace, the final goal of all those blind flights.

After short, incoherent days, partly spent in sleeping, the nights opened up like an enormous, populated motherland. Crowds filled the streets, turned out in public squares, head close to head, as if the top of a barrel of caviar had been removed and it was now flowing out in a stream of shiny buckshot, a dark river under a pitch-black night noisy with stars. The stairs broke under the weight of thousands, at all the upper floor windows little figures appeared, matchstick people jumping over the rails in a moon-struck fervor, making living chains, like ants, living structures and columns— one astride another's shoulders—flowing down from windows to the platforms of squares lit by the glare of burning tar barrels.

I must beg forgiveness if in describing these scenes of enormous crowds and general uproar, I tend to exaggerate, modeling myself unwittingly on certain old engravings in the great book of disasters and catastrophes of the human species. But they all create a pre-image and the megalomanic exaggeration, the enormous pathos of all these scenes proved that we had removed the bottom of the eternal barrel of memories, of an ultrabarrel of myth, and had broken into a prehuman night of untamed elements, of incoherent anamnesis, and could not hold back the swelling flood. Ah, these nights filled with stars shimmering like fishscales! Ah, these banks of mouths incessantly swallowing in small gulps, in hungry draught, the swelling undrunk streams of those dark rain-drenched nights! In what fatal nets, in what miserable trammels did those multiplicated generations end?

Oh, skies of those days, skies of luminous signals and meteors, covered by the calculations of astronomers, copied a thousand times, numbered, marked with the water-marks of algebra! With faces blue from the glory of those nights, we wandered through space pulsating from the explosions of distant suns, in a sidereal brightness— human ants, spreading in a broad heap on the sandbanks of the milky way spilled over the whole sky—a human river overshadowed by the cyclists on their spidery machines. Oh, stellar arena of night, scarred by the evolutions, spirals and leaps of those nimble riders; oh, cycloids and epi-cycloids executed in inspiration along the diagonals of the sky, amid lost wire spokes, hoops shed with indifference, to reach the bright goal denuded, with nothing but the pure idea of cycling! From these days dates a new constellation, the thirteenth group of stars, included forever in the zodiac and resplendent since then in the firmament of our nights: THE CYCLIST.

Part III
Not in Vain the Distance Beckons!

Introduction

Not in vain the distance beckons.
Forward, forward let us range.
Let the great world spin for ever
Down the ringing grooves of change.

Alfred, Lord Tennyson,
"Locksley Hall"

According to Flann O'Brien, "[a] journey is an hallucination." Such hyperbole is typical of Flann O'Brien. But it is no exaggeration to affirm that a journey by bicycle is like none other; it is a thing apart; it has a tempo and a style of its own; it is demonstrably unique.

A bicycle trip may be a lonely, even a daring, adventure, but the companionship of two wheels under foot establishes a silent and fortifying partnership. A bicycle¹ journey may be longer and more arduous than travel by car, but, with time, distance evaporates in the elation of personal achievement. A bicycle tour may be faster than travel by foot, but its speed is the measured, rhythmic pace of one who, after James Stephens, has "quit forever more the brick-built den" that hides us from all contact with our fellow men. It is instinct with the viatic excitement of one whose cycle of learning is fulfilled in the steady, wind-inherited knowledge that we are better than we thought and "equal to the peaks of our desire."

A bicycle journey can be brief or extended. To a large extent the length, duration and place of bicycle travel determine the items that should be carried on it. A bicyclist intending to cross the North American continent, without the aid of a "sag wagon," could hardly be expected to emulate Lawrence of Arabia in carrying a voluminous dictionary on the order of Viollet-le-Duc's *Dictionnaire raisonné* for his leisure-time reading. Woodrow Wilson, it is related, was fond of bicycling "about the villages of the Lake Country with the *Oxford Book of English Verse* in his pocket." That is more manageable reading material, at least in terms of size and weight and as keyed to the purpose of the outing. Thomas de Quincey and William Wordsworth, among other English Lake Country poets, would have been pleased to know, I am sure, that Wilson bicycled through their Lake Country haunts reading their poetry. In the summer of 1944, another Wilson, Edmund this time, bicycled through the same Lake Country "and in the evenings I read Wordsworth's *Prelude*."[1]

—avoir l'apprenti dans le soleil.—

"The world lies right beyond the handlebars of any bicycle." (From *The Man Who Loved Bicycles* by Daniel Behrman)

Touring bicyclists generally worry less about the books they plan to read along the way than about the equipment they will need to effect necessary repairs. And it is right that they should do so. Bicyclists are, of course, as disparate in their judgments on what tools should be carried as they are on whether "sew-ups" should be used on long-distance travel. For example, Ian Hibbell, the famed, even fabled, bicycle explorer, never thought it necessary to carry a freewheel remover on his ventures. And, by all reports, the lack of a remover never caused him any grief.

But, for me, the freewheel remover is essential luggage on any long-distance bicycle travel, that is, at least since one day in Washington, Kansas. It was in Washington, Kansas, in the summer of 1971 that my daughter broke two spokes in her rear wheel, as always, on the freewheel side. At the time three of my children and I were traveling by bicycle to California from our home in the Washington, D.C., suburbs. Until Washington, Kansas, the lightening of our load by the absence of a freewheel remover had been a blessing to us, modest though it was.

Washington, Kansas is small in size and remote from the technological demands of the ten-speed bicycle. The local machine shop was our only hope for assistance in removing my daughter's Atom freewheel, so we were told by persons at the town's Western Auto.

The machine shop was peopled by two persons, grimed by years of welding this and brazing that. Laconic and sparse of words though they were, they were willing and even anxious to help without delay. Bending to the task, they puzzled over what they might have that would fit inside the freewheel snugly enough to break it loose from the hub. After casting about in boxes of rusted metal parts, assembled in an entirely helter-skelter fashion, they set about locating bolts with heads large enough to fit the Atom's center cavity.

One bolt after another broke as its shaft was twisted in an effort to loosen the freewheel. When the last bolt of proper size was about to be used, the owner, or so he seemed to be, told the younger one to heat the bolt under the torch and then to immerse it in water—in short, to temper it. He did; the bolt held; the freewheel was dislodged and the spokes were replaced.

Even today, this home-crafted freewheel puller is cherished by me as a formidable example of prairie-land bricolage, which is defined by Claude Levi-Strauss as "the art of the do-it-yourself handyman who must solve problems given only limited tools and his own ingenuity."

The contemporary American poet Kenneth Rexroth's Parisian garagist was of the same stripe as this rural Kansas machinist. As Rexroth describes him in *The Dragon and the Unicorn*, he was

> A little wiry garagist
> Red-faced, bright eyed, three times
> Given up for dead with consumption,
> Three years in concentration camps.[2]

This garagist appears near the end of Rexroth's long poem at a farewell party in

Paris, hosted by the poet's friend Lèontine. Rexroth has just completed a bicycle tour through France to Italy and he is about to bid adieu to the continent.

At the party the garagist proves himself to be not only an inventor but inventive in more colorful, engaging and social ways as well.

> The garagist cuts loose. His
> Repertory is formidable.
> "La Poule qu'etait batie trop étroite,"
> "Toute la nuit sur la Tour Eiffel,"
> "L'Hirondelle avec les hemorriodes seches,"
> [Hirondelles are bicycle cops]
> And especially for the shepherd,
> "Pompadour, ma belle angele."
> Leontine says, "He writes them all
> Himself.". . .
> The garagist raises his glass,
> And says, "Ki Yi Yippee Yi Yi!"
> He has come back from his own room,
> Bringing a sheaf of drawings, and
> A box of beautiful models.
> As he shows them to me his face
> Lights with exaltation, and his
> Movements grow entranced and still
> More quick. I am dumbfounded.
> He has managed to discover
> A fundamentally new
> Application of a double
> Torsion. I cannot tell through his
> Excited language if he is
> Aware of this or not.
> He has perfect models of a
> Stabilizer for the latest
> Ford, a coupling for heavy trailers,
> A gimmick for jet airplanes
> I do not quite understand,
> And last—"I hoped this at least
> Could be sold in France"—a brake
> For a bicycle, which is so
> Revolutionary and
> Efficient, I ask him if he
> Can have it copied for me
> In a model shop. "I do not
> Use a model shop. I make them
> Myself, in my spare time in the
> Garage." "What do you do in the
> Garage?" "I wash cars." No one speaks.
> At last Lèontine says, "There is
> No place for a man like him
> In France. No one will invest
> Any money. They want big
> Profits from the old machinery,
> Making the old junk. The money

They put in gold in boxes
In the banks in Buenos Aires."
I looked at him. He is in rags.
His cheeks are like splotches
Of red ink. In a year or so
He will be dead. If he had gone
To America in his youth,
Today he would be on the
Cover of Time magazine. But
He would never have written the
Poem about the midinette
And the camel, or the song
About the nuns who got drunk.
If only poverty was not
Killing him. I write an address.
"You can mail those plans to Detroit.
I am sure they would give you
A job. But like M'sieu le berger,
You would not like America."
When we leave the card is crumpled
On the floor. It is the law
Of the falling rate of profit.[3]

As if to prove that there is nothing new under the sun, Bernard Newman, the prolific English author, reported having an experience while bicycling in England which was very similar to mine in Washington, Kansas. Newman's incident occurred in 1944 as he bicycled, aboard "George III," through the English countryside as an emissary of the British Ministry of Information. His smithy was my welder, was Rexroth's garagist.

My journey carried me irregularly from corner to corner of the West Riding. As I rode south to Selby, the cold rain made cycling anything but a pleasure. Suddenly my front hub began to click: then to make an angry spluttering sound. I diagnosed a broken ball-bearing, but the rain did not suggest a halt.

Here was a village smithy: its notice-board proclaimed "Cycles repaired." I disturbed the smith at his legitimate occupation of shoeing a horse.

"Could you do a small repair for me?"

"Well, it's my son who does the bicycles. I do the horses."

"Oh, isn't he in?"

"No, he isn't."

"How long will he be?"

"Well, I don't exactly know. You see, he's in the army, in Italy. But I can mend a puncture for you."

I could do that myself: he finished his horse, then we tackled George together. My diagnosis was not quite correct: a few drops of water had penetrated into the hub.

"Are you this man I was reading about in the paper?" the blacksmith asked. I admitted that I might be. Then a considerable argument ensued—he did not wish to charge me for his work.

"No. I reckon I've learned something about hubs this morning."

"Of course, I insisted, and rode on.[4]

The security of the bicycle is another concern of the touring bicyclist. But no garagist or anyone else has yet invented a safety device providing at once both the maximum in protection and the minimum in bulk and weight acceptable to the bicyclist on tour. This anxiety for the safety of one's bicycle is not a vagrant fancy without basis in demonstrated fact or in creative fiction.

I recall one summer Saturday evening bicycling alone into Gordon, Nebraska, on the prowl for a self-service laundry into which to unload my dirty-clothes-laden panniers. Upon stopping at an intersection, I asked a couple of dour-faced Saturday-night gawkers for directions. Almost immediately, I felt my bicycle being pulled out from under me from behind. Upon turning, I confronted the alcohol-sodden face of a native American attempting to dislodge me from my bicycle. I turned to my handlebar bag in a futile scramble to locate my security blanket, better known as a Swiss Army knife. But, too late, another Saturday-night reveler was alternately grabbing at my handlebars and leering drunkenly at me. And a third member of the group was lurching directly toward me from the side.

I realized at once that I was outnumbered and soon to be overpowered. Force was out and persuasion was in. I quickly and firmly protested that they would do well not to steal my bicycle, for it was like stealing a man's horse, a hanging offense. They momentarily desisted. I repeated, my voice cracking: a horse—a hanging offense. They looked at each other in bewilderment and backed off long enough for me to regain control of my bicycle and to make a wobbly escape. A kryptonite bicycle lock would have been worthless weight in that encounter.

In the annals of literature, a similar solicitude for bicycle security is occasionally discovered. Raman, the painter of signs of Narayan's novel of that name, found his eager and fervent amour chilled briefly by an ill-timed concern for the safety of his bicycle, as the excerpt in part three of this book discloses.

Again, in Ernest Hemingway's taut short story, "A Way You'll Never Be," Nick Adams is depicted as a soldier of uncertain allegiance, either Italian or American, bicycling disguised as an American soldier through the blood, the bodies and the sham bravado of a combat zone. Nick happens upon the encampment of his friend Para, Captain Paravicini, who welcomes him and offers him a respite from his grim bicycling duty. Nick sorely needs the rest for combat fatigue has overcome him. But before he lies down, Para asks:

> Where did you leave your bicycle?
> Inside the last house.
> Do you think it will be all right?
> Don't worry, Nick said. I'll go in a little while.
> Lie down a little while, Nicolo.
> All right.[5]

But his slumber was but a brief and painful dream, cut short by Nick's decision to return to "that damned bicycle," which, unhappily for him, no Henry Fleming had seen fit to seize in an effort to desert.

Bicyclists can take precautions against the theft of their bicycles, whether they are touring or not. But nothing can be done to divert or to discourage a headwind. For travelers from east to west, it is the prevailing westerly that torments them. And for those who reverse their direction to profit from the prevailing westerly, the wind, pixielike, confounds them by becoming a prevailing easterly.

Most bicyclists realize that only rarely is any wind an asset in their travels. As the saying goes among bicyclists, if the wind is not against you, it is not blowing.

Kenneth Rexroth, once again in his poem *The Dragon and the Unicorn,* remarks on the dread wind, which even makes a downhill run a wearisome chore. His descent to the Mediterranean against a headwind recalls for me a similar experience in entering Salt Lake City from the east down the canyon. As Rexroth saw it:

> Heavy bicycling all morning,
> Down hill in second gear against
> A pounding southeast wind from the
> Mediterranean, millions
> Of cubic miles of transparency
> With millions of tons of pressure
> Rushing up from Africa.
> At the watershed they change the
> Trees on the canal to cypress
> Because of the constant wind.[6]

The touring bicyclist, whether traveling singly or in a group, must expect the humdrum of the road to be unrelenting and, at times, unnerving. Long-distance travel cannot sustain the initial excitement for days and miles of incessant pedaling, particularly where there are no hills or down dales to soften the monotony.

Every touring bicyclist concocts one or more devices to leaven the weary hours of bicycling. Counting the milepost markers on well-traveled roads is a pastime of limited value, for each marker is just another boulder for the bicyclist to bear, Sisyphus-like. Watching milepost markers becomes an obsession that obscures everything else and wears the anxious watcher down. U.S. Route 2, for example, across Montana has 667 conspicuous green markers. The last one at each end was missing in 1974. The results of the furious frenzy of a number-crazed bicyclist, no doubt.

And in California the county roads add to the milepost torment by inserting markers for fractions of a mile in between each milepost sign. The eye is fixed and mesmerized by an endless sea of numerals and markers. The brain is dizzied and the monotony is not in the least lessened.

Another ploy to relieve the boredom involves a counting game, with the milepost markers used only to start and end the counting. With this gambit, suppose a water tower (omnipresent on the plains) or grain elevator is spied in the distance. Guess the number of miles from the location of first sighting to the landmark itself. The object is to test the accuracy of the guess by mentally noting the nearest milepost marker when the distant landmark is first seen and checking the marker nearest the landmark upon arrival there. Of course, the game assumes the road does not take an unexpected turn, leaving the landmark unattainable off in some different direction.

Junking is another cunning caper that can backfire. Junking is the art of eagle-eyeing the shoulder of the road for usable items that have been lost or abandoned which can then be retrieved and salvaged. This game is demanding and invariably provocative. It takes care to note items on the abutting shoulder while simultaneously keeping to the road and avoiding its ruts. This is particularly the case on downhill runs.

And what could be more imponderable than the number of hair combs found along the roads in the eastern United States or the number and variety of sports shirts lying by the road in the Russian River resort area in northern California? Yet a stray kitten may be sighted, as happened to my son Jim in North Dakota, and a pannier flap becomes a roof for a restive kitten over long miles of meowing until a farmer is found who will rescue cat and bicyclist from each other. Or how does one trundle along by bicycle after finding a portable tape recorder that plays authentic Indian tribal chants? And when the added weight is borne over mile upon laborious mile, it is likely to be stolen, as happened to my son Charlie, when the days were run and the "fearful trip is done."

One of the most unique and amusing prescriptions to counteract the boredom of long-distance bicycling is that of a poet, not an apothecary, Samuel Hoffenstein. Songs they are and songs of a most peculiar kind. *Songs to Break the Tedium of Riding a Bicycle, Seeing One's Friends, or Heartbreak:*

> Along the country roads there grow
> Willow-trees and Texaco,
> Mobiloils and marigold
> And other fruits of men and mould.
> Oh, how my town-tried heart desires
> To know the peace of Kelly Tires,
> To hear the robin in the grass
> Sing, "Socony," as I pass!
> Some day I shall fly the rut
> And build a small, bucolic hut,
> Trim a hedge and hop a stile,
> Walk my Camel for a mile,
> Milk a mid-Victorian cow—
> Eventually, but not now.

*   *   *

> When trouble drives me into rhyme,
> Which is two-thirds of all the time,
> What peace a thought like this can give—
> Great is the age in which we live!
> My heart is heavy, but I know
> They're working on the radio;
> That letters, by aerial post,
> Go every day from coast to coast.
> I may be sunk beyond repair,
> Drunk less on liquor than despair,
> And yet my heart leaps up when I

Behold Sweet Caporal in the sky.
Though winter-bare my solitude,
Though heartbreak in its branches broad,
I know that future wars will be
Fought by super-chemistry,
And, therefore, loneliness and loss
Are but a mask for applesauce;—
For I am lord of life and death,
Who flaunt this flaming shibboleth:—
No matter what the morrow brings,
Inventors are inventing things![7]

Bicyclists who travel alone over extended distances indulge in some rather strange flights of fancy. The personification of the bicycle by giving it a name is one of these. It may be that a bicycle with a name is more of a real-life companion to the lonely bicyclist. For whatever reason, touring bicyclists have had their naming day. Harold Elvin called his bicycle Sir Walter, undoubtedly because it was manufactured by Raleigh. A Georgia attorney, Fred Birchmore, who trundled around the world in 1938 in order to fulfill a childhood dream, rode a bicycle called Bucephalus (after Alexander the Great's Thracian war-horse?). A young Irishwoman, Dervla Murphy, traveled from Dunkirk to India on a three-speed with stand-up handlebars that she named Rozinante [*sic*] after Don Quixote's horse.

Bernard Newman dubbed his most recently acquired bicycle George III. He has explained his naming process as follows:

My constant companion on the journey was George. He is my third bicycle, George III. The first was murdered by Mussolini, who did not pretend to like me, the second I gave to a Roumanian prince when the Russians refused to admit him to their country. George III came to me only in 1938, to make a ride all around the Baltic. Since then he has seen the world.[8]

The lot of the touring bicyclist is not a litany of unrelieved trials and tribulations. That would be a decidedly false understanding. The wind will abate, the monotony can be cracked, and the pavement will not always sizzle in the sun.

Even on chill mornings, the warmth of being on the road, under your own power, in anticipation of the next rise and what lies beyond stirs the heart. A good deal more than the pioneer spirit is awakened. A unique sense of communion with the scenes observed and the events experienced elevates the spirit. It is the freedom of the eagle as it flies that captivates.

Edmund Wilson saw all of this and more as he bicycled down Prospect Hill taking in

the autumn landscape where the barns showed a red almost as soft, and unlike the sharp bright red of clear air, as the deep red of the petals of a rose—or rather, like the cheeks of a Baldwin apple otherwise green, as did the great red stain of a tree still around the stain, and exactly matching the color of the barns, above which the bushy leafage of a tree, at once faded and enriched, where the irregular high grass and clumps of shrubs and trees seemed interesting, as if somehow with the autumn they seemed to conceal some special life, vegetable, animal or human?—the impression was indistinctly blended—ended in the rough dense or feathery tree-tops, through which a window of a house behind the trees glittered silver from the top of the hill—it glittered as I rode, extinguished now and then by the trees; and to the left of the road stood the white bole and crooked limbs of an old buttonwood tree, still green but dying at the top from a fish hawk's nest, while on the right the reddened leaves of poison ivy wound around the trunk of a tree that was dead.[9]

As Wilson intuitively understood, the world of the touring bicyclist cannot be seen with eyes fixed on the solid white line down the side of the road. It is not only a replica of the Eiffel Tower in a Kansas wheatfield that will be missed by the eye that is glued to the white line. There are also gypsy moments that will pass undetected. The road west of Last Chance, Colorado, was such a place in the summer of 1972, and the eye was alert to the occasion.

It was morning, very early in the morning, and a low, chill mist wrapped the road in silence. As I topped a rise, certainly not a hill, I eased out of the down position on the handlebars and prepared to glide into a descent. There, on the apron of the road to my right, where the mist had retreated before the clear air of the morning, was a pronghorn antelope and its offspring, leisurely grazing. My shifting down must have startled them, for there was no one else and no other noise to bring their heads smartly to attention. We were just short feet apart, each waiting in quiet anxiety for the other's first reaction. It was no one's turn but they took to their heels as I started downhill. The race was on, though neither of us was primed for it. Mother and offspring seemed confused, for they raced in a parallel line to my right, keeping pace with me and I with them.

My wits regrouped, I chatted with them, switching back to the racing posture in order to test my steed against them. And then, before either of us could claim to be victor, they moved off diagonally to the right into the open fields. Theirs was the advantage, and I could not follow. More's the shame; the moment was sudden, and short, without an introduction or even an adieu.

My brief meeting with these antelopes in Colorado recalls Robert Frost's sighting, in "The Wood-Pile," of a small bird that flew before him as he walked "in the frozen swamp one gray day." This winged stranger, after a wary glance and a watchful eyeing, was carried off "without so much as wishing him good-night."[10] No good-byes or good-nights exist to break the hold that such encounters claim on those who invite and embrace them.

There is no telling what new acquaintances may be struck, fleeting though they may be, on a bicycle journey. The unexpected is often part of the enlivening promise which tempts and impels the touring bicyclist. The memories of a trip are haunting, poignant, and a goad to be on the road again. After all, this, too, may be your last chance.

Stranger than strange was Harold Elvin's mysterious observation of a horsed giant as he bicycled towards Kiruna, the capital of Swedish Lapland. As he has related the incident, he had just crossed over the Arctic Circle beyond Rovaniemi and

I was cycling towards Pello on the Swedish border on this knife-bright morning when I saw in front of me a stationary horseman. He was a giant and his horse was a

giant and something about him frightened me. A side road ran into my highway and
he stood still there at the junction, he being in the bye-road. It was a lonely stretch;
there was no sense in waiting for a car or cart as company. I must hurry past by
myself. As I closed the gap I put pressure on the pedals and decided to dash by in
top gear, though this Satan's own road might throw me.

The figure was dark skinned. I presumed he was gypsy as most of the gypsies I
had seen in other journeys in Finland have been deeply swarthy. He had a black
patch over one eye, a brilliant neckerchief about his head, high jackboots, and a
cutlass! He looked 500 years out of time and a thousand miles out of place. He was
wild certainly. He sat high, erect, stiff. He was waiting, waiting at the junction of
the roads. As I passed I gave a quick glance at him. His face was that of a giant that
housed a fiend: yet that face was calm and that calm gave that fiend a dignity. He
did not see me! The horse made a shy-ing movement of its head but there were no
more re-actions from either man or beast. I pressed hard down on the pedals and
darted onwards, expecting any minute that the horseman would give chase and cut
me down. I have been chased by gypsies on horseback before and, hurray, my cycle
has won. That bye-road had been odd: it had been the width of a road but it had led
nowhere and it died into the fields twenty yards down.[11]

Less sinister and more customary are the human contacts the bicycle generates. For
"bikes talk to each other like dogs, they wag their wheels and tinkle their bells, the
riders let their mounts mingle."[12] There is a sociability in the conspicuous nature of
bicycle travel. The bicyclist is not anonymous like the motorist whose license plate is
even a nameless cipher. Daniel Behrman could bicycle, hubbed by Paris and spoked
on all sides by congeniality.

A cyclist with a load of *Le Mondes* on his handlebars asks me how much I paid for
my black bike, the one that a bike racer's son made up for me for city riding and
occasional country sprinting, not a Ferrari but still an Alfa. I tell him; he thinks i
got a good buy. A Portuguese laborer catches me on the squirrel cage at
Longchamp; I speed up, we go round together, he asks me where I am riding next
Sunday. We have a lot in common, we are both cyclists, we are both foreigners. I
sneak up on a young man in the Bois de Vincennes. I get into his slip-stream, then I
race by him in the hope that he won't be able to get into mine, but he does. He's a
salesman, it's not an easy life, he has heard that things are better in America. I give
him the embassy's phone number.

On the banks of the Yonne, seventy miles from Paris, I stop to look at the river
from a paved section of the towpath. A cyclist, an older man with young blue eyes,
is looking at it, too. We talk about the river and our bikes. He lives three miles
away along my route. We ride together, he invites me in for a glass of white wine; it
comes from a friend, a retired colonel, who grows it himself. We make a date to ride
again. He is a coal miner's son from the south of France; he came up to Paris as a
mason's helper, a hod carrier. He went into plumbing and came out on top or, at
least, high enough to be comfortable. A few apartment houses here and there, a
country house, a modest car but a beautiful bicycle, a wide range of reading, the
self-educated man who does not stop his education when he stops going to school. It
was he who taught me the first law of cycling: on a bicycle, you never have the wind
with you—either it is against you or you're having a good day.[13]

Even motorists are occasionally within the compass of a traveling bicyclist's surge of
conviviality. Daniel Behrman, again, tells us

I was once riding down Rue de Sèvres, a Left Bank artery in the vein of Carnaby Street, when I pulled up at a red light next to a panel truck with a donkey inside. The driver told me he sold sachets of lavender, bottles of lavender toilet water in the street from a big basket on the donkey's back. The donkey provided an authentic touch of Haute Provence, where the lavender grows. The light changed, the truck moved off slowly. The driver said he was looking for a place to park. I asked him why he did not use the new underground parking lot that had been gouged out below Boucicaut Square, leaving the square with a layer of pallid grass and puny trees trying to grow over the scene of the crime. Oh no, said the lavender-truck driver, the donkey didn't like to go under the ground, he balked in the darkness where the shoppers parked. He may have been a donkey, he was no ass.[14]

With or without the benefit of new friends, "travel," as Sinclair Lewis proclaims, "broadens the mind. It also quickens the sympathies and bestows on one a ready fund of knowledge. And it is useful to talk about when you get back home." Lewis made these comments in his short story "I'm a Stranger Here, Myself" in introducing "J. Johnson & Wife." This complete couple from "Northernapolis, G.C." (for God's Country), U.S.A. was so fatuous and pompous that the only broadening and quickening travel gave them enabled Lewis to satirize them in the most slashing Swiftian fashion.[15]

Even travelers who are genuinely interested in being broadened and quickened may find deep-rooted obstacles in their way. Harold Elvin, in describing his two-thousand-mile ride to Chandigarh to view the new city designed by Le Corbusier and Jeanneret at the foothills of the Himalayas rues his undisciplined craving for speed at any cost.

I come across a Salvation Army chapel so like one in Essex that I feel that I must go in and shake their hands there. But my legs and a silly something in me cry out for knocking the milestones down one by one and stopping at nothing. For years I have been telling myself that it's not the miles in the life that count but the life in the miles, but still this silly restlessness hurries me on.[16]

The impulse to speed at any cost is innate among bicyclists, even among those touring bicyclists who, by age and occupation, should be able to harness the impulse. H. G. Wells, in *The Wheels of Chance*, has captured this flaw among bicyclists in his recounting of the conversation of the anonymous "middle-aged man in a drab cycling suit" with the lemon squash cooler. This cyclist is encountered for the first and only time at the Marquis of Granby Inn at Esher where he has retired for refreshment after a round of hard cycling. Hoopdriver, the protagonist of the book, happens to be at the inn when the perspiring and loquacious cyclist arrives. And it is to Hoopdriver that the cyclist laments:

"There's no hurry, sir, none whatever. I came out for exercise, gentle exercise, and to notice the scenery and to botanise. And no sooner do I get on that accursed machine than off I go hammer and tongs; I never look to right or left, never notice a flower, never see a view—get hot, juicy, red—like a grilled chop. Here I am, sir. Come from Guildford in something under the hour. Why, sir?"

Mr. Hoopdriver shook his head.

"Because I'm a damned fool, sir. Because I've reservoirs and reservoirs of muscular energy, and one or other of them is always leaking. It's a most interesting road, birds and trees, I've no doubt, and wayside flowers, and there's nothing I should enjoy more than watching them. But I can't. Get me on that machine, and I have to go. Get me anything, and I have to go. And I don't want to go a bit. Why should a man rush about like a rocket, all pace and fizzle? Why? It makes me furious. I can assure you, sir, I go scorching along the road, and cursing aloud at myself for doing it. A quiet, dignified, philosophical man, that's what I am—at bottom; and here I am dancing with rage and swearing like a drunken tinker at a perfect stranger—"

"But my day's wasted. I've lost all that country road, and now I'm on the fringe of London. And I might have loitered all the morning! Ugh! Thank Heaven, sir, you have not the irritable temperament, that you are not goaded to madness by your endogenous sneers, by the eternal wrangling of an uncomfortable soul and body. I tell you, I lead a cat-and-dog life. But what is the use of talking? It's all of a piece!"

He tossed his head with unspeakable self-disgust, pitched the lemon squash into his mouth, paid for it, and without any further remark strode to the door. Mr. Hoopdriver was still wondering what to say when his interlocutor vanished. There was a noise of a foot spurning the gravel, and when Mr. Hoopdriver reached the doorway the man in drab was a score of yards Londonward. He had already gathered pace. He pedalled with ill-suppressed anger, and his head was going down. In another moment he flew swiftly out of sight under the railway arch, and Mr. Hoopdriver saw him no more. [17]

Speed is not the only foolishness with which touring bicyclists are afflicted. Bicycling by night transgresses the eleventh commandment of journeymen bicyclists: Thou Shalt Not Take Thy Life in Thine Own Hands. This admonition, prudent though it is, deprives the bicyclist of a most exhilarating adventure of incomparable moment. Stijn Streuvels, while bicycling at night, would report feeling like Faust being spirited away by Mephisto. Sean O'Faoláin has captured the tingling essense of nighttime bicycling in his description of the return of a group of bicyclists from a wake.

The journey back was even more eerie than the journey out, the moon now behind them, their shadows before, and as they climbed the hills the mountains climbed before them as if to bar their way and when they rushed downward to the leaden bowl that was the lake, and into the closed gulley of the coom, it was as if they were cycling not through space but through a maw of Time that would never move. [18]

If bicycling after dark is sinful, then long-distance bicycling in the eighth month of pregnancy must be incomprehensible. Yet Marie Curie, in August of 1897 at the age of twenty-nine, joined by her husband Pierre, did just that. As her biographer, her daughter Eve, relates it,

With the thoughtlessness of the insane—or rather of the scientist—the pair went off (from Port Blanc) to Brest on their bicycles, covering stages as long as they usually did. Marie declared that she felt no fatigue, and Pierre was quite willing to believe her. He had a vague feeling that she was a supernatural being, who escaped from human laws.

This time, just the same, the young wife's body had to beg for mercy. Marie was forced, in great humiliation, to cut short the trip and go back to Paris, where she gave birth to a daughter on September 12: Irene, a beautiful baby and a future Nobel prize winner. [19]

There is a little of J. Johnson & Wife in all touring bicyclists. Nothing, for example, surpasses the inherent one-upmanship among bicycle travelers who have succumbed to the braggadocio of the achiever. A ten-day, thousand-mile bicycle trip, in the telling, becomes a five-day, two-thousand-mile trip. A day's ride, part of a longer journey, over eighty-five miles is rounded off to the nearest hundred miles. A bicyclist's divagations are only exceeded by his prevarications.

On occasion, the touring bicyclist may be straightforward and honest in the belief that his performance is unexcelled. Perish the thought and swallow the statement. The incomparable Thomas Stevens did the impossible. As to him, we are but wrens catching a ride on an eagle's shoulder.

Stevens highwheeled it across the United States in 1884 in one hundred three and a half days. He started from Oakland, California, on April 22, 1884, and ended in Boston, Massachusetts, on August 4 after wheeling 3700 miles, as he said, "to deliver the message." This incredible feat was performed at a time when there were few, if any, roads west of the Mississippi, but ample deserts to cross and mountains to climb. Stevens then continued his bicycle trek around the world and wrote about the whole astonishing journey in two volumes published in 1887 under the title *Around the World on a Bicycle*. [20]

In 1974, I got my comeuppance when I learned, while bicycling through Ohio en route to Spokane, Washington, that a cross-country roller skater, Clint Shaw by name, was days ahead of me. And if that were not humbling enough, I was informed in Minnesota that two girls, on horseback no less, were also journeying to Spokane along the same route I had chosen. My pride was somewhat salvaged when I passed them, in the racing posture of course, just a day or two from Spokane.

The people along the route of the touring bicyclist rarely do anything to fortify his sense of self-importance either. I remember two occasions when my ego was flattened by well-placed verbal jabs from the local townsfolk.

One occurred in Iowa, when I had stopped for water at a farmhouse well. In the hope that the accommodating farmer would ask those important questions about how far I'd come and how far I had yet to travel, I struck up a conversation by asking:

"Can you tell me why it is that the wheat on one side of the road out here is so tall and healthy-looking in contrast to the short, scrubby wheat on the other side?"

"Sure," he said, rubbing his face with the back of his hand. "The seeds for the short wheat were planted upside down—by accident."

Only later, my ears still red, did I learn that the short wheat was really a crop of soybeans.

At another time, much farther west, I had stopped to rest from the blazing heat at the familiar bicyclist's oasis, a gas station, when a lady in a rather overblown American car leaned out to ask why I would be so foolish as to bicycle in such torrid weather. I smart-alecked her by answering that I did it to lose weight, adding that when I left Washington, D.C., I was over two hundred pounds.

She stared at my one-hundred-and-sixty-pound sweaty and grimy body, most of which was exposed to the sun, and called excitedly to her husband. When he heard her retell my lie, he strode over to me, as coolly as you please, handed me a silver dollar and said: "Here, go buy yourself a hamburger; you need it."

Humble pie, when taken in large doses, is quite indigestible.

At another time, while bicycling with my son, Liam, on the East Coast Bicycle Trail, I seemed to be getting the better of things—for a while. Whenever I was asked to explain Liam's presence, I would chortle and announce that I had brought him along to pull me up the hills. Later I noticed that Liam was carrying a monstrously thick and lengthy strand of rope which he had found while junking. I unmercifully needled him about carting such excess baggage until the next time that why-is-he-along question popped up. My response was as usual but Liam was no longer content to suffer in silence. "Yes," he said, "and here's the rope I use to do the job."

Hoisted by my own son's rope!

The well-timed, deft riposte is, however, very much there for the finding. My experience teaches that I just had difficulty finding it. Dylan Thomas, on the contrary, was a master of the quick retort in life as well as in death. His death, it was said in the medical examiner's protocol, was caused by an "insult to the brain." That pathological condition, previously unknown to medical authorities, typified the baffling and amusing quality of Thomas's writings—writings which, according to his daughter, he penned after his wife had locked him in his bicycle shed.

In one of his short stories, "Who Do You Wish Was with Us," Raymond Price and he, "flannelled and hatless, with sticks and haversacks, set out together to walk to the Worm's Head." Along their heady way, these brash hikers meet

A party of cyclists [who] had pulled up on the roadside and were drinking dandelion and burdock from paper cups. I saw the empty bottles in a bush. All the boys wore singlets and shorts, and the girls wore open cricket shirts and boys' long grey trousers, with safety-pins for clips at the bottoms.

"There's room for one behind, sonny boy," a girl on a tandem said to me.

"It won't be a stylish marriage," Ray said.

"That was quick," I told Ray as we walked away from them and the boys began to sing.

Later in the day, along the same dusty road,

the cycling party rode by, three boys and three girls and the one girl on the tandem, all laughing and ringing.

"How's Shanks's pony?"

"We'll see you on the way back."

"You'll be walking still."

"Like a crutch?" they shouted.

Then they were gone. [21]

Rare are the touring bicyclists who have not succumbed to the temptation to memorialize their exploits in print. The card catalog at the Library of Congress is crammed with books extolling this hero or that of cross-country or round-the-world bicycle travel. One husband-and-wife team even went so far as to claim the round-trip cross-country speed title for a tandem. I too have yielded in this introduction to this very natural impulse to recapture events that the bicycle made possible and singular.

In this chapter, a very conscious effort has been made to avoid selections that simply indulge in diaristic writing. If anyone wishes a bicycle Baedeker, the much-published Bernard Newman's books canvas almost any land into which one might wish to bicycle. Instead of personal recollections or memoirs of bicycle jaunts, I have selected materials that seemed to explore the unique possibilities in bicycle travel.

The architectural discovery of Lawrence of Arabia, related by John F. Mack, is one of these. And romantic enchantments, either real or imagined, as in *The Wheels of Chance* and *Crome Yellow*, are others. Jerome K. Jerome provides the kind of grassroots, no-nonsense advice that any bicycle-traveling novice requires.

1

Monica Starrs

"Bicycles Made for More Than Twoness Shaped for Only One"

This poem by my daughter Monica is a previously unpublished poem that she wrote after completing a trans–United States bicycle journey at the age of fifteen.

Pick up those burrowed thoughts,
   as you scrape out pieces of caged-in mind.
Seek out and attack that point of no return
   where you'll smother empty smiles
   with spreading wings
   to pass secluded car dreams
On a 10-speed freedom flyer.

2

Jerome K. Jerome

Meditations on Planning a Bicycle Tour

From *Three Men on the Bummel*

Bicycle touring has long been an established pastime for those with the time and the inclination to seek adventure on the open road. With the advent, in 1976, of the 4000-mile-plus backroads bicycle trail across the breadth of the United States, it has become deceptively easy to think of bicycle touring over long distances as a very recent happening. Yet that is a delusion fostered by those who want nothing but an unexcelled experience. It is a chastening fact to realize that there have been countless Thomas Stevenses and Ian Hibbells, both sung and unsung, who have wheeled down the same or different pathways according to their own style or fancy. All were alike in one respect: they had to prepare for their journey.

The planning of a bicycle tour involves many preparations which the neophyte might overlook and others which he or she might overdo. I remember one young man who traveled with me from the Washington, D.C., suburbs to Montana carrying a full roll of toilet paper and a long, menacing bowie-type knife. When asked why he was carrying these heavy and bulky items, he explained that "you never can tell what you might need for protection." On that thinking, the enumeration of the items to be hauled by bicycle while touring would constitute an endless potpourri, including both the essential and the frivolous.

In Three Men on the Bummel, *a tale of an escapist-type bicycle trip in 1900 through the Black Forest, Jerome K. Jerome presents the indispensable method for determining what is to be carried on a bicycle tour and what is to be discarded.*

From Jerome K. Jerome, *Three Men on the Bummel* (New York: Dodd, Mead and Co., 1900), pp. 192–93, 203–4, 296–302.

"Always, before beginning to pack," my uncle would say, "make a list."

He was a methodical man.

"Take a piece of paper"—he always began at the beginning—"put down on it everything you can possibly require; then go over it and see that it contains nothing you can possibly do without. Imagine yourself in bed; what have you got on? Very well, put it down—together with a change. You get up; what do you do? Wash yourself. What do you wash yourself with? Soap; put down soap. Go on till you have finished. Then take your clothes. Begin at your feet; what do you wear on your feet? Boots, shoes, socks; put them down. Work up till you get to your head. What else do you want besides clothes? A little brandy; put it down. A corkscrew; put it down. Put down everything, then you don't forget anything."

That is the plan he always pursued himself. The list made, he would go over it carefully, as he always advised to see that he had forgotten nothing. Then he would go over it again, and strike out everything it was possible to dispense with.

Then he would lose the list.

To the bicycle tourer, one minute's realism is worth an hour's imaginings, preparatory to the event. There is no end to the resolutions one can make on the kitchen drawing board. But on the road resolutions are, so to speak, thrown to the winds. As Samuel Beckett has said, "resolutions are like precautions. They are to be taken with precaution."

So if you think that you can surely average ten miles an hour while touring or that you will be off tooling along at 6 A.M. each day; indeed, if you believe, as a stranger once put it to me, that bicycle touring involves nothing but having enough available time, then you will need the enlightenment of Jerome K. Jerome.

Again in Jerome's novel Three Men on the Bummel, *a sequel to his most famous work,* Three Men in a Boat, *the three very unherolike characters, George, Harris, and J. (for Jerome, obviously), are concocting a bicycle tour of the Black Forest, more for the excuse it gives them to escape from their wives (two of them are married) and their other duties than for the enjoyment of bicycling. But the planning is not without its recognition of the problems that lie ahead and the suggestion of ingenious solutions for them.*

"I have it!" exclaimed Harris; "a bicycle tour!"

George looked doubtful.

"There's a lot of uphill about a bicycle tour," said he, "and the wind is against you."

"So there is downhill, and the wind behind you," said Harris.

"I've never noticed it," said George.

"You won't think of anything better than a bicycle tour," persisted Harris.

I was inclined to agree with him.

"And I'll tell you where," continued he: "through the Black Forest."

"Why, that's all uphill," said George.

"Not all," retorted Harris; "say two-thirds. And there's one thing you've forgotten."

He looked round cautiously and sunk his voice to a whisper.

"There are little railways going up those hills, little cogwheel things that—"

And when the time comes for them to put their plans to the test, the practicalities of the real world intrude.

We did not succeed in carrying out our programme in its entirety, for the reason that human performance lags ever behind human intention. It is easy to say and believe at three o'clock in the afternoon that: "We will rise at five, breakfast lightly at half past, and start away at six."

"Then we shall be well on our way before the heat of the day sets in," remarks one.

"This time of the year, the early morning is really the best part of the day. Don't you think so?" adds another.

"Oh, undoubtedly."

"So cool and fresh."

"And the half-lights are so exquisite."

The first morning one maintains one's vows. The party assembles at half past five. It is very silent; individually, somewhat snappy; inclined to grumble with its food, also with most other things; the atmosphere charged with compressed irritability seeking its vent. In the evening the Tempter's voice is heard:

"I think if we got off by half past six, sharp, that would be time enough?"

The voice of Virtue protests, faintly: "It will be breaking our resolution."

The Tempter replies: "Resolutions were made for man, not man for resolutions." The devil can paraphrase Scripture for his own purpose. "Besides, it is disturbing the whole hotel; think of the poor servants."

The voice of Virtue continues, but even feebler: "But everybody gets up early in these parts."

"They would not if they were not obliged to, poor things! Say breakfast at half past six, punctual; that will be disturbing nobody."

Thus, Sin masquerades under the guise of Good, and one sleeps till six, explaining to one's conscience, who, however, doesn't believe it, that one does this because of unselfish consideration for others. I have known such consideration extend until seven of the clock.

Likewise, distance measured with a pair of compasses is not precisely the same as when measured by the leg.

"Ten miles an hour for seven hours: seventy miles. A nice easy day's work."

"There are some stiff hills to climb?"

"The other side to come down. Say eight miles an hour, and call it sixty miles. *Gott in Himmel!* If we can't average eight miles an hour, we had better go in bath-chairs." It does seem somewhat impossible to do less, on paper.

But at four o'clock in the afternoon the voice of Duty rings less trumpet-toned:

"Well, I suppose we ought to be getting on."

"Oh, there's no hurry! don't fuss. Lovely view from here, isn't it?"

"Very. Don't forget we are twenty-five miles from St. Blasien."

"How far?"

"Twenty-five miles, a little over if anything."

"Do you mean to say we have only come thirty-five miles?"

"That's all."

"Nonsense. I don't believe that map of yours."

"It is impossible, you know. We have been riding steadily ever since the first thing this morning."

"No, we haven't. We didn't get away till eight, to begin with."

"Quarter to eight."

"Well, quarter to eight; and every half-dozen miles we have stopped."

"We have only stopped to look at the view. It's no good coming to see a country and then not seeing it."

"And we have to pull up some stiff hills."

"Besides, it has been an exceptionally hot day to-day."

"Well, don't forget St. Blasien is twenty-five miles off, that's all."

"Any more hills?"

"Yes, two; up and down."

"I thought you said it was downhill into St. Blasien?"

"So it is for the last ten miles. We are twenty-five miles from St. Blasien here."

"Isn't there anywhere between here and St. Blasien? What's that little place there on the lake?"

"It isn't St. Blasien, or anywhere near it. There's a danger in beginning that sort of thing."

"There's a danger in overworking oneself. One should study moderation in all things. Pretty little place, that Titisee, according to the map; looks as if there would be good air there."

"All right, I'm agreeable. It was you fellows who suggested our making for St. Blasien."

"Oh, I'm not so keen on St. Blasien! poky little place, down in a valley. This Titisee, I should say, was ever so much nicer."

"Quite near, isn't it?"

"Five miles."

General chorus: "We'll stop at Titisee."

George made discovery of this difference between theory and practice on the very first day of our ride.

"I thought," said George—he was riding the single, Harris and I being a little ahead on the tandem—"that the idea was to train up the hills and ride down them."

"So it is," answered Harris, "as a general rule. But the trains don't go up every hill in the Black Forest."

"Somehow I felt a suspicion that they wouldn't," growled George; and for a while silence reigned.

"Besides," remarked Harris, who had evidently been ruminating the subject, "you would not wish to have nothing but downhill, surely. It would not be playing the game. One must take a little rough with one's smooth."

Again there returned silence, broken after a while by George this time.

"Don't you two fellows over-exert yourselves merely on my account," said George.

"How do you mean?" asked Harris.

"I mean," answered George, "that where a train does happen to be going up these hills, don't you put aside the idea of taking it for fear of outraging my finer feelings. Personally, I am prepared to go up all these hills in a railway train, even if it's not playing the game. I'll square the thing with my conscience; I've been up at seven every day for a week now, and I calculate it owes me a bit. Don't you consider me in the matter at all."

We promised to bear this in mind, and again the ride continued in dogged dumbness, until it was again broken by George.

"What bicycle did you say this was of yours?" asked George.

Harris told him. I forget of what particular manufacture it happened to be; it is immaterial.

"Are you sure?" persisted George.

"Of course I am sure," answered Harris, "Why, what's the matter with it?"

"Well, it doesn't come up to the poster," said George, "that's all."

"What poster?" asked Harris.

"The poster advertising this particular brand of cycle," explained George. "I was looking at one on a hoarding in Sloane Street only a day or two before we started. A man was riding this make of machine, a man with a banner in his hand: he wasn't doing any work, that was clear as daylight; he was just sitting on the thing and drinking in the air. The cycle was going of its own accord, and going well. This thing of yours leaves all the work to me. It is a lazy brute of a machine; if you don't shove, it simply does nothing. I should complain about it, if I were you."

When one comes to think of it, few bicycles do realize the poster. On only one poster that I can recollect have I seen the rider represented as doing any work. But then this man was being pursued by a bull. In ordinary cases the object of the artist is to convince the hesitating neophyte that the sport of bicycling consists in sitting on a luxurious saddle, and being moved rapidly in the direction you wish to go by unseen heavenly powers.

Generally speaking, the rider is a lady, and then one feels that, for perfect bodily rest combined with entire freedom from mental anxiety, slumber upon a water-bed cannot compare with bicycle-riding upon a hilly road. No fairy travelling on a summer cloud could take things more easily than does the bicycle girl, according to the poster. Her costume for cycling in hot weather is ideal. Old-fashioned landladies might refuse her lunch, it is true; and a narrow-minded police force might desire to secure her, and wrap her in a rug preliminary to summoning her. But such she heeds not. Uphill and downhill, through traffic that might tax the ingenuity of a cat, over road surfaces, calculated to break the average steam-roller she passes, a vision of idle loveliness; her fair hair streaming to the wind, her sylph-like form poised airily, one foot upon the saddle, the other resting lightly upon the lamp. Sometimes she condescends to sit down on the saddle; then she puts her feet on the rests, lights a cigarette, and waves above her head a Chinese lantern.

Less often, it is a mere male thing that rides the machine. He is not so accomplished an acrobat as is the lady; but simple tricks such as standing on the saddle and waving flags, drinking beer or beef-tea while riding, he can and does perform. Something, one supposes, he must do to occupy his mind: sitting still hour after hour on this machine, having no work to do, nothing to think about, must pall upon any man of active temperament. Thus it is that we see him riding on his pedals as he nears the top of some high hill to apostrophize the sun, or address poetry to the surrounding scenery.

Occasionally the poster pictures a pair of cyclists; and then one grasps the fact how much superior for purposes of flirtation is the modern bicycle to the old-fashioned parlour or the played-out garden gate. He and she mount their bicycles, being careful, of course, that such are of the right make. After that they have nothing to think about but the old sweet tale. Down shady lanes, through busy towns on market days, merrily roll the wheels of the "Bermondsey Company's Bottom Bracket Britain's Best," or of the "Camberwell Company's Jointless Eureka." They need no pedalling; they require no guiding. Give them their heads, and tell them what time you want to get home, and that is all they ask. While Edwin leans from his saddle to whisper the dear old nothings in Angelina's ear, while Angelina's face, to hide its blushes, is turned towards the horizon at the back, the magic bicycles pursue their even course.

And the sun is always shining, and the roads are always dry. No stern parent rides behind, no interfering aunt beside, no demon small boy brother is peeping round the corner, there never comes a skid. Ah me! Why were there no "Britain's Best" nor "Camberwell Eurekas" to be hired when we were young?

Or maybe the "Britain's Best" or the "Camberwell Eureka" stands leaning against a gate; maybe it is tired. It has worked hard all the afternoon, carrying these young people. Mercifully minded they have dismounted, to give the machine a rest. They sit upon the grass beneath the shade of graceful boughs; it is long and dry grass. A stream flows by their feet. All is rest and peace.

That is ever the idea the cycle poster artist sets himself to convey—rest and peace.

But I am wrong in saying that no cyclist, according to the poster, ever works. Now I come to reflect, I have seen posters representing gentlemen on cycles working very hard—overworking themselves, one might almost say. They are thin and haggard with the toil, the perspiration stands upon their brow in beads; you feel that if there is another hill beyond the poster they must either get off or die. But this is the result of their own folly. This happens because they will persist in riding a machine of an inferior make. Were they riding a "Putney Popular" or "Battersea Bounder," such as the sensible young man in the centre of the poster rides, then all this unnecessary labour would be saved to them. Then all required of them would be, as in gratitude bound, to look happy; perhaps, occasionally to back-pedal a little when the machine in its youthful buoyancy loses its head for a moment and dashes on too swiftly.

You tired young men, sitting dejectedly on milestones, too spent to heed the steady rain that soaks you through; you weary maidens, with the straight, damp hair, anxious about the time, longing to swear, not knowing how; you stout bald men, vanishing visibly as you pant and grunt along the endless road; you purple, dejected matrons, plying with pain the slow, unwilling wheel; why did you not see to it that you bought a "Britain's Best" or a "Camberwell Eureka"? Why are these bicycles of inferior make so prevalent throughout the land?

Or is it with bicycling as with all other things: does Life at no point realize the Poster?

3

The First Bicycle "Trip"

In 1943, Albert Hofmann at the Sandoz laboratories in Switzerland discovered the bizarre effects of the hallucinogen LSD-25 when he accidentally ingested a small amount of it and then set off by bicycle for his home. The experience resulted in a unique bike trip. As he later recounted it,

My field of vision swayed and objects appeared distorted, like images in curved mirrors. I felt fixed to the spot, although my assistant told me afterwards we were cycling at a good speed. I recall the most outstanding symptoms as vertigo and visual disturbance; the faces of those around me appeared as grotesque colored masks. I recognized my condition clearly and sometimes, as if I were an independent neutral observer, saw that I babbled half insanely and incoherently. Occasionally I felt out of my body. When I closed my eyes endless colorful, realistic and fantastic images surged in on me. Acoustic perceptions, such as the noise of a passing car, were transformed into optical effects, every sound evoking a corresponding colored hallucination constantly changing in shape and color.

From Ergot Vining, "The Taming of a Medieval Pestilence," *Technology Review* 81 (December 1978–January 1979): 69.

4

Gavin Casey

"That Day at Brown Lakes"[1]

A bicycle ride can be a memorable occasion, especially when viewed from the hindsight of time and maturity. The memory of it is there for the recalling. For Adam Dalgleish, P.D. James's popular detective, it was a gale at three-fifteen in the morning as he slept in his car that brought him to wandering in the night wind and to musing on days long past.

He felt as he had as a boy on one of his solitary cycling trips when he would leave his small tent to walk in the night. It had been one of his greatest pleasures, this sense of complete loneliness, of being not only without a companion but with the knowledge that no one in the world knew exactly where he was. It was a solitude of the spirit as well as of the body. Shutting his eyes and smelling the rich dampness of grass and earth, he could imagine himself back in childhood, the smells were the same, the night was familiar, the pleasure was as keen.[1]

Nothing so dramatic as gale-force winds in the loneliness of a parked car in a dark lay-by is necessary to call up the comforting balm of fond memories. Elizabeth West, in recounting her lifeways in the remote reaches of Wales, could recall, without apparent urging, one "hot summer's day" as she and her husband rested after bicycling to

the top of a hill on the "old" road not far out of Colwyn Bay. With the bikes leaning up against a farm gate, we were sitting at the roadside munching apples. The scent of wild rose and honey-suckle filled the air and the sounds of summer were all around us. I felt absolutely in my right element. I was not just living through a summer's afternoon—I was part of it. Suddenly a car came round the bend and drove on towards Colwyn Bay. A woman looked out of the side window and for an instant our eyes met. We would have been about the same age. I imagined what it must have felt like to be her, sitting inside that car—all clean, tidy, nylon-tighted and upright, with the hot interior-car smell of fumes and warm plastic. What would

From Gavin Casey, *Short Shift Saturday and Other Stories* (Sydney, Australia: Angus & Robertson, 1973), pp. 93–98.

150

they do when they got to Colwyn Bay? She would get stiffly out of the car, straighten her dress and find her handbag. They would walk around for a bit, go into a cafe and have tea, and then drive home. I lay back in the grass; I was dusty, sweaty and absolutely content. I would not, under any circumstances, wish to change places with that woman. And she, looking out at me sitting on my backside at the edge of the road, probably felt exactly the same.[2]

And Gavin Casey, in "That Day at Brown Lakes," could relive a day's bicycle outing and its place in his scheme of things as he sat in comfort and in congeniality over a beer. Casey, the only Australian writer represented in this anthology, drops colloquialisms like bat, crib, quid, *and* double-gees *as unobtrusively as he stirs us to reflect on where, the wind being always at our back, we have ventured.*

I wonder if you remember the day we pedalled out to the Brown Lakes?

It was a good day, that, one of those memorable days that are pretty much like a lot of others but that stand out in your mind because of something or other. It was a whole day that went with your mood and completed itself in weariness and peace.

It started right when I got to your place and your mother was packing a couple of apple-pies in your crib. At that time I used to reckon that those apple-pies of your mother's were better than anything my old lady could make. My mum was the best around the place when there was anything wrong with me; but when everything was O.K. she was just a woman, and it was a pity she couldn't make apple-pies like the juicy ones, with flaky pastry, that came from your place.

I filled my waterbag at your tank and tied it between the bars of my bike, and you strapped your twenty-two along the top bar, and we got off in the early morning, with our bags full of good food and the long day ahead of us.

"Now be careful!" your mother said. "I'm sure I don't know what you want to go away out there for. You'll tire yourselves out for nothing, and get home about midnight, I suppose, with every one worried to death about what's happened to you."

"Aw, we'll be all right," you said. "We've pushed our bikes further than that in the bush. We know how to look after ourselves."

Then we were off, pedalling side by side through the streets of the town, and though I couldn't tell what you're thinking now, even if it was worth a million, I knew then, all right. You were feeling like me—impatient and patronizing towards women who didn't know why a man wanted to pedal so far and tire himself out for nothing. I was feeling impatient with the town, and with my humdrum work at Simpson's, too. I was thinking that it was better to be setting out for the Brown Lakes with you than it would have been with Darky Green or Sid Wilson or even Larry Summerville, though I used to knock about with him so much in town.

The day started right.

Up Parson's Hill we stood on the pedals, and we both began to sweat. When we got to the top we had a spell, and I was mighty glad to find that you could do with a breather, too. We squatted on a couple of big rocks on top of the hill, with the whole town spread out on one side of us and the endless stretch of bush, with the ribbon of road running through it, on the other. In the town the chimneys were dribbling smoke, and in the scrub Jackson's dairy was huddled and some cows were milling and mooing in a yard, but nothing else stirred for miles. It was pretty flat country except for Parson's Hill.

I remember looking at you then and feeling nervous, just for a moment, wondering if I'd be able to hold my own all right on the long ride. You had thick, strong legs when you were a kid, as brown and powerful-looking as a grown man's. Anyway, I had no need to get the wind up, and my fear was only momentary, because, though I was skinny and light, I knew from experience that I could push a bike with the best of 'em.

We coasted down the hill and then settled down to a good steady bat that rolled the miles out behind us. For the first fifteen of them the road was broad and straight to the old diggings, and the surface wasn't too bad. As we went, the trees at the roadside pulled their shadows in toward themselves, the sun rose high and fierce, and we were soon sweating again. But it wasn't the breathless, uncomfortable sweat that had poured out of us at the top of Parson's Hill. It was a good flow of lubricant for our moving muscles, a sweat that cooled and refreshed on the skin.

While we pedalled that easy fifteen miles we talked. We could ride abreast, and we must have averaged about two words to the yard. We both said things we wouldn't ever put into words when there was any one around—even the best of the mob like Larry Summerville. What we said then wasn't of much consequence, pretty silly, really, I suppose, and we got it out of us along with our good sweat, and it mixed with the sunlight and the air we were breathing, to form part of the pattern of a good day.

After the old diggings the track was bad. For twenty miles it wound between rock outcrops, and where there weren't stones there was sand. It was narrow, too, and whenever a car passed us, full of men with beer and shotguns, we cursed the dust and wobbled and sometimes took to the bush and fell off. But we enjoyed it, every minute of it. At Wrigley's Soak you shook your fist at the road and roared all the bad language you knew into the quiet bush in a fine fluent stream. I cursed and swore, too, and we called ourselves fools, but we wouldn't have been anything else for quids. We ate your mother's apple-pies and filled the waterbag from the soak. The bag was still nearly full of good tank water, but we emptied that out because the weedy, strong soak water seemed to us to be the stuff to keep life and energy in proper bushmen and pioneers.

From there on it was hard work getting through the sand and stones and double-gees, and it was single-file riding and we didn't talk much. You made the pace and you put your back into it. I could see you wanted to shake me off in the rough going, and for a mile or so my muscles ached and I hated you. But then I found that I could keep up all right and didn't have to burst myself, and I felt a sort of patronizing affection for you as you strained away in front with your big muscles bulging. When we came out among the Brown Lakes we were tired, but we felt we'd done something. We felt good.

You mightn't be able to remember that day even if I reminded you of it, but surely you sometimes remember the Brown Lakes? It was a public holiday in town, and the news that there was good shooting out there must have got around. Every one who owned a shotgun and could get a ride in a car seemed to be there, and the ducks were being kept on the move. Most of the crowd had come out the previous night, and there were camps all around the two-mile stretch of shallow, rusty inland water. There were parties at all the outlying waterholes and claypans, too, booming away and keeping the weary, puzzled birds on the wing most of the time. It was hard shooting, and a pretty cruel shooting, too, but we were blood-thirsty enough for it.

"Cripes!" I said, excited. "Y' never get a sitting shot. We'll never pot one of those with a rifle."

"We'll give 'em a fright, anyway," you said, getting the twenty-two off your bike. "We won't get 'em if we don't try, that's sure."

But then a chap came across from one of the camps and put an end to that. "You kids can't shoot here with a rifle," he said. "You'll murder someone. Can't you see there's more people than ducks?"

That nearly spoiled the day properly, but when he said we could tag along with his crowd it made it perfect. If you don't remember all the tramping and wading and excitement of that day, you ought to remember when he gave us each a shot out of his double-barrelled gun, anyway. I can tell you I shoved the butt hard against the muscles of my shoulder as I'd always been told to do with a gun that kicked. And I don't mind admitting now that I shut my eyes when I pulled the trigger. Any duck was safe from me that wasn't pretty unlucky. I was content enough and proud enough to find myself still standing upright after I'd done the job.

That was all good, exciting and strenuous, the whole day of it, pedalling and tramping and eating and shooting and yarning as we did. But do you remember going home? Do you remember the first five miles after we'd reached the good road, when we were dog weary and pedalling slowly, but not too tired to talk? It was cooler then, just beginning to get dark, and we got on to talking about girls. We were full of curiosity about girls, but we were sentimental and frightened and respectful too. We were decent kids underneath all the bluff we had to put up to convince the mob that we were tough and ruthless. When there was just the two of us, after such a fine day, it was different, and that day you said things you haven't lived up to, if that leery dial of yours means anything. Perhaps I've fallen short of a few of the things I said myself.

It was a hard ride back, with all the cars that had been around the lake on the road together going home, and one of them bumped us into the bush about every half mile in the bad section and the air was thick with red dust; but it was all right. We were young and tough and full of illusions. We reckoned war was heroic and business was romantic, and that the world never meant us any more harm than we meant it. It was a good day. But it was after dark, after the last car had passed us on its way to town, when we had our lamps lit, and I had three punctures in a mile, and then the back tube pulled in half, that it was best of all for me. It was ridiculous and childish and unfair to our parents and altogether mad, but it was deeply satisfying.

I wonder if you remember? It was six or seven miles from town where the case got hopeless and we decided that my bike was unrideable. We'd been working, patching the tube in the yellow of our lamps, with the busy shadowy and cool and dark all around and the crickets mocking us in a chorus, and we'd been cursing our luck and really enjoying the bit of adventure not too far from home.

"Well, that's that!" I said. "You'd better ride on to town to let 'em know we're all right. I'll walk and wheel the bike, and if my dad's home he can drive out in the car to meet me."

"Gosh, no!" you said. "Here, you go on, on my grid, an' I'll do the walking."

"Don't be silly!" I said. "Your bike's all right. Hop on and ride it!"

"Look," you pointed out, "you don't know for sure if your dad'll be home. You might have to walk all the way. I don't mind that. I'm as fresh as a daisy."

"Who do you think isn't?" I demanded indignantly. "If you think I can't keep up with you, ridin' *or* walkin', you've got another think comin'."

"Aw, I didn't mean it that way," you said. "Only we're in this together. I'm not going to leave you out here just because you had a bit of bad luck any one might have had. I'll toss you for it if you like."

When we tossed I won, but I wouldn't take your bike. I felt pretty heroic about it, and the excitement of our crazy argument had driven all the fatigue out of my bones. I was wide awake and determined, and I was depending on you, too. In the first place I'd quite expected that you'd ride on and I'd walk to town; but once the argument started you'd have disappointed me, Dick, if you'd given way. I reckoned mates had to stick together. I was stupid enough for anything, with just a few miles between us and home, but we were only kids and that was how I felt. When you stuck out and we eventually set off on the tramp along the dark, silent road wheeling our bikes, it was the perfect end to a perfect day for me. I was elated, full of talk and friendship and not giving a damn about our parents worrying their heads off at home when we finished up with that seven-mile walk on the day we pedalled out to the Brown Lakes.

You didn't disappoint me then, but would you now? I must be afraid you would, or I'd have said it aloud, told you all I remembered about it instead of just thinking it as we sit here over our beer. That day—practically the whole of that day—you and I were pretty much the same; but we're different now. You'd probably think I was mad. The years we haven't seen each other, that we've both spent chasing the hopes we had that day, have done a lot to us. You don't look my kind now, Dick. You're thick and fat and dressed up and stamped with prosperity and anxiety, but even so you might be a better man than I am. I don't know. I only know that you're different.

But perhaps I'm wrong. You've been silent for a long time now, just sitting there staring at your beer while I've been remembering all this, and for all I know you might have been thinking about the day we pedalled out to the Brown Lakes too.

5

Aldous Huxley

The Bard and the Bicycle

From *Crome Yellow*

Unquestionably, touring by bicycle opens up entirely unexplored and even novel reflec-
tions. To a Lawrence of Arabia, the bicycle is only the vehicle by which thoughts are put
into action. More commonly, the bicycle frees the mind for ruminations which the
workaday world suppresses. Without the bicycle to liberate such thoughts, they might
well go unnoticed and uninvestigated.

Ernest Hemingway gave voice to this feature of bicycling in his novel To Have and
Have Not. *Richard Gordon, a touristlike journalist in the Keys, first encounters Marie,*
the wife of ill-fated rumrunner Harry Morgan, while bicycling from Freddie's Bar in
Key West.

As Hemingway put it:

Riding his bicycle, he passed a heavy-set, big, blue-eyed woman, with bleached-
blonde hair showing under her old man's felt hat, hurrying across the road, her eyes
red from crying. Look at that big ox, he thought. What do you suppose a woman like
that thinks about? What do you suppose she does in bed? How does her husband
feel about her when she gets that size. Who do you suppose he runs around with in
this town? Wasn't she an appalling looking woman? Like a battleship. Terrific.[1]

But it is not only the mind that is activated by bicycling. Sense perceptions awaken as
well. Sounds and sights previously encountered take on a new dimension. With the
deliberate speed of the bicycle, the scents of land and air mingle so that even the
commonplaces of honeysuckle and rain contrive a new sensory experience.

Any touring bicyclist can relate the feeling of carefree abandon and catharsis that
pedaling evokes as layers upon layers of mental and emotional encrustations are shed.

From Aldous Huxley, *Crome Yellow* (New York: Perennial Library, 1974), pp. 1–3.

Each turn, each hill is another discovery illuminating a place, a sensation and a perception until then hidden from view. Nothing is so utterly alive and well as the spirit of the touring bicyclist, until fatigue or boredom takes control.

To a poet, whether fledgling or seasoned, bicycling can be the source of new inspiration. And so it was for the twenty-three-year-old apprentice poet Denis Stone in Aldous Huxley's first novel Crome Yellow. *The book details Denis's experiences during a vacation from the routine of city life in London to a rural retreat of baronial majesty at Crome. Denis escapes from London not only for a moment's respite but also to see Anne Wimbush, niece of Henry and Priscilla Wimbush, who are the proprietors of the manor at Crome. Anne may be Denis's love but the feeling is in no sense mutual. Indeed, Anne does her despicable best to humiliate Denis on every occasion that he seeks to demonstrate his affection for her.*

This novel was the first of Aldous Huxley's social satires, of which Brave New World *is the best-known example. In* Crome Yellow, *Huxley satirizes the affluence of pseudointellectuals who live uselessly cloistered lives in the munificence of English castledom. Henry Wimbush is the most inert of the lot, spending his every waking hour toiling over the monumental* History of Crime. *Why, even the seven dozen oysters that his ancestor, Sir Ferdinand Lapith, ate 350 years before captivate his interest.*

Priscilla Wimbush, in her turn, sits in her boudoir day after day spinning webs from her horoscope. Henry has consigned her to this method of playing the horses in order to avert bankruptcy from her fervid gambling. The cast of Dresden-china characters also includes Gombauld, the thirtyish artist of Byronic visage whose days of devotion to Cubism are but shortly ended. He is painting a portrait of Anne, but with more lifelike representations than she might find tolerable.

Mr. Scogan is another Crome-harnessed personality. He is a contemporary of Henry's, but there the resemblance ends. Scogan is the high-powered and sardonic intellectual with the acerbity of an Oscar Wilde who jibes and rails on life and love, suffering, and whatnot. And, of course, there is Ivor Lombard, the dashing Lothario of the bunch, who arrives in a cloud of dust in his yellow motorcar. He is, naturally, handsome, brilliant, educated, and athletic. But most of all he is amorous. He entrances Mary Bracegirdle, of Malthusian fame and inclination, after performing feats of daredevilry on the parapets of Crome. He comes and goes with a flourish, mimicking the butterfly, yellow of course, in all but his inability to depart without leaving a trace.

And, most importantly, we are introduced to yellow-haired Denis Stone, a just-published poet, who in this summer of 1918 decides that his soul is "a pale, tenuous membrane" and that life lies in the magic mix of words. His rapture with words leads him, on occasion, to outlandish fits of fancy that cost him dearly. One poem is utterly destroyed when he exalts passion as "carminative as wine." Unfortunately and unforgivably, neither wine nor passion should be carminative to be satisfying. On this occasion as on so many others, Denis's poetic genius just runs out of gas.

Denis is not often a man of action. The passage below from the book's first chapter is an exception that is repeated at the end when he hastily departs from Crome. There is a certain symmetry in portraying Denis in action only in the beginning and at the end, but Huxley apparently forgets that Denis arrived by bicycle, for he leaves by car, with nary a thought or mention of his bicycle. Neither the book nor the parvenus it depicts are flawless. But the reader is spared these unsightly conclusions if all that he knows is that

The train came bumpingly to a halt. Here was Camlet at least. Denis jumped up, crammed his hat over his eyes, deranged his pile of baggage, leaned out of the window and shouted for a porter, seized a bag in either hand, and had to put them down again in order to open the door. When at last he had safely bundled himself and his baggage on to the platform, he ran up the train towards the van.

"A bicycle, a bicycle!" he said breathlessly to the guard. He felt himself a man of action. The guard paid no attention, but continued methodically to hand out, one by one, the packages labelled to Camlet. "A bicycle!" Denis repeated. "A green machine, cross-framed, name of Stone. S-T-O-N-E."

"All in good time, sir," said the guard soothingly. He was a large, stately man with a naval beard. One pictured him at home, drinking tea, surrounded by a numerous family. It was in that tone that he must have spoken to his children when they were tiresome. "All in good time, sir." Denis's man of action collapsed, punctured.

He left his luggage to be called for later, and pushed off on his bicycle. He always took his bicycle when he went into the country. It was part of the theory of exercise. One day one would get up at six o'clock and pedal away to Kenilworth, or Stratford-on-Avon—anywhere. And within a radius of twenty miles there were always Norman churches and Tudor mansions to be seen in the course of an afternoon's excursion. Somehow they never did get seen, but all the same it was nice to feel that the bicycle was there, and that one fine morning one really might get up at six.

Once at the top of the long hill which led up from Camlet station, he felt his spirits mounting. The world, he found, was good. The far-away blue hills, the harvests whitening on the slopes of the ridge along which his road led him, the treeless skylines that changed as he moved—yes, they were all good. He was overcome by the beauty of those deeply embayed combes, scooped in the flanks of the ridge beneath him. Curves, curves: he repeated the word slowly, trying as he did so to find some term in which to give expression to his appreciation. Curves—no, that was inadequate. He made a gesture with his hand, as though to scoop the achieved expression out of the air, and almost fell off his bicycle. What was the word to describe the curves of those little valleys? They were as fine as the lines of a human body, they were informed with the subtlety of art. . . .

Galbe. That was a good word; but it was French. *Le galbe evase de ses hanches:* had one ever read a French novel in which that phrase didn't occur? Some day he would compile a dictionary for the use of novelists. Galbe, gonflé, goulu: parfum, peau, pervers, potelé, pudeur: vertu, volupté.

But he really must find that word. Curves, curves. . . . Those little valleys had the lines of a cup moulded round a woman's breast; they seemed the dinted imprints of some huge divine body that had rested on these hills. Cumbrous locutions, these; but through them he seemed to be getting nearer to what he wanted. Dinted, dimpled, wimpled—his mind wandered down echoing corridors of assonance and alliteration ever further and further from the point. He was enamoured with the beauty of words.

Becoming once more aware of the outer world, he found himself on the crest of a descent. The road plunged down, steep and straight, into a considerable valley. There, on the opposite slope, a little higher up the valley, stood Crome, his destination. He put on his brakes; the view of Crome was pleasant to linger over. The facade with its three projecting towers rose precipitously from among the dark trees of the garden. The house basked in full sunlight; the old brick rosily glowed. How ripe and rich it was, how superbly mellow! And at the same time, how austere! The hill was becoming steeper and steeper; he was gaining speed in spite of his brakes. He loosed his grip of the levers, and in a moment was rushing headlong down. Five minutes later he was passing through the gate of the great courtyard. The front door stood hospitably open. He left his bicycle leaning against the wall and walked in. He would take them by surprise.

6

H. G. Wells

A Bolt of Blue

From *The Wheels of Chance*

Walter Mitty is alive and well in the person of Hoopdriver. Hoopdriver, the twenty-three-year-old draper's assistant cum knight-errant of The Wheels of Chance, *is on a ten-day cycling holiday when he becomes the hero of a romantic escapade. True, he doesn't go over Niagara Falls on his bicycle, nor does he bicycle through the enemy lines seeking help nor does he stand back to the wall, bicycle by his side, calmly awaiting death by the firing squad. But, like Thurber's hero, he is an irrepressible romantic, a Walter Mitty on wheels.*

A draper's assistant is not the stuff from which heroes are customarily drawn. In the Middle Ages, all manner and variety of consumer frauds were practiced by drapers. John Gower's description in the Mirour de l'omme *is a classic portrait of the crooked merchant.*

Sometimes Trick is a draper. . . . Men tell us (and I believe it) that whatsoever is dark by nature hateth and avoideth the light: wherefore when I see the draper in his house, methinks he hath no clear conscience. Dark is the window where he bargaineth with thee, and scarce canst thou tell the green from the blue; dark too are his ways, none may trust his word for the price of his goods. Darkly will he set thee his cloth at double price, and clinch it with an oath; darkly thus will he beguile thee all the worse, for he would persuade that he hath done thee a friendship, wherein he hath the more cozened thee, saying that he hath given thee the stuff at cost price to get thy further custom; but the measure and the market price will tell thee afterwards another tale.[1]

Hoopdriver is a draper's assistant because his creator was a draper's assistant, albeit

From H. G. Wells, *The Wheels of Chance: A Cycling Holiday Adventure* (London: J. M. Dent & Sons Ltd., 1896), pp. 124–30, 138–44.

reluctantly and temporarily. Moreover, Wells "rode wherever Mr. Hoopdriver rode in that story." When Wells fell during his learning to ride a bicycle, "I wrote down a description of the state of my legs which became the opening chapter of the Wheels of Chance."[2] *The book's autobiographical content does not eclipse its interest as a solid yarn of warmth and humanity in which any traveling bicyclist may be the principal, faint-hearted though he be.*

Hoopdriver's bicycling adventures are those of everyone who, in escape, finds discovery. The Walter Mittys and the Phineas Foggs of fiction would not be as instantly and perpetually popular as they are if the seeds of bold adventure did not lie dormant in all of us, to be enlivened by the right occasion.

The right occasion, for twelve-year-old Denis in Frank O'Connor's story "Masculine Protest,"[3] was his rebellion against his parents—his mother who treated him with curt disdain, as if he were still in knickers, and his father whose bowler hat bespoke his meek and ineffectual ways. Denis took to the road on a bicycle "equipped with dynamo lamp and everything—a smasher" for a one day's journey of twenty miles to prove, if nothing else, that he was a man.

Along the way his sudden awareness of the "fragility of [his] tyres compared with the rough surface of the road" nearly panics him. "Whacked" though he is from pedaling along a road where "wide green rivers rose up and slipped away again under [his] tyres," he draws support from his having successfully run away, on his bicycle, without funds, food or family to sustain him. But enough is sometimes too much, so he buses home to a father whose bowler hat no longer conceals his quiet strength and understanding. That recognition, Denis sensed, was "the real sign of [his] manhood." Hoopdriver too, on the high road to adventure, has his own growing pains to endure.

The story finds Hoopdriver's bicycling path constantly crisscrossing that of a young Lady in Grey who is traveling along by bicycle with a man in brown. Hoopdriver is suspicious of the relation between the two, and rightfully so. The man in brown is a thirtyish, married Mr. Bechamel who is assisting the Lady in Grey, eighteen-year-old Jessie Milton, to escape a cruel stepmother. All is harmony between them until Jessie realizes that Mr. Bechamel intends to seduce her.

Jessie is confronted with a choice between succumbing to Bechamel or returning to the repression of her stepmother. A truce is declared between them while she considers which is the lesser of the two evils.

Meanwhile, Hoopdriver is being far more decisive. His courage is up. His intention is fixed. Miss Milton must be rescued, though he still does not know the full extent of her plight. He gives chase, as any Walter Mitty would.

The following episode opens with Hoopdriver at Mrs. Wardor's boarding house in Midhurst on the watch for Bechamel and the Lady in Grey, who have spent the night next door at the Angel Hotel.

And now to tell of Mr. Hoopdriver, rising with the sun, vigilant, active, wonderful, the practicable half of the lead-framed window stuck open, ears alert, an eye flicker-

ing incessantly in the corner panes, in oblique glances at the Angelic front. Mrs. Wardor wanted him to have his breakfast downstairs in her kitchen, but that would have meant abandoning the watch and he held out strongly. The bicycle, *cap-à-pie*, occupied, under protest, a strategic position in the shop. He was expectant by six in the morning. By nine horrible fears oppressed him that his quest had escaped him, and he had to reconnoitre the Angel yard in order to satisfy himself. There he found the ostler (How are the mighty fallen in these decadent days!) brushing down the bicycles of the chase, and he returned relieved to Mrs. Wardor's premises. And about ten they emerged, and rode quietly up the North Street. He watched them until they turned the corner of the post-office, and then out into the road, and up after them in fine style! They went by the engine-house, where the old stocks and the whipping-posts are, and on to the Chichester road, and he followed gallantly. So this great chase began.

They did not look round, and he kept them just within sight, getting down if he chanced to draw closely upon them round a corner. By riding vigorously he kept quite conveniently near them, for they made but little hurry. He grew hot indeed, and his knees were a little stiff to begin with, but that was all. There was little danger of losing them, for a thin chalky dust lay upon the road, and the track of her tire was milled like a shilling, and his was a chequered ribbon along the way. So they rode by Cobden's monument and through the prettiest of villages, until at last the downs rose steeply ahead. There they stopped awhile at the only inn in the place, and Mr. Hoopdriver took up a position which commanded the inn door, and mopped his face and thirsted, and smoked a Red Herring cigarette. They remained in the inn for some time. A number of chubby innocents returning home from school, stopped and formed a line in front of him, and watched him quietly but firmly for the space of ten minutes or so. "Go away," said he, and they only seemed quietly interested. He asked them all their names then, and they answered indistinct murmurs. He gave it up at last, and became passive on his gate, and so at length they tired of him.

The couple under observation occupied the inn so long that Mr. Hoopdriver, at the thought of their possible employment, hungered as well as thirsted. Clearly they were lunching. It was a cloudless day, and the sun at the meridian beat down upon the top of Mr. Hoopdriver's head, a shower-bath of sunshine, a huge jet of hot light. It made his head swim. At last they emerged, and the other man in brown looked back and saw him. They rode on to the foot of the down, and dismounting, began to push tediously up that long, nearly vertical ascent of blinding white road. Mr. Hoopdriver hesitated. It might take them twenty minutes to mount that. Beyond was empty downland perhaps for miles. He decided to return to the inn and snatch a hasty meal.

At the inn they gave him biscuits and cheese, and a misleading pewter measure of sturdy ale, pleasant under the palate, cool in the throat, but leaden in the legs, of a hot afternoon. He felt a man of substance as he emerged in the blinding sunshine, but even by the foot of the down the sun was insisting again that his skull was too small for his brains. The hill had gone steeper, the chalky road blazed like a magnesium light, and his front wheel began an apparently incurable squeaking. He felt as a man from

Mars would feel if he were suddenly transferred to this planet, about three times as heavy as he was wont to feel. The two little black figures had vanished over the forehead of the hill. "The tracks'll be all right," said Mr. Hoopdriver.

That was a comforting reflection. It not only justified a slow progress up the hill, but at the crest a sprawl on the turf beside the road, to contemplate the Weald from the south. In a matter of two days he had crossed that spacious valley, with its frozen surge of green hills, its little villages and townships here and there, its copses and cornfields, its ponds and streams like jewelry of diamonds and silver glittering in the sun. The North Downs were hidden, far away beyond the Wealden Heights. Down below was the little village of Cocking, and half-way up the hill, a mile perhaps to the right, hung a flock of sheep grazing together. Overhead an anxious peewit circled against the blue, and every now and then emitted its feeble cry. Up here the heat was tempered by a pleasant breeze. Mr. Hoopdriver was possessed by an unreasonable contentment; he lit himself a cigarette and lounged more comfortably. Surely the Sussex ale is made of the waters of Lethe, of poppies and pleasant dreams. Drowsiness coiled insidiously about him.

He awoke with a guilty start, to find himself sprawling prone on the turf with his cap over one eye. He sat up, rubbed his eyes, and realised that he had slept. His head was still a trifle heavy. And the chase? He jumped to his feet and stooped to pick up his overturned machine. He whipped out his watch, and saw that it was past two o'clock. "Lord love us, fancy that!—But the tracks'll be all right," said Mr. Hoopdriver, wheeling his machine back to the chalky road. "I must scorch till I overtake them."

He mounted and rode as rapidly as the heat and a lingering lassitude permitted. Now and then he had to dismount to examine the surface where the road forked. He enjoyed that rather. "Trackin'," he said aloud, and decided in the privacy of his own mind that he had a wonderful instinct for "spoor." So he came past Goodwood station and Lavant, and approached Chichester towards four o'clock. And then came a terrible thing. In places the road became hard; in places were the crowded indentations of a recent flock of sheep, and at last in the throat of the town cobbles and the stony streets branching east, west, north, and south, at a stone cross under the shadow of the cathedral the tracks vanished. "O Cricky!" said Mr. Hoopdriver, dismounting in dismay and standing agape. "Dropped anything?" said an inhabitant at the kerb. "Yes," said Mr. Hoopdriver, "I've lost the spoor," and walked upon his way, leaving the inhabitant marvelling what part of a bicycle a spoor might be. Mr. Hoopdriver, abandoning tracking, began asking people if they had seen a Young Lady in Grey on a bicycle. Six casual people hadn't, and he began to feel the inquiry was conspicuous, and desisted. But what was to be done?

Hoopdriver was hot, tired, and hungry, and full of the first gnawings of a monstrous remorse. He decided to get himself some tea and meat, and in the Royal George he meditated over the business in a melancholy frame enough. They had passed out of his world—vanished, and all his wonderful dreams of some vague, crucial interference collapsed like a castle of cards. What a fool he had been not to stick to them like a leech! He might have thought! But there!—what *was* the good of that sort of thing now?

He thought of her tears, of her helplessness, of the bearing of the other man in brown, and his wrath and disappointment surged higher. "What *can* I do?" said Mr. Hoopdriver aloud, bringing his fist down beside the teapot.

What would Sherlock Holmes have done? Perhaps, after all, there might be such things as clues in the world, albeit the age of miracles was past. But to look for a clue in this intricate network of cobbled streets, to examine every muddy interstice! There was a chance by looking about, and inquiry at the various inns. Upon that he began. But of course they might have ridden straight through, and scarcely a soul have marked them. And then came a positively brilliant idea. "'Ow many ways are there out of Chichester?" said Mr. Hoopdriver. It was really equal to Sherlock Holmes— that. "If they've made tracks, I shall find those tracks. If not—they're in the town." He was then in East Street, and he started at once to make the circuit of the place, discovering incidentally that Chichester is a walled city. In passing, he made inquiries at the Black Swan, the Crown, and the Red Lion Hotel. At six o'clock in the evening, he was walking downcast, intent, as one who had dropped money, along the road towards Bognor, kicking up the dust with his shoes and fretting with disappointed pugnacity. A thwarted, crestfallen Hoopdriver it was, as you may well imagine. And then suddenly there jumped upon his attention—a broad line ribbed like a shilling, and close beside it one chequered, that ever and again split into two. "Found!" said Mr. Hoopdriver, and swung round on his heel at once, and back to the Royal George, helter skelter, for the bicycle they were minding for him. The ostler thought he was confoundedly imperious, considering his machine. . . .

Hoopdriver has now tracked his quarry to Bognor. Jessie is in a dither. Bechamel's importunities have become an ultimatum. She is desperate.

And now without in the twilight, behold Mr. Hoopdriver, his cheeks hot, his eye bright! His brain is in a tumult. The nervous, obsequious Hoopdriver, to whom I introduced you some days since, has undergone a wonderful change. Ever since he lost that "spoor" in Chichester, he has been tormented by the most horrible visions of the shameful insults that may be happening. The strangeness of new surroundings has been working to strip off the habitual servile from him. Here was moonlight rising over the memory of a red sunset, dark shadows and glowing orange lamps, beauty somewhere mysteriously rapt away from him, tangible wrong in a brown suit and an unpleasant face, flouting him. Mr. Hoopdriver for the time was in the world of Romance and Knight-errantry, divinely forgetful of his social position or hers; forgetting, too, for the time any of the wretched timidities that had tied him long since behind the counter in his proper place. He was angry and adventurous. It was all about him, this vivid drama he had fallen into, and it was eluding him. He was far too grimly in earnest to pick up that lost thread and make a play of it now. The man was

living. He did not pose when he alighted at the coffee-tavern even, nor when he made his hasty meal.

As Bechamel crossed from the Vicuna toward the esplanade, Hoopdriver, disappointed and exasperated, came hurrying round the corner from the Temperance Hotel. At the sight of Bechamel his heart jumped, and the tension of his angry suspense exploded into, rather than gave place to, an excited activity of mind. They were at the Vicuna, and she was there now alone. It was the occasion he sought. But he would give Chance no chance against him. He went back round the corner, sat down on the seat, and watched Bechamel recede into the dimness up the esplanade, before he got up and walked into the hotel entrance. "A lady cyclist in grey," he asked for, and followed boldly on the waiter's heels. The door of the dining-room was opening before he felt a qualm. And then suddenly he was nearly minded to turn and run for it, and his features seemed to him to be convulsed.

She turned with a start, and looked at him with something between terror and hope in her eyes.

"Can I—have a few words—with you, alone?" said Mr. Hoopdriver, controlling his breath with difficulty. She hesitated, and then motioned the waiter to withdraw.

Mr. Hoopdriver watched the door shut. He had intended to step out into the middle of the room, fold his arms, and say, "You are in trouble. I am a Friend. Trust me." Instead of which he stood panting, and then spoke with sudden familiarity, hastily, guiltily, "Look here. I don't know what the juice is up, but I think there's something wrong. Excuse my intruding—if it isn't so. I'll do anything you like to help you out of the scrape, if you're in one. That's my meaning, I believe. What can I do? I would do anything to help you."

Her brow puckered as she watched him make, with infinite emotion, this remarkable speech. *"You!"* she said. She was tumultuously weighing possibilities in her mind, and he had scarcely ceased when she had made her resolve.

She stepped a pace forward. "You are a gentleman," she said.

"Yes," said Mr. Hoopdriver.

"Can I trust you?"

She did not wait for his assurance. "I must leave this hotel at once. Come here."

She took his arm and led him to the window. "You can just see the gate. It is still open. Through that are our bicycles. Go down, get them out, and I will come down to you. Dare you?"

"Get your bicycle out in the road?"

"Both. Mine alone is no good. At once. Dare you?"

"Which way?"

"Go out by the front door and round. I will follow in one minute."

"Right!" said Mr. Hoopdriver, and went.

He had to get those bicycles. Had he been told to go out and kill Bechamel he would have done it. His head was a Maelstrom now. He walked out of the hotel, along the front, and into the big, black-shadowed coachyard. He looked round. There were no bicycles visible. Then a man emerged from the dark, a short man in a short, black, shiny jacket. Hoopdriver was caught. He made no attempt to turn and run for it. "I've

been giving your machines a wipe over, sir," said the man, recognising the suit and touching his cap. Hoopdriver's intelligence now was a soaring eagle; he swooped on the situation at once. "That's right," he said, and added, before the pause became marked, "Where is mine? I want to look at the chain."

The man led him into an open shed, and went fumbling for a lantern. Hoopdriver moved the lady's machine out of his way to the door, and then laid hands on the man's machine and wheeled it out of the shed into the yard. The gate stood open, and beyond was the pale road and a clump of trees black in the twilight. He stooped and examined the chain with trembling fingers. How was it to be done? Something behind the gate seemed to flutter. The man must be got rid of anyhow.

"I say," said Hoopdriver, with an inspiration. "Can you get me a screwdriver?"

The man simply walked across the shed, opened and shut a box, and came up to the kneeling Hoopdriver with a screwdriver in his hand. Hoopdriver felt himself a lost man. He took the screwdriver with a tepid "Thanks," and incontinently had another inspiration.

"I say," he said again.

"Well?"

"This is miles too big."

The man lit the lantern, brought it up to Hoopdriver, and put it down on the ground. "Want a smaller screwdriver?" he said.

Hoopdriver had his handkerchief out and sneezed a prompt *atichew*. It is the orthodox thing when you wish to avoid recognition. "As small as you have," he said, out of his pocket handkerchief.

"I ain't got none smaller than that," said the ostler.

"Won't do, really," said Hoopdriver, still wallowing in his handkerchief.

"I'll see wot they got in the 'ouse, if you like, sir," said the man. "If you would," said Hoopdriver. And as the man's heavily nailed boots went clattering down the yard, Hoopdriver stood up, took a noiseless step to the lady's machine, laid trembling hands on its handle and saddle, and prepared for a rush.

The scullery door opened momentarily and sent a beam of warm, yellow light up the road, shut again behind the man, and forthwith Hoopdriver rushed the machines towards the gate. A dark grey form came fluttering to meet him. "Give me this," she said, "and bring yours."

He passed the thing to her, touched her hand in the darkness, ran back, seized Bechamel's machine, and followed.

The yellow light of the scullery door suddenly flashed upon the cobbles again. It was too late now to do anything but escape. He heard the ostler shout behind him, and came into the road. She was up and dim already. He got into the saddle without a blunder. In a moment the ostler was in the gateway with a full-throated "*Hi!* sir! That ain't allowed;" and Hoopdriver was overtaking the Young Lady in Grey. For some moments the earth seemed alive with shouts of, "Stop 'em!" and the shadows with ambuscades of police. The road swept round, and they were riding out of sight of the hotel, and behind dark hedges, side by side.

She was weeping with excitement as he overtook her. "Brave," she said, "brave!" and he ceased to feel like a hunted thief. He looked over his shoulder and about him, and saw that they were already out of Bognor—for the Vicuna stands at the very westernmost extremity of the sea front—and riding on a fair wide road.

7

John E. Mack

Not Castles in the Air

From *A Prince of Our Disorder*

Some touring bicyclists waste their time and efforts watching the white line along the edge of the road. Others go in search of castles in Spain or in France or in . . . T. E. Lawrence, known popularly as Lawrence of Arabia, was one of the more imaginative latter group.

Lawrence of Arabia, after whom the popular movie was named, was born Thomas Edward Lawrence on August 16, 1888, in Wales. Ned, as his parents called him, was the second of five illegitimates born to a governess with whom his father had eloped (and for whom he had changed his name) rather than remain in Dublin with his lawful daughters and under the sway of his puritanical wife. For a time, as a child, Lawrence lived in Kirkcudbright, Scotland, the scene of Dorothy Sayers's Lord Peter Wimsey novel The Five Red Herrings.

Lawrence was introduced to the bicycle by his father, who took him on summer bicycle tours in England and France during his teenage years. He and his brothers could often be seen bicycling in a regimented line to and from Oxford High School. At one point, when Lawrence was twelve or thirteen, he took to bicycling in order to strengthen his leg muscles after he had broken a bone in his leg during an altercation with another boy.

Most often the bicycle was to Lawrence what the pole is to a pole-vaulter—the means to test his strength and to facilitate his achievements. It is reported that he was a hill climber of a most unusual sort. He would pick the most difficult hills to surmount and, having done so, he would walk his bicycle down the other side. But even today the bicycle is used in such endurance tests. Los Angeles's Fargo Street, where a one hundred

From John E. Mack, *A Prince of Our Disorder: The Life of T. E. Lawrence* (Boston: Little, Brown and Co., 1976), pp. 48–55.

169

fifty-yard hill with a 33 percent grade tempts the most fanatic bicyclists, is often the site of such individual contests of will and determination.

But Lawrence went still further in seeking out challenging experiences with his bicycle. He was known to bicycle nonstop until he collapsed in exhaustion by the roadside.

Even in his later years, the bicycle was the means Lawrence chose to achieve his ends. When he was released from the Royal Air Force in 1935, after his search for anonymity there under the pseudonym of Aircraftsman Shaw had proved futile, he was pictured bicycling off into civilian life. It seems that his motorcycle, a Brough Superior, was in disrepair at the time. The bicycle was a convenient and handy substitute.

Strangely, the bicycle even played a role in Lawrence's tragic and untimely death at the age of forty-seven in 1935. According to uncontroverted accounts of his death, he was fatally injured en route to his cottage at Clouds Hill in Dorset when his motorcycle swerved to avoid two delivery boys on bicycles.

As Lawrence was in his lifetime, so he is after his death—a legend and an enigma. He has been described, glowingly, as "a white Arab, Prince of Mecca, and uncrowned King of Damascus," which he was instrumental in liberating from the Turks. To Winston Churchill, he was "one of the greatest beings of our time" and he predicted that "whatever our need we shall never see his like again." The visitor to St. Paul's Cathedral will find his bust in the company of those of Nelson and Wellington. Some thirty books in at least four languages have been written about his life and times.

"Crusader Castles," Mack's chapter title for the following selection, was taken from the title given Lawrence's Oxford thesis, which presented his findings from his bicycle tour, when published by the Golden Cockerel Press in 1936. As submitted to Oxford, his paper was entitled "The Military Architecture of the Crusades." In this research, Lawrence proved that the bicycle could be an aid to scholarship as well as a medium for enjoying life.

At thirteen Lawrence began to go on bicycle trips in England to visit medieval castles and churches. Often he went alone, but sometimes he would be accompanied by his father and other family members, or by his friend C. F. C. Beeson. According to Beeson, Lawrence was interested in the design of military buildings as early as 1905. Toward the end of that year the two friends had exhausted the accessible examples in England, and they read during the winter of 1905–1906 in the Radcliffe and Ashmolean libraries in preparation for the investigation of the ruins and restorations of France. . . .

The trips to France that concern us here are the bicycle tours Lawrence made during the summer holidays of 1906, 1907 and 1908 when he was eighteen, nineteen and twenty. On the 1906 trip, which lasted four weeks, he was accompanied by Beeson. In April 1907, during his Easter holiday, he visited the medieval castles of North Wales, not far from his birthplace. In August 1907, Lawrence traveled with his father for part of the month, and their shared interest in photography stimulated

Lawrence's picture-taking. On the 1908 trip, which lasted six weeks, he was alone.

Lawrence traveled on the latest model of high-speed bicycle, with dropped handles and an unusually high top-gear ratio, specially built to his order in a shop in Oxford. During 1906 Lawrence and Beeson ("Scroggs") confined themselves to the parts of Brittany near Dinard, Saint-Malo and the Channel coast. In 1907 Lawrence reached the Loire. In 1908 he traveled the length and breadth of France, reaching Champagne, the Mediterranean, the Pyrenees and the western part of the country. The plan to undertake eventually a detailed study of the military architecture of the Crusades may have begun to take shape during the 1906 and 1907 trips, both made before Lawrence began his studies at Jesus College, but only the 1908 tour was specifically devoted to this purpose.

The published accounts do not bring out the extent to which these travels, like so many of the ventures of Lawrence's youth, were a personal preparation, a testing of his body and his spirit for future trials. Beeson noted how his friend, whom he had known for about two years before their trip to France, "had to prove himself." Lawrence was "always making himself tough, always climbing, always testing the limits of his powers." Beeson also felt strongly Lawrence's leadership qualities. Once in Brittany they visited a castle ruin with a moat that was crossed by a bridge. According to Beeson, Lawrence had to jump the moat instead of using the bridge. Lawrence seemed to the more cautious man to take unusual, even reckless, chances when climbing about old walls with loose stones. An image has stayed in Beeson's mind of Lawrence atop some rocks in France with his foot trembling as he tried to find a footing. Beeson warned, "You'll fall," and offered to help. But Lawrence would not let him. Beeson was also impressed with his friend's resourcefulness. On one occasion when his tire was punctured, he became quite troubled about the possible delay in the trip. But Lawrence was not frustrated or irritated. He knew someone "around the corner" who could fix it. Lawrence frequently repaired his own tires. . . .

On his trips Lawrence wrote proudly home of how lightly he could travel, how little he could get by with eating, and how cheaply he could live in the most meager of surroundings. His letters contain long accounts of his thrift. For instance, in 1906: "My silk shirt was a blessing. It took up no space, and every day I used to roll it tightly around my other articles, and it used to hold them all in place. Thus my luggage was never larger or longer than my carrier. Father will be very interested to learn this, for the carrier is a small one. It went through the trip excellently and gave absolutely no trouble. I carried two pairs of socks and wore a third. Next time I would only carry one pair and would not trouble to bring a sponge. A spare pair of trousers is useful and in fact necessary: also a spare shirt. A coat is quite useless if a cape is carried: by this means the weight can be reduced to practically nil."

According to Beeson, his friend was not fastidious about food and would eat most of what was available in the countryside. When they went to a farmhouse for a meal, T. E. would be greeted as a familiar friend (which suggests that he had made at least one previous visit to Brittany since his early childhood years in Dinard). When the food in France was really unfamiliar or bad, Lawrence could complain colorfully. He once described the food of the Tarn district of the south: "Their food is weird and wonderful (*omelette aux pommes de terre* yesterday and other articles unspecified and indescribable), the bread tastes like . . . can you imgine leather soaked in brine, and then boiled till soft: with an iron crust, and a flavour like a brandy-snap? It takes me considerable mental and physical effort to 'degust' a mouthful: milk has not been heard of lately, butter has a smell like cream cheese, but a taste like Bruyere (thank goodness for the Roquefort, 'tis the district, and its strength would make palatable (or indiscoverable) a cesspool), and in fact a dinner for me is like an expedition into Spain, Naples, the North and Antarctic regions. Central Australia, Japan, etc."

Lawrence's letters from France, though pedantic with detail at times (especially the long descriptions of churches and castles), are suffused with the excitement and pleasure of discovery. They show an enormous range of interests, from the position of the grandmother in the French family ("she is all powerful . . . an affront to her usually causes a 'counseil de famille'") to tipping (or not tipping) castle guides. Lawrence begins here to show the descriptive powers that were later to characterize his literary work. Little of the cynicism that embittered his spirit after the war is evident in these enthusiastic, sometimes joyous and frequently poetic accounts. He found "a special joy" in Carcassonne: "One does not need a guide with one, all is free and open except some of the towers: there are guides, but no fees." His ecstatic reverence for the beauties of Chartres gave his mother special pleasure, although she misinterpreted his aesthetic raptures. George Bernard Shaw appreciated Lawrence's description of Chartres, which Lord Carlow had privately printed in an elaborate edition after Lawrence's death. But Shaw chided Lawrence for omitting the stained-glass windows. . . .

[His letters] contain in particular long descriptions of the crudeness of the lives and habits of the people in Brittany, which contrasted sharply with the Arthurian "Matiere de Bretagne" and other romantic French medieval literature in which Lawrence was simultaneously steeping himself. He was disparaging of the drunkenness, poor manners, overeating and ignorance of the Bretons, although he showed an understanding and fondness for particular individuals. "A child is always the person to ask for directions as to the road, or distances; they know better than their elders here," he wrote in irritation. . . .

Although these letters do not reveal much of Lawrence's inmost feelings, they are filled with conscientious and affectionate concern for each member of the family, and inquiries about Oxford neighbors. He shares a great deal about his interests with his family and considerately selects particular topics that he knows will match the interests of each one. For his mother, in addition to the poetic sharing of lines of Tennyson and the raptures over Chartres Cathedral, Lawrence seems to go to endless pains to find a petticoat of the type she has asked for. To his father, to whom only two letters are specifically addressed, he writes of politics, of cycling (a beach for doing "a little speed work on the sands"), of false teeth and medieval architecture. . . . To his friend Beeson, in addition to providing details about medieval towns and architecture, Lawrence compared the women of Arles ("glorious") and Tarascon ("hideous, exactly like grey horses").

Lawrence took advantage of a new university regulation that allowed him to submit a thesis as an additional part of his final examinations for his degree. He chose as his topic the influence of the Crusades on European military architecture to the end of the twelfth century, not an unexpected choice. We have seen already how extensively Lawrence traveled in England, Wales and France from 1905 to 1908 visiting the important castles. He felt that it was essential to examine and photograph their architectural features at first hand in order to establish the influence of one form of building upon another, to determine by comparisons the periods in which particular developments occurred, and to fix the dates of various transitions. He now needed to study the castles of Syria and Palestine "from their own evidence" and accordingly visited the Middle East for the first time in the summer of 1909. But his keen desire to go there had been awakened the previous summer when he reached the Mediterranean and wrote to his mother in excitement: "I felt that at last I had reached the way to the South, and all the glorious East. Greece, Carthage, Egypt, Tyre, Syria, Italy, Spain, Sicily, Crete . . . they were all there, and all within reach . . . of me. I fancy I know now better than Keats what Cortes felt like, 'silent upon a peak in Darien.' Oh I must go down here,—farther out—again! Really this getting to the sea has almost overturned my mental balance; I would accept a passage for Greece tomorrow."

Lawrence's travels gradually made him doubt the traditional view, propounded particularly by the nineteenth-century authorities C. W. C. Oman and E. G. Rey, that the Crusaders drew their excellence in castle building from the East, and that Syrian workmen were imported even to build Château-Gaillard, the masterpiece of Richard I. Particularly "in treating of Latin Fortresses in Syria itself," Lawrence insisted that "documentary evidence of building is absolutely valueless. Medieval fortresses must in every case be dated from their own evidence."

In the limited time available to him he scrambled over endless fortifications, steps, towers and ruins making notes and plans and taking photographs for his thesis. Mosquitoes, indigestible food, snakes and assault by suspicious natives were among the obstacles he encountered. In the course of his personal examinations of castles and cathedrals (his need was always, as his friend E. F. Hall phrased it, "to see for himself"), Lawrence would delight in finding errors in the guidebooks ("Mondoubleau which the guidebooks called ix cent. Really it was an enormous keep of the latest xii"). And he gave way to a boyish delight in the discovery of a "beautiful" latrine at a castle in Brittany during one of the earlier explorations, and chided his prudish older brother for not appreciating it when he visited there: "By the way, did not Bob, (many thanks for the post card) go and see the castle? What could he have been thinking about not to mention those most attractive domestic conveniences?"

The excitement of discovery comes through vividly in Lawrence's letters, as his suspicions regarding the castle builders of southern Europe are confirmed by his own findings. " 'Eureka,' " he wrote Beeson, from France in 1908, "I've got it at last for the thesis: the transition from the square keep form: really it's too great for words."

The need to come to startling conclusions—what he called "my rather knight-errant style of tilting against all comers in the subject,"—or, more importantly, to overturn the position of the "regulars," Oman and Rey, led Lawrence to overstate somewhat the implications of his findings. "There is no evidence," he wrote, "that Richard borrowed anything great or small, from any fortress which he saw in the Holy Land: it is not likely that he would do so, since he would find better examples of everything in the South of France, which he knew so well. There is not a trace of anything Byzantine in the ordinary French castle, or in an English one: while there are evident signs that all that was good in Crusading architecture hailed from France and Italy. A summing up of the whole matter would be the statement that 'the Crusading architects were for many years copyists of the Western builders.' "

Yet Lawrence himself acknowledges the possibility of mutual influence, "the transfer of trifling detail," because East-West interchange among the upper classes was constant.

The actual writing of the thesis was done in the winter of 1909–1910 and completed by the end of March. Despite its somewhat overly sweeping conclusion, his tutor was so impressed with the work that he gave a dinner for the examiners to celebrate it.

According to Lawrence he refused to have his thesis printed because it was only a preliminary study, "not good enough to publish." In 1929 he wrote of it: "An elementary performance, and I think it has been destroyed or left behind somewhere, in the course of my life. At any rate, I haven't a notion where it is—but a strong memory that it was worthless." This self-disparaging view of the work, so characteristic of Lawrence, was directly contradicted by the statement of Professor Ernest Barker, one of Lawrence's medieval history teachers, who had studied and written about various aspects of the Crusades himself. Barker read the thesis when Lawrence submitted it and concluded: "It proved conclusively, so far as I could judge, that the old theory of the influence of the castles of Palestine on western military architecture must be abandoned, and that instead of the East affecting the West, it was the West that had affected the East."

Lawrence's fundamental point, that the early Crusaders from Southern Europe took a lot of knowledge about military castle building with them when they went to the East, and did not learn the art from Byzantine examples, has been largely sustained by subsequent writers. These writers also agree that there was more interchange and mutual influence between East and West than Lawrence acknowledges, that there is much that is not known about who influenced whom, and that more firsthand comparison, based on direct examinations of the evidence from the castles themselves, is needed to achieve accurate dating and to learn fully the history of military castle building.

A letter to his parents of January 24, 1911, indicates that Lawrence was then contemplating writing a "monumental work on the Crusades." If he had done such a book, it would have included further considerations of these questions, and he wrote later to his biographers that his "basic intention in exploring Syria" during his youth "was always to write a strategic study of the Crusades" or to write a history of the Crusades.

One unhappy byproduct of these years of exploration was malaria. Lawrence was subject to recurrent bouts of it through most of his life. He probably contracted the disease in 1908 in the south of France when he was nearly twenty.

Part IV

Head over Wheels in Love

Introduction

Romance, of course, takes many different forms. It ranges from the passionate and meretricious, as in D. H. Lawrence's *Lady Chatterley's Lover*, to the fumbling and puerile, exemplified by the pulp novels on newsstands everywhere. The touching and epic romances of Tristan and Isolde and of Eloise and Abelard add grace, dignity, and poignancy to this literary genre.

The literature of the bicycle includes all of these types of romantic fact and fiction and others too. The cycling Romeo can be of the J. P. Donleavy type—lusty and audacious. Such a one is Sexton, the one-eyed horticulturist of Andromeda Park in Donleavy's *The Destinies of Darcy Dancer, Gentleman*. Sexton is described by Catherine the Cook, in most reproachful terms, as "cycling up to the young girls at every crossroad all over the countryside. To get them to take a ride with you across your dirty, filthy handlebars."

"What better than to hire bicycles, disappear with her along the road, way out of sight and around the corner, whisked!" (From "An Interlude" by William Sansom)

The bicycle might seem to be an unlikely and odd sex symbol. But not to Donleavy, to whom everything seems to be grist for the sexual mill. Indeed, at one point when Darcy Dancer manifests one of his recurring erections, Donleavy tells us that his hero was "lit up like a bicycle lamp." More conventionally, a bicycle lamp could evoke recollections of "eyes that twinkled like bicycle lights in a mist," as Tom Robbins puts it in *Even Cowgirls Get the Blues*.

On other occasions in the literature of romance, the bicycle is simply the bridge that brings the lovers together. That was, for example, the use of the bicycle in Frederick L. Keefe's far-less-than-captivating story entitled "The Bicycle Rider." In that tale, a G.I. is waiting in London during World War II to embark for the war front in France when he is accidentally injured and hospitalized as he returns from a

177

bicycle ride. This very fortuitous circumstance introduces the soldier to Isabel
Fletcher, whom he very politely romances during his recuperation. His romancing is
enhanced by his use of a second-hand bicycle, which he discards when Isabel elopes
unsuspectingly with another military man. The bicycle is just a prop in the plot, but
not enough to hold it up.

A bicycle ride can, on the contrary, spell the end of a romance, or, as in the case of
Bertrand Russell, seven years of marriage. Russell gave two lectures at Cambridge in
the autumn of 1901 which "contained the outline of [his] Principia Mathematica."
During that time, as he tells us, he

> went out bicycling one afternoon, and suddenly, as I was riding along a country
> road, I realized that I no longer loved Alys [his first wife]. I had had no idea until
> this moment that my love for her was even lessening.[1]

That fateful bicycle ride also first brought to mind many of her traits and attitudes
which he found repugnant.

The bicycle may be put to ominous purposes when the romantic impulse is con-
verted into a fury for revenge. So, in D. H. Lawrence's *The Fox*, it is the bicycle that
enables Henry Grenfel to dash madly and angrily over "sixty miles of wet and muddy
crossroads" to the Bailey farm to have his revenge on Jill Banford. It is Banford whom
he blames for Nellie March's renouncing him. And it is Banford who must and does
die for it in a pretended accident when Henry fells a tree directly into the path where
Banford stands.

More frequently, the bicycle can be seen as an ally in the cause of giving expression
to love. For "Diamond Jim" Brady, this meant the gift of a gold-plated bicycle
complete with mother-of-pearl handlebars and spokes encrusted with chips of diamonds, emeralds, rubies, and sapphires to actress Lillian Russell. This bicycle, then
valued at $10,000, traveled with Miss Russell in "a blue plush-lined morocco case."
The Book of Lists considers this gift to be one of fifteen most well-known love offerings.
This union of a bicycle's freedom and a lover's quite openly abandoned commitment is
best expressed in Kenneth Koch's poem "To You":

> I think I am bicycling across an Africa of green and white fields
> Always to be near you, even in my heart[2]

The bicycle can add a descriptive color to the person with whom it appears. A
romantic interest may, in that way, be awakened. To Marcel Proust, Albertine
Simonet, upon a first acquaintance, was a "bacchante with the bicycle." A "throbbing
chord of happiness" pulsed in him, stirred by the sight of her "as though by the
pressure of a pedal." When he saw her outside the Grand Hotel at Balbec, he was
initially impressed with her, in his customary nineteen-to-the-dozen phrasing, as

> a girl with brilliant, laughing eyes and plump, colourless cheeks, a black polo-cap
> pulled down over her face, who was pushing a bicycle with so exaggerated a
> movement of her hips, with an air borne out by her language, which was so typically

of the gutter and was being shouted so loud, when I passed her (although among her expressions I caught that irritating "live my own life") that, abandoning the hypothesis which her friend's hooded cape had made me construct, I concluded instead that all these girls belonged to the population which frequents the racing-tracks, and must be the very juvenile mistresses of professional bicyclists.[3]

This assessment would not prevent Proust, or did it rather tempt him, to seek out this enigmatic Albertine and to go bicycling with her on the cliffs at Balbec. Later, this "dark cyclist with the bright eyes" would lay claim to his most endearing, and most quixotic, impulses.

The grace and charm of the bicycle lend added warmth and contour to the persons of the lovers it joins. This facet of the bicycle can be discerned in a number of the selections in this chapter, particularly in Nabokov's *Mary*. In others the bicycle generates a gentle mirth which seems hospitable to the romantic relationship in which it appears. In all of them, one can find the bicycle's rhythmic motion imbuing the atmosphere of romance with a new and enhanced dimension.

These selections are connected by a somewhat casual but always intriguing nexus. The first two manifest youth in the service of Cupid. There is an obvious and delightful humor in the excerpt from *The Red and the Green* which is found repeated in the far different and distant situs of Narayan's *The Painter of Signs*. More subtly, a wry humor pervades the selection from *Cakes and Ale* as well as the I-can-do-anything-you-can-do-better attitude of Ariel Durant in *A Dual Autobiography*.

On the other hand, Nabokov's *Mary* should be read in conjunction with *The Third Book about Achim*. These selections are remembrances of early romances; the one, of *Achim*, clearly fictional by design; the other, of *Mary*, fictional only by the accident of memory. Both, however, focus on the dilemma of the correspondence between the real and the remembered. The extent to which memory plays hob with facts is a recurrent theme in life as it is in literature. But rarely do we find an author like Uwe Johnson willing to stop the narrative to observe, parenthetically, "that was an error." Generally the errors of memory, transformed by time, go uncorrected. And, well they might, if the recollection is of a love long lost whose total recall would be too grievous to bear. That is the impression one may draw from the portrait of young love Nabokov renders in *Mary*.

All the selections in this chapter are of a piece in the sometimes unique and always pleasurable way in which the bicycle is insinuated or simply partakes in the development of the plot.

These selections are just that—choices from a larger array of tales in which the bicycle is integral to the romantic theme. Unfortunately, space limitations prevented the inclusion of other very engaging tales of young love. In one, "The Scandal Detectives" by F. Scott Fitzgerald, the author appears as Basil Duke Lee, the chief rapscallion in a group, still in short pants, who are styled "The Scandal Detectives," later known as the Goosrah. This story, according to Fitzgerald's own account in his ledger, depicts his first "faint sex attraction." It tells of affection stirred, unrewarded, and then revenged in a way that is so ineptly devised that its failure was assured at the outset. The episode occurred in Fitzgerald's own life in the spring of 1911.

The tale finds Basil D. Lee and his fourteen-year-old coconspirator, Riply Buckner, Jr., scheming in Buckner's attic over their lemon-juice-inked (to provide invisibility) "Book of Scandal." This book is their journal of neighborhood indiscretions, on hand as ammunition in case of need. They are distracted by Margaret, Imogene, and Connie, thirteen, twelve, and thirteen years old respectively, who pass through the alley below their lair. The girls are chewing "gum with a purpose" to conceal the telltale traces of Mrs. Bissel's cigarettes, which the girls had been smoking on the sly.

The girls' attitude of mild abandon sets the boys to action. They leave the attic, mount their bicycles, and escort the girls to Wharton's yard—where all day long there were "deep shadows . . . and ever something vague in bloom, and patient dogs around, and brown spots worn bare by countless circling wheels and dragging feet."

In a manner as inexplicable as the spontaneity of youth, Basil and Imogene are attracted to each other. He tells her he likes her "better than anybody." In his delirium he offers to return that night and present his school ring to her in exchange for

> "What?" Her color spread; she knew.
> "You know. Will you trade?"
> Imogene looked around uneasily. . . .
> "You're awful," she whispered. "Maybe. . . . Goodby."[4]

That night, back at Wharton's yard, Basil excitedly awaits Imogene who is now more to him than a "distraction." When she arrives, she is squired by Hubert Blair. This proves to be a fatal omen.

Hubert entrances Imogene with the dexterity of his roller skating. And Imogene misapprehends Basil's secret conversation with Margaret Torrence, in which Basil seeks the return of his school ring so as to present it to Imogene. Hubert embarrasses Basil by publicly labeling him "Basil the Boozle," to the merriment of all. The upshot is that Basil loses Imogene to Hubert.

In revenge, Basil schemes with his Scandal Detectives to assault and frighten Hubert, after leaving vaguely threatening notes at his home. When the hour arrives for the Scandal Detectives, dressed in various artlessly conceived disguises, to carry out their plan to put Hubert into an ashcan, they either lose their nerve or their interest. Consequently, the plot is foiled. Yet, Basil knew that in this episode

> the vague and restless yearnings of three long spring months were somehow satisfied. They reached combustion in that last week—flared up, exploded and burned out. His face was turned without regret toward the boundless possibilities of summer.[5]

In another omitted short story Stephen Crane, in his *Whilomville Stories,* also treats us to an exposé of the frenzied foibles of young love. One of the short tales in this collection, "Showin' Off," is a pure comedy rendering of an episode that could have happened in any village or town where boys and girls primp and posture in the throes of growing up.

Jimmie Trescott could not wait to get to school. It was not education but Abbie, the "little girl in a red hood," who made school such a passion for him. For three weeks, Jimmie had been in love. This love was encouraged, not by whispered conversations between the lovers, since "it was not customary to speak to girls." Instead, they "exchanged glances at least two hundred times in every school-hour."

The day arrived when Jimmie decided to walk little Abbie home from school. She was not consulted on the question. Jimmie just knew she would not object. En route to the alien land of Oakland Park, a suburb of Whilomville, which claimed the residence of his Abbie, Jimmie performed prodigious leaps calculated to win the admiration of his red-hooded love. Safely shepherded to her home, Abbie disappears inside while Jimmie idles about in the hope that she will reappear.

Enter Tommie Semple, one of those "weaklings" among Jimmie's classmates "who made friends with the fair sex." Jimmie must now outdo himself to prove his worth. Just then, Horace Glenn comes tooling along on his new velocipede.

Of course, Jimmie is called upon to assert that his velocipede is bigger and better than Horace's machine. But more is demanded if Jimmie is to outclass Horace. After all, little Abbie is now on the scene, watching every maneuver with grim anticipation.

"I've rode mine down Bridge Street hill. Yessir," says Jimmie. For a moment, Horace is hopeless and speechless. Then, not to be outdone, he replies in a display of "a spirit for climbing up again."

"Oh, you can do wonders!" he said, laughing. "You can do wonders! I s'pose you could ride down that bank there?" he asked, with art. He had indicated a grassy terrace some six feet in height which bounded one side of the walk. At the bottom was a small ravine in which the reckless had flung ashes and tins. "I s'pose you could ride down that bank?"

All eyes now turned upon Jimmie to detect a sign of his weakening, but he instantly and sublimely arose to the occasion. "That bank?" he asked, scornfully. "Why, I've ridden down banks like that many a time. Ain't I, Clarence?"

This was too much for the company. A sound like the wind in the leaves arose; it was the song of incredulity and ridicule. "O-o-o-o-o!" And on the outskirts a little girl suddenly shrieked out, "Story-teller!"

Horace had certainly won a skirmish. He was gleeful. "Oh, you can do wonders!" he gurgled. "You can do wonders!" The neighborhood's superficial hostility to foreigners arose like magic under the influence of his sudden success, and Horace had the delight of seeing Jimmie persecuted in that manner known only to children and insects.

Jimmie called angrily to the boy on the velocipede, "If you'll lend me yours, I'll show you whether I can or not."

Horace turned his superior nose in the air. "Oh no! I don't ever lend it." Then he thought of a blow which would make Jimmie's humiliation complete. "Besides," he said, airily, "'tain't really anything hard to do. I could do it—easy—if I wanted to."

But his supposed adherents, instead of receiving this boast with cheers, looked upon him in a sudden blank silence. Jimmie and his retainer pounced like cats upon their advantage.

"Oh," they yelled, "You *could*, eh? Well, let's see you do it, then! Let's see you do it! Let's see you do it! Now!" In a moment the crew of little spectators were gibing at Horace.

The blow that would make Jimmie's humiliation complete! Instead, it had boomeranged Horace into the mud. He kept up a sullen muttering:

"'Tain't really anything! I could if I wanted to!"

"Dare you to!" screeched Jimmie and his partisans. "Dare you to! Dare you to! Dare you to!"

There were two things to be done—to make gallant effort or to retreat. Somewhat to their amazement, the children at last found Horace moving through their clamor to the edge of the bank. Sitting on the velocipede, he looked at the ravine, and then, with gloomy pride, at the other children. A hush came upon them, for it was seen that he was intending to make some kind of an ante-mortem statement.

"I—" he began. Then he vanished from the edge of the walk. The start had been unintentional—an accident.

The stupefied Jimmie saw the calamity through a haze. His first clear vision was when Horace, with a face as red as a red flag, arose bawling from his tangled velocipede. He and his retainer exchanged a glance of horror and fled the neighborhood. They did not look back until they had reached the top of the hill near the lake. They could see Horace walking slowly under the maples towards his home, pushing his shattered velocipede before him. His chin was thrown high, and the breeze bore them the sound of his howls.[6]

1

Vladimir Nabokov

The Summer of '15

From *Mary*

In marked respects, Vladimir Nabokov's first novel, Mary, *is of the literary genre which Katherine Anne Porter's* The Ship of Fools *exemplified and made popular.*

It is the tale of persons thrown together for a time under unusual and often trying circumstances. The focus is not so much on individuals as such but on individuals within a small and rather unique social setting.

The situation in Mary *is simple. Russian émigrés are gathered together in a pension (or boardinghouse) in Berlin in 1925. But the personalities of the characters are complex. Ganin, the protagonist, is twenty-five years old and drifting listlessly from job to job after a tour of duty as a Russian soldier in the Crimean War. Klara, also twenty-five, and frequently described as "full busted," decries the mundanity of her life as a clerk-typist and pines wistfully over her unrequited love for Ganin. Podtyagin, the septuagenarian of the group, is a poet of some renown who is moved by a single-minded passion to visit France which his fumbling ways and ailing health frustrate at every turn. Alfyorov, who brims with health, and apparent finances, is a faucet of conversation which cannot be shut off. And finally there are the effeminate ballet dancers, Kolin and Gorantsvetov, who bubble while life in the boardinghouse simmers about them.*

Above all, though, the novel centers on Ganin. And Ganin, as Nabokov admits in his preface, is a fictionalized self-image. A more realistic version of the incidents in Mary *is portrayed in Nabokov's partial autobiography,* Speak, Memory.

As we learn there, the bicycle was a constant companion in Nabokov's youth. His father was, as he recalls him, a "dedicated cyclist" whom he joined on bicycle rides. Even the Galliwogg of his children's stories went on a Maurice Sendak-type bicycle trip,

From Vladimir Nabokov, *Mary* (New York: McGraw-Hill Book Company, 1959), pp. 34, 44–48, 67–68, 71–73.

fraught with wild danger and haunting adventure. A chum visited him after traversing many miles on a bicycle. One of his many tutors, Max by name, was assisted by a fully accessoried bicycle to a "remote trysting place" for his meetings with an Irish lass. And Nabokov himself used the bicycle to venture into his butterfly haunts. On more boyishly daring excursions, we are told by Nabokov's biographer, Andrew Field, of young Nabokov's "being caught by a narrowing strip of beach at Biarritz between a clayey cliffside and the surf with his brother on bicycles in 1909 as the bikes slipped and foundered and the swift tide rushed in." Naturally, therefore, the bicycle will claim a place in his novels, particularly those of an evident autobiographical turn like Mary.

The setting for Nabokov's youthful romance, fictionalized in Mary, was his family's summer house at Vyra, their retreat after the winters endured at 47 Morskaya, St. Petersburg. As Andrew Field, in his Nabokov: His Life in Part, *recounts the events of those days*

Life in the city was quite formal, and there were restrictions of class and times. It was natural that first love should appear in the relaxed and much more open atmosphere of Vyra. . . . The romance lasted almost exactly one year, from the end of the summer of 1915 to the end of the following summer. Many years afterward the girl's sister appeared in emigration, and thereby some information as to the fate of his youthful love did reach Nabokov, but rather uncertain and secondhand.

She was one year younger than Nabokov, had at least a brother and two sisters, one a beauty very like her but slightly older and taller and slimmer. In 1915 their mother (the father was an estate manager who appears not to have figured very much in the life of his family at this time) rented a summer *dacha* for the family near the Rozhestvenskaya church. In the early part of the first summer Nabokov had his first encounter with a member of the family when he rode to the *dacha* together with his tutor to extend permission—at the same time declining to participate himself—for a soccer match that her older brother, then in officers' school, wished to arrange on one of the meadows belonging to the Nabokovs. Unknown to Nabokov his future love sat high up in the branches of an apple tree and looked down on the three as they talked. Her Russian nickname, oddly enough, was the exact equivalent of the French name Lucette.

That autumn and winter Nabokov would meet her in the Tavrichesky Gardens, a park at one end of Sergievskaya Street, a handsome residential street where the family lived in a flat, perhaps belonging to some relative, for the Sh's are not listed in *All Petrograd*—no matter, Vladimir Vladimirovich never went there with her, and she never went to 47 Morskaya with him. In writing about his first romance and the at first scarcely perceptible decline that it suffered upon its transfer to St. Petersburg, Vladimir Vladimirovich seems not to have taken into account a simple term and phenomenon: summer romance.[1]

This youthful romance was of such "particular primacy in the young Vladimir's affection and memory" that it appears again in his ethereal, mystical, and mystifying The Real Life of Sebastian Knight. *On one, simplistic, view of the plot, Sebastian Knight, the novelist, had died leaving a half-brother, six years younger, who is determined to give identity to the life of Sebastian. In the course of his evidence gathering, he tracks the woman whose "dark love" caused his brother so much anguish in his later years. The quest unexpectedly reveals aspects of Sebastian's first love that mesh, in important aspects, with the Vyra romance of Nabokov's own youth. As these incidents are transmuted into* The Real Life of Sebastian Knight, *Sebastian was sixteen and so was his "dark love." They are alone in the sight of a sky overflowing with stars. He asks if she must go. But she makes no response.*

Sebastian, still not alone, is seated on the white-and-cinder-grey trunk of a felled tree. His bicycle rests, its spokes a-glitter among the bracken. A Camberwell Beauty skims past and settles on the kerf, fanning its velvety wings. Back to town to-morrow, school beginning on Monday.

"Is this the end? Why do you say that we shall not see each other this winter?" he asks for the second or third time. No answer. "Is it true that you think you've fallen in love with that student chap?—*vetovo studenta?*" The seated girl's shape remains blank except for the arm and a thin brown hand toying with a bicycle pump. With the end of the holder it slowly writes on the soft earth the word "yes," in English, to make it gentler.[2]

In Mary, *Nabokov's summer of 1915 at Vyra becomes the focus on Ganin's reminiscences as he wanders, with well-directed aimlessness, in a public garden in Berlin in April 1925. He recalls that summer when his first and still greatest love set fire to his veins. He was then sixteen and recovering from typhoid fever. In his condition of weakness and recuperation, he was fair game for the new and unfathomable sensations that his Mary would stir in him.*

The contrast between his remembered happiness in his Russian boyhood and his present rootlessness as an émigré in a Berlin boardinghouse is so deep and so disturbing that it moves him to reflect:

"And where is it all now?" mused Ganin. "Where is the happiness, the sunshine, where are those thick skittles of wood which crashed and bounced so nicely, where is my bicycle with the low handlebars and the big gear? It seems there's a law which says that nothing ever vanishes, that matter is indestructible; therefore the chips from my skittles and the spokes of my bicycle still exist somewhere to this day. The pity of it is that I'll never find them again—never. I once read about the 'eternal return.' But what if this complicated game of patience never comes out a second time? Let me see—there's something I don't grasp—yes, this: surely it won't all die when I do? Right now I'm alone in a foreign city. Drunk. My head's buzzing from beer laced with cognac. I have tramped my fill. And if my heart burst, right now, then my whole world bursts with it? Cannot grasp it."[3]

Ganin's plaintive reflections are those of lovers everywhere and at all times when they realize that the singularity of their first love has slipped into the obscurity of a pallid memory. There is nothing unique, in literature or in life, about the lamentations of Ganin. Turgenev, Nabokov's compatriot and predecessor, has given us Vladimir Piotrovich, who at forty is called upon to relate the details of the summer of 1833 when, as a rather brash sixteen-year-old, he experienced his First Love. *Like Ganin, Vladimir, or "M'sieur Voldemar" as his love terms him, rails at the evanescence of the joys of first love.*

O gentle feelings, tender sounds, the benignity and assuagement of the deeply moved soul, the melting joy of love's first emotions—where are you now, where are you now?[4]

Mary might have remained nothing but an infrequent and searing memory for Ganin if it had not been for the puckishness of Alfyorov. Alfyorov, Ganin's immediate neighbor in the rooming house, could not hold his tongue on the matter of the imminent arrival of his wife, or on any other subject. As a consequence of that verbal impetuosity, Ganin learns that Alfyorov's wife is also the Mary of his youth. He immediately soars into a wonderland where Mary's pending arrival resurrects a summer which he is convinced, in the quixotic way of the romantic heart, he is destined to relive.

But memory is elusive, halting and deceptive and that of the lover all the more so. So Ganin discovers as he seeks to recall the exact details of his summer with Mary.

That evening in July Ganin had pushed open the creaking iron front door and walked out into the blue of the twilight. The bicycle ran with special ease at dusk, the tire emitting a kind of whisper as it palpated each rise and dip in the hard earth along the edge of the road. As he glided past the darkened stables they gave off a breath of warmth, a sound of snorting and the slight thud of a shifting hoof. Further on, the road was enveloped on both sides by birch trees, noiseless at that hour; then like a fire smouldering on the threshing-floor a faint light shone in the middle of a field and dark streams of people straggled with a festive hum toward the lone-standing barn.

Inside a stage had been knocked up, rows of seats installed, light flooded over heads and shoulders, playing in people's eyes, and there was a smell of caramels and kerosene. A lot of people had turned up; the back was filled with peasant men and women, the dacha folk were in the middle, while in front, on white benches borrowed from the manorial park, sat about twenty patients from the military hospital in the village, quiet and morose, with hairless patches blotching the gray-blue of their very round, shorn heads. Here and there on the walls, decorated with fir branches were cracks through which peeped the starry night as well as the black shadows of country boys who had clambered up outside on tall piles of logs.

The opera bass from Petersburg, a gaunt man with a face like a horse, gave forth a cavernal boom; the village school choir, obedient to the melodious flick of a tuning fork, joined in with the refrain.

Amid the hot yellow glare, amid the sounds that took on visible form in the folds of crimson and silvery headscarves, fluttering eyelashes, black shadows on the roof beams shifting whenever there was a puff of the night breeze, amid all this glitter and popular music, among all the heads and shoulders in the large, crowded barn, Ganin saw only one thing: he stared ahead at a brown tress tied with a black bow, slightly frayed at the edges, and his eyes caressed the dark, smooth, girlish sheen of the hair at her temple. Whenever she turned her face sideways to give the girl sitting beside her one of her rapid smiling glances, he could also see the strong color in her cheek, the corner of a flashing, Tartar eye, the delicate curve of her nostril alternately stretching and tightening as she laughed. Later, when the concert was over, the Petersburg bass was driven away in the local mill owner's huge car which cast a mysterious light over the grass and then, with a sweep of its beam, dazzled a sleeping birch tree and the footbridge over a brook; and when the crowd of fair vacationists, in a festive flutter of white frocks, drifted away through the blue darkness across the dew-laden clover, and someone lit a cigarette in the dark, holding the flaring match to his face in cupped hands—Ganin, in a state of lonely excitement, walked home, the spokes of his bicycle clicking faintly as he pushed it by the saddle. . . .

He could not remember when it was he saw her next, whether it was the following day or a week later. At sunset, before evening tea, he had swung himself onto the wedge of sprung leather, had bent forward over the handlebars and ridden off straight into the western flow. He always chose the same circular route, through two hamlets divided by a pine wood, and then along the highway, between fields and back home through the big village of Voskresensk which lay on the river Oredezh, sung by Ryleev a century before. He knew the road by heart, now narrow and flat, with its compact margin running alongside a dangerous ditch, now paved with cobblestones which made his front wheel bounce, elsewhere scored with treacherous ruts, then smooth, pink and firm—he knew that road by feel and by sight, as one knows a living body, and he rode expertly along it, pressing resilient pedals into a rustling void.

The evening sun banded the rough trunks of a pine coppice with red fire; from dacha gardens came the knocking of croquet balls; midges kept getting into one's mouth and eyes.

Occasionally on the highway he would stop by a little pyramid of roadbuilding stone above which a telegraph pole, its wood peeling in grayish strips, gave off a gentle, desolate hum. He would lean on his bicycle, looking across the fields at one of those forest fringes only found in Russia, remote, serrated, black, while above it the golden west was broken only by a single long lilac cloud from under which the rays spread out like a burning fan. And as he stared at the sky and listened to a cow mooing almost dreamily in a distant village, he tried to understand what it all meant—that sky, and the fields, and the humming telegraph pole; he felt that he was just on the point of understanding it when suddenly his head would start to spin and the lucid languor of the moment became intolerable.

He had no idea where he might meet her or overtake her, at what turn of the road, in this copse or the next. She lived in Voskresensk and would go out for a walk in the deserted sunny evening at exactly the same time as he. Ganin noticed her from a distance and at once felt a chill round his heart. She walked briskly, blue-skirted, her hands in the pockets of her blue serge jacket under which was a white blouse. As Ganin caught up with her, like a soft breeze, he saw only the folds of blue stuff stretching and rippling across her back, and the black silk bow like two outstretched wings. As he glided past he never looked into her face but pretended to be absorbed in cycling, although a minute earlier imagining their meeting, he had sworn that he would smile at her and greet her. In those days he thought she must have some unusual, resounding name, and when he found out from the same student that she was called Mary he was not at all surprised, as though he had known it in advance—and that simple little name took on for him a new sound, an entrancing significance.

"Mary," Ganin whispered, "Mary." He took a deep breath and held it, listening to the beating of his heart. It was about three o'clock in the morning, the trains did not run, and as a result the house seemed to have come to a standstill. On the chair, its arms flung out like a man struck rigid in the middle of a prayer, there hung in the darkness the vague white shape of his cast-off shirt.

"Mary," Ganin repeated again, trying to put into those two syllables all the music that they had once held—the wind, the humming of telegraph poles, the happiness—together with another, secret sound which gave that word its very life. He lay on his back and listened to his past. And presently from the next room came a low, gentle, intrusive tu-tu- tu-tu-: Alfyorov was looking forward to Saturday. . . .

As lovers will, Ganin and Mary set apart their own special place where the secrecy of their trysting could add an uninterrupted and unique glitter to their romance. Their rendezvous was on the terrace of a deserted white mansion across the river from the estate of Ganin's parents.

And now, in the darkness and gloom of an early spring night in Berlin, Ganin is reminded of that secluded place and the love he savored there. The unromantic aroma of carbide from a garage which he passes while strolling to avoid the conversational inanity of Alfyorov recalls his hurried and excited nocturnal bicycle trips, illuminated by a carbide lamp, to the deserted mansion and the waiting there for his Mary.

Straight out of the bright country house, he would plunge into the black, bubbling darkness and ignite the soft flame of his bicycle lamp; and now, when he inhaled that smell of carbide, it brought back everything at once: the wet grasses whipping against his moving leg and wheel spokes; the disk of milky light that imbibed and dissolved the obscurity; the different objects that emerged from it—now a wrinkled puddle, or a glistening pebble, then the bridge planks carpeted with horse dung, then, finally, the turnstile of the wicket, through which he pushed, with the rain-drenched pea-tree hedge yielding to the sweep of his shoulder.

Presently, through the streams of the night, there became visible the slow rotation of columns, washed by the same gentle whitish beam of his bicycle lamp; and there on the six-columned porch of a stranger's closed mansion Ganin was welcomed by a blur of cool fragrance, a blend of perfume and damp serge—and that autumnal rain kiss was so long and so deep that afterward great luminous spots swam before one's eyes and the broad-branching, many-leaved, rustling sound of the rain seemed to acquire new force. With rain-wet fingers he opened the little lantern's glass door and blew out the light. Out of the darkness a humid and heavy pressure of gusty air reached the lovers. Mary, now perched on the peeling balustrade, caressed his temples with the cold palm of her little hand and he could make out in the dark the vague outline of her soggy hairbow and the smiling brilliance of her eyes.

In the whirling blackness the strong, ample downpour surged through the limes facing the porch and drew creaks from their trunks, which were banded with iron clasps to support their decaying might. And amid the hubbub of the autumn night, he unbuttoned her blouse, kissed her hot clavicle; she remained silent—only her eyes glistened faintly, and the skin of her bared breast slowly turned cold from the touch of his lips and the humid night wind. They spoke little, it was too dark to speak. When at last he struck a match to consult his watch, Mary blinked and brushed a wet strand of hair from her cheek. He flung his arm around her while impelling his bicycle with one hand placed on its saddle, and thus slowly walked away in the night, now reduced to a drizzle; first there was the descent along the path to the bridge, and then the farewell there, protracted and sorrowful, as though before a long separation. . . .

But the inevitable moment came when the lovers were separated and then reunited in a different place and time and separated once again. Out of each other's presence and that of their deserted mansion, their love fluctuated between moments of rekindled emotion and others more moribund, without flame and nearly without fire.

And then the reunion which would determine the course and current of their love was signalled by a telephone conversation between them.

Her voice crackled weakly from a great distance, a noise hummed in the telephone as in a seashell, at times an even more distant voice on a crossed line kept interrupting, carrying on conversations with someone else in the fourth dimension—the telephone in their country house was an old one with a hand crank—and between Mary and him lay thirty miles of roaring darkness.

"I'll come to see you," Ganin shouted into the receiver. "I'm saying I'll come. On my bicycle. It'll take a couple of hours."

"—didn't want to stay at Voskresensk again. D'you hear? Papa refused to rent a dacha at Voskresensk again. From your place to this town it's thirty—"

"Don't forget to bring those boots," interrupted a low, unconcerned voice.

Then Mary was heard again through the buzzing, in miniature, as if she were speaking from the wrong end of a telescope. And when she had vanished altogether Ganin leaned against the wall and felt that his ears were burning.

He set off at about three o'clock in the afternoon, in an open-necked shirt and football shorts, rubber-soled shoes on his sockless feet. With the wind behind him he rode fast, picking out the smooth patches between sharp flints on the highway, and he remembered how he used to ride past Mary last July before he ever knew her.

After ten miles or so his back tire burst, and he spent a long time repairing it, seated on the edge of a ditch. Larks sang above the fields on both sides of the road; a gray convertible sped by in a cloud of gray dust, carrying two military men in owlish goggles. The tire mended, he pumped it up hard and rode on, aware that he had not allowed for this and was already an hour behind time. Turning off the highway he rode through a wood along a path shown to him by a passing muzhik. Then he took another turning, but a wrong one this time, and continued for a long while before getting back onto the right road again. He rested and had a bite to eat in a little village, and then, when he only had some eight miles to go, he ran over a sharp stone and once more the same tire expired with a whistle.

It was already getting dark when he reached the small town where Mary was spending the summer. She was waiting for him at the gates of the public park, as they had agreed, but she had already given up hope of his coming as she had been waiting since six o'clock. When she saw him she stumbled with excitement and almost fell. She was wearing a diaphanous white dress which Ganin did not know. Her black bow had gone, and, in result, her adorable head seemed smaller. There were blue corn-flowers in her piled-up hair.

That night, in the strange stealthily deepening darkness, under the lindens of that spacious public park, on a stone slab sunk deep in moss, Ganin in the course of one brief tryst grew to love her more poignantly than before and fell out of love with her, as it seemed then, forever.

At first they conversed in a rapturous murmur—about the long time they had not seen each other, about the resemblance of a glowworm that shone in the moss to a tiny semaphore. Her dear, dear Tartar eyes glided near his face, her white dress seemed to shimmer in the dark—and oh, God, that fragrance of hers, incomprehensible, unique in the world!

"I am yours," she said, "do what you like with me."

In silence, his heart thumping, he leaned over her running his hands along her soft, cool legs. But the public park was alive with odd rustling sounds, somebody seemed to be continuously approaching from behind the bushes, the chill and the hardness of the stone slab hurt his bare knees; and Mary lay there too submissive, too still.

He stopped; then emitted an awkward short laugh. "I keep feeling that someone's around," said Ganin and got up.

Mary sighed, rearranged her dress—a whitish blur—and stood up, too.

As they walked back to the park gate along a moon-flecked path, she stooped over the grass and picked up one of the pale green lampyrids they had noticed. She held it upon the flat of her hand, bending over it, examining it closely, then burst out laughing and said in a quaint parody of a village lass, "Bless me, if it isn't simply a cold little worm."

It was then that Ganin, tired, cross at himself, freezing in his thin shirt, decided that it was all over, that he was no longer enamored of Mary. And a few minutes later, when he was cycling in the moonlight haze homeward along the pale surface of the road, he knew that he would never visit her again.

Ganin's prediction proved to be correct, for the lovers never did visit again, either before or after Ganin's departure from Russia. A fleeting and happenstance railway-station meeting was all that followed this last encounter.

2

D. H. Lawrence

The Bitter Ecstasy of Young Love

From *Sons and Lovers*

When Paul Morel, at eighteen, went to Willey Farm, he went by bicycle. Miriam Leivers, whom Paul was tutoring in French, would await his arrival with eyes fixed on the minute hand. The pupil was devoted more to the young teacher than to the subject he taught.

Movement is an evident theme in D. H. Lawrence's Sons and Lovers. *Travel by train, tram, foot and bicycle occurs more than the full-time clerkship of Paul and his part-time commitment to painting would seem to permit. Movement is also used to highlight the transitions in the action as Paul matures. He moves from a groping, arm's-length love for Miriam to a fiery but frustrating passion for the worldly Mrs. Clara Dawes. It is only from his doting mother that Paul does not and cannot move.*

Paul's bicycling serves a number of artistic purposes. When Paul is described as coming "into the yard [at Willey Farm] with his bicycle, which glittered as he walked," Paul's person is enhanced by the presence of the bicycle. Again, the bicycle is enlivened by its proximity to Paul. So, "he walked in a nonchalant fashion, and his bicycle went with him as if it were a live thing."

When Paul suffers the indignity of a drubbing by the cuckolded Baxter Dawes, he exhorts his mother to "say it was a bicycle-accident." The lie makes the wounds more tolerable. Later, when Paul visits Baxter Dawes at Colonel Seely's Home, where he is invalided, a friendship arises between them. When Baxter asks "What made that scar on

Excerpted from D. H. Lawrence, *Sons and Lovers* (New York: Thomas Seltzer, Inc.), pp. 223–25, 255, 266, 431.

your mouth?," Paul "put his hand hastily to his lips and looked over the garden. 'I had a bicycle accident,' he said." The lie makes the friendship more durable.

The bicycle also is witness to and part of the coming and the going of Paul's love for Miriam. After one session, at which Verlaine is featured, Paul prepares to leave the Willey Farm at ten o'clock with "dark and shining" eyes and "a kind of fascination about him."

When he went into the barn for his bicycle he found the front wheel punctured.

"Fetch me a drop of water in a bowl," he said to her. "I shall be late, and then I s'll catch it."

He lighted the hurricane lamp, took off his coat, turned up the bicycle, and set speedily to work. Miriam came with the bowl of water and stood close to him, watching. She loved to see his hands doing things. He was slim and vigorous, with a kind of easiness even in his most hasty movements. And busy at his work, he seemed to forget her. She loved him absorbedly. She wanted to run her hands down his sides. She always wanted to embrace him, so long as he did not want her.

"There!" he said, rising suddenly. "Now, could you have done it quicker?"

"No!" she laughed.

He straightened himself. His back was towards her. She put her two hands on his sides, and ran them quickly down.

"You are so *fine!*" she said.

He laughed, hating her voice, but his blood roused to a wave of flame by her hands. She did not seem to realize *him* in all this. He might have been an object. She never realized the male he was.

He lighted his bicycle-lamp, bounced the machine on the barn floor to see that the tires were sound, and buttoned his coat.

"That's all right!" he said.

She was trying the brakes, that she knew were broken.

"Did you have them mended?" she asked.

"No!"

"But why didn't you?"

"The back one goes on a bit."

"But it's not safe."

"I can use my toe."

"I wish you'd had them mended," she murmured.

"Don't worry—come to tea tomorrow, with Edgar."

"Shall we?"

"Do—about four. I'll come to meet you."

"Very well."

She was pleased. They went across the dark yard to the gate. Looking across, he saw through the uncurtained window of the kitchen the heads of Mr. and Mrs. Leivers in the warm glow. It looked very cosy. The road, with pine-trees, was quite black in front.

"Till tomorrow," he said, jumping on his bicycle.

"You'll take care, won't you?" she pleaded.

"Yes."

His voice already came out of the darkness. She stood a moment watching the light from his lamp race into obscurity along the ground. She turned very slowly indoors. Orion was wheeling up over the wood, his dog twinkling after him, half smothered. For the rest, the world was full of darkness, and silent, save for the breathing of cattle in their stalls. She prayed earnestly for his safety that night. When he left her, she often lay in anxiety, wondering if he had got home safely.

He dropped down the hills on his bicycle. The roads were greasy, so he had to let it go. He felt a pleasure as the machine plunged over the second, steeper drop in the hill. "Here goes!" he said. It was risky, because of the curve in the darkness at the bottom, and because of the brewers' waggons with drunken waggoners asleep. His bicycle seemed to fall beneath him, and he loved it. Recklessness is almost a man's revenge on his woman. He feels he is not valued, so he will risk destroying himself to deprive her altogether.

The stars on the lake seemed to leap like grasshoppers, silver upon the blackness, as he spun past. Then there was the long climb home. . . .

But later, when Clara has dimmed his ardor for Miriam, he arrives at Willey Farm to find Miriam nervous, watchful and querulous.

"You were late," she said.

"Was I?" he answered.

There was silence for a while.

"Was it rough riding? she asked.

"I didn't notice it."

She continued quickly to lay the table. When she had finished—

"Tea won't be for a few minutes. Will you come and look at the daffodils?" she said.

He rose without answering. They went out into the back garden under the budding damson-trees. The hills and the sky were clean and cold. Everything looked washed, rather hard. Miriam glanced at Paul. He was pale and impassive. It seemed cruel to her that his eyes and brows, which she loved, could look so hurting.

"Has the wind made you tired?" she asked. She detected an underneath feeling of weariness about him.

"No, I think not," he answered.

"It must be rough on the road—the wood moans so."

"You can see by the clouds it's a south-west wind; that helps me here."

"You see, I don't cycle, so I don't understand," she murmured.

"Is there need to cycle to know that?" he said. . . .

Paul's cruelty to Miriam brings him to an early departure from Willey Farm, for he knows that whatever fondness beyond friendship they had had is ended.

Miriam sat in the rocking-chair, and did not speak. He hesitated, expecting her to rise and go with him to the barn as usual for his bicycle. She remained as she was. He was at a loss.

"Well—good-night all!" he faltered.

She spoke her good-night along with all the others. But as he went past the window he looked in. She saw him pale, his brows knit slightly in a way that had become constant with him, his eyes dark with pain.

She rose and went to the doorway to wave good-bye to him as he passed through the gate. He rode slowly under the pine-trees, feeling a cur and a miserable wretch. His bicycle went tilting down the hills at random. He thought it would be a relief to break one's neck.

3

Uwe Johnson

Learning to Endure

From *The Third Book about Achim*

A road racer without endurance is like a bicycle without wheels. Neither is equal to the task for which it is intended. For both, that task is motion, but for the road racer it is motion of a most punishing and demanding kind. It is motion in extremis over long distances, for the success of which a total commitment to physical training and mental concentration is essential.

Like the road racer, the young lover must learn to endure, in that case, the pains and penalties of loves that flourish for a moment, then languish and die. Achim T. was a road racer, so Uwe Johnson tells us in his novel of the writing of the third biography of Achim. And Achim's young manhood was spend in a Germany that first demanded quickstepping allegiance to the Hitler movement and later to the Communist Party, at least as to those like Achim, living in East Germany.

Achim lived to see and to believe in the Hitlerian ideology. He also lived to outgrow that fanaticism into a new dedication to the regime of communism. All of this transpired while Achim was sixteen and experiencing the normal stirrings of interest in romance.

Achim reflects the confusion and the uncertainty of his time and his place. He wants to be like the others of his age and have a girlfriend of his own. But he also wishes to excel, in this case, as a bicyclist. In all respects, he shies from the embarrassment of failing either in romance or in bicycling.

There is no necessary incompatibility between his romantic aspirations and his bicycling. Indeed, the distance he must bicycle to visit his young love teaches him to practice at bettering his bicycling style and time day by day. The challenge of his bicycling so preoccupies him that it seems ultimately that he is bicycling less to be with his nameless

From Uwe Johnson. *The Third Book about Achim* (New York: Harcourt Brace Jovanovich, 1967), pp. 125–33.

love than to be bicycling against the clock. His time trialing succeeds where his amorous quest fails. But it is all of a piece—flat and unemotional—mirroring the burned out character of the time and the place in which Achim lived.

What does it mean: He was alone?

For a while he was alone. After the armistice the school in the neighboring village opened its doors again (not in this village then; that was an error). It was an hour's walk, but Achim rode over on the bicycle he had been given. The upper grades sat huddled together in the low run-down room whose windows looked out on the church square. They were taught two hours in succession, one group watching the other. Diagonally in front of Achim was the neck of a girl between stiff black braids. They'd jerk each time she moved her head. After some time he'd feel inexplicably startled when he saw the outlines of her face from the side against the November light with the temples in the shadow above the eyes. Once every two weeks his father would send him a picture postcard. They showed the opera house the way it no longer looked and the market square without the rubble and the central station intact. Achim answered: We took the turnips in. I'm fine. He had no idea why they were estranged.

He enjoyed working his grandfather's fields. He liked feeling tired. He remembered where he had seen the girl who sat in front of him in class. He had passed her on his bicycle, coming back from the meadow with a pitchfork in one hand. She was herding the cows home that belonged to the farmer with whom her mother had found lodging. She had to herd the cows. The hoofs of the thin beasts with their brown and white markings were rubbing low dust clouds off the path. She was following them, barefoot in the swirling sand, the stick dangling loosely in her arm. The path sloped gently down toward the first houses, the bushes on either side were white with sand, her skirt was torn and full of spots. She looked up when he passed. He would have liked to say something. She lifted her head and looked at him, quietly, gaily. Tiny curls fell from her part onto her forehead. After a while he turned to look back and saw her trim little figure leap over the fence around the pasture. The bushes along the path were silhouetting the slope against the sky, her surprising glance lay in the shadow of the colored evening light. All the boys his age had a girl friend.

In the winter his father stopped sending cards for some weeks, but people would come from the cities with their woolen clothes and optical instruments in knapsacks, to be exchanged for potatoes or maybe turnips. The grandmother had begun to ask Achim every time she bought or gave away something; he was sixteen now, he was the man in the house. He sat with a fozen woman close to the stove, questioning her while the grandmother filled the shabby shopping bag. She was grateful, she took him for the farmer. She told about the dead American soldiers lying face-down around the last Hitler fortress, not one of them shot in the back. The streetcars were running again every now and then. The Soviet headquarters had been installed in the town hall. The troops weren't distributing food any more, but the bakers still didn't have enough flour. The pillaging was over, but the streets were still unsafe at night. They've just cleared the rubble at the corner of the market square. Many many thanks. Do you want me to take a letter? Achim shook his head. He lived as though he couldn't feel. He saw everything, but he couldn't put it together in his mind. He hoped his uniform had burned up. Sometimes he felt like writing long letters to his mother.

After the Christmas vacation he passed the cow girl several times on the way home. She didn't always walk with the others. He rode quickly past her. He saw her worn-out shoes on the crunching path and the clouds of her breath in the icy air. Then he turned around and barred her path with his bicycle.—No need to walk: he said clumsily.

She looked up, questioningly, friendly. Her frosted shawl fluttered about her head. She hadn't understood what he said. She was a refugee.

—Do you know how to ride a bicycle? he asked. She nodded. He took his satchel from the handlebars and held the bike out to her. Let's take turns: he said. He looked after her, wobbling off on the swaying bicycle. The saddle was too high for her, she had to stand on the pedals. He was prepared to be happy. He was disappointed. After two hundred yards she leaned the bicycle against a tree and went on walking. She had her hands in her pockets. When he passed her, she looked up with a quiet laugh. He waved to her when he got off again and left the bike for her on the path. She waved back. For three miles they took turns that way. She had already reached the end of the little forest down the long slope close to the first houses when he saw three men in uniforms come out of a path. They barred the road, waiting for her with outspread arms, stopped her by the handle bars, made her get down and walked off with the bicycle. The confusion of small black creatures in the snow looked very graceful seen from the top of the hill. They tried to ride all three at once, one on the handle bars, one on the saddle, and one on the rack, at the bend they disappeared out of sight. Achim was already running. When he reached her, she was still standing at the same spot, hugging her satchel, in tears. She was fourteen.

—But it isn't your fault: said Achim. He tried to wipe the tears from her face, but he hurt her with his stiff frozen glove. He took it off. He felt happy touching the skin around her eyes. And when she raised her head. For a year and a half he went with her, always waiting for the pulsing in his temples to return, but it would only come as a memory or when he thought of her, not when they were together. He thought he ought to trust her now.—So your mother is dead? she said placidly, she had seen lots of people dead or dying, during her flight. He hadn't been able to say it. And he didn't like to speak about the destruction in the city and war games in uniform. The only thing that remained from those days was his sure, hard-hitting fist that defended her and himself against the teasing and the jealousy of their classmates; that was one useful thing he had learned.

He asked his grandmother to allow her and her mother to stay in the living room. She had to work so hard in the farmer's house, and the farmer screamed at her, once he had beaten her even. But nothing came of it. One day Achim found his father sitting in the kitchen when he returned from the fields. Both of them were embarrassed, they hardly looked at each other when they shook hands. The high embarrassed tone of the question made Achim forget himself.

—Yes: he said. I'll come with you.

Then it struck him that he had forgotten her. That time they both had gone to the Soviet headquarters together and described how they had lost the bicycle. In their awkward Russian each of them had tried to explain to the lieutenant that it hadn't been a German bicycle any more. That it had been a gift. The lieutenant laughed a great deal about their way of speaking. Finally he allowed them to go out in the yard and find their bicycle among the others.

When they came back, they saw him standing on the stairs, jiggling his hands in his pockets.—You've got a very pretty girl: he said to Achim in Russian.

—Yes: said Achim. Now he had a girl. Like all the other boys his age. And she was even prettier than the others. He felt sorry for her because he was leaving. Only much later did it occur to him that he could have stayed.

—I'll come to see you: he said. That was the same evening at the fence, he had called her out of the stable. She was holding on to the slats with both hands and paid no attention to the farmer who kept shouting for her. She didn't cry. She looked at him inaccessibly and said: So it's over.

—I'll really come to see you: Achim said distractedly. He wasn't sure where he actually belonged, perhaps he couldn't take her seriously. . . .

And how did he get into racing?

Until the following spring he rode over to see her. It was a little less than four hours by bicycle. He'd get there before noon, eat lunch with his grandmother and do for her whatever chores remained to be done (the water buckets were beginning to be some-what heavy for her and when she chopped firewood she'd often have to rest against the block). In the afternoon he'd try to see his girl. Her mother liked him; she thought him faithful for riding all that way to see her, she'd send her daughter out to him. Then it was as she had said: over.

—I came on my bike.

—Did you?

—Three and a half hours.

—And halfway down the hill the chain popped off.

—Did you see my father the day he was here?

—No.

For hours she could walk beside him and never say a word. But she didn't look angry; almost content, with her hands in her coat pockets, letting him do the talking. He couldn't get through to her. Her firm fifteen-year-old silhouette that seemed so tender in his memory grew less familiar when he saw her, more indispensable from a distance. When he shook her hand in the evening, she'd turn and run. His hand would remember the shy polite pressure of her fingers on the ride home through the night, blindly raging against himself he'd pedal faster and faster and keep seeing her from the back, sometimes behind closing eyelids.

Three and a half hours? Why not less? He was happy getting up alone on Sunday mornings, tiptoeing past his sleeping father to the door of the shed. The garden lay cool and untouched. He'd ride toward her in the very early morning, the air still moist with dew along deserted road ribbons and Sunday villages. Trade school and building lots, the strangers in their house, orders from the Soviet headquarters would form an irritating indistinguishable mixture in his head; suddenly he'd wake up and notice that he was pedaling very slowly, as though his legs were hesitating, pondering. Only when he'd concentrate all his attention on the relationship of body and bicycle (the sensation of motion) and speed up his pedaling, carefully breathing, until he'd experience a bearable and pleasant feeling of exertion, would his contentment be complete. He'd feel in tune with himself. Rushing downhill, sometimes with the wind coming from a certain angle, this feeling would soar very high.

The ride back was unhappy. He was clumsy enough to bring it up.

—Can't you forget it? he said, he was already lying, he couldn't forget it either. But he could only imagine how it felt to live four weeks of disappointment. He felt obliged to feel guilty.

In a fury she kept slapping his face, his lips were taut and attentive as though she were accomplishing a difficult task. She was still crying when they came back to the village, it made him feel ashamed because of the people. The next time he came, she seemed to have been waiting for him.

Four and a half (and when I told her what the foreman had said, her eyes wandered and swam a bit and then she did say that she'd had a girl friend in East Prussia wherever that is who hadn't come along. Or perhaps that was some other time, before. What did she mean, and when I stopped talking, she looked quite friendly in the face, still I, hell well I don't know) hours. The roads were thick with snow, he had to keep in the car tracks. Then he'd get onto untraveled stretches where the narrow tires sank into the hard snow, he'd topple back and forth over the front wheel. For ten minutes he lay in the ditch and didn't care in the soft soaking cold. Then a truck came by and cleared a track for him. The sky was completely dark, the forest so very black.

He should have touched her

. . . Three hours and a quarter. Three hours and twenty minutes. All of a sudden she had forgiven him. She no longer protested when they teased her at school or in the village square about her lover from the city; Sunday mornings she'd wait along the road and in the evening she'd ride with him for a bit on the handle bars and wouldn't run back into the forest before he was completely out of sight behind the bend of the road at the three big rocks: She'd asked him never to turn around.

And yet he couldn't wait for the feeling of hard joy that came at the fast ride into the city under the first street lamps between sporadically mushrooming house fronts: he was home again, here he knew everything, here he was safe.

Three hours and five minutes, but that was an accidental result: someone on a bicycle passed him during the last thirty miles. It had never happened before, that's why he tried to catch up with him, to show the guy, and he was surprised how much effort it took.

He saw the apparently effortless spinning of the other guy's feet, his bicycle sounded different. For the first time Achim noticed a slim free-wheeling clutch shining beside three black toothy disks, wires ran along the frame, the whole structure looked much thinner and curved differently. That's easy. The other guy turned his head through one bent arm and nodded encouragement. Achim flattened his back like the other one and pedaled like mad. The other guy was wearing a sweat shirt under the puffed-out collar of his windbreaker; he let himself drift so that Achim could catch up. He was watching him.—Too angular, the way you pedal, too angular: he said. After a while he shook his head, regretfully. He spoke calmly with ease, while Achim panted. Sorry, man: he said: I'm in training. And pulled away, simply vanished (Achim said with a laugh, wanting to express how dumb and surprised he'd been ten years ago), quickly he was out of reach, impossible to catch up with, pedaled away smaller and smaller, disappeared as a dot on a straight stretch of road. A few more times Achim tried to pedal in the same frequency of tread as during the few minutes they had ridden side by side, but each time he'd fall back, more and more out of breath.

Those three hours and five minutes must have stuck in his bones until the clammy Monday mornings that fell and reasserted themselves as a memory; when loads of bricks and mortar tore his arms out of their sockets, when he sat behind the frosted glass of the trade-school windows, it may have occurred to him that everything was quite different: every idle second could be compressed into the heightened sensation of complete absorption, the obediently laboring bicycle would draw body and attention into a proud speedy solitude, cut through villages and leave them behind, rush through unknown forests, pass horse carts, tractor convoys, bicycling peasant women, more nimbly on the only road. Arriving meant delay, the skin around a girl's eyes tight with expectation arrested him and threw him back, finally, in the spring, the ride had become an aim in itself and expelled the image of the arrival: a child in a Sunday dress who'd appear out of the colorful grass, grave and happy she'd walk toward the clearing with demanding steps—

. . . after twenty-two miles in one hour the stop ought to be allowed to settle undisturbed with softly clasping brakes into the comforting exhaustion and the memory of a steep curve that had swallowed him up with a roar, crushed and dismissed him. Approximately the same distance in the opposite direction took him three hours, without stopping; he turned around at once.

4

Will and Ariel Durant

The Captain
and the Stoker

From *A Dual Autobiography*

In tandem parlance, the captain is the front runner and the stoker brings up the rear. That description is not nearly an accurate characterization of the relationship between Will and Ariel Durant. In their case, they seemed to shift roles without design or discomfort. Ariel, although thirteen years younger than Will, was in no sense dominated by him. Theirs was a union in which the back seat was either vacant or in constant rotation from one to the other.

Without Will and Ariel Durant, The Story of Civilization *never would have been written. And the story of their lives together, entitled* A Dual Autobiography, *might never have been written if Will had not bicycled from New York City some 150 miles to Albany, New York. Will's bicycle trip was his retreat from Ariel so that, in separation from her, he could decide if their relationship was to be made formal by marriage.*

Unfortunately for bicyclists, if not also for romantics, we know nothing of Will's 1913 trip to Albany by bicycle, except that it took three days and that he used "an old bicycle which had survived from my irresponsible years." So much do we learn from his partial and ill-disguised (under the pseudonym John Le Maire) autobiography entitled Transition. *On the other hand, we know a great deal of the return trip by canoe from Albany for he did, in* Transition, *write extensively of its hazards and hardships.*

Whereas Will used his bicycle trip to find solitude and time for quiet reflection, Ariel later embarked on a bicycle trip of her own to Boston from New Dorp, Staten Island, in order to speak her mind concerning Will's postmarital neglect of her.

From Will and Ariel Durant, *A Dual Autobiography* (New York: Simon and Schuster, 1977), pp. 53–54, 63–64.

If the Albany bicycle trip moved them to marry, the even longer Boston excursion kept the marriage intact.

When we returned to New York Will saddened me by arranging to bicycle all the way to Albany (150 miles), alone. Later he confessed that he had wanted a week in which to think, in quiet solitude, just what our relationship should be in the coming years. He had decided to spend four years in graduate studies at Columbia University, should he complete those years before venturing on marriage? He has told, in *Transition*, how he pedaled his way to Albany, climbing so many hills that he had no time to think of me; how, at Albany, he exchanged his bicycle for a canoe; how he paddled his way 150 miles down the Hudson, facing so many buffets from the waves made by steamboats and winds that he had no time to weigh all the pros and cons of marriage. In any case, he arrived in a storm, lodged his canoe at 186th Street on the Hudson, and came to me so exhausted that he collapsed at my feet with his head on my knees, and fell asleep. When he awoke we quietly assumed that we were pledged to each other forever. . . .

Two years later, in 1915, Will and Ariel have made their marital home in New Dorp, Staten Island, New York.

In retrospect it seems that we were happy in that far-out-of-the-way Eskimo retreat. A picture taken of us in 1915 shows no sign of misery, though it surprises me by proving that Will had already grown a beard—perhaps through unwillingness to shave himself in the cold mornings of those New Dorp winters. But looking back now I wonder that Will, usually considerate, could leave me alone through so many bitter days, with only one neighbor in the street—an old Victorian lady who never seemed to make up her mind whether I was a legal wife or a tramp who had found a winter's lodging with a fool. In any case I soon came to dread those occasions when Will would go off to Columbia, or to lecture in Brooklyn or the Bronx, or Philadelphia or Bethlehem, Pennsylvania. On such days I hardly dared move more than a few feet from the stove. I missed the wild freedom of Manhattan streets, and the exciting contacts and events at the Ferrer Center.

After reading half a hundred books I was ripe for rebellion. Some of the books fell in with my restless mood. Wedekind's *Awakening of Spring* seemed to call to me; Artsybashev's *Breaking Point* was almost a warning that I might go mad in that prison of love. In any case, one morning when Will was presumably watching paramecia rub bellies in the biological laboratory at Columbia, I packed a small bundle, jumped upon my bicycle, rode to the ferry, crossed to the Battery, and pedaled through the traffic of I don't remember what streets, and then along the Boston Post Road until, somewhere in Connecticut, one of my tires gave out. I stood desolate as the traffic passed by, heedless of my thumb. Then a truck stopped, and the driver asked did I need help. "Yes," I answered; "could you take me and my bike into the next town, where I can get a puncture fixed?" He agreed, but "First," he said, "come with me and let's have some fun," and he tried to pull me into the roadside woods. I resisted so lustily and loudly that he retired to his truck and drove on. Soon a passing motorist took me to a service station, and my tire was repaired. One bad man, one good man.

I rode on until my legs gave way. On the outskirts of a village I knocked at a door and asked for a night's lodging. I wore a divided skirt, and my hair was bobbed. The woman who answered my ring judged that I was just another disreputable vagrant; she closed the door in my face. At the next house I made sure to show my money, and I was given a room. On the following day I reached Boston, so tired that I almost collapsed on a park bench. I had the address of a Boston acquaintance, Dorothy Parrott, whom I had met in the birth control movement in New York, but I was in no condition to invade her rooms. A prim lady sat nearby; I feared that she was one of those Bostonians who spoke only to God; but I broke some ice between us by talking with her child. I asked her just to let me into her home to wash up before presenting myself to Miss Parrott, who lived nearby at 33 Bellingham Place. She agreed, and presently I found, with Dorothy's help, a room and some new friends, including Michael Gold. Now, however, I began to long for Will, and to wonder how he had taken my leaving him without a word of explanation. I wired him, and he came at once; he took me in his arms, and sympathized with my wish to avoid further incarceration in New Dorp. Soon, he promised, he would get me some habitation nearer to the traffic and ideologies of Manhattan. I think he loved me a little more now; it seems easier to love a sinner than a saint.

5

Iris Murdoch

Too Many Suitors

From *The Red and the Green*

Ireland-born and England-domiciled author Iris Murdoch has given the bicycle its head in more than one of her numerous novels. Indeed, the more convoluted the love affairs she concocts, the more the bicycle appears.

In The Sandcastle, *for example, Bill Mor, middle-aged housemaster at St. Bride's School, and his wife, Nan, have managed fairly tolerably in keeping their marital frictions under wraps until youthful Rain Carter reveals the fragility of their union. Rain, a portrait painter, has been commissioned to put to canvas the craggy visage of cantankerous Demoyte, former Headmaster of St. Bride's. Demoyte lives at Brayling's Close, a Georgian house some three miles from the school. Ms. Carter takes up lodging there, the better to be near the subject of her task. It is to Brayling's Close, at first out of affection for Demoyte and later for Rain, that Bill Mor is forever taking his cycling journeys. The master's bicycle shed at St. Bride's is but one stiff climb to the railway bridge away from the Close.*

Mor's first, earnest interest in Ms. Carter appears at a luncheon party to which he has cycled bearing the complete works of Demoyte in his bicycle basket, to fulfill a promise to Ms. Carter. At the party, Mor's jealousy is aroused by Rain's conversational intimacy with Bledyard, the art master at St. Bride's. Firm, principled Bledyard is soon to become Mor's sardonic, closet rival for the affections of Rain. Mor seems to suspect as much for, as he leaves the party, he renounces his bicycle for a Rain-chauffeured ride home in her car. As they depart from Brayling's Close, we are favored by an instance of Iris Murdoch's sly, catch-you-by-surprise humor.

From Iris Murdoch, *The Red and the Green* (New York: The Viking Press, 1965).

. . . she started the engine. As they began to move slowly forward a curious apparition passed them. It was Bledyard, riding his own bicycle and pushing Mor's. He went by at speed, with head down, and turned off the drive on to the cycle track that led back to the school.

The impudence of him! thought Mor. He hoped Miss Carter would not realize the significance of the spectacle.[1]

Comically ironic twists of a similar flavor occur throughout Ms. Murdoch's later historical novel The Red and the Green. *It is a compelling tale of romance and patriotism, focusing on the week preceding the Irish Easter uprising against the British in 1916. At center stage stands Lady (familiarly called Aunt) Millicent Kinnard, a femme fatale if Ireland ever produced one. Aunt Millie is spoiled rich, plumply beautiful, and a gun-toting independent. Friends and relatives alike are constantly at her feet or in her bed or wishing to be so. She seems to have no scruples about whom she romances or whom she corrupts. She has flirted with and seduced Barnabus Drumm from his priestly vocation. She entices her nephew, Lieutenant Andrew Chase Smith, of the King Edward's Horses, with promises of amour and then some. She has lately pledged her troth to the wealthy Christopher Bellman, knowing full well that his daughter, Frances, is all but engaged to Andrew Chase Smith. Her interest in Christopher derives from his affluence and the staying power that it will assure her in her claims and conquests.*

As the days count down to the Easter Monday rebellion, Aunt Millie becomes more and more romantically rambunctious. The pyramiding passion of the patriots is matched by the escalation of her amorous adventures. It is now the night of Holy Saturday and the uprising, scheduled for Easter Sunday, has been, at least temporarily, canceled. Pat Dumay, captain in the Irish Volunteers, with romantic visions of Millie dancing in his head, has bicycled the fifteen miles south from Dublin to Aunt Millie's estate at Rathblane. He arrives to find Andrew's bicycle at the door and Andrew tucked in bed with Millie. As he leaves, in a panic of despair and disgust, he notices another bicycle standing by. Unknown to him, his stepfather, Barnabas Drumm, has bicycled to Rathblane to stand, hound-dog-like, in the shadow of Millie. Next Christopher enters—sans bicycle. And the scene is set for a comic-opera confrontation.

Christopher Bellman had suddenly decided that he absolutely must see Millie. After her wonderful "yes" to him, he had felt happy and at peace and quite content not to see her for a while. He had felt her to be delightfully stored up and safe, a prize reserved and labelled, a perfume sealed, and he had returned to his work and felt more serene, he thought, than ever in his life. This serenity had been disturbed by two things. First, he had been extremely excited and upset by the news of the projected rebellion, which had been followed so soon by the news of its cancellation. This sudden glimpse of another Ireland, so close and yet so hidden, filled him with a distress which seemed like guilt. For a second he had felt the warm, quick movement of Irish history risen out of books alive, alive-o. He was stirred, magnetized, then disappointed, relieved. The second thing was that Frances, later that afternoon, had told him that she was not going to marry Andrew. Then it became essential to see Millie.

He set off on his bicycle and would have arrived at Rathblane earlier in the evening, only just as he was beginning to get into the mountains he had a puncture. He left the bicycle and walked on, imagining that the distance was shorter than it was. Then it became dark and he missed his way. When, very tired and drenched with rain, he at last reached Millie's front door he was extremely startled at being jumped upon by a man suddenly issuing from the doorway. As he picked himself up it seemed that the man, who had now faded into the moonlight, was Pat Dumay. He went in through the open door.

The hall was very dark and as soon as he came in it seemed to him that someone who was standing in the darkness moved away, with a soundless displacement of air, into one of the rooms. Almost at once a moving light was seen up above and Millie appeared, wearing a white gown. She began to glide quickly down the stairs, carrying the lamp, her gown flowing out behind her, her loose hair lifted. When she was halfway down, the lamplight showed her Christopher and she stopped abruptly.

"Millie, what on earth's happening? Somebody rushed out at me. I thought it was—"

"Hello, Christopher," said Millie. "Good evening." She put the lamp down on the stairs and sat down beside it. Then she began to laugh helplessly. She rocked quietly to and fro, moaning with laughter.

"I'm sorry I've come so late," said Christopher. "I'd have got here much earlier, only I got a puncture and had to walk the last bit. But, Millie, what—"

Millie stopped laughing. "Please, Christopher, would you go into the drawing-room and wait there? I'll put on some clothes and join you in a few minutes." She went back up the stairs, taking the lamp with her and leaving Christopher in darkness.

Christopher fumbled his way to the drawing-room door and fell through it, knocking his head on the big Chinese screen whose position just inside the door he had forgotten. There was no fire, and the room smelt of damp textile and turf ash. He stood still until he could discern the squares of the windows and shuffled towards them. There was a sound of scuffling overhead, and he thought he heard voices.

Christopher was feeling very confused. During his long walk along the dark mountain road he had been all the time anxious simply to arrive. He disliked walking. The mountains were frightening at night; there were sounds, presences. He had hurried on, looking forward to finding Millie up, a blazing fire, a welcoming glass of whiskey. But the uphill walk had taken such a long time. And now here he was, hustled away, left in the dark and the cold, not looked after in the least. And who was that person who had rushed out of the door and knocked him down? He realized that his arm was hurting from the fall and his head was aching from the encounter with the Chinese screen. Was it Pat Dumay? What was he doing bursting out of the house as if the devil was after him? And who was the mysterious moving figure in the hallway? And what was all that curious scuffling going on in the room above? Christopher felt very puzzled and very ill-used. He pawed several tables, looking for matches, but only succeeded in overturning something which fell onto the floor with a crash. It sounded as if it was broken. He began to feel his way back to the door.

Before he could reach it, Millie came in with the lamp. She was wearing her plainest grey walking dress, with a red woollen shawl over her head. She put the lamp down, carefully pulled the curtains, and then lit another lamp.

"Please sit down, Christopher."

"I'm so sorry, I've broken that vase. I was looking for the matches."

"It doesn't matter. It's only Ming or something. For God's sake, Christopher, sit down."

"My dear Millie, I'm only too anxious to sit down once you've given me time to take off this extremely damp mackintosh. And I think you might give me some whiskey. I've had a very long walk."

"Oh, yes, of course, whiskey, there's some in the cupboard. Wait a moment. Here you are."

"Millie, is something funny going on here? Was that Pat Dumay? And is there somebody else in the house? I thought I saw someone in the hall as I came in."

"No, there's no one here but me. The maids all sleep in the annexe."

"What was Pat doing here and why did he push me like that? I nearly broke my arm. I'm sorry I came so late, but as I told you I had a puncture and—"

"I should think he pushed you like that because you were in his way when he wanted to go out of the door. I'm sorry about your arm and I'm sorry about your bicycle and I'm sorry—"

"But what did he *want?*"

"What did he want? He wanted me." Millie laughed. She kicked a piece of the broken vase across the floor and turned to stare at Christopher.

He now took in her elated, excited face, flushed with an onset of laughter or tears. Her hair was plaited in a single plait, which she had drawn forward over her shoulder and was convulsively clutching and tugging together with the folds of the red shawl.

"What on earth do you mean?"

"He came here to seduce me."

"Millie! Surely you hadn't given him any reason to think—"

"No, of course I hadn't given him any reason to think. I sent him away with a flea in his ear."

"But he can hardly just have taken it into his head—"

"Why shouldn't he just have taken it into his head? Or do you think I'm not attractive enough?"

"Of course I think you're attractive enough—"

"Then there's nothing more to explain, is there?"

"Millie, I'm very surprised indeed."

"Well, I can't help that. Nothing happened. I just sent him off. That's why he was in such a hurry. You do believe me, don't you?"

"Of course I believe you. But, as I say—"

"Why did *you* take it into your head to come, Christopher?"

"I had to see you. So many things have been happening. I'm sorry to arrive so late, but as I told you—"

"Yes, yes, your bike. Tell me some of the things that have been happening."

"Well—Frances has decided not to marry Andrew."

"Ah—" Millie let go of the red shawl, which fell in a heap behind her. She moved forward and began quickly picking up the fragments of the Chinese vase. "It's so cold in here, we could do with a fire, couldn't we." She put the fragments of the vase on the table. She advanced on the fireplace and bent to put a match to the paper and sticks. "Hand over a couple of those little logs, would you?"

"Millie, did you hear what I said?"

"Of course I did, but what am I supposed to say about it? I'm sorry."

"It won't make any difference to us, of course. That's what I wanted to come and tell you. I'll manage about Frances."

"Have you told Frances about us?"

"No."

"That's just as well, perhaps."

"Why?"

"Christopher, I think I can't marry you after all."

"Millie, what on earth are you talking about?"

"I just can't. I'd be no use to you."

"Is this because of Frances?"

"No, it's nothing to do with Frances. I just can't do it, it would be wrong. Please forgive me. I should never have let the idea exist at all."

"Millie, I can't let you say this—" He got awkwardly and stiffly to his feet stretching out his arms towards her. Millie continued to stare down at the crackling sticks, whose light flickered on her face, showing a serene exhausted smile.

"Millie, my darling—" Christopher took her hand, lifting it from her side. It was heavy and limp. Her hand was familiar to him, and as he touched her his fingers became aware of something unusual. He looked down and saw that she was wearing a ring adorned with diamonds and rubies. He recognized the ring.

When Millie saw Christopher's expression and saw what he was looking at she withdrew her hand with an exclamation and moved away from him.

"Millie, why are you wearing Andrew's ring?"

She pulled it quickly off and laid it on the table. "Because Andrew has been wearing my ring."

"I don't understand."

"Well, why should you, with such an awful lot going on? I've just seduced your would-be son-in-law. I didn't mean to tell you. I just forgot about the ring. I never seem to be able to do wrong with impunity. What an unlucky girl I am!"

"Millie, do you actually mean that you—"

"Yes. I was in bed with Andrew when Pat turned up. I'd invited Pat to be my lover, only I didn't think he would oblige, so I made do with Andrew instead. It was all most unfortunate, and I'm a very disappointed woman."

"Millie, are you seriously saying that you and Andrew—"

"Yes! I've said it as clearly as I can. Do you want me to say it again?"

"How can you talk in that tone?"

"Well, a woman caught in my situation has got to adopt some tone, and it's not easy to combine devastating frankness with calm dignity. What tone do you suggest?"

"I just can't believe you."

"Have a good try. The fact is I'm in love with Pat, I'm desperately in love with Pat and I have been for ages, only of course it's hopeless, and it would have been hopeless even if Andrew hadn't been here tonight. And our thing would have been hopeless even if you hadn't found out about Andrew. I really think you'd better go, Christopher. Oh, hang it, you can't, you haven't got a bike. . . ."

6

W. Somerset Maugham

Falling in Love

From *Cakes and Ale*

The experience of mastering the fine art of riding a bicycle is today nothing of the chore that it was during the age of the "boneshaker." The apprentice bicyclist in those days certainly had his ups and downs and the downs were always embarrassing and often bruising, as well.

Mark Twain saw the experience as a source of gentle mirth while W. Somerset Maugham used it as the means of introducing Willie Ashenden, the then sixteen-year-old narrator of the novel Cakes and Ale, *to Edward Driffield, "one of the greatest of the later Victorian novelists" and to Driffield's first wife, Rosie. Ashenden recalls the incident at the urging of Alroy Kear, an opportunist turned novelist, who has been commissioned to write the biography of the lately deceased Edward Driffield.*

But, as a reading of the entire novel makes clear, Ashenden's introduction to Ted Driffield also saw the first stirrings of his later love affair with Driffield's wife, Rosie. The course of Willie's romance with Rosie, it turns out, was almost as forbidding as his first bicycling lesson. Rosie not only was untrue to Ted with Willie, but she also cuckolded Willie for Lord George Kemp and others. In the doing, Rosie left both Ted and Willie in England and eloped with Lord George to New York, leaving behind unfulfilled expectations and unpaid debts.

This moderately tangled tale of star-crossed romance all began with Ashenden's chance meeting with the Driffields, while he was attempting to learn the technique of holding fast to a bicycle.

From W. Somerset Maugham, *Cakes and Ale* (New York: Random House, Inc., 1950), pp. 62–68, 133–34.

211

It was true that Edward Driffield had taught me to bicycle. That was indeed how I first made his acquaintance. I do not know how long the safety bicycle had been invented, but I know that it was not common in the remote part of Kent in which I lived and when you saw someone speeding along on solid tires you turned round and looked till he was out of sight. It was still a matter for jocularity on the part of middle-aged gentlemen who said Shank's pony was good enough for them, and for trepidation on the part of elderly ladies who made a dash for the side of the road when they saw one coming. I had been for some time filled with envy of the boys whom I saw riding into the school grounds on their bicycles, and it gave a pretty opportunity for showing off when you entered the gateway without holding on to the handles. I had persuaded my uncle to let me have one at the beginning of the summer holidays, and though my aunt was against it, since she said I should only break my neck, he had yielded to my pertinacity more willingly because I was of course paying for it out of my own money. I ordered it before school broke up and a few days later the carrier brought it over from Tercanbury.

I was determined to learn to ride it by myself and chaps at school had told me that they had learned in half an hour. I tried and tried and at last came to the conclusion that I was abnormally stupid (I am inclined now to think that I was exaggerating), but even after my pride was sufficiently humbled for me to allow the gardener to hold me up I seemed at the end of the first morning no nearer to being able to get on by myself than at the beginning. Next day, however, thinking that the carriage drive at the vicarage was too winding to give a fellow a proper chance, I wheeled the bicycle to a road not far away which I knew was perfectly flat and straight and so solitary that no one would see me making a fool of myself. I tried several times to mount, but fell off each time. I barked my shins against the pedals and got very hot and bothered. After I had been doing this for about an hour, though I began to think that God did not intend me to ride a bicycle, but was determined (unable to bear the thought of the sarcasms of my uncle, his representative at Blackstable) to do so all the same, to my disgust I saw two people on bicycles coming along the deserted road. I immediately wheeled my machine to the side and sat down on a stile, looking out to sea in a nonchalant way as though I had been for a ride and were just sitting there wrapped in contemplation of the vasty ocean. I kept my eyes dreamily averted from the two persons who were advancing toward me, but I felt that they were coming nearer, and through the corner of my eye I saw that they were a man and a woman. As they passed me the woman swerved violently to my side of the road and, crashing against me, fell to the ground.

"Oh, I'm sorry," she said. "I knew I should fall off the moment I saw you."

It was impossible under the circumstances to preserve my appearance of abstraction and, blushing furiously, I said that it didn't matter at all.

The man had got off as she fell.

"You haven't hurt yourself?" he asked.

"Oh, no."

I recognized him then as Edward Driffield, the author I had seen walking with the curate a few days before.

"I'm just learning to ride," said his companion. "And I fall off whenever I see anything in the road."

"Aren't you the vicar's nephew?" said Driffield. "I saw you the other day. Galloway told me who you were. This is my wife."

She held out her hand with an oddly frank gesture and when I took it gave mine a warm and hearty pressure. She smiled with her lips and with her eyes and there was in her smile something that even then I recognized as singularly pleasant. I was confused. People I did not know made me dreadfully self-conscious, and I could not take in any of the details of her appearance. I just had an impression of a rather large blond woman. I do not know if I noticed then or only remembered afterward that she wore a full skirt of blue serge, a pink shirt with a starched front and a starched collar, and a straw hat, called in those days, I think, a boater, perched on the top of a lot of golden hair.

"I think bicycling's lovely, don't you?" she said, looking at my beautiful new machine which leaned against the stile. "It must be wonderful to be able to ride well."

I felt that this inferred an admiration for my proficiency.

"It's only a matter of practice," I said.

"This is only my third lesson. Mr. Driffield says I'm coming on wonderful, but I feel so stupid I could kick myself. How long did it take you before you could ride?"

I blushed to the roots of my hair. I could hardly utter the shameful words.

"I can't ride," I said. "I've only just got this bike and this is the first time I've tried."

I equivocated a trifle there, but I made it all right with my conscience by adding the mental reservation: except yesterday at home in the garden.

"I'll give you a lesson if you like," said Driffield in his good-humoured way. "Come on."

"Oh, no," I said. "I wouldn't dream of it."

"Why not?" asked his wife, her blue eyes still pleasantly smiling. "Mr. Driffield would like to and it'll give me a chance to rest."

Driffield took my bicycle, and I, reluctant but unable to withstand his friendly violence, clumsily mounted. I swayed from side to side, but he held me with a firm hand.

"Faster," he said.

I pedalled and he ran by me as I wobbled from side to side. We were both very hot when, notwithstanding his struggles, I at last fell off. It was very hard under such circumstances to preserve the standoffishness befitting the vicar's nephew with the son of Miss Wolfe's bailiff, and when I started back again and for thirty or forty thrilling yards actually rode by myself and Mrs. Driffield ran into the middle of the road with her arms akimbo shouting, "Go it, go it, two to one on the favourite," I was laughing so much that I positively forgot all about my social status. I got off of my own accord, my face no doubt wearing an air of immodest triumph, and received without embarrassment the Driffields' congratulations on my cleverness in riding a bicycle the very first day I tried.

"I want to see if I can get on by myself," said Mrs. Driffield, and I sat down again on the stile while her husband and I watched her unavailing struggles.

Then, wanting to rest again, disappointed but cheerful, she sat down beside me. Driffield lit his pipe. We chatted. I did not of course realize it then, but I know now that there was a disarming frankness in her manner that put one at one's ease. She talked with a kind of eagerness, like a child bubbling over with the zest of life, and her eyes were lit all the time by her engaging smile. I did not know why I liked it. I should say it was a little sly, if slyness were not a displeasing quality; it was too innocent to be sly. It was mischievous rather, like that of a child who has done something that he thinks funny, but is quite well aware that you will think rather naughty; he knows all the same that you won't be really cross and if you don't find out about it quickly he'll come and tell you himself. But of course then I only knew that her smile made me feel at home.

Presently Driffield, looking at his watch, said that they must be going and suggested that we should all ride back together in style. It was just the time that my aunt and uncle would be coming home from their daily walk down the town and I did not like to run the risk of being seen with people whom they would not at all approve of; so I asked them to go on first, as they would go more quickly than I. Mrs. Driffield would not hear of it, but Driffield gave me a funny, amused little look, which made me think that he saw through my excuse so that I blushed scarlet, and he said:

"Let him go by himself, Rosie. He can manage better alone."

"All right. Shall you be here to-morrow? We're coming."

"I'll try to," I answered.

They rode off, and in a few minutes I followed. Feeling very much pleased with myself, I rode all the way to the vicarage gates without falling. I think I boasted a good deal at dinner, but I did not say that I had met the Driffields.

7

R. K. Narayan

No Greater Love

From *The Painter of Signs*

It would be hard to conceive of a contemporary movie with, as the admen say, fast-paced action without the use of the automobile as a symbol and instrument to enhance the development of the plot. Action implies movement and movement, according to the modern appraisal, requires the automobile. But this situation, deplorably unimaginative as it is, is peculiarly the creation of the Western mind and its culture.

In other places and other climes, the bicycle might substitute for the automobile in serving the needs of a less action-packed plot line. Such is the case in *R. K. Narayan's* recent short novel The Painter of Signs, *in which the bicycle appears on twenty-seven of the book's 183 pages. Most often these references simply indicate that Raman, the most accomplished sig.ι painter of Malgudi, is making his rounds, either in his business or for his pleasure in trysting with Daisy, the official in the population control movement by whom Raman is smitten.*

This book, by India's most renowned living novelist, lacks the storytelling depth and psychological insight of Narayan's earlier novels of the life and times of his mythical city of Malgudi, such as, for example, The Financial Expert. *But it is a desultory afternoon's reading for those who ask no more of literature than a distracting moment without demands or commitments.*

Raman is Malgudi's most successful painter of signs, known to some of its inhabitants as an "artist in lettering." He lives with his aged aunt, who has cared for him since his infancy. The bicycle is his means of transportation around town. In due course of business, Raman undertakes to paint a sign for the offices of the population control movement. He receives his commission from Daisy, who is portrayed as fanatically and mechanically dedicated to the purposes of population control. But Raman sees her only

From R. K. Narayan, *The Painter of Signs* (New York: The Viking Press, 1976), pp. 143–44.

as his gossamer goddess whom he must love and obey after his most abject and simpering fashion.

The following excerpt shows Raman, in an unusually courageous mood, seeking, as the blushing would say, to force his attentions on Daisy. Daisy's reaction reveals that concern for the bicycle is a more compelling force than even the ardor of young love, at least to one of Daisy's "caste."

Now Raman had a fine excuse to knock on the door of Number Seven, Third Cross, that night. Daisy let him in.

He said, "I won't keep you long, only a quarter of an hour." She looked rather drawn and tired. Overworked, actually, with no relief, poor girl, he thought. If you had stood by the door and eavesdropped as did an urchin who had brought her her dinner from a near-by restaurant, you would have heard his voice: "I just came to enquire, on behalf of a friend, if you are offering nylon bangles to village women who—"

"Rubbish!" said her voice. "We don't believe in that kind of conversion. They must understand what they are doing, and not be enticed in this childish manner. Tell your friend to keep his bangles. I know him. He came here twice with a few samples, and I asked him to pack up and go. I gave him only two minutes. This sort of thing maddens me, I tell you." A pause and some movement of feet. Her voice: "No, no, you will be in trouble again. Be sensible."

"I used to be the most sensible person known at one time. Full of good sense, logic, reason. I could talk the most irrational fellow back into sense."

"Not to my knowledge," said the female voice. "Why not give me also the pleasure of watching your logic and reason at work? I see you only as a rash, head-strong . . . H'sh, don't be childish, let go, you are hurting me; behave like an adult."

"But you let me touch you on the river-step the other evening!"

"Oh, that! That was different, it was dark there."

"I can switch off the light here too."

And then one heard a scuffle and a struggle to reach the switch, feet and hands reaching for the switch, and a click of the switch, off. The eavesdropper applying his eye to the keyhole at this point would see nothing. A stillness followed before the light went up again, the female voice saying, "If you must stay, please bring your bicycle in. I don't want it to be stolen, or worse, seen on my veranda at this hour."

"You command, I'm ever your slave."

"Don't you feel ashamed to say it?"

"No, proud and happy." And as the door bolt is heard drawn, the eavesdropper vanishes, leaving Daisy's food at the threshold.

Part V

Not Just Ordinary Humor

Introduction

When a stray dog attacks me as I bicycle it is usually at a time when I least expect it—while I am climbing a hill and am least able to defend myself against the assault. The canine caper is a well-known hazard for bicyclists with almost as many suggested remedies as there are breeds and sizes of dogs to mount the attack.

My wife's solution seems to me to be the most unique and individualistic and the only one that I have seen work unfailingly every time. She simply talks to the dog, calmly but firmly, and without evincing the fear that she must be harboring. And the dog backs off in puzzlement while she briskly bicycles past, never slipping a link.

For myself, howling, ravenous dogs craving a bicyclist always remind me of Pudd'nhead Wilson, in Mark Twain's book of that name. It is little known that Pudd'nhead's rightful given name was David. He lost that the first day of his stay in Dawson's Landing, Missouri.

As Mark Twain tells it, Wilson was conversing with a group of citizens from Dawson's Landing when he was interrupted and irked by the yelping and howling of an unseen dog. Wilson commented, "I wish I owned half of that dog." To which a villager asked, "Why?" And Wilson replied, "Because I would kill my half." Only a pudd'nhead would make such an outlandish statement, according to the good citizens of Dawson's Landing. And the nickname stuck for twenty years.[1]

Whenever I see a dog on the prowl as I bicycle, I too wish I owned half. And I'd do with my half what Pudd'nhead Wilson wanted to do with his.

Apparently there is no aspect of bicycling that does not have its humorous side, even the common danger of the marauding dog. This chapter's selections are proof of that.

But dogs are not the only hazard for bicyclists. There are also stones. Not just any stones. White stones.

On occasions too numerous to count, many a bicyclist has suddenly and mysteriously caromed into a roadside ditch or found a tire flat with no apparent cause. My daughter Mary Alice, for one, is always complaining of her rear tire, which, at the oddest times, most inexplicably goes flat. Upon investigation, the tube is seen to be intact and the tire well-treaded and sound. The only plausible explanation is the white stones. They must be responsible.

The portentous power of white stones is ingrained in Celtic mythology. Robert Gibbings, in *Lovely Is the Lee*, relates:

"It was a very confused bicycle. . . ." (From *The Third Policeman* by Flann O'Brien)

White stones are unlucky, especially in a boat. No fisherman on the west coast will take them as ballast. "Them's no good." "Them's unlucky." "Hens lay them." I heard a man trying to persuade the priest that it was a white stone that had thrown him from his bicycle. The priest did not think so, but the man, who was not present at the accident, was convinced of it. Whatever the origin of the belief may be, the association of white pebbles with the dead goes back a very long way, for we find these stones a constantly recurring feature in bronze age burials, placed beside the cremated remains. The belief in their magic power is not confined to Ireland. In Strathnaver, in Scotland, "an old woman did many marvellous things by means of a white pebble." In Sandsting parish in the Shetlands a quartz pebble about the size of an egg was used to cure sterility. The stone was placed in running water and the would-be mother washed her feet in water drawn from the stream.[2]

For myself, I am not convinced that white stones have all the magic that folklore attributes to them. Yet, I never bicycle on a road where I find a white stone. It is a result of a vow and prudence. It makes no sense to tempt fate.

Yes, humor can be fanciful and exaggerated. And bicycle humor is no exception. Who would believe, for example, that a patent was granted on May 22, 1900,[3] for a bicycle-seat attachment intended to harpoon potential bicycle thieves. The invention provides for holes in the bicycle seat through which sharp needles or barbs are extended upward when the bicycle is not in use. While the bicycle is being ridden the needles are retracted in a manner "beyond the possibility of accidental raising," so the patent specification unconvincingly asserts. Nothing is known of the success or failure of this Orwellian device, but it apparently takes the view of most bicyclists that hanging is too good for bicycle thieves.

A more contemporary example of the same kind of solemn statement, blessed with unintentional whimsy, appeared in the 1976 report of the influential Peyrefitte Committee in France, which is entitled "Résponses à la violence." The report documents the extraordinary rise in the crime rate in France and lists a number of remedies for it. Among them is a suggestion that "there should be more bicycle paths."[4] Now there is an argument for bicycle paths that has never before been heard or even imagined.

As the circus teaches with its bears and stunt men on bicycles and unicycles and just plain wheels, the bicycle is a likely prospect for slapstick humor. One might wish that Laurel and Hardy had lived in the age of the "wheelie." Their bicycling antics surely would have been sidesplitting. Norman Mailer, in *Of a Fire on the Moon*, illustrates this type of humor in his description of the "talented" merry-andrew Eddie Bonetti.

Eddie was also capable while riding a bicycle down the main street (if he saw a friend driving behind him) of jumping his bike off the street across the sidewalk and into the bushes, where he would take a wild dive over the handlebars into the grass, just to give his friends the craziest laugh of the week. Bonetti could say, "I'm worried about my heart," and fall immediately on his back, there to wink at you. Bonetti was a prodigy of talent.[5]

Marcel Pagnol, in *The Glory of My Father* (Memories of Childhood), recalls a similar and nonfictional incident in his own youth.

It was a park of shady lanes, ancient sycamore trees and wild thickets, a park of lawns and guards who did not let anyone sprawl in the inviting grass, while small armadas of ducks plowed the waters of its ponds.

In those days, a number of people also visited this refreshing place to try their wings on a bicycle. Looking straight ahead, clenching their teeth, they would suddenly escape the grip of the instructor, zoom across the lane, plunge into a bush and reappear shortly with their vehicles draped around their necks. An interesting sight, a sight that would make me laugh to tears. But my aunt would not let me stay for long in this danger zone: she would drag me off—still engrossed in the spectacle behind me—to a quiet corner by the pond.[6]

To speak of antics is to be reminded of the absentminded bicyclist, whose foibles could even amuse Rasputin. G. K. Chesterton was one of this type.

A story was told of him that . . . dressing in his Battersea flat to go to an important dinner, he was stopped only just in time from setting off in full evening clothes and cycling shoes. He changed them, but was soon back in the flat. He had gone on the wrong day.[7]

On another occasion, Chesterton's friend, Major Maurice Baring, was seen to arrive on a bicycle for a country-house weekend.

He rode absent-mindedly past his hosts awaiting him on the entrance steps and out into the road again, not to reappear until twenty-four hours later.[8]

Forgetfulness was not the mark of James Gordon Bennett, Commodore of the New York Yacht Club, publisher of the then *New York Herald*, leading American sportsman and nineteenth-century grandee who had sent Henry Stanley to Africa to find Dr. David Livingstone. Bennett is reported to have bicycled "around his Fifth Avenue block, pausing as he passed his town-house for refreshments supplied by a butler, who stood on the sidewalk with a silver tray bearing a glass of brandy."[9] A silver-plated pit stop, no less!

Bicycles can be the occasion for puns too, both the skillful and pedestrian. It is quintessential Joyce to see him remark in his letter to Harriet Shaw Weaver of June 13, 1925: "Gromwelling I said and what? O, ah! Bisexcycle that was the bunch."[10] The following story is within the spirit, if not the letter, of Joyce's pun.

The somewhat ribald story is told of the young Welsh miner who was hailed into court on the charge of impregnating some twenty-two girls living in widely separated parts of the county. He pleaded guilty. Before passing sentence the astonished judge asked him how in heaven's name he had been able to manage all that. The man hung his head and replied, "Your Honor, it was really quite simple. I had a bicycle."[11]

The poet, John Ashbery, found a pun helpful in explaining his use of the sestina, a form of lyric poetry, "as a probing tool."

I once told somebody that writing a sestina was rather like riding downhill on a bicycle and having the pedals push your feet. I wanted my feet to be pushed into places they wouldn't normally have taken.[12]

Good and bad puns there are, but it is certainly the dregs of humor to ask, "Do you know why a bicycle cannot run?" And to reply, "Because it is too tired."

The bicycle even appears in certain idiomatic uses that have a humorous twist. According to a French saying, if you do not know what you are talking about, *vous pedalez dans le choucroute*.

Mrs. Homewood, an English woman who bicycled around the world in 1910 at the age of sixty-six, has recorded in her *Recollections of an Octogenarian* two amusing bicycling experiences on her travels. The wit of the first is lost to all but those who have a firm grasp on idiomatic usages in French (I am not one of them). As she has told them:

Once, on arrival at a country inn in France, which I had previously sampled and found comfortable and extremely moderate in price, I was disappointed to find it already beset by a rather rowdy wedding party. I had counted on spending the night there, but under the circumstances I just partook of some coffee and remounted my cycle. The wit of the party—I think it was the bridegroom—called out, "Madame, vous avez une roue qui tourne," and I replied, "Oui, Monsieur, j'ai même deux roues qui tournent," much to his astonishment and I think to the increased merriment of the guests, who laughed loudly at his expense!

Cycling on a very muddy road in England, I politely asked a man who was leading a horse in a farm cart to go to his proper side of the road and allow me to pass. His reply was, 'Go to Hell!' But on my saying that I would rather not, as I should meet him there, he went to the right side of the road to allow me to pass. Later in the day I again had to pass him, and he did not repeat his polite remark.[13]

Humor of a sly and subtle persuasion has also focused on the bicycle, when it was not otherwise engaged. Among legislators, T. M. Healy was the Everett McKinley Dirksen of his age. His silver tongue was a necessary asset since he represented the colony of Ireland in the inhospitable English House of Commons. On one occasion at the turn of the century a bill was submitted to require bicycles in Ireland to carry bicycle lamps. Healy's speech in opposition to this discriminatory class legislation was a gem of low-keyed humor couched in phrases that lawyers, with their sophistry, would understand and applaud.

The cyclist has just as much right to be protected from being run down as a carriage. Why should I be run down in the dark by a carriage which carries no lamps, or by a car that refuses to carry anything? Carriages with india rubber tyres are becoming very popular, and they are becoming noiseless like bicycles; therefore, I think it is essential, if this law is to be applied to one section of the community on wheels it is only right to apply it to all sections. . . . I would not object to cyclists being compelled to carry lights if it is also made to apply to the grocer's cart and the milkman's cart, as well as to every cyclist. . . . If a man is driving a car or a cart, he is not often injured in case of accidents, although his horse may be injured; but the bicyclist is nearly always injured if anything runs into him. He is riding at his peril, and that is far more than can be said of the man on the car or cart. If you consider the way in which bicyclists are treated as a rule by those in charge of cars or carriages, I venture to say that the necessity for regulations is in the opposite direction, for the danger is rather the other way about. On the magisterial bench in Ireland there seem to be a number of old gouty gentlemen who themselves are unable to ride and they seem to have the very strongest prejudice against any cyclist who happens to be brought before them, and this Amendment will give them a chance of coming down on cyclists in general with a very severe voice.[14]

The same brand of wily, tongue-in-cheek humor appears in Kurt Vonnegut's *Cat's Cradle*. At one point the narrator has enplaned for San Lorenzo and finds himself in the company of an American businessman who is preparing to manufacture "Bicycles for Afghanistan." This conversational vignette does nothing to shore up the sagging, popular image of the American businessman.

There was a small saloon in the rear of the plane and I repaired there for a drink. It was there that I met another fellow American, H. Lowe Crosby of Evanston, Illinois, and his wife, Hazel.

They were heavy people, in their fifties. They spoke twangingly. Crosby told me that he owned a bicycle factory in Chicago, that he had had nothing but ingratitude from his employees. He was going to move his business to grateful San Lorenzo.

"You know San Lorenzo well?" I asked.

"This'll be the first time I've ever seen it, but everything I've heard about it I like," said H. Lowe Crosby. "They've got discipline. They've got something you can count on from one year to the next. They don't have the government encouraging everybody to be some kind of original pissant nobody every heard of before."

"Sir?"

"Christ, back in Chicago, we don't make bicycles any more. It's all human relations now. The eggheads sit around trying to figure out new ways for everybody to be happy. Nobody can get fired, no matter what; and if somebody does accidentally make a bicycle, the union accuses us of cruel and inhuman practices and the government confiscates the bicycle for back taxes and gives it to a blind man in Afganistan."

"And you think things will be better in San Lorenzo?"

"I know damn well they will be. The people down there are poor enough and scared enough and ignorant enough to have some common sense!"[15]

The varieties of humor that have amused, titillated, rollicked or even startled their readers are apparently boundless and inexhaustible. But the one species of humor which is more macabre than merry is black humor. It has such a perversely absurd and even a funereal pallor that is so extravagant and outrageous as to be comical.

Samuel Beckett's *Mercier and Camier* presents incident after incident where we laugh in spite of ourselves at the daft and dizzy doings of its two besotted stumblebums who are traveling not far but long. At one point, Mercier and Camier recollect that their bicycle is missing, having been chained and locked to a railing one week earlier while they tarried at a nearby pub. The pub's proprietor, a "publican" according to Beckett's neat double entendre, had banned their bicycle from his premises. This suddenly reawakened interest in their bicycle brings Mercier to inquire:

You remember our bicycle? said Mercier.

Just, said Camier.

Speak up, said Mercier, I'm not deaf.

Yes, said Camier.

Of it there remains, said Mercier, securely chained to the railing, as much as may reasonably remain, after a week's incessant rain, of a bicycle relieved of both wheels, the saddle, the bell and the carrier. And the tail-light, he added, I nearly forgot. He struck his forehead a blow. What an addle-pate to be sure! he said.

And the pump of course, said Camier.

Believe it or not, said Mercier, it's all one to me, our pump has been spared.

And it such a fine pump, said Camier. Where is it?

Thinking it was a mere oversight, said Mercier, I left it where it was. It seemed the right thing to do. What is there for us to pump up now? That is to say I turned it upside down, I don't know why.

Does it fit as well so? said Camier.

Oh quite as well, said Mercier, quite, quite as well.

They went out. It was blowing.[16]

Blacker still than the humor of Beckett in *Mercier and Camier* is that of J. P. Donleavy in *The Ginger Man*. At one point in the novel, Sebastian Dangerfield, a most irrepressibly irreverent person, posts a letter from Dublin to Kenneth O'Keefe, his one-eyed rascally friend, who has hied off to the continent. The letter is vintage Donleavy, which, in part, says:

> I have bought myself a second hand bicycle and have painted it black and put a little black flag on the handle bars and I take up the rear of all funerals going to the Grange. I have found that some people laugh at me for doing this and think that perhaps this man is a little mad but I say O aye and go on about my little tortured business. [17]

Black humor is not so far removed from subtle irony. Once again Samuel Beckett, a master of the deftly and absurdly ambiguous, provides a stunning example of this relationship in his radio play *All That Fall*. In the play, Beckett's preoccupation with motion, by whatever means—horse-cart, bicycle, or foot—and sharp verbal byplay stand out in bold relief. The action finds Mrs. Rooney, a lady in her seventies, en route on foot to the railway station to meet her blind husband, Dan, when she meets Mr. Tyler, a retired bill broker, who is traveling in the same direction by bicycle.

Dragging feet. Sound of bicycle-bell. It is old Mr. Tyler coming up behind her on his bicycle, on his way to the station. Squeak of brakes. He slows down and rides abreast of her.

MR. TYLER: Mrs. Rooney! Pardon me if I do not doff my cap, I'd fall off. Divine day for the meeting.

MRS. ROONEY: Oh, Mr. Tyler, you startled the life out of me stealing up behind me like that like a deerstalker! Oh!

MR. TYLER: *(playfully)* I rang my bell, Mrs. Rooney, the moment I sighted you I started tinkling my bell, now don't you deny it.

MRS. ROONEY: Your bell is one thing, Mr. Tyler, and you are another. What news of your daughter?

MR. TYLER: Fair, fair. They removed everything, you know, the whole . . . er . . . bag of tricks. Now I am grandchildless.

Dragging feet.

MRS. ROONEY: Gracious how you wobble! Dismount, for mercy's sake, or ride on.

MR. TYLER: Perhaps if I were to lay my hand lightly on your shoulder, Mrs. Rooney, how would that be? *(Pause.)* Would you permit that?

MRS. ROONEY: No, Mr. Rooney, Mr. Tyler I mean, I am tired of light old hands on my shoulders and other senseless places, sick and tired of them. Heavens, here comes Connolly's van! *(She halts. Sound of motor-van. It approaches, passes with thunderous rattle, recedes.)* Are you all right, Mr. Tyler? *(Pause.)* Where is he? *(Pause.)* Ah there you are! *(The dragging steps resume.)* That was a narrow squeak.

MR. TYLER: I alit in the nick of time.

MRS. ROONEY: It is suicide to be abroad. But what is it to be at home, Mr. Tyler, what is it to be at home? A lingering dissolution. Now we are white with dust from head to foot. I beg your pardon?

MR. TYLER: Nothing, Mrs. Rooney, nothing, I was merely cursing, under my breath, God and man, under my breath, and the wet Saturday afternoon of my conception. My back tire has gone down again. I pumped it hard as iron before I set out. And now I am on the rim.

MRS. ROONEY: Oh what a shame!

MR. TYLER: Now if it were the front I should not so much mind. But the back. The back! The chain! The oil! The grease! The hub! The brakes! The gear! No! It is too much!
Dragging feet.[18]

In no other area of literature, save possibly in the literature of travel, has the bicycle assumed such a dominant role as in the literature of humor. It is easy to see why. The design and use of the bicycle bespeaks an essential movement which naturally evokes humorous episodes. The bicycle may be graceful, but it can also be frolicsome. Clowning is just another way in which the bicycle gives enjoyment, as you shall see.

1

Short Sketches

In the category of quips and shorter humorous "takes" on the exploits of bicycles and bicyclists, the following are especially worth enjoying.

Free Wheeling

I was enjoying a ride on my new ten-speed bicycle when the sky suddenly blackened and a few drops of rain fell. Realizing that I would never reach home before the storm broke, I decided to take the bus.

"How much is the fare?" I asked the driver.

"Twenty-five cents," he said.

To my relief I found a solitary quarter in my pocket. "Can I take my bike on the bus?" I asked.

"Well," he said, "I suppose if you paid a separate fare for it, it would be all right."

"All I have is a quarter," I confessed. He frowned as a loud peal of thunder sounded, and I resigned myself to a long, wet ride home.

"That bicycle looks brand-new," he commented as I turned to go.

"It is," I replied.

"In that case," he said jovially, "bring it aboard. Children under six years old ride free."

From Steven Divide, *Reader's Digest*, April 1977, p. 101.

Mounting and . . .

"As you are perfectly aware the right is much more tricky than the left, you would be surprised at all the right pitfalls there are. We are only at the beginning of our knowledge of the right, there is nothing more deceptive to the unwary."

"I did not know that."

The Sergeant opened his eyes wide in surprise.

"Did you ever in your life," he asked, "mount a bicycle from the right?"

"I did not."

"And why?"

"I do not know. I never thought about it."

He laughed at me indulgently.

"It is nearly an insoluble pancake," he smiled, "a conundrum of inscrutable potentialities, a snorter."

From Flann O'Brien, *The Third Policeman* (New York: Walker and Company, 1967), p. 153.

Dismounting

Smilzo, one of the Communist inhabitants of an Italian village, brings an invitation to the village priest, Don Camillo, to attend the inauguration ceremonies for the newly constructed People's Palace. Gentle verbal sparks fly in this brief encounter.

Smilzo rode up on his racing bicycle and braked it in the American manner, which consists of letting the backside slip off the seat backwards and sit astride the wheel.

Don Camillo was reading the newspaper, seated upon the bench in front of the presbytery. He raised his head. "Does Stalin hand you down his trousers?" he inquired placidly.

Smilzo handed him a letter, touched his cap with a forefinger, leaped on to his bicycle and was just about to disappear round the corner of the presbytery when he slowed down for an instant. "No, the Pope does that," he bawled, then stood on his pedals and was gone in a flash.

From Giovanni Guareschi, *The Little World of Don Camillo*, Trans. Una Vincenzo Troubridge (London: Victor Gollancz, Ltd., 1951), p. 111.

A Slow Puncture

"I remember well," he said, "a dream that I had six years ago on the twenty-third of November next. A nightmare would be a truer word. I dreamt if you please that I had a slow puncture."

"That is a surprising thing," I said idly, "but not astonishing. Was it the work of a tintack?"

"Not a tintack," said the Sergeant, "but too much starch."

"I did not know," I said sarcastically, "that they starched the roads."

"It was not the road, and for a wonder it was not the fault of the County Council. I dreamt that I was cycling on official business for three days. Suddenly I felt the saddle getting hard and lumpy underneath me. I got down and felt the tyres but they were unexceptionable and fully pumped. Then I thought my head was giving me a nervous outbreak from too much overwork. I went into a private home where there was a qualified doctor and he examined me completely and told me what the trouble was. I had a slow puncture."

He gave a coarse laugh and half-turned to me his enormous backside.

"Here, look," he laughed.

"I see," I murmured.

From Flann O'Brien *The Third Policeman* (New York: Walker and Company, 1967), pp. 120–21.

First Things First

The gas rationing and other privations imposed during World War II gave the bicycle an importance that it has lost in peacetime. The story is told of an Englishman who loaned his very aged but much cherished bicycle to an R.A.F. flight sergeant who was billeted with the bicycle owner's family. The sergeant would daily pedal across the English countryside to the airport where he was stationed.

All went well until one day the sergeant returned to his lodgings without the bicycle. He had been prevailed upon to hitch a ride to avoid a thorough soaking from a chill rain. The bicycle was left snug within the largest hangar at the airport.

That night Jerry's aircraft came in force and bombed everything in sight, including the airport where the sergeant was employed. The very next day the sergeant again returned home without the bicycle, but this time his somber face told the tale. The bombs had destroyed the hangar and the bicycle with it.

A few days later, during another air raid, the owner of the bicycle had taken refuge in an air-raid shelter when another occupant of the shelter announced, in a state of much excited agitation, "the Japanese have bombed Pearl Harbor." Whereupon the bicycle owner, without hesitation, replied: "And the Germans have blown up my bike."

Adapted from Bob Mace, "By Enemy Action," *Cycle Touring*, June–July, 1978: 121–22.

Bait and Switch I

A girl was bicycling alone through the Ozarks when she had the misfortune of having a puncture. For some time she stood by the side of the lonely, lightly trafficked road puzzling over what she might do to repair the tube. To her delight a young farm boy driving a pickup truck stopped to offer her assistance.

"What seems to be the trouble?" he asked.

"It's my tube," she said. "It's gone flat and I have no tools or patches to repair it."

"Never you mind," he said, cutting short her tale of woe. "I'll have it fixed in no time."

The boy then proceeded to remove the tube, find and patch the tear, and reassemble the tire so that she was soon ready for the road again.

In an excess of gratitude for his help, she offered to pay him whatever he would like, at the same time reaching into the pocket of her jeans for some loose change.

The boy, however, with a wave of his hand, refused any such payment, commenting, "Ma'am, in these parts, we don't take money for the good deeds we do. We just swap."

For a moment, but only a moment, the girl hesitated until she thought she caught the drift of his meaning. With a nod, she motioned to him to follow her off the road into the trees. In a clearing some distance from the road, she started to disrobe.

After she had removed all of her clothes, the boy looked at her for a long second, rubbed his chin, and said,

"I think I'll take the bike."

Bait and Switch II

A United States Customs agent at the Mexican border was much perplexed. Each day for weeks a man had bicycled up to the border from Mexico carrying a weighty sack over his shoulder. And each day the same ritual had been performed. The agent had required the man to open the sack for inspection before permitting him to cross the border. Each time the sack contained sand, nothing but sand.

Finally, in desperation, the Customs agent begged, pleaded, and even promised immunity from prosecution if the man would reveal what he was smuggling across the border. With a wry smile, the man beckoned to the agent and bending his head whispered: bicycles.

Hang the Bicycle

"The last hanging we had in this parish," he [Sergeant Pluck] said, "was thirty years ago. It was a very famous man called MacDadd. He held the record for the hundred miles on a solid tyre. I need to tell you what the solid tyre did for him. We had to hang the bicycle."

"Hang the bicycle?"

"MacDadd had a first-class grudge against another man called Figgerson but he did not go near Figgerson. He knew how things stood and gave Figgerson's bicycle a terrible thrashing with a crowbar. After that MacDadd and Figgerson had a fight and Figgerson—a dark man with glasses—did not live to know who the winner was. There was a great wake and he was buried with his bicycle. Did you ever see a bicycle-shaped coffin?"

"No."

"It is a very intricate piece of wood-working, you would want to be a first-class carpenter to make a good job of the handlebars to say nothing of the pedals and the back-step. But the murder was a bad piece of criminality and we could not find MacDadd for a long time or make sure where the most of him was. We had to arrest his bicycle as well as himself and we watched the two of them under secret observation for a week to see where the majority of MacDadd was and whether the bicycle was mostly in MacDadd's trousers *pari passu* if you understand my meaning."

"What happened?"

"The Sergeant gave his ruling at the end of the week. His position was painful in the extremity because he was a very close friend of MacDadd after office hours. He condemned the bicycle and it was the bicycle that was hanged. We entered a *nolle prosequi* in the day-book in respect of the other defendant. I did not see the stretching myself because I am a delicate man and my stomach is extremely reactionary."

From Flann O'Brien, *The Third Policeman* (New York, Walker and Company, 1967), pp. 104–105.

A Soft Saddle Is Hard to Come By

"Then, there are saddles," I went on—I wished to get this lesson home to him. "Can you think of any saddle ever advertised that you have *not* tried?"

He said: "It has been an idea of mine that the right saddle is to be found."

I said: "You give up that idea; this is an imperfect world of joy and sorrow mingled. There may be a better land where bicycle saddles are made out of rainbow, stuffed with cloud; in this world the simplest thing is to get used to something hard. There was that saddle you bought in Birmingham; it was divided in the middle, and looked like a pair of kidneys."

He said: "You mean that one constructed on anatomical principles."

"Very likely," I replied. "The box you bought it in had a picture on the cover, representing a sitting skeleton—or rather that part of a skeleton which does sit."

He said: "It was quite correct; it showed you the true position of the—"

I said: "We will not go into details; the picture always seemed to me indelicate."

He said: "Medically speaking, it was right."

"Possibly," I said, "for a man who rode in nothing but his bones. I only know that I tried it myself, and that to a man who wore flesh it was agony. Every time you went over a stone or a rut it nipped you; it was like riding on an irritable lobster. You rode that for a month."

"I thought it only right to give it a fair trial," he answered.

I said: "You gave your family a fair trial also; if you will allow me the use of slang. Your wife told me that never in the whole course of your married life had she known you so bad tempered, so unchristian-like, as you were that month. Then you remember that other saddle, the one with the spring under it."

He said: "You mean 'the Spiral.'"

I said: "I mean the one that jerked you up and down like a jack-in-the-box; sometimes you came down again in the right place, and sometimes you didn't. I am not referring to these matters merely to recall painful memories, but I want to impress you with the folly of trying experiments at your time of life."

From Jerome K. Jerome, *Three Men on the Bummel* (New York: Dodd, Mead & Co., 1900), pp. 207–8.

Going to the Devil

There once was a bicyclist whose quick-witted tomfoolery knew no bounds. To teach him a lesson, his wife decided to dress in a ghost's costume to scare him upon his arrival at home. As he bicycled up to the door of his house, she leaped from the nearby bushes and wailed at him in a ghastly moan.

Whereupon the bicyclist asked: "And who might you be?" And the disguised wife replied: "The devil." And the husband retorted: "Well, then, devil, come into the house and meet your sister."

In Stitches

And then there was the girl who, being late for church, mounted her bicycle and rode madly off. As she arrived at the church, she careened into a tree and fell helter-skelter onto the pavement. When a young man descended the church's steps to assist her, she asked, in much embarrassment, "Is mass out?" "No," he replied, "but you've got quite a rip in your stocking."

Colossal Collisions

Stephen Dedalus, in Joyce's A Portrait of the Artist as a Young Man, *was knocked to the cinderpath by a cyclist, "a fellow out of second of grammar," and "his spectacles had been broken in three places and some of the grit of the cinders had gone into his mouth." There was no humor in that, certainly, but there was a certain irony in his upstaging Father (Baldyhead) Dolan upon Dedalus's complaint to the rector that Father Dolan had unjustly taken the switch to him for failing to prepare his lessons, when Baldyhead knew he could not do so without his glasses.*[1]

Simone de Beauvoir and George Bernard Shaw, bicyclists both, could turn serious bicycle crashes in which they were participants into occasions for merry mirth.

I (Simone de Beauvoir)

On a beautiful sunny morning we [Jean-Paul Sartre and Simone de Beauvoir] undertook the last leg of our [bicycle] journey which was to bring us to Colette Audry's house at Grenoble. We had lunch at the top of a pass, and I drank some white wine: not much, but because of the bright sun, it was enough to make my head spin ever so slightly. We started to glide down the slope; Sartre was riding about twenty yards ahead of me. Suddenly I unexpectedly met two bicyclists who, like myself, were riding in the middle of the road, even a trifle on my side. To pass them I pulled to my left where there was still some free space while they moved to their right. This manoeuvre brought us face to face again. My brakes did not function properly and it was impossible for me to stop. Once again, I pulled to the left and I slid on the gravel, stopping just short of the cliff. I thought, for a second, "this is what death is like." And I died. When I opened my eyes again, I was standing up and Sartre was bracing me with one arm. I recognized him but only as through a glass darkly. We managed to reach a house where I was given a glass of "marc" [strong coffee]. Someone washed my face while Sartre pedaled to the next village in search of a doctor who, it happened, refused to return with him. When he came back, I had recovered a little bit. I recalled that we were travelling by bicycle to visit Colette Audry. Sartre suggested that we mount our bicycles again since there was less than fifteen miles left and all of that downhill. Nevertheless, I felt as if all the cells of my body were fighting with one another. I could not see myself on my bicycle again. So we took a train on a little railway. People stared at me, horrified. When I knocked at Colette Audry's door, she gasped at my condition and did not even recognize me. I looked at myself in a mirror. I was quite a sight. I had lost a tooth, one of my eyes was closed and my face was swollen to twice its size and my skin was badly scratched. Not even a grape could pass between my swollen lips. I went to bed without dinner, hoping that my face would return to normal, although it then seemed impossible.

I awoke looking just as repulsive as I had the night before, but I gathered sufficient courage to mount my bicycle. It was Sunday, and hordes of bicyclists had converged on the road towards Chambery. Those who passed me whistled or laughed rudely at me. On the ensuing days, every time I went into a store I was the object of stares.

One woman asked me with concern: "Did you have an accident?" For a long time, I regretted not having retorted "No, I was born this way." One afternoon, I was bicycling ahead of Sartre and was waiting for him at a crossroads. A man, who was also standing there, after observing me intently burst into laughter and said: "And you are still waiting for him after all that he has done to you!"[2]

II (GBS)

George Bernard Shaw, according to Olivia Collidge, one of his many biographers, "who always thought of himself as a nervous specimen without much physical courage, was a mad cyclist. Over and over again he risked his life by putting up his feet in the days before free-wheelers and tearing down hill around blind corners as though possessed."[3]

On one occasion, in 1898, Shaw demonstrated his renowned eccentricity and his fanaticism for the bicycling rage by riding a bicycle with one foot, while his other foot was on the mend from a most incapacitating disease which had left him with thoughts of amputation and a long travail on crutches. His one-footed bicycling feat was less successful than that of Samuel Beckett's Molloy, who is represented as bicycling with crutches. Shaw, for his part, "fell over, sprained his ankle badly, and had to be confined to a wheelchair."[4]

At another time, Shaw was involved in a two-bicycle collision with Bertrand Russell. As Russell tells it in his Portraits from Memory:

At this time he and I were involved in a bicycle accident, which I feared for a moment might have brought his career to a premature close. He was only just learning to ride a bicycle, and he ran into my machine with such force that he was hurled through the air and landed on his back twenty feet from the place of the collision. However, he got up completely unhurt and continued his ride; whereas my bicycle was smashed, and I had to return by train. It was a very slow train, and at every station Shaw with his bicycle appeared on the platform, put his head into the carriage and jeered. I suspect that he regarded the whole incident as proof of the virtues of vegetarianism.[5]

2

Jerome K. Jerome

The Amateur and the Bon Vivant

From *Three Men on the Bummel*

There are two ways you can get exercise out of a bicycle: you can "overhaul" it, or you can ride it. On the whole, I am not sure that a man who takes his pleasure overhauling does not have the best of the bargain. He is independent of the weather and the wind; the state of the roads troubles him not. Give him a screw-hammer, a bundle of rags, an oil-can, and something to sit down upon, and he is happy for the day. He has to put up with certain disadvantages, of course; there is no joy without alloy. He himself always looks like a tinker, and his machine always suggests the idea that, having stolen it, he has tried to disguise it, but as he rarely gets beyond the first milestone with it, this, perhaps, does not much matter. The mistake some people make is in thinking they can get both forms of sport out of the same machine. This is impossible; no machine will stand the double strain. You must make up your mind whether you are going to be an "overhauler" or a rider. Personally, I prefer to ride, therefore I take care to have near me nothing that can tempt me to overhaul. When anything happens to my machine I wheel it to the nearest repairing shop. If I am too far from the town or village to walk, I sit by the roadside and wait till a cart comes along. My chief danger, I always find, is from the wandering overhauler. The sight of a broken-down machine is to the overhauler as a wayside corpse to a crow; he swoops down upon it with a friendly yell of triumph. At first I used to try politeness. I would say:

"It is nothing; don't you trouble. You ride on, and enjoy yourself, I beg it of you as a favour; please go away."

From Jerome K. Jerome, *Three Men on the Bummel* (London: J. M. Dent and Sons, 1900), pp. 209–15.

Experience has taught me, however, that courtesy is of no use in such an extremity. Now I say:

"You go away and leave the thing alone, or I will knock your silly head off."

And if you look determined, and have a good stout cudgel in your hand, you can generally drive him off.

And if you are without a club or other source of forceful resistance to the blandishments of the friendly bicycle mechanic, then prepare to suffer through an experience similar to the following:

There was a man at Folkestone; I used to meet him on the Lees. He proposed one evening we should go for a long bicycle ride together on the following day, and I agreed. I got up early, for me; I made an effort, and was pleased with myself. He came half an hour late; I was waiting for him in the garden. It was a lovely day. He said:

"That's a good-looking machine of yours. How does it run?"

"Oh, like most of them!" I answered; "easily enough in the morning; goes a little stiffly after lunch."

He caught hold of it by the front wheel and the fork, and shook it violently.

I said: "Don't do that; you'll hurt it."

I did not see why he should shake it; it had not done anything to him. Besides, if it wanted shaking, I was the proper person to shake it. I felt much as I should had he started whacking my dog.

He said: "This front wheel wobbles."

I said: "It doesn't if you don't wobble it." It didn't wobble, as a matter of fact—nothing worth calling a wobble.

He said: "This is dangerous; have you got a screw-hammer?"

I ought to have been firm, but I thought that perhaps he really did know something about the business. I went to the tool shed to see what I could find. When I came back he was sitting on the ground with the front wheel between his legs. He was playing with it, twiddling it round between his fingers; the remnant of the machine was lying on the gravel path beside him.

He said: "Something has happened to this front wheel of yours."

"It looks like it, doesn't it?" I answered. But he was the sort of man that never understands satire.

He said: "It looks to me as if the bearings were all wrong."

I said: "Don't you trouble about it any more; you will make yourself tired. Let us put it back and get off."

He said: "We may as well see what is the matter with it, now it is out." He talked as though it had dropped out by accident.

Before I could stop him he had unscrewed something somewhere, and out rolled all over the path some dozen or so little balls.

"Catch'em!" he shouted; "catch 'em! We mustn't lose any of them." He was quite excited about them.

We grovelled round for half an hour, and found sixteen. He said he hoped we had got them all, because, if not, it would make a serious difference to the machine. He said there was nothing you should be more careful about in taking a bicycle to pieces than seeing you did not lose any of the balls. He explained that you ought to count them as you took them out, and see that exactly the same number went back in each place. I promised, if ever I took a bicycle to pieces I would remember his advice.

I put the balls for safety in my hat, and I put my hat upon the doorstep. It was not a sensible thing to do, I admit. As a matter of fact, it was a silly thing to do. I am not as a rule addleheaded; his influence must have affected me.

He then said that while he was about it he would see to the chain for me, and at once began taking off the gear-case. I did try to persuade him from that. I told him what an experienced friend of mine once said to me solemnly:

"If anything goes wrong with your gear-case, sell the machine and buy a new one; it comes cheaper."

He said: "People talk like that who understand nothing about machines. Nothing is easier than taking off a gear case."

I had to confess he was right. In less than five minutes he had the gear-case in two pieces, lying on the path, and was grovelling for screws. He said it was always a mystery to him the way screws disappeared.

We were still looking for the screws when Ethelbertha came out. She seemed surprised to find us there; she said she thought we had started hours ago.

He said: "We shan't be long now. I'm just helping your husband to overhaul this machine of his. It's a good machine; but they all want going over occasionally."

Ethelbertha said: "If you want to wash yourselves when you have done you might go into the back kitchen, if you don't mind; the girls have just finished the bedrooms."

She told me that if she met Kate they would probably go for a sail; but that in any case she would be back to lunch. I would have given a sovereign to be going with her. I was getting heartily sick of standing about watching this fool breaking up my bicycle.

Common sense continued to whisper to me: "Stop him, before he does any more mischief. You have a right to protect your own property from the ravages of a lunatic. Take him by the scruff of the neck, and kick him out of the gate!"

But I am weak when it comes to hurting other people's feelings, and I let him muddle on.

He gave up looking for the rest of the screws. He said screws had a knack of turning up when you least expected them, and that now he would see to the chain. He tightened it till it would not move; next he loosened it until it was twice as loose as it was before. Then he said we had better think about getting the front wheel back into its place again.

I held the fork open, and he worried with the wheel. At the end of ten minutes I suggested he should hold the forks, and that I should handle the wheel; and we changed places. At the end of his first minute he dropped the machine, and took a short walk round the croquet lawn, with his hand pressed together between his thighs. He explained as he walked that the thing to be careful about was to avoid getting your fingers pinched between the forks and the spokes of the wheel. I replied I was convinced, from my own experience, that there was much truth in what he said. He wrapped himself up in a couple of dusters, and we commenced again. At length we did get the thing into position; and the moment it was in position he burst out laughing.

I said: "What's the joke?"

He said: "Well, I am an ass!"

It was the first thing he had said that made me respect him. I asked him what had led him to the discovery.

He said: "We've forgotten the balls!"

I looked for my hat; it was lying topsyturvy in the middle of the path, and Ethelbertha's favourite hound was swallowing the balls as fast as he could pick them up.

"He will kill himself," said Ebbson—I have never met him since that day, thank the Lord; but I think his name was Ebbson—"they are solid steel."

I said: "I am not troubling about the dog. He has had a bootlace and a packet of needles already this week. Nature's the best guide; puppies seem to require this kind of stimulant. What I am thinking about is my bicycle."

He was of a cheerful disposition. He said: "Well, we must put back all we can find, and trust to providence."

We found eleven. We fixed six on one side and five on the other, and half an hour later the wheel was in its place again. It need hardly be added that it really did wobble now; a child might have noticed it. Ebbson said it would do for the present. He appeared to be getting a bit tired himself. If I had let him, he would, I believe, at this point have gone home. I was determined now, however, that he should stop and finish; I had abandoned all thoughts of a ride. My pride in the machine he had killed. My only interest lay now in seeing him scratch and bump and pinch himself. I revived his drooping spirits with a glass of beer and some judicious praise. I said:

"Watching you do this is of real use to me. It is not only your skill and dexterity that fascinates me, it is your cheery confidence in yourself, your inexplicable hopefulness, that does me good."

Thus encouraged, he set to work to refix the gear-case. He stood the bicycle against the house, and worked from the off side. Then he stood it against a tree, and worked from the near side. Then I held it for him, while he lay on the ground with his head between the wheels, and worked at it from below, and dropped oil upon himself. Then he took it away from me, and doubled himself across it like a pack-saddle, till he lost his balance and slid over on to his head. Three times he said:

"Thank heaven, that's right at last!"

And twice he said:

"No, I'm damned if it is after all!"

What he said the third time I try to forget.

Then he lost his temper and tried bullying the thing. The bicycle, I was glad to see, showed spirit; and the subsequent proceedings degenerated into little else than a rough-and-tumble fight between him and the machine. One moment the bicycle would be on the gravel path, and he on top of it; the next, the position would be reversed—he on the gravel path, the bicycle on him. Now he would be standing flushed with victory, the bicycle firmly fixed between his legs. But his triumph would be short-lived. By a sudden, quick movement it would free itself, and, turning upon him, hit him sharply over the head with one of its handles.

At a quarter to one, dirty and dishevelled, cut and bleeding, he said: "I think that will do"; and rose and wiped his brow.

The bicycle looked as if it also had had enough of it. Which had received most punishment it would have been difficult to say. I took him into the back kitchen, where, so far as was possible without soda and proper tools, he cleaned himself, and sent him home.

The bicycle I put into a cab and took round to the nearest repairing shop. The foreman of the works came up and looked at it.

"What do you want me to do with that?" said he.

"I want you," I said, "so far as is possible, to restore it."

"It's a bit far gone," said he; "but I'll do my best."

He did his best, which came to two pounds ten. But it was never the same machine again; and at the end of the season I left it in an agent's hands to sell. I wished to deceive nobody; I instructed the man to advertise it as a last year's machine. The agent advised me not to mention any date. He said:

"In this business it isn't a question of what is true and what isn't; it's a question of what you can get people to believe. Now, between you and me, it don't look like a last year's machine; so far as looks are concerned, it might be a ten-year-old. We'll say nothing about date; we'll just get what we can."

I left the matter to him, and he got me five pounds, which he said was more than he had expected.

3

Jerome K. Jerome

Who's in Front; What's in the Rear

From *Three Men on the Bummel*

There is always unpleasantness about this tandem. It is the theory of the man in front that the man behind does nothing; it is equally the theory of the man behind that he alone is the motive power, the man in front merely doing the puffing. The mystery will never be solved. It is annoying when Prudence is whispering to you on the one side not to overdo your strength and bring on heart disease; while Justice into the other ear is remarking: "Why should you do it all? This isn't a cab. He's not your passenger": to hear him grunt out:

"What's the matter—lost your pedals?"

Harris, in his early married days, made much trouble for himself on one occasion, owing to this impossibility of knowing what the person behind is doing. He was riding with his wife through Holland. The roads were stony, and the machine jumped a good deal.

"Sit tight," said Harris, without turning his head.

What Mrs. Harris thought he said was, "Jump off." Why she should have thought he said "Jump off," when he said "Sit tight," neither of them can explain.

Mrs. Harris puts it in this way: "If you had said, 'Sit tight,' why should I have jumped off?"

Harris puts it: "If I had wanted you to jump off, why should I have said 'Sit tight'?"

The bitterness is past, but they argue about the matter to this day.

Be the explanation what it may, however, nothing alters the fact that Mrs. Harris

From Jerome K. Jerome, *Three Men on the Bummel* (London: J. M. Dent and Sons, 1900), pp. 200–203.

did jump off, while Harris pedalled away hard, under the impression she was still behind him. It appears that at first she thought he was riding up the hill merely to show off. They were both young in those days, and he used to do that sort of thing. She expected him to spring to earth on reaching the summit, and lean in a careless and graceful attitude against the machine, waiting for her. When, on the contrary, she saw him pass the summit and proceed rapidly down a long and steep incline, she was seized, first with surprise, secondly with indignation, and lastly with alarm. She ran to the top of the hill and shouted, but he never turned his head. She watched him disappear into a wood a mile and a half distant, and then sat down and cried. They had had a slight difference that morning, and she wondered if he had taken it seriously and intended desertion. She had no money; she knew no Dutch. People passed, and seemed sorry for her; she tried to make them understand what had happened. They gathered that she had lost something, but could not grasp what. They took her to the nearest village, and found a policeman for her. He concluded from her pantomime that some man had stolen her bicycle. They put the telegraph into operation, and discovered in a village four miles off an unfortunate boy riding a lady's machine of an obsolete pattern. They brought him to her in a cart, but as she did not appear to want either him or his bicycle they let him go again, and resigned themselves to bewilderment.

Meanwhile Harris continued his ride with much enjoyment. It seemed to him that he had suddenly become stronger, and in every way a more capable cyclist. Said he to what he thought was Mrs. Harris:

"I haven't felt this machine so light for months. It's this air, I think; it's doing me good."

Then he told her not to be afraid, and he would show her how fast he could go. He bent down over the handles, and put his heart into his work. The bicycle bounded over the road like a thing of life; farmhouses and churches, dogs and chickens came to him and passed. Old folks stood and gazed at him, the children cheered him.

In this way he sped merrily onward for about five miles. Then, as he explains it, the feeling began to grow upon him that something was wrong. He was not surprised at the silence; the wind was blowing strongly, and the machine was rattling a good deal. It was a sense of void that came upon him. He stretched out his hand behind him, and felt; there was nothing there but space. He jumped, or rather fell off, and looked back up the road; it stretched white and straight through the dark wood, and not a living soul could be seen upon it. He remounted, and rode back up the hill. In ten minutes he came to where the road broke into four; there he dismounted and tried to remember which fork he had come down.

While he was deliberating, a man passed, sitting sideways on a horse. Harris stopped him, and explained to him that he had lost his wife. The man appeared to be neither surprised nor sorry for him. While they were talking another farmer came along, to whom the first man explained the matter, not as an accident, but as a good story. What appeared to surprise the second man most was that Harris should be making a fuss about the thing. He could get no sense out of either of them, and cursing them he mounted his machine again, and took the middle road on chance. Half-way up, he came upon a party of two young women with one young man between them. They appeared to be making the most of him. He asked them if they had seen his wife. They asked him what she was like. He did not know enough Dutch to describe her properly; all he could tell them was she was a very beautiful woman, of medium size. Evidently this did not satisfy them, the description was too general; any man could say that, and by this means perhaps get possession of a wife that did not belong to him. They asked him how she was dressed; for the life of him he could not recollect.

I doubt if any man could tell how any woman was dressed ten minutes after he had left her. He recollected a blue skirt, and then there was something that carried the dress on, as it were, up to the neck. Possibly, this may have been a blouse; he retained a dim vision of a belt; but what sort of a blouse? Was it green, or yellow, or blue? Had it a collar, or was it fastened with a bow? Were there feathers in her hat, or flowers? Or was it a hat at all? He dared not say, for fear of making a mistake and being sent miles after the wrong party. The two young women giggled, which in his then state of mind irritated Harris. The young man, who appeared anxious to get rid of him, suggested the police station at the next town. Harris made his way there. The police gave him a piece of paper, and told him to write down a full description of his wife, together with details of when and where he had lost her. He did not know where he had lost her; all he could tell them was the name of the village where he had lunched. He knew he had her with him then, and that they had started from there together.

The police looked suspicious; they were doubtful about three matters: Firstly, was she really his wife? Secondly, had he really lost her? Thirdly, why had he lost her? With the aid of a hotel-keeper, however, who spoke a little English, he overcame their scruples. They promised to act, and in the evening they brought her to him in a covered wagon, together with a bill for expenses. The meeting was not a tender one. Mrs. Harris is not a good actress, and always has great difficulty in disguising her feelings. On this occasion, she frankly admits, she made no attempt to disguise them.

4

Ring Lardner

"My Kingdom for a Horse," but Ring Prefers a Bicycle

TO THE EDITOR:

This week they was a big argument around the neighborhood broughten about by the parents of a young male boy wondering should they get him a horse or a bicycle for a birthday present, those being the 2 articles which he had expressed a desire for and they could not afford to give him both. They enquired amongst all the parents nearby of which they seems to be a great number and the opinions was split about even, most of the mothers declaring in favor of the horse and most of the fathers choosing the bicycle, which proves what I have always contended, namely that girls will be girls.

The arguments put forth by the horse fanciers was in substance as follows

1. That a horse gets attached to you and vice versa, whereas wile you may learn to love a bicycle the last named don't never reciprocate.

2. A horse lasts a whole lot longer than a bicycle.

3. A horse is a pet wile a bicycle is just a mechanical toy.

4. You don't have to carry a tool box with a horse and they don't never have tire trouble.

5. You can show a horse at a horse show and maybe get a blue ribbon.

Reprinted from the *San Francisco Examiner*, August 2, 1925, p. E4.

Bicycle vs. Horse

In opposition to these arguments some of we male parents give evidence in rebuttal as follows:

1. You don't have to show a bicycle at a horse show and you can buy a blue ribbon at pretty near any notion store for 3 cents a yard.

2. If you like your boy, why you may as well know that the motorists who infest these parts seem to have no compunctions vs. running into a horse, whereas the instance they see anybody on a bicycle they promptly slow down to practically nothing.

3. You can get a great bicycle for $40.00, but if you buy a $40.00 horse onlookers is going to begin talking about you.

4. Bicycles come all ready named, whereas you half to pick out a name for a horse and sometimes it all but racks your brains and then look at the results. Like for instants a well known cartoonist friend of mine called Bud Fisher or something got a hold of a horse and thought and thought and thought and in the final analysis as they say, he named the horse Swope.

5. Now in regards to keeping a bicycle. My own kiddies has a couple of them and on rainy nights they keep them in what I jokingly call my office and when they want to use them, they take them out, without putting no harnass on them or curring them or nothing. And during the time they are in there they don't never disturb me at what the critics refer to as my work.

Do you think I could work in the same office as a horse? All the time I would be saying to myself I can't work like a horse so why work at all. But I would always know that I can work as good as a bicycle because they's genally always something wrong with them, either they creak or they are rusty just like their room mate.

He Meant Well, Anyway

6. On the other hand if you have got a horse you half to find room for him in the stable and personly the only place we could room a horse would be in the next stable to our cow and how do you know that a horse and cow is going to get along under the same roof? Whereas I never met a cow that couldn't remain for years on friendly terms with a bicycle.

7. Finely I have never met a horse that did not holler murder if he was kept without food or gin for 2 days at the outside, wile on the other hand I have set in my office with the bicycles all winter long and the only noise in the room was me beating away on a typewriter.

That is the gist of the argument and I would like to hear expressions whether from partisans or neutrals in regards to what they think of the proposition as it has became very important in our little community and maybe one of you boys or girls could advance a thesis that would put the finishing touches on the argument.

5

Dylan Thomas

No Horsing Around

From *Me and My Bike*

In 1948, during his screenwriting days, Dylan Thomas wrote the first part of what he planned to be a much longer film operetta entitled Me and My Bike. *Unfortunately, at least for bicycle lovers, if not for the literati, he went no further with his original design.*

According to the foreword to the published version of Me and My Bike, *Dylan Thomas had envisioned an operetta about a man who rode "penny-farthings, tandems, tricycles, racing bikes—and when he dies at the end, he rides on his bike up a sunbeam straight to heaven, where he's greeted by a heavenly chorus of bicycle bells." But what we have as a finished product includes only the penny-farthing phase and then that appears nearly at the end of the script itself.*

Most of the remnant which we have of his original conception concerns the pettifoggery of the lavishly landed household of Sir Gregory Grig, where horsiness is next to godliness. Sir Gregory is all horse and to the marrow, even to the point that the author has "a chorus of horses, singing hoarsely in Yorkshire accents," hurrying Sir Gregory's young stable boy, Fred, about his manure-piling and other tasks. We are told that "Man's Best Friend is the horse" and this "Everybody knows. . . ." Indeed, the horse and hunt set so predominates Sir Gregory's household and that of the surrounding region that the local schoolchildren learn the alphabet according to horse races as follows:

A for Ascot
B for Bangor
C for Caesare witch
D for Derby

From Dylan Thomas, *Me and My Bike* (New York: McGraw-Hill Book Co., 1965), pp. 39, 43–52.

E for Epsom
G for Galway Races
[F *is omitted in original. Apparently no horse-racing place names begin with* F.]
H for Horse

The bicycle would seem to be an alien menace in such an environment and so it proves to be as Augustus Wilberforce, our bicycling hero, enters the stage on his penny-farthing, to the accompaniment of background music for the theme song "Me and My Bike," *as the Honourable Georgina Grig is singing (or is it pining?) at her boudoir window.*

"The cold, cold, deep river
That runs in the dale
Behind the tall bushes

Now tells an old tale,
With a ripple and quiver
O lover to be,
The lovely green rushes
Are singing to me.

Wherever he be
Under the sky,
In a far country,
Or riding by
On the green homely hill
Beyond my window sill
I am made for him and he is made for me.

Whoever he be
Under the sun,
A man of the sea,
Or a countryman
On the green homely hill
Beyond my window sill
I am dear to him and he is dear to me—"

In the far distance, a young man on a penny-farthing bicycle is riding down the slope of a country lane. He is clad in full bicycling costume of the eighties and rides his fearful machine with an attempt at debonair confidence, whistling the tune of "Me and my bike" as he wheels down the slope, but wincing as the rubberless wheels bump in each rut.

Georgina is still at her window and her harp, singing—

> The bees in their hives
> The leaves in their clusters
> Are humming and strumming
> My true lover's coming—

Suddenly, as she looks through the window, she ends the verse with a glad cry.

> Oh, darling Augustus!

Augustus on his penny-farthing is coming up the drive. We see his head above the bushes as he bicycles along in a hubbub of dogs barking and chickens squawking. Georgina is racing down the great stairs, her skirts billowing. She runs through the hall and opens the front door. On the steps, she stands to welcome Augustus. Augustus's head is bobbing up and down above the bushes of the drive. And now we see him, penny-farthing and all, ride up to the steps. A loud crowd of dogs barks, bays, bellows about the wheels. He wobbles. He alights. He raises his bicycling cap, and bows, stiffly and creakingly to Georgina. He stands at his penny-farthing's side, while Georgina exclaims in delight—

> Augustus!
> Georgina!

And the two lovers burst into a kind of song, half operatic, and recitative.

GEORGINA. How stern you appear
          With your penny-farthen,
          Augustus my dear,
          So imposing astride it
          and not scared a bit
          Oh, I'd have a fit
          If I even tried it!
AUGUSTUS. For you I would ride it,
          Georgina my dear,
          From here to Carmarthen.
GEORGINA. Oh how brave you are then
          On your penny-farthen!
AUGUSTUS. Though it is, I admit,
          Very sharp where you sit.
GEORGINA. How impressively you pedal!
AUGUSTUS. How excessively it shakes!
GEORGINA. Your monster made of metal
AUGUSTUS. And every whisker aches.
GEORGINA. How aggressively you pedal!
AUGUSTUS. Though it hasn't any brakes.

Georgina turns from Augustus and addresses the audience—

> How handsome my love
> Upon his boneshaker!
> How high up above!
> How the winds reel behind!
> But the day I get on it
> I'll eat my best bonnet
> And the small wheel behind.

AUGUSTUS. Oh for a steel behind!
              Then I would take her
              From here to Jamaica.
GEORGINA. Oh he'd never take her
              Upon his boneshaker.
AUGUSTUS. Bicycles rot 'em, yes!
              Hell is not bottomless!
GEORGINA. How swivelly
              You are then
AUGUSTUS. Oh my liverly
              And lights
GEORGINA. On your nasty penny-farthen
AUGUSTUS. Where the saddle sits and bites
GEORGINA. How busily
AUGUSTUS. How dizzily
GEORGINA. How knobbily
AUGUSTUS. How hobbily
GEORGINA. You wobble and you sway!
AUGUSTUS. O speedily
GEORGINA. Indeedily
BOTH.   Take the brute away!

As they reach the last lines of the song, the butler comes out on the steps. They direct the last injunction to him, and tell him with gestures, to remove the penny-farthing. With dignity, the butler comes down the steps, takes the penny-farthing from Augustus, who pushes it disgustedly towards him, and holds it at arm's length. Augustus whispers craftily in the butler's ear, and then he and Georgina, arm in arm, move off towards the shrubbery. Their faces are turned to one another as they go; her skirts sweep the ground; he walks with a creaking limp, slightly bowed in the tight-trousered legs. We follow them through the shrubbery paths towards the lawn, and hear their loving whispers.

"Come, my wasp-waisted treasure."

"But what if Papa returns, my prince?"

"Have no fear. I saw him but a short while ago, halfway between Magnum Tipling and Little Swig."

"But what if Papa observes your penny-farthing? He does not approve of modern inventions. He does not even believe in the balloon."

"Trust me, my whale-boned swan. Your papa will not see the penny-farthing. I have bribed the butler. Come, to our badminton!"

And they go on to the lawn.

The butler, outside the servants' quarters, passes at arm's length, and with a look of well-bred loathing, the penny-farthing to a footman.

> Take this hobject away.
> It's a heysore to horsemen.

Now the footman, with repugnance, is passing it to an under-footman.

> Take this error away.
> To 'orsemen it's 'ell.

Now the under-footman is passing it, with a scandalised expression, to a parlour-maid.

> Take this 'otch potch away.
> It's a insult to 'orseflesh.

Now the parlourmaid is passing it, with upturned nose and a refined accent, to an under-parlourmaid.

> Take this engine away.
> All bicycles smell.

The under-parlourmaid passes the penny-farthing to Nell and she, pushing it into the stable yard, eggs Fred on to ride it. She twits him with having no sense of adventure or daring. Fred looks with tempted longing at the penny-farthing as he tentatively turns the pedals and pushes it just a very little way along the cobbles of the yard. But Nell's scorn becomes increasingly derisive and at last and with difficulty, and with her assistance, he manages to get on to the back of the fearful machine. He begins to wobble across the yard, a look of mingled ecstasy and awe upon his face.

Augustus and Georgina are on the lawn playing badminton and singing—

> Back and fore
> Back and fore
> Battledore and shuttlecock
> Shuttlecock and battledore
> Back and fore
> Back and fore
> Oh what a battle for

Shuttlecock and battledore!
Oh what a subtle knock
Battledore and shuttlecock!
Back and fore
Back and fore
Oh what a shuttle for
Battlecock and shuttledore!
Oh what a battlecock!
Back and fore
Back and fore—

They stop suddenly as they see Fred on the penny-farthing wobbling down the drive. Astonished gardeners pop up their heads from bushes and borders as Fred careers down the drive. We follow him on his erratic course. Around the corner of the drive comes, at a spanking pace, Sir Gregory Grig in his gig. Fred, the penny-farthing out of control, goes faster and faster. We see Nell, at the top of the drive, her mouth wide open in horror. We see Augustus and Georgina fluttering with horror on the lawn. One by one the gardeners shut their eyes . . . CRASH!

This is the end of Dylan Thomas's script.

6

J. G. Farrell

The Constable's
Double Fault

From *Troubles*

In July of 1919, Major Brendan Archer finds himself among the very extraordinary residents of the once majestic Majestic Hotel standing or, rather, in the process of decaying on a peninsula at Kilnalough, Ireland. The hotel's current owner is Edward Spencer; Major Archer has sought out the Majestic for the purpose of wedding Angela Spencer, one of the owner's two daughters.

Ripon Spencer, Edward's son, is another inhabitant of the hotel at a time of troubles for the English with the Irish and the Bolsheviks and in the colonies, i.e., India.

Ripon had attached himself to the Major and had begun to tell him about a curious incident that had occurred at a tennis party not far away at Valebridge a few days earlier. A heavily armed bicycle patrol had surprised two suspicious individuals (no doubt Sinn Feiners) tampering with the canal bridge. One of them had fled across the fields and made good his escape. The other, who had a bicycle and was disinclined to leave it, had been confident that he could outpedal the Royal Irish Constabulary. Although for the first fifty yards the fugitive, pedalling desperately, had swerved to and fro in front of the peelers almost within grabbing range, he had then slowly pulled away. By the time they had slowed their pursuit to draw their revolvers the Sinn Feiner

From J. G. Farrell, *Troubles* (New York: Alfred A. Knopf, 1970), pp. 28–31.

had increased his lead to almost a hundred yards. He slowed too, however, when the first shots began to whistle round his ears and had possibly even decided to give himself up when disaster struck his pursuers. One of the Constables had removed both hands from the handlebars in order to take a steady, two-handed aim at the cyclist ahead. Unfortunately, just as he was squeezing the trigger he had veered wilding, colliding with his companions. The result was that all three had taken a nasty fall. As they had painfully got to their feet and dusted themselves off, expecting to see their quarry vanishing over the brow of the hill, they saw to their surprise that he too was slowing down. They hurriedly straightened their handlebars and, standing on the pedals to accelerate, sped towards the Sinn Feiner; the chain had come off his bicycle. Instead of awaiting capture he had abandoned his bicycle and fled into the drive of the house where the tennis party was going on. What a shock the tennis players and spectators had got when all of a sudden a shabbily dressed young man had sped out of the shrubbery and across the court to gallop full tilt into the wire netting (which he evidently hadn't seen)! Under the impact—he had crumpled to his knees. But though he seemed stunned, almost immediately he began to pull himself up by gripping the wire links with his fingers. Then someone had hurled a tennis ball at him. He had turned round as if surprised to see so many faces watching him. Then another tennis ball had been thrown, and another—at this the man had come to his senses and veered along the netting in search of an opening. Not finding one he had leaped up and clung to the netting to drag himself upwards. But by now everyone was on their feet hurling tennis balls. Then one of the women had joined in, throwing an empty glass but he still managed to pull himself up. Someone (Ripon thought it might have been old Dr. Ryan, the "senile old codger" they had been having tea with) had shouted for them to stop. But nobody paid any attention. A tennis racket went revolving through the air and only missed by inches. Someone tore off his tennis shoes and threw them, one of them hitting the fugitive in the small of the back. He had paused now to gather strength. Then he was climbing again. A beer bottle shattered against one of the steel supports beside his head and a heavy walking-shoe sruck him on the arm. Then, at last, a racket press had gone spinning through the air to hit him in the back of the head. He had dropped like a sack of potatoes and lay there unconscious. But when the breathless, red-faced peelers had finally arrived panting to arrest their suspect it was to find the tennis players and their wives still hurling whatever they could find at the prone and motionless Sinn Feiner. . . .

"Good heavens!" exclaimed the Major. "What an incredible story! Frankly, I find it a bit hard to believe that people would throw things at an unconscious man. Did you see all this happen yourself?"

"Well, no, I wasn't actually present. But I've spoken to a lot of people who were there and . . . but what I wanted to say . . ."

"I must ask Dr. Ryan, the 'senile old codger' as you call him."

"But I haven't finished," cried Ripon. "The thing is, it turned out later that this fellow wasn't a Shinner at all. He was just repairing the bridge with another workman."

7

Stephen Crane

New York's Bicycle Speedway

Few would imagine that the author of The Red Badge of Courage *(1895) would also be the author of "New York's Bicycle Speedway," published in the* New York Sun *on July 5, 1896, under the title "Transformed Boulevard." Yet the writings of Stephen Crane manifest how versatile and prolific he was.*

Crane, at his death in 1900 at the age of twenty-nine, could lay claim to the authorship of ten printed volumes, as well as to his journalistic pieces for the New York Herald. *As a reporter for the* New York Herald, *he would have had to be blind or cloistered to miss the escapades of the then omnipresent bicyclists.*

Even though tilts between bicyclists and the police might have been madcap fun in the 1890s, the relationship between the police and bicyclists today is more solemn and often more acerbic as well. Indeed, according to a recent New York Times *editorial, the campus police at Central Washington University in Ellensburg, Washington, have decided to use radar to catch speeding and hit-and-run bicyclists using campus roads and paths. The officials in blue in the bicycle's heyday were also irked by the "take charge" attitude of bicyclists. This irritation, as Stephen Crane recounts, could be the source of much "hellzapoppin" mirth.*

Just as the police and the bicycle have never reached an entente cordiale, so the truck driver and the bicyclist have forever been feuding. It is not often that the bicycle bests the behemoth, but Crane's article on the "speedway" reveals that there was a time and a place where bicycle power ousted and even terrorized truckers, at least the horse-drawn variety. Unfortunately, Mack and the internal combustion engine have made those idyllic days matters of legend rather than current fact.

From R. W. Stallman and E. R. Hagemann, eds., *The New York City Sketches of Stephen Crane and Related Pieces* (New York: New York University Press, 1966), pp. 149–51.

NEW YORK, July 3, 1896.—The Bowery has had its day as a famous New York street. It is now a mere tradition. Broadway will long hold its place as the chief vein of the city's life. No process of expansion can ever leave it abandoned to the cheap clothing dealers and dime museum robbers. It is too strategic in position. But lately the Western Boulevard which slants from the Columbus monument at the southwest corner of Central Park to the river has vaulted to a startling prominence and is now one of the sights of New York. This is caused by the bicycle. Once the Boulevard was a quiet avenue whose particular distinctions were its shade trees and its third foot-walk which extended in Parisian fashion down the middle of the street. Also it was noted for its billboards and its huge and slumberous apartment hotels. Now, however, it is the great thoroughfare for bicycles. On these gorgeous spring days they appear in thousands. All mankind is a-wheel apparently and a person on nothing but legs feels like a strange animal. A mighty army of wheels streams from the brick wilderness below Central Park and speeds over the asphalt. In the cool of the evening it returns with swaying and flashing of myriad lamps.

The bicycle crowd has completely subjugated the street. The glittering wheels dominate it from end to end. The cafes and dining rooms or the apartment hotels are occupied mainly by people in bicycle clothes. Even the billboards have surrendered. They advertise wheels and lamps and tires and patent saddles with all the flaming vehemence of circus art. Even when they do condescend to still advertise a patent medicine, you are sure to confront a lithograph of a young person in bloomers who is saying in large type: "Yes, George, I find that Willowrum always refreshes me after these long rides."

Down at the Circle where stands the patient Columbus, the stores are crowded with bicycle goods. There are innumerable repair shops. Everything is bicycle. In the afternoon the parade begins. The great discoverer, erect on his tall grey shaft, must feel his stone head whirl when the battalions come swinging and shining around the curve.

It is interesting to note the way in which the blasphemous and terrible truck-drivers of the lower part of the city will hunt a bicyclist. A truck-driver, of course, believes that a wheelman is a pest. The average man could not feel more annoyance if nature had suddenly invented some new kind of mosquito. And so the truckdriver resolves in his dreadful way to make life as troublous and thrilling for the wheelman as he possibly can. The wheelman suffers under a great handicap. He is struggling over the most uneven cobbles which bless a metropolis. Twenty horses threaten him and forty wheels miss his shoulder by an inch. In his ears there is a hideous din. It surrounds him, envelopes him.

Add to this trouble, then, a truckman with a fiend's desire to see dead wheelmen. The situation affords deep excitement for everyone concerned.

But when a truck-driver comes to the Boulevard the beautiful balance of the universe is apparent. The teamster sits mute, motionless, casting sidelong glances at the wheels which spin by him. He still contrives to exhibit a sort of a sombre defiance, but he has no oath nor gesture nor wily scheme to drive a 3 ton wagon over the prostrate body of some unhappy cyclist. On the Boulevard this roaring lion from down town is so subdued, so isolated that he brings tears to the sympathetic eye.

There is a new game on the Boulevard. It is the game of Bicycle Cop and Scorcher. When the scorcher scorches beyond the patience of the law, the bicycle policeman, if in sight, takes after him. Usually the scorcher has a blissful confidence in his ability to scorch and thinks it much easier to just ride away from the policeman than to go to court and pay a fine. So they go flying up the Boulevard with the whole mob of wheelmen and wheelwomen, eager to see the race, sweeping after them. But the bicycle police are mighty hard riders and it takes a flier to escape them. The affair usually ends in calamity for the scorcher, but in the meantime fifty or sixty cyclists have had a period of delirious joy.

Bicycle Cop and Scorcher is a good game, but after all it is not as good as the game that was played in the old days when the suggestion of a corps of bicycle police in neat knickerbockers would have scandalized Mulberry street. This was the game of Fat Policeman on Foot Trying to Stop a Spurt. A huge, unwieldy officer rushing out into the street and wildly trying to head off and grab some rider who was spinning along in just one silver flash was a sight that caused the populace to turn out in a body. If some madman started at a fierce gait from the Columbus monument, he could have the consciousness that at frequent and exciting intervals, red-faced policemen would gallop out at him and frenziedly clutch at his coat-tails. And owing to a curious dispensation, the majority of the policemen along the boulevard were very stout and could swear most graphically in from two to five languages.

But they changed all that. The un-police-like bicycle police are wonderfully clever and the vivid excitement of other days is gone. Even the scorcher seems to feel depressed and narrowly looks over the nearest officer before he starts on his frantic career.

The girl in bloomers is, of course, upon her native heath when she steers her steel steed into the Boulevard. One becomes conscious of a bewildering variety in bloomers. There are some that fit and some that do not fit. There are some that were not made to fit and there are some that couldn't fit anyhow. As a matter of fact the bloomer costume is now in one of the primary stages of its evolution. Let us hope so at any rate. Of course every decent citizen concedes that women shall wear what they please and it is supposed that he covenants with himself not to grin and nudge his neighbor when anything particularly amazing passes him on the street but resolves to simply and industriously mind his own affairs. Still the situation no doubt harrows him greatly. No man was ever found to defend bloomers. His farthest statement, as an individual, is to advocate them for all women he does not know and cares nothing about. Most women become radical enough to say: "Why shouldn't I wear 'em, if I choose." Still, a second look at the Boulevard convinces one that the world is slowly, solemnly, inevitably coming to bloomers. We are about to enter an age of bloomers, and the bicycle, that machine which has gained an economic position of the most tremendous importance, is going to be responsible for more than the bruises on the departed fat policemen of the Boulevard.

8

Giovanni Guareschi

Flying Skirts

From *The Little World of Don Camillo*

The gentle and engrossing humor of Guareschi's Don Camillo series of books has delighted countless thousands of readers over the years. References to the bicycle appear quite regularly in them, particularly in The Little World of Don Camillo. *And this is not unexpected, for the locale of this story is a village "somewhere in the valley of the Po River" in Northern Italy where bicycles are as profuse as bees at a Sunday afternoon's summer picnic.*

The simplicity of the story is as refreshing as the humor. Don Camillo is a vigorous, assertive parish priest in a village peopled by Communists, whose mayor is the Communist Peppone. The subjects of the individual chapters, which can, in most cases, stand independently of each other, are the incessant feuds of the Church, represented by Don Camillo against the Communists, in the person of Peppone.

In spite of these constant squabbles, it is clear that Don Camillo and Peppone, if not the best of friends, are not the worst of enemies, either. Certainly, their having been allies and companions as resistance fighters against the Fascists ensures their benign tolerance of each other, at the very least.

The entente cordiale between them surfaces when Peppone fires at an assassin who seeks to kill Don Camillo. And, in his turn, Don Camillo jumps into the ring to floor an upstart prizefighter who has downed Peppone at the festivities celebrating the dedication of a new People's Palace building in the village. In these disputes, Don Camillo always seems to have the last word, that is, save for that of the Lord who, from his position on the cross in the village's church, gives kindly guidance and, often, mild remonstrance to Don Camillo.

From Giovanni Guareschi, *The Little World of Don Camillo* (London: Victor Gollancz, 1951), pp. 32–36.

Don Camillo had let himself go a bit in the course of a little sermon with a local background, allowing himself some rather pointed allusions to *"certain people"* and it was thus that on the following evening, when he seized the ropes of the church bells— the bell-ringer having been called away on some pretext—all hell broke out. Some damned soul had tied crackers to the clappers of the bells. No harm done, of course, but there was a shattering din of explosions, enough to give the ringer heart failure.

Don Camillo had not said a word. He had celebrated the evening service in perfect composure, before a crowded congregation from which not one was absent, with Peppone in the front row and every countenance a picture of fervour. It was enough to infuriate a saint, but Don Camillo was no novice in self-control and his audience had gone home disappointed.

As soon as the big doors were closed, Don Camillo snatched up an overcoat and on his way out went to make a hasty genuflection before the altar.

"Don Camillo," said the Lord, "put it down."

"I don't understand," protested Don Camillo.

"Put it down!"

Don Camillo drew a heavy stick from beneath his coat and laid it in front of the altar.

"Not a pleasant sight, Don Camillo."

"But, Lord! It isn't even oak; it's only poplar, light and supple . . ." Don Camillo pleaded.

"Go to bed, Don Camillo, and forget about Peppone."

Don Camillo had raised his arms and had gone to bed with a temperature. And so when on the following evening Peppone's wife made her appearance at the presbytery, he leaped to his feet as though a cracker had gone off under his chair.

"Don Camillo," began the woman, who was visibly greatly agitated. But Don Camillo interrupted her. "Get out of my sight, sacrilegious creature!"

"Don Camillo, never mind about that foolishness. At Castellino there is that poor wretch who tried to support Peppone! They have turned him out!"

Don Camillo lighted a cigar. "Well, what about it, comrade? I didn't make the amnesty. And in any case, why should you bother about it?"

The woman started to shout. "I'm bothering because they came to tell Peppone, and Peppone has gone rushing off to Castellino like a lunatic. And he has taken his tommy-gun with him!"

"I see; then you have got concealed arms, have you?"

"Don Camillo, never mind about politics! Can't you understand that Peppone is out to kill! Unless you help me, my man is done for!"

Don Camillo laughed unpleasantly. "Which will teach him to tie crackers to the clappers of my bells. I shall be pleased to watch him die in gaol! You get out of my house!"

Ten minutes later, Don Camillo, with his skirts tucked up almost to his neck, was pedalling like a lunatic along the road to Castellino astride a racing bicycle belonging to the son of his sacristan.

There was a splendid moon and when he was about four miles from Castellino Don

Camillo saw by its light a man sitting on the low parapet of the little bridge that spans the Fossone. He slowed down, since it is always best to be prudent when one travels by night, and halted some ten yards from the bridge, holding in his hand a small object that he happened to have discovered in his pocket.

"My lad," he inquired, "have you seen a big man go by on a bicycle in the direction of Castellino?"

"No, Don Camillo," replied the other quietly.

Don Camillo drew nearer. "Have you already been to Castellino?" he asked.

"No. I thought it over. It wasn't worth while. Was it my fool of a wife who put you to this trouble?"

"Trouble? Nothing of the kind . . . a little constitutional!"

"Have you any idea what a priest looks like on a racing bicycle?" sniggered Peppone.

Don Camillo came and sat beside him on his wall. "My son, you must be prepared to see all kinds of things in this world."

Less than an hour later, Don Camillo was back at the presbytery and went to make his report to the Lord.

"All went well according to Your instructions."

"Well done, Don Camillo, but would you mind telling me who it was that instructed you to take him by the feet and tumble him into the ditch?"

Don Camillo raised his arms. "To tell you the truth, I really can't remember exactly. As a matter of fact, he appeared to dislike the sight of a priest on a racing bicycle, so it seemed only kind to prevent him from seeing it any longer."

"I understand. Has he got back yet?"

"He'll be here soon. Seeing him fall into the ditch, it struck me that as he would be coming home in a rather damp condition he might find the bicycle in his way, so I thought it best to bring it along with me."

"Very kind of you, I'm sure, Don Camillo," said the Lord with perfect gravity.

Peppone appeared just before dawn at the door of the presbytery. He was soaked to the skin, and Don Camillo asked if it was raining.

"Fog," replied Peppone with chattering teeth. "May I have my bicycle?"

"Why, of course. There it is."

"Are you sure there wasn't a tommy-gun tied to it?"

Don Camillo raised his arms with a smile. "A tommy-gun? And what may that be?"

"I," said Peppone as he turned from the door, "have made one mistake in my life. I tied crackers to the clappers of your bells. It should have been half a ton of dynamite."

"*Errare humanum est,*" remarked Don Camillo.

9

Ernest Hemingway

Saddlesores
for Early Birds

From *The Sun Also Rises*

Autobiographical details are commonplace in Hemingway's fiction. As a result, his
commentators have almost made a game of picking the persons who were the prototypes
for the characters in his works. The Sun Also Rises, *being one of his earliest novels, is*
more susceptible to this pastime than some of his later books.

Jake Barnes, the protagonist, is modeled, to a large extent, after Hemingway him-
self. Jake is a free-lance journalist (stringer). Most significantly, Jake's physical in-
juries, which made him impotent, were the result of war wounds very much like those
suffered by Hemingway but without the disabling effect upon his procreative powers
which Jake experienced. Lady Brett Ashley, who is rather profligate with her affections,
is said to be identified with Lady Duff Twysden.

The Pamplona bullfights, the Paris scene, and the Lost Generation, who are so
generously represented, are all sliced from Hemingway's own life. The characters are
tragic, but, according to the author, "the real hero was the earth and you get the sense
of its triumph in abiding forever."[1] But, even in tragedy, Hemingway could have a
sense of humor, broadly speaking. The following excerpt captures something of this
aspect of his creativity. Indeed, even in the real life of Lady Duff, Hemingway could
find the kind of tragicomedy which causes unpremeditated laughter, for instance, when
a fat man is seen running after a departing bus. Lady Duff died at forty-three.

Her pallbearers had all been her lovers. On leaving the church, where she had had

From Ernest Hemingway, *The Sun Also Rises* (New York: Charles Scribner's Sons, 1926), pp. 234–37.

a proper service, one of the grieving pallbearers slipped on the church steps and the casket dropped and split open.

Jake's conduct, in the following excerpt, typifies the frailty of his personality, as his maiming signifies the incompleteness of his manhood. At another time, after introducing the innocent bullfighter, Romero, to the Circe-like Lady Brett, Jake goes swimming for two days off the beach at San Sebastian. Although he sees and dwells upon the open sea beyond the breakers and the headlands across the harbor, he will not (or is it cannot?) venture out into the open sea or across the harbor. Jake's flawed personality even enables him to accept the infidelities of Lady Brett taciturnly. Unlike Jake, Romero is a character with a code that he courageously lives. Bicycle road racers too have a special brand of courage, which Jake could recognize, even though he could not join it—at the 5:45 A.M. starting time.

Even on a hot day San Sebastian has a certain early-morning quality. The trees seem as though their leaves were never quite dry. The streets feel as though they had just been sprinkled. It is always cool and shady on certain streets on the hottest day. I went to a hotel in the town where I had stopped before, and they gave me a room with a balcony that opened out above the roofs of the town. There was a green mountainside beyond the roofs.

I unpacked my bags and stacked my books on the table beside the head of the bed, put out my shaving things, hung up some clothes in the big armoire, and made up a bundle for the laundry. Then I took a shower in the bathroom and went down to lunch. Spain had not changed to summer-time, so I was early. I set my watch again. I had recovered an hour by coming to San Sebastian.

As I went into the dining-room the concierge brought me a police bulletin to fill out. I signed it and asked him for two telegraph forms, and wrote a message to the Hotel Montoya, telling them to forward all mail and telegrams for me to this address. I calculated how many days I would be in San Sebastian and then wrote out a wire to the office asking them to hold mail, but forward all wires for me to San Sebastian for six days. Then I went in and had lunch.

After lunch I went up to my room, read a while, and went to sleep. When I woke it was half past four. I found my swimming-suit, wrapped it with a comb in a towel, and went down-stairs and walked up the street to the Concha. The tide was about half-way out. The beach was smooth and firm, and the sand yellow. I went into a bathing-cabin, undressed, put on my suit, and walked across the smooth sand to the sea. The sand was warm under bare feet. There were quite a few people in the water and on the beach. Out beyond where the headlands of the Concha almost met to form the harbor there was a white line of breakers and the open sea. Although the tide was going out, there were a few slow rollers. They came in like undulations in the water, gathered weight of water, and then broke smoothly on the warm sand. I waded out. The water was cold. As a roller came I dove, swam out under water, and came to the surface with all the chill gone. I swam out to the raft, pulled myself up, and lay on the hot planks. A boy and girl were at the other end. The girl had undone the top of her bathing-suit and was browning her back. The boy lay face downward on the raft and talked to her. She laughed at things he said, and turned her brown back in the sun. I lay on the raft in the sun until I was dry. Then I tried several dives. I dove deep once, swimming down to the bottom. I swam with my eyes open and it was green and dark. The raft made a dark shadow. I came out of water beside the raft, pulled up, dove once more, holding it for length, and then swam ashore. I lay on the beach until I was dry, then went into the bathing-cabin, took off my suit, sloshed myself with fresh water, and rubbed dry.

I walked around the harbor under the trees to the casino, and then up one of the cool streets to the Cafe Marinas. There was an orchestra playing inside the cafe and I sat out on the terrace and enjoyed the fresh coolness in the hot day, and had a glass of lemon-juice and shaved ice and then a long whiskey and soda. I sat in front of the Marinas for a long time and read and watched the people, and listened to the music.

Later when it began to get dark, I walked around the harbor and out along the promenade, and finally back to the hotel for supper. There was a bicycle-race on, the Tour du Pays Basque, and the riders were stopping that night in San Sebastian. In the dining-room, at one side, there was a long table of bicycle-riders, eating with their trainers and managers. They were all French and Belgians, and paid close attention to their meal, but they were having a good time. At the head of the table were two good-looking French girls, with much Rue du Faubourg Montmartre chic. I could not make out whom they belonged to. They all spoke in slang at the long table and there were many private jokes and some jokes at the far end that were not repeated when the girls asked to hear them. The next morning at five o'clock the race resumed with the last lap, San Sebastian–Bilbao. The bicycle-riders drank much wine, and were burned and browned by the sun. They did not take the race seriously except among themselves. They had raced among themselves so often that it did not make much difference who won. Especially in a foreign country. The money could be arranged.

The man who had a matter of two minutes lead in the race had an attack of boils, which were very painful. He sat on the small of his back. His neck was very red and the blond hairs were sunburned. The other riders joked him about his boils. He tapped on the table with his fork.

"Listen," he said, "to-morrow my nose is so tight on the handlebars that the only thing touches those boils is a lovely breeze."

One of the girls looked at him down the table, and he grinned and turned red. The Spaniards, they said, did not know how to pedal.

I had coffee out on the terrasse with the team manager of one of the big bicycle manufacturers. He said it had been a very pleasant race, and would have been worth watching if Bottechia had not abandoned it at Pamplona. The dust had been bad, but in Spain the roads were better than in France. Bicycle road-racing was the only sport in the world, he said. Had I ever followed the Tour de France? Only in the papers. The Tour de France was the greatest sporting event in the world. Following and organizing the road races had made him know France. Few people know France. All spring and all summer and all fall he spent on the road with bicycle road-racers. Look at the number of motor-cars now that followed the riders from town to town in a road race. It was a rich country and more *sportif* every year. It would be the most *sportif* country in the world. It was bicycle road-racing did it. That and football. He knew France. *La France Sportive*. He knew road-racing. We had a cognac. After all, though, it wasn't bad to get back to Paris. There is only on Paname. In all the world, that is. Paris is the town the most *sportif* in the world. Did I know the *Chope de Negre?* Did I not. I would see him there some time. I certainly would. We would drink another *fine* together. We certainly would. They started at six o'clock less a quarter in the morning. Would I be up for the depart? I would certainly try to. Would I like him to call me? It was very interesting. I would leave a call at the desk. He would not mind calling me. I could not let him take the trouble. I would leave a call at the desk. We said good-bye until the next morning.

In the morning when I awoke the bicycle-riders and their following cars had been on the road for three hours.

Part VI

Bang of the Last Lap Bell

Introduction

—Barang!
Bang of the last lap bell spurred the half mile wheelmen to their sprint.

James Joyce,
Ulysses

The word is out. Arsène Lupin, the gentleman-burglar, and Godot, for whom everyone is waiting, have been unmasked.

Arsène Lupin, the irrepressible burglar who could enter the residence of Baron Schormann but depart empty-handed, leaving a card announcing: "Arsène Lupin, the gentleman-burglar, will return when the furniture is genuine"; Arsène Lupin, "the man of a thousand disguises: in turn a chauffeur, detective, bookmaker, Russian physician, Spanish bull-fighter, commercial traveler, robust youth, or decrepit old man"; Arsène Lupin "was the bicyclist who won the Grand Prix de l'Exposition, received his ten thousand francs, and was never heard of again." Of course, that is only one of many explanations of his pedigree. He is also reputed to have been "the person who saved so many lives through the little dormer-window at the Charity Bazaar; and, at the same time, picked their pockets."[1]

And Godot!

As the story is told, Samuel Beckett

encountered a large group of people standing on a street corner one afternoon during the annual Tour de France bicycle race and he asked what they were doing. 'Nous attendons Godot,' they replied, adding that all the competitors had passed except the oldest, whose name was Godot.[2]

Yet other interpretations for the origin of Godot abound. Some would find *God* in *Godot*. Others would note that there is a rue Godot in Paris, where Beckett, so it is said, was accosted by a prostitute. According to this probably apocryphal story, the spurned prostitute, in a tantrum, asked Beckett if he was so selective that he was "waiting for Godot?" Godot is also close to the French slang *godillot*, *godasse*, which means boot, signifying the prevalence of movement by foot in "Waiting for Godot." Beckett seems to savor this philological mystery, for he has himself offered the rue Godot and bicycle racer Godot explanations with "a wry smile."[3]

Le Tour de France se gagne au lit. (A French proverb)

In contemporary America, if Godot and Lupin were bicycle racers, the public would be oblivious to them. Bicycle racing (on this there is no doubt) is not the sport in America that it once was. The American people, by and large, neither understand nor witness the strategy and excitement of road or track racing. And the press coverage of the sport is either lackluster or, worse, abysmal. When the "Junior Worlds" came to Washington, D.C., in 1978, returning to the United States after an absence of many years, *Sports Illustrated* could not find the space to include an article on this race which had a massed, breath-catching photo finish of fourteen bicyclists clocked in the same time over the seventy-six-mile route.

Fourth fiddle was not always the place of bicycle racing in this country. From the turn of the century to the mid-1930s, bicycle dromomaniacs could be found anywhere on and off the track. The names of some of the American racers became legendary throughout the world. Major Taylor, Mile-a-Minute Murphy, and Bobby Waltham, Sr., are just a few of our fabled greats.

This disinterest in bicycle racing is a peculiarly American anomaly. The rest of the world reacts to bicycle racing with the frenzy and delight that Americans reserve for baseball and football. And it is no wonder. Bicycle racing, to say the least, evokes colorful imagery. Joyce's Bloom sees a bicycle poster as depicting a

cyclist doubled up like a cod in a pot. Damn bad ad. Now if they had made it round like a wheel. Then the spokes: sports, sports, sports: And the hub big: college. Something to catch the eye.[4]

At a later point in *Ulysses* the "lacquey" at the door of Dillon's auction rooms shakes his handbell and

—Barang!
Bang of the last lap bell spurred the half mile wheelmen to their sprint. [The racers,] their stretched necks wagging, negotiated the curve by the College Library.[5]

Maurice Shadbolt, in his tragic tale of petty minds at large in a small New Zealand town, describes the start of a bicycle race in similarly spirited tones.

A whistle shrilled, a pistol banged, and the senior race began. Headgeared, taut-faced, the riders leapt from their saddles, jerking pedals, making speed, zipping past.[6]

"Skeleton-functional as their machines"[7]; such is the look of bicycle racers, especially in the momentum of a pack.
Save for the pursuit race, and motor-paced bicycle racing, most bicycle racing involves bodies and bikes bunched into a balled pack. The pack is a kaleidoscope of colorful action. It is dizzying, death-menacing motion. It is

a big flashing flock, their stockinged legs, blue, red, green, pumping up and down, up and down, like pistons; their feet attached to the pedals so that their ankles work like bearings, the big wheels with the chrome spokes winking at the sun, sending motes over blue, green, red stockings.[8]

One of the principal advantages of riding in a pack is that it constitutes a man-made windbreak. The phalanx enables those in the rear to be drawn along, nearly effortlessly, in the slipstream of those in front. The common term denoting this tactic is drafting.
It is an extreme challenge to break away from the pack. The wind bears down on the leaders while the followers just go along for the ride. Daniel Behrman, however, tells of one racer who had a knack for winning—by a nose.

There is one little fellow at Longchamp who can leave me behind. He uses a liniment to warm up his thigh muscles and it lays a barrage of reek right behind his rear wheel. No one can get near him; he rushes around Longchamp at the head of the flock, invincible in his liniment. We can only pick him up on the backstretch where the wind turns; now it buoys us along, we whir at twenty-five miles per hour as if we were sitting in our living rooms; the air is still, the Flying Skunk loses most of his advantage, we can put him behind.[9]

Drafting appears in contexts totally removed from bicycling. Those who understand the principles of drafting in bicycling have instant access to new insights in these other areas of endeavor. Roger Vailland in *The Law* uses bicycle drafting as a metaphor to elucidate the art of mullet fishing. His method is contingent upon the fact that

Mullets attract one another. The difficulty lies only in catching the first and in the chances of its being plump, robust, full of life, full of attraction. This first mullet, which is known as the *richiamo*, the bait, is thrown back into the sea, attached to a line long enough for it to move freely about inside the net, but too short to allow it to reach the wall of the cliff. . . .

A second mullet would come along (or had already come along) to join the first—the one attached to the line, the bait—and attach himself to him, slightly to the rear, his head level with the dorsal fins, in exactly the same way as, in the course of a race, one cyclist attaches himself to another cyclist, his front wheel against the other's back wheel. The second mullet would describe the same circles, ovals, arabesques, zigzags as the bait, heading towards the rocks with him, returning with him vertically below the lookout, slowing and accelerating with him, attached to him.[10]

Bicycle riders tend to be dreamers. All seem to be united under one banner—the craving to excel. Either they are racers or they want to be. Sometimes the dream is father to the reality. And sometimes not.

Mick, in Maurice Shadbolt's "Love Story," found that his dreams had an evanescent and misleading promise of future successes on the bicycle track.

He thought, as he often did, of his single visit to the city: of the crowded stadium and the silky interweaving colours of the riders flashing around the long banked floodlit oval of concrete. That part of his memory always talked bright things to his tired mind. One day soon, not far away now, he would go to the city and find a job; and ride the floodlit track. He would do well: everyone seemed agreed on that. They said it was remarkable how a boy with so little competition on a rough grass track in a country town could develop so quickly and record such good times. He would, they predicted, be a champion.[11]

The same delusional trait appears in the ill-fated, one-dimensional Martin with whom we suffer in the selection from Marcel Aymé's "The Last." Both Homer Macauley and Professor Jeffrey, in the excerpts from William Saroyan and John D. MacDonald, respectively, are dreamers, except that Homer's dream becomes a sad reality, while Professor Jeffrey dreams of a grandeur that age has put beyond his ken. Paul Morand's "Six-Day Night" is less a dream than a nightmare as the torture of the six-day races, in the good ol' days, always was. And Alfred Jarry's dialectic makes us pause to wonder, as dreams often do.

1

Ernest Hemingway

On the Right Track!

From *A Moveable Feast*

The sport of bicycle racing in all its many forms—from the criterium to the cyclocross—has never really caught on in this country. The six-day bike races of years ago were the exception. But they have long since departed from the scene and so has the old Madison Square Garden, the citadel for the six-day bike races in their heyday.

There are various explanations for the failure of bicycle racing to attract a wide audience in the United States. Some would see it as bicycle racing's lack of a television presence. The autophobe would cast the blame on the internal combustion engine. Others reason that the long-delayed finish of a typical bicycle race is without the glamour and the excitement that an American sports audience demands. And yet that is also true of long-distance foot racing, which seems to interest the public at large in, say, for example, the annual Boston marathon. But America has no Tour de France (the Red Zinger is a wastrel cousin) nor does it seem capable of supporting one—at this time.

Yet other countries and other peoples have shown nearly a zealot's dedication to bicycle racing. European velodromes are the equivalent of football stadiums in this country. Bicyclists are, in other countries, national heroes to be feted and compensated like super-bowl champions. In fact, elsewhere, bicycling is a way of life in or out of competitive cycling. And that might just explain the inadequacy of bicycle racing in America.

To Ernest Hemingway, in any event, the sport of bicycle racing would seem to have been a natural source of literary inspiration. As reflected in much of his writing, Hemingway was a sports fanatic. Boxing, bullfighting, horse racing, and his ever-most-cherished deep-sea fishing were constant material for his authorial inventiveness. His enthusiasm for the spontaneity, the quickened pulse and the individuality in those

From Ernest Hemingway, *A Moveable Feast* (New York: Charles Scribner's Sons, 1964), pp. 62–65.

sports would lead one to expect a similar response from his artistry to bicycle racing. And yet, sadly, his published writings do not often serve the cause of bicycle racing, nor does bicycle racing often engage his creative genius.

There are references, here and there, it is true. In The Sun Also Rises,[1] *we are treated to a short evening's frank and friendly revelry among a group of road racers who are stopping at an over-nighter during a stage race. And in one of his collected journalistic reports,[2] he captures the quiddity of bicycling when he remarks that only the bicyclist knows the lay of the land, for he must sweat up hills and dry on the downhill runs.*

And, on another occasion, in his Nick Adams short story entitled "A Pursuit Race," Hemingway explains the genesis for the title to his story as follows:

> In a pursuit race, in bicycle racing, riders start at equal intervals to ride after one another. They ride very fast because the race is usually limited to a short distance and if they slow their riding another rider who maintains his pace will make up the space that separated them equally at the start. As soon as a rider is caught and passed he is out of the race and must get down from his bicycle and leave the track. If none of the riders are caught the winner of the race is the one who has gained the most distance. In most pursuit races, if there are only two riders, one of the riders is caught inside of six miles.[3]

Yet this story has nothing to do with bicycle racing. On the contrary, it describes the pathetic end of William Campbell, an advance man for a road touring burlesque show. The burlesque show, in the person of its manager, Mr. Turner, catches up to Campbell in Kansas City. Campbell lies in a hotel-room bed, zonked from the combined effects of drugs, taken intravenously, and alcohol. The manager finds Campbell drawn and all but quartered in his bed and fires him on the spot, but only reluctantly, due to some unexplained liking for him. Eventually Nick Adams comes to replace Campbell as the group's advance man.

The most Hemingway ever wrote about bicycle racing appeared in the chapter from A Moveable Feast *that is excerpted below. The book is very autobiographical, and, although published posthumously, it is vintage Hemingway. In it he recounts his experiences in Paris in the 1920s and among those was "The End of an Avocation."*

The day I gave up racing I went over to the other side of the river and met my friend Mike Ward at the travel desk in the Guaranty Trust which was then at the corner of the rue des Italiens on the Boulevard des Italiens. I was depositing the racing capital but I did not tell that to anyone. I didn't put it in the checkbook though I still kept it in my head.

"Want to go to lunch?" I asked Mike.

"Sure, kid. Yeah I can do it. What's the matter? Aren't you going to the track?"

"No."

We had lunch at the square Louvois at a very good, plain bistro with a wonderful white wine. Across the square was the Bibliothèque Nationale.

"You never went to the track much, Mike," I said.

"No. Not for quite a long time."

"Why did you lay off it?"

"I don't know," Mike said. "Yes. Sure I do. Anything you have to bet on to get a kick isn't worth seeing."

"Don't you ever go out?"

"Sometimes to see a big race. One with great horses."

We spread paté on the good bistro bread and drank the white wine.

"Did you follow them a lot, Mike?"

"Oh yes."

"What do you see that's better?"

"Bicycle racing."

"Really?"

"You don't have to bet on it. You'll see."

"That track takes a lot of time."

"Too much time. Takes all your time. I don't like the people."

"I was very interested."

"Sure. You make out all right?"

"All right."

"Good thing to stop," Mike said.

"I've stopped."

"Hard to do. Listen kid, we'll go to the bike races sometime."

That was a new and fine thing that I knew little about. But we did not start it right away. That came later. It came to be a big part of our lives later when the first part of Paris was broken up.

But for a long time it was enough just to be back in our part of Paris and away from the track and to bet on our own life and work, and on the painters that you knew and not try to make your living gambling and call it by some other name. I have started many stories about bicycle racing but have never written one that is as good as the races are both on the indoor and outdoor tracks and on the roads. But I will get the Vélodrome d'Hiver with the smoky light of the afternoon and the high-banked wooden track and the whirring sound the tires made on the wood as the riders passed, the effort and the tactics as the riders climbed and plunged, each one a part of his machine; I will get the magic of the *demi-fond*, the noise of the motors with their rollers set out behind them that the *entraîneurs* rode, wearing their heavy crash helmets and leaning backward in their ponderous leather suits, to shelter the riders who followed them from the air resistance, the riders in their lighter crash helmets bent low over their handlebars their legs turning the huge gear sprockets and the small front wheels touching the roller behind the machine that gave them shelter to ride in, and the duels that were more exciting than anything, the *put-put*ting of the motorcycles and the riders elbow to elbow and wheel to wheel up and down and around at deadly speed until one man could not hold the pace and broke away and the solid wall of air that he had been sheltered against hit him.

There were so many kinds of racing. The straight sprints raced in heats or in match races where the two riders would balance for long seconds on their machines for the advantage of making the other rider take the lead and then the slow circling and the final plunge into the driving purity of speed. There were the programs of the team races of two hours, with a series of pure sprints in their heats to fill the afternoon, the lonely absolute speed events of one man racing an hour against the clock, the terribly dangerous and beautiful races of one hundred kilometers on the big banked wooden five-hundred-meter bowl of the Stade Buffalo, the outdoor stadium of Montrouge where they raced behind big motorcycles, Linart, the great Belgian champion that they called "the Sioux" for his profile, dropping his head to suck up cherry brandy from a rubber tube that connected with a hot water bottle under his racing shirt when he needed it toward the end as he increased his savage speed, and the championships of France behind big motors of the six-hundred-and-sixty-meter cement track of the Parc du Prince near Auteuil, the wickedest track of all where we saw that great rider Ganay fall and heard his skull crumple under the crash helmet as you crack a hard-boiled egg against a stone to peel it on a picnic. I must write the strange world of the six-day races and the marvels of the road-racing in the mountains. French is the only language it has ever been written in properly and the terms are all French and that is what makes it hard to write. Mike was right about it, there is no need to bet. But that comes at another time in Paris.

2

William Saroyan

"Death, Don't Go to Ithaca!"

From *The Human Comedy*

If there is enduring greatness in anything, it is in the simplicity of the lives of common folk, or so Saroyan seems to say in The Human Comedy.

At fourteen years of age, Homer Macauley is a messenger for a telegraph company in Ithaca, California, as well as the staff which supports his mother, his four-year-old brother, Ulysses, and his older sister, Bess. Homer's brother, Marcus, is away in the Great War (World War II), leaving Homer to be the man of the family in Ithaca. The constant family fear is for Marcus's welfare.

Homer's experiences as a telegraph messenger bring maturity to a rapid boil in him. He delivers messages of death from the War Department with reluctance and regret. He witnesses sensitivity at a brothel to which his duties take him. And he discovers vapidity at the Ithaca Parlor Lecture Club, where Miss Rosalie Simms-Peabody, a burned-out case if ever there was one, awaits his delivery of a staged telegram, which is almost as postured and bogus as she is.

The challenges of Homer's life are not confined to the telegraph office, however. At Ithaca High School, Homer learns ancient history from old Miss Hicks, while he yearns to conquer the low hurdles in his quest for the admiration of his classmate, Helen Eliot. But Hubert Ackley III, who is the coach's pet, is also enamored of Helen Eliot. And Coach Byfield takes a dim view of Homer's jeopardizing the status and prestige of Hubert Ackley III in the 220 low hurdles.

From William Saroyan, *The Human Comedy* (New York: Harcourt, Brace and Company, Inc., 1943), pp. 158–61.

The abundant confusions and apparent contradictions of his young life give Homer no rest, even as he sleeps. And so he dreams.

Homer Macauley was in bed at last, tossing and turning. He dreamed he was running the two-twenty low hurdles again, but every time he got to a hurdle, Byfield was there to stop him. He hurdled anyway and they went down. At every hurdle Byfield was there. Finally the injury to Homer's leg was so painful that when he tried to run, he fell. He got up and pasted Byfield in the mouth. He shouted out to the man, "Byfield, you can't stop me. You can never stop me—low hurdles, high hurdles, any kind of hurdles."

He began to run again, limping at first but soon running well, but the next hurdle was inhumanly high—eight feet—nevertheless, Homer Macauley, perhaps the greatest man in Ithaca, California, went over the hurdle with perfect form.

Next in the dream he was in his uniform riding his bicycle swiftly down a narrow street. Suddenly Byfield stood in the way. But Homer pushed toward the man more

swiftly than ever. "Byfield," he shouted, "I told you—you can't stop me." He lifted upward on the handlebars of his bicycle, and the bicycle began to rise and fly. It flew directly over Byfield's head and came down lightly on the other side of him. But just as it reached the pavement, Byfield stood in the way again. Again the bicycle left the street and began to fly over the man. But this time it stayed aloft, suspended twenty feet over Byfield's head. The man stood in the street, amazed and displeased. "You can't do that," he shouted at the messenger. "You're breaking the law of gravity."

"What do I care about the law of gravity?" Homer shouted down at the man in the street, "or the law of averages, or the law of supply and demand, or any other law? *You can't stop me.* You can't stop me, that's all. Worm, rust and rot—I have no time for you." The messenger rode on through space, leaving the ugly man alone in the street, as inferior as any inferiority could ever be.

Now Homer flew high on his bicycle, among dark clouds. As the messenger rode through the sky, he watched another bicycle rider in a messenger's uniform very much like his own but moving even faster than himself, push out of black cloud. The second messenger, strangely, seemed to be Homer himself, but at the same time he seemed to be someone Homer feared. Therefore Homer raced after the second messenger to find out who he really was.

The two riders raced a good long distance before Homer began to catch up. Suddenly the other messenger turned to look at Homer, and Homer was amazed that the messenger looked exactly like himself, but at the same time was unmistakably— not so much in appearance as in feeling—the messenger of Death. The riders were swiftly coming to Ithaca. Homer raced after the messenger of Death, moving swifter than ever before. Far down in the distance he could see the lonely lights of the town and the beautiful lonely streets and houses. Homer was determined to head off the other messenger, to keep him away from Ithaca. Nothing in the whole world was more important than to keep this messenger from reaching Ithaca.

The two riders raced hard and decently, with no tricks of any kind. They were both tiring now, but at last Homer was alongside the other rider, and was heading him away from Ithaca. Then, with a sudden burst of speed, the other messenger drew away and turned back toward the little town. Deeply disappointed in himself but still racing with all his might, Homer watched the other messenger ride on toward Ithaca, leaving Homer far behind. Now Homer could race no longer. There was no energy left with which to chase the messenger of Death. The boy almost collapsed on his bicycle, sobbing bitterly. The bicycle began to fall, and Homer began to cry out to the other messenger. "Come back. Don't go to Ithaca. Leave them alone. Come back."

The boy sobbed with terrible grief.

3

Alfred Jarry

"The Passion Considered as an Uphill Bicycle Race"

Barabbas, slated to race, was scratched.

Pilate, the starter, pulling out his clepsydra or water clock, an operation which wet his hands unless he had merely spit on them—Pilate gave the send-off.

Jesus got away to a good start.

In those days, according to the excellent sports commentator St. Matthew, it was customary to flagellate the sprinters at the start the way a coachman whips his horses. The whip both stimulates and gives a hygienic massage. Jesus, then, got off in good form, but he had a flat right away. A bed of thorns punctured the whole circumference of his front tire.

Today in the shop windows of bicycle dealers you can see a reproduction of this veritable crown of thorns as an ad for puncture-proof tires. But Jesus's was an ordinary single-tube racing tire.

The two thieves, obviously in cahoots and therefore "thick as thieves," took the lead.

It is not true that there were any nails. The three objects usually shown in the ads belong to a rapid-change tire tool called the "Jiffy."

We had better begin by telling about the spills; but before that the machine itself must be described.

The bicycle frame in use today is of relatively recent invention. It appeared around 1890. Previous to that time the body of the machine was constructed of two tubes

From R. Shattuck and Simon Watson Taylor, eds., *Selected Works of Alfred Jarry* (New York, 1965), pp. 122–24.

soldered together at right angles. It was generally called the right-angle or cross bicycle. Jesus, after his puncture, climbed the slope on foot, carrying on his shoulder the bike frame, or, if you will, the cross.

Contemporary engravings reproduce this scene from photographs. But it appears that the sport of cycling, as a result of the well-known accident which put a grievous end to the Passion race and which was brought up to date almost on its anniversary by the similar accident of Count Zborowski on the Turbie slope—the sport of cycling was for a time prohibited by state ordinance. That explains why the illustrated magazines, in reproducing this celebrated scene, show bicycles of a rather imaginary design. They confuse the machine's cross frame with that other cross, the straight handlebar. They represent Jesus with his hands spread on the handlebars, and it is worth mentioning in this connection that Jesus rode lying flat on his back in order to reduce his air resistance.

Note also that the frame or cross was made of wood, just as wheels are to this day.

A few people have insinuated falsely that Jesus's machine was a *draisienne*,* an unlikely mount for a hill-climbing contest. According to the old cyclophile hagiographers, St. Briget, St. Gregory of Tours, and St. Irene, the cross was equipped with a device which they name *suppedaneum*. There is no need to be a great scholar to translate this as "pedal."

Lipsius, Justinian, Bosius, and Erycius Puteanus describe another accessory which one still finds, according to Cornelius Curtius in 1643, on Japanese crosses: a protuberance of leather or wood on the shaft which the rider sits astride—manifestly the seat or saddle.

This general description, furthermore, suits the definition of a bicycle current among the Chinese: "A little mule which is led by the ears and urged along by showering it with kicks."

We shall abridge the story of the race itself, for it has been narrated in detail by specialized works and illustrated by sculpture and painting visible in monuments built to house such art.

There are fourteen turns in the difficult Golgotha course. Jesus took his first spill at the third turn. His mother, who was in the stands, became alarmed.

His excellent trainer, Simon the Cyrenian, who but for the thorn accident would have been riding out in front to cut the wind, carried the machine.

Jesus, though carrying nothing, perspired heavily. It is not certain whether a female spectator wiped his brow, but we know that Veronica, a girl reporter, got a good shot of him with her Kodak.

The second spill came at the seventh turn on some slippery pavement. Jesus went down for the third time at the eleventh turn, skidding on a rail.

The Israelite *demimondaines* waved their handkerchiefs at the eighth.

The deplorable accident familiar to us all took place at the twelfth turn. Jesus was in a dead heat at the time with the thieves. We know that he continued the race airborne—but that is another story.

*A two-wheeled, bicycle-like machine without pedals fashionable in 1818. The rider straddled it and paced along with part of his weight on the seat. [Translator's note.]

4

John D. MacDonald

A Century Ride Is Not a
Race, Is Not a Race . . .

From *Condominium*

John MacDonald's Condominium, *a Book-of-the-Month Club selection, is no Travis McGee thriller, not nearly. But it has the same aura of suspense, intrigue, and mystery as the plot tracks the lives of those who are condominium-cloistered on the keys in the Gulf of Mexico near Sarasota, Florida. The book is of the muckraker variety, with the boom in condominium development as its target. Nearly everyone in the book who stands to profit is corrupted by the condominium craze, to the extent that the shoddy construction of four condominiums on Fiddler Key leaves them unsafe and unprotected from the impending ravages of Hurricane Ella.*

As MacDonald moralizes and Hurricane Ella festers in the tropics, we meet Professor Roger Jeffrey, retired after thirty years of teaching comparative religion at Syracuse University, who, with his wife Maurine, resides in apartment Five-B at the Golden Sands condominium. Professor Jeffrey is no Travis McGee, not by a long shot. But he has the same crafty crustiness toward those who are short, brutish, and nasty. He employs this trait most effectively to con the tipsy widow, Peggy Brasser, into paying $825 to replace his Schwinn Voyageur when her automobile dismantles it in the Golden Sands garage.

The good professor may have retired from college teaching to learn, as his fin-de-siècle mentality toward the century ride makes distressingly evident. In the 1890s, the heyday of the bicycling craze in this country, it was very much the passion to excell in

From John D. MacDonald, *Condominium* (Philadelphia: J. B. Lippincott Company, 1977), pp. 313–17.

280

riding one hundred miles in less than one day. The Century Riding Club of America fueled the fad by awarding a gold bar each time the feat was accomplished—at least for a time.

The press, however, did not support the fever, considering its devotees to be as witless as gargantuan pie-eaters at county fairs. Undaunted, the fad spread to the point where bicyclists would vie with one another to see who could ride the most centuries on consecutive days. In 1898, a New Yorker named Teddy Edwards rode a total of 250 consecutive centuries before quitting under a doctor's orders when he developed typhoid fever. And Edwards could not even claim a place in the book of records, for John Noble had ridden 253 centuries the year before. Most astounding of all was the feat of Walter McGrath, who completed four centuries in 1897—at the age of seven.[1]

Today the century is still in vogue among bicyclists, although its lunatic aspects have abated. Annually, the month of September is designated by the League of American Wheelmen as National Century Month. Each year thousands turn out to test their mettle in this endurance contest. And some, confident of their ability, seek either to better their previous time or to be among the front runners. Seventy-one-year-old Professor Jeffrey was among those who do the century for the joy of winning and not merely for the satisfaction of having finished it.

By ten o'clock on Saturday morning, retired Professor Roger Jeffrey had reached the second checkpoint of the Summer Invitational Century. As a member of the Route Committee of the Athens Cycle League he had helped lay out the hundred-mile course which began and ended in the big empty parking lot of Kennedy High School. The kids at the checkpoint had parked the van in the shade. They grinned and waved him on. Jeffrey squinted off into the heat waver on the long flat stretch of county road and could see, at least a mile ahead, the bright clothing of the pack of young people who had started out at much too fast a pace. He had gained a little on them, and as the day wore on he knew he would gain more. A lot of them would never finish, taken out by cramps, exhaustion, or bad falls.

This was the first real test of the machine he had purchased with the check from Mrs. Brasser. He felt a pang of guilt when he remembered how he had extorted eight hundred and twenty-five dollars from the wretched woman. She had been too obviously afraid of his reporting her destruction of the Voyageur. The guilt feeling had lessened with her death, and since the visit from one Frederick Brasser, a vulgar lout who became almost insulting in his demands to know why his mother had written him a check in that amount, the guilt was almost undetectable.

The new machine was lovely. A Panasonic Touring DeLuxe in a beautiful deep wine red, with a mirror finish. Shimano Dura-Ace cotterless alloy cranks, alloy quick-release hubs, pedals, and Oro freewheel. A Shimano Crane GS rear derailleur, and Titlist front gear wheel. Alloy micro-adjusting seat post, Dia-Compe brakes, Gran Compe alloy stem with recessed bolt and alloy drop bars. By the time the dealer had altered the basic machine to fit the professor's requirements, the total cost came to six hundred and thirty-five. The only thing old on it was the comfortable leather seat rescued from the shattered Voyageur.

He had begun to sweat heavily in the morning heat. Without breaking his cadence or speed, he took two salt tablets with several swallows of water from his water bottle, took the terrycloth pad from under his Bell helmet, soaked it with water once again and shoved it back under the helmet. Within ten minutes he was less conscious of the heat. Maurine had told him quite a few times that he was an old fool to do a century in Florida in August. He told her he was quite competent to take care of himself. He told her he had been doing it for seventy-one years and planned to keep on indefinitely. He told her she was a tottery baleful old woman married to a spry dirty old man, and she could spend Saturday in the cool gloom watching that tube until her brain turned to fish paste if she chose but he was going to be on the open road, with the wind in his hair, under the broad blue of God's sky.

"Hey, Prof!"

The loud voice startled him. He had not heard the bike coming up beside him. "Hello, Rich." Rich coached track at Kennedy and was perhaps the best and most durable bicyclist in the League.

"Aren't you pouring it on a little heavy for this kind of heat?"

"Not so far."

"Don't you push it too much, hear? Hey, you got the padded tape, I see. How's it working?"

"Great. No numb hands."

"The whole machine looks great, Prof. Fits you great. How much you carrying in those gumwalls?"

"Eighty-five."

"Should be about right."

They came upon a young man and woman at the side of the road. He was sitting down, wearing an agonized expression. She was kneading and knuckling the calf muscles of his right leg.

"See you later," Rich said and braked and turned off to help the pair.

Cramps would take some of them all the way out, and slow down some of the others. The toes of his right foot felt odd. He reached down and loosened the strap on the leather-covered clip, then pulled the plastic knob and tightened it again, but not as much as before. He wiggled his toes while stroking and in a little while they were normal again.

From time to time he shifted his position on the handle-bars. He counted his cadence against the sweep second hand on his watch and found that he was precisely on sixty-five, right where he should be. At this gear ratio, he knew from his memorized chart that he should be making 20.5 miles per hour. His record century time was six hours seven minutes, or 6.116 hours. That translated to an averge speed of 16.35 miles per hour. If he really wanted to be an old fool, he would try to best his previous time. To best it in this heat would mean riding right through the customary rest stop at the fifty-mile mark.

A small pain appeared in his left knee and began to sharpen with each stroke. He experimented, changing slightly the angle of his foot against the rat-trap pedal. He did not like cleats because they ruled out these small adjustments. The pain diminished and went away, as did his anxiety.

Ahead the pack was closer, more visible. The road went behind fenced ranchlands. Lazy cattle, drowsing in the heat, would lift their heads sharply, stare at the lead pack, then wheel and go thundering across the pastureland. He wanted to be the lead machine, the one to startle the cattle. The cattle were used to cars and trucks, took them for granted, were startled out of their bovine wits by quiet gleaming wheels hissing down upon them.

Sweat ran into his left eye and he toweled it away. There were a lot more machines behind him than ahead of him, he knew. One hundred and thirty-one starters. And maybe fifteen ahead of him. All young. Ah, youth, that precious commodity always wasted on the young.

A giant beetle bounced off his lips, stinging him and making his eyes water.

Time? Ten forty. Breathe deeply. The muscles need the oxygen. Suck it in. Just air. No beetles.

The century, he thought. A cheap analogy for life. One of those tiresome comparisons Hawkinson was probably still pulling back there in some classroom. Little pains happen. You adjust. A lot of it is dull stuff indeed, but you make the effort. Man and machine become one organism, stroking away, correcting, favoring, compensating, and trying to enjoy the little moments of magic that come along. At the end of it, you get off the bike, or fall off, or are pushed off, and that is that. Peggy Brasser did not get off, or fall off, or get pushed off. She rode into a wall. Or over a cliff.

Golden Sands was full of people riding their private machines to God knows where. All upset now. Committees and protests and confrontations. Any man who has spent most of his life on a faculty cannot get very concerned about committees and protests and confrontations. You do that when you are young—instructor or assistant professor. In time you learn that if you make the right-sounding excuses at the right time, all the others will be out there in front of you, driving off the wild animals, killing snakes, draining the swamps. Those whose interests are the same as yours will usually do all the work necessary to protect yours as well as their own. Can't help doing so. When their job is done, thank them with great earnestness and sincerity, and that will ready them to go out and do the chores the next time too.

He caught up with the next straggler from the group ahead. A fat girl. One of the little group of housewives who had joined the League. Bright red straining face, mouth agape. She had a heavy machine, an old black Raleigh three-speed. He could hear her breathing.

"Take a break in the shade," he called to her. She seemed not to hear him. A little while later he looked back for her and she was not there. He thought she had sought the shade of one of the infrequent pine trees, and then saw her far back, flattened on the road, the bike down nearby. He missed one stroke as he debated turning back, then realized how soon the others would be along. And in a few more minutes he would be among the pack of leaders. He counted them. Eleven machines. And the professor makes one dozen. Some of them were singing. Good, he thought. Takes a lot of good breath to sing. About six miles to the halfway point, where we turn south. They'll all stop. Get off there and fill the water bottles. Keep moving around. Get back on. Leave as inconspicuously as possible.

5

Marcel Aymé

"The Last"

*White jersey, green jersey, yellow jersey, even a polka-dot jersey (white with red spots)
mark the winners of the various races within the annual Tour de France, but the maillot
jaune (yellow jersey) is the most prestigious and the most coveted of all.*

*But the Tour de France is not only a colorful spectacle. It would not be the crème de
la crème of bicyclists, the World Series of bicycle racing, the King Kong of professional
road races, the ne plus ultra of stage races, the race for which there is no suitable epithet
without its three weeks and up to 3000 miles of a course (carrière) of fierce winds,
torturous mountains, and sun-blistering level stretches that is varied each year. Everyone who participates in the Tour de France is a hero, the winner only slightly more so.
Even the person who reaches the Champs Elysée (the race always ends in Paris) last gets
a prize—the lanterne rouge or red lamp. That is a prize that Martin in Marcel Aymé's
short story "The Last" would have been overjoyed to achieve.*

*Since 1903, when the first Tour de France was run, it has become the legendary test
of a professional bicyclist's courage and stamina. It has its own legends and tragedies.
It is more than a spectator sport for those who line the route by the thousands are often so
belligerently partisan that they can and do interrupt its progress or even sabotage the
riders. An out-of-favor rider can find the spectators to be his Montezuma's revenge. In
1905, for example, 125 kilograms of nails were spread along the road.*

*The Tour de France is a uniquely European affair. It is so imbued in European life
and literature that when it appears in humorous episodes, the humor is lost without an
understanding of the stature and traditions of the Tour de France. A beach-side conversation of two local toughs in Roger Vailland's* The Law *is illustrative.*

"You know," said Pizzaccio, "if I was Chief Attilio I'd slap that Giuseppina's
ears back . . ."

From Marcel Aymé, *The Proverb*, trans. Norman Denny (New York: Atheneum 1961), pp. 279–87.

"Would you?" said Matteo Brigante. "I'd give her a yellow swimsuit."
"Why a yellow one?"
"Like the winner of the Tour de France."
"Why the winner?"
"Because she's champion."
"She swims well," said Pizzaccio. "That's true."
"Idiot," said Matteo Brigante.[1]

*The Tour de France is so distinctively European that no American has ever par-
ticipated in it. And few from the British Isles have met the measure of its demands. Tom
Simpson was one who did, but he is now remembered only for his death on the volcanic
Mont Ventoux on July 13, 1967, during the thirteenth stage of the race. Amphetamines
and heat, which reached 55 degrees centigrade (131 Fahrenheit), sufficient to burst the
thermometer at the Chalet Reynard, had combined to kill the twenty-nine-year-old
Simpson. His has been the only fatality in the history of the Tour de France. But
Simpson was not the last coureur (as the bicyclists are called) to seek the boost that
doping can give. Most recently, it is said that the French two-time Tour winner Bernard
Thevenet's health has been threatened by his use of massive doses of cortisone for that
extra lift.*

*Terry Davenport, a principal in Ralph Hurne's The Yellow Jersey, was also a British
bicycle racer. He might have been modeled after Barry Hoban, a Britisher now living in
Belgium, who in 1978 participated in his twelfth Tour de France. Davenport, however,
is fictional, as are his romantic escapades with nineteen-year-old Bobbie, twenty-one-
year-old Susan, and her thirty-nine-year-old mother, Paula. Davenport, a thirty-seven-
year-old ex-professional bicyclist and roué living in Ghent, Belgium, is described as a
"sensualist, bon vivant, radical, cyclist extraordinaire, light work done with horse and
trap."[2] He is also managing Romain Hendrickx, a professional bicyclist of much
potential as a Tour de France champion.*

*Davenport reluctantly joins Hendrickx's team for the Tour de France, simply as a
domestique (one who is at the leader's beck and call), after much inducement by
Hendrickx's promoters. All goes well in Davenport's shepherding Hendrickx along until
the level stretches of the sixteen stage from Toulouse to Beziers. At a pit stop Davenport
casually observes the actions of the members of the competing teams when his suspicions
are aroused.*

It's only after I've drunk my tea and, like everyone else, tossed the bottle, that
I notice something about Audaire. I happen to ride near him and see his bidon of
tea stuffed in the rear pocket of his vest. Big think. A man only keeps a drink if he's
going to need it later on, also Audaire is at his strongest on long flat stages. Then
he's got one of his mates already up the road well placed to help him. I look round
for Romain, but he's riding quite a way back next to Bert and Beach Boy. If I drop
behind and warn him, then Audaire will be sure to go and I'll have lost contact. I try
to beckon to Romain to join me but I can't catch his eye and my actions are making
the other suspicious.

We come to a dodgy patch of road. There are a series of tight bends and the tar is
melting on the road's surface. Ahead I can see the French team car cruising as near

to the front of the peloton as it dare. Suddenly I see the team director remove his cap and wave it, and as one Audaire and two of his team sprint from the bunch and ride for all they're worth. I sit right on Audaire's wheel and go with him, taking with me a member of the Spanish team.[3]

The breakaway is on. Davenport clings to the others, heaving and sighing, until he literally tumbles into Beziers. The rest of the competitors have been left miles, and more importantly minutes, in their wake. Davenport is resting in his hotel room when he learns that Audaire and his followers have been disqualified upon failing the drug tests. He is awarded the maillot jaune. The Tour is now his to win. But, at thirty-seven, Davenport is no Lucien Van Impe (the little Piston, who in 1976 surprised the world and exchanged his polka-dot jersey for the cherished maillot jaune). Terry Davenport makes a gallant effort but the Frank Merriwell in him has long since been played out. He freezes in his pedals, dogged but dazed, after a frenzied sprint. He collapses, another "also ran."

Terry Davenport never sensed the glory of finishing the Tour. It is at the finish of any stage or of the Tour itself that the excitement peaks in the bow-taut tension of the sprint. Yes, the Alps and the Pyrenees are bone-crushing, nerve-wrenching experiences. But, for pure animal pleasure, the end counts most as the occasion for a dramatic denouement. A spectator could do no better than to be a witness to the finish of any stage. Alistair Reed has written of his stirring introduction to bicycle racing as he waited for the pack to enter Pau, the capital city of Béarn, at the conclusion of the Tour's seventeenth étape. The famed multiple Tour winner Jacques Anquetil (nicknamed Jacquot) was wearing the yellow jersey at the time and had been from the first day of the race. Could he continue as leader?

The hoopla of advertising vans, flower vendors, exhibitions of talent from the world's champion lady accordion player, and other Hollywood-type fanfare was over. Anxious waiting was all that remained.

The roar began far away and rippled in waves towards us; then, sure enough, over the top of the fences appeared three white-capped heads, sweeping round the bend. After the animals, they seemed to me to be going at a tremendous speed. Two cyclists in gray jerseys, wheel to wheel, were keeping back a third with a green stripe round his middle. They were crouched over their handlebars, pumping the pedals furiously. They zipped towards us, whoosh whoosh whoosh, and were past, out of sight on the right. We were all cheering wildly. "That's the sprint," yelled my neighbor. "That's what kills them!" I had barely time to get my head round again before a cluster of heads appeared at the bend and were on us, whoosh whoosh whoosh whoosh whoosh, a group of seventeen or so, although nobody without an electric eye could have counted them at that speed.[4]

The whoosh of the sprint was on, and Anquetil had it in his pocket again.

The Tour de France is the most renowned of all the stage races. Bicycle-racing fervor is at its height during it. Other tours, like the Peace Race from Warsaw to Berlin to Prague or the Giro d'Italia (Tour of Italy) are challenging, but not inhumanly so like "le tour." The one-day classics, like the 170-mile Milan–San Remo race, also demand concentration, endurance, and spirit, but they are merely the proving grounds for those who would compete in the Tour de France.

Martin, the protagonist in the selection from Marcel Aymé which follows, was a stage-race bicyclist with time for nothing else. His single-minded determination to achieve the impossible left him a caricature of the champion he sought to be. There is a little of Martin in all professional racing bicyclists as well as in some bicyclists who are not professionals. Martin exudes the distinctive "bittersweet tragicomic world" of which Marcel Aymé so often wrote with blistering irony.

There was once a racing cyclist named Martin who always came in last, and the onlookers laughed to see him so far behind the others. He wore a vest of tender blue with a small periwinkle embroidered on the left breast. Doubled over the handlebars and with a handkerchief gripped between his teeth, he pedalled no less courageously than the winner, attacking the steepest slopes with so much fervour that a flame gleamed in his eyes; and seeing that clear and candid gaze and the muscles knotted with exertion, people said to one another:

"Well, Martin seems to be in form today. That's good. Perhaps this time he'll arrive at Tours (or Bordeaux, or Orléans, or Dunkirk) somewhere in the middle."

But every time was like every other time and Martin was always last. He never lost hope of doing better, but he worried a little because he had a wife and children to support and there is not much to be made out of coming in last. He worried, but no one ever heard him complain that fate was treating him unjustly. When he arrived at Tours (or Marseilles or Cherbourg) he would be welcomed with laughter and jesting by the crowd.

"Hullo, Martin! You're first, starting at the wrong end!"

And Martin, hearing these words, never displayed the slightest ill-humour. If he glanced round it was with a gentle smile, as though to say, "Yes, here I am, Martin. I'm last again, but next time I shall do better."

The other competitors would nudge one another and say:

"Well, how's it going, Martin? Are you satisfied with the result?"

"Yes," Martin would reply. "I'm not dissatisfied."

He did not see that they were making fun of him, and when they laughed he laughed with them. He watched without envy as they went off surrounded by their friends and admirers, feted and flattered, although he was left alone, for there was never anyone to greet him at the winning-post. His wife and children lived in a village on the road between Paris and Orléans, and he only saw them at rare intervals, and just in passing, when the race happened to go that way. Clearly if one lives for an ideal one cannot expect to live like other people; Martin loved his wife and children but he was a racing cyclist and he raced, only pausing to rest between the stages. He sent a little money home when he had any and he often thought of his family, never during the race when he had more important things to think about, but in the evenings while he massaged his tired legs after the long day's ride.

Before he went to sleep Martin made his prayer to God, telling Him all about the stage he had covered during the day, without ever pausing to consider that he might be trying the Divine patience. He took it for granted that God was as much interested in bicycle-racing as in anything else, and he was right: for if God had not a thorough understanding of all pursuits He would not know how hard it is for a man to keep his soul in order.

"Dear God," said Martin, "the same thing happened again today. I don't know why it is, but it's always the same. Yet I've got a good bike and it's no use saying I haven't. The other day I wondered if perhaps there was something a bit wrong with the pedals, so I stripped it down, every bit, calmly and methodically, the way I'm talking to You now. I found that there was nothing wrong with the pedals, or with anything else. If anyone tries to say it isn't a good bike I can only answer that it *is* a good bike, in good order, a good, sound make. Well, then? Well, of course, there's the question of the man—the muscles, the will-power, the intelligence. But the man, God, is Your affair. That's what I tell myself, and that's why I don't complain. I know perfectly well that someone has to be last, and it's nothing to be ashamed of. I'm not complaining. I just thought I'd mention it."

After which he closed his eyes and slept soundly till morning; and when he awoke he said happily:

"Today I'm going to be first."

He laughed in delight, thinking of the little girl who would present him with a bunch of flowers when he came in first, and the money he would send to his wife. He pictured the newspaper headlines—"Martin Takes the Poligny-Strasbourg Stage: Wins in a Sprint after a Hard-Fought Race." And thinking of this he felt sorry for the runners-up and the ones who came in nowhere, especially the last, whom he loved like a brother without knowing him.

That evening he arrived at Strasbourg in his usual place, amid the jesting and the laughter. He was disappointed and a little surprised, but in the morning he started on the next stage as sure as ever that he would win. Every morning and every departure saw the renewal of that miracle of hope.

On the eve of the Paris-Marseilles race a rumour spread through bicycling circles that Martin was preparing a sensational surprise for the public, and fifty-three reporters rushed to interview him.

"My views on the theatre?" said Martin. "Well, once when we stopped the night at Carcassonne I went to see *Faust* at the Municipal Theatre and I couldn't help feeling sorry for that girl, Marguerite. What I say is, if Faust had known what it means to have a decent bike he wouldn't have been at a loose end the way he was, and he wouldn't have gone making trouble for the poor girl and she'd have found herself a good husband. That's what I think. And now if you want to know who's going to be first at Marseilles I'll tell you without making any bones about it—I shall be the winner."

After the reporters had left Martin received a scented missive, inviting him to tea, from a lady named Liane. She was a woman of loose life such as are all too numerous, as deficient in morals as she was in correct behaviour. Martin went to keep the appointment in all innocence, going straight from the race-track, where he had been riding a few practice-laps to make sure his machine was in good order, and taking with him a small case containing his cycling kit.

He chatted artlessly about racing, the tactics to be pursued and the care that must be taken of one's bike and one's person, while the seductress plied him with cunning questions.

"Tell me, Monsieur Martin, how do you massage a leg?"

Saying which she offered him a leg as it were for the purpose of demonstration. But Martin merely grasped that limb of perdition with no more concern than if it had belonged to a fellow-cyclist and explained calmly:

"Well, you see, you start at the calf and work your way up, like this. Of course, it's more difficult in the case of a woman because of the layer of adipose tissue."

"Yes, I see. How cleverly you do it. What firm hands you have. Well, now, when it comes to the stomach-muscles . . ."

But we will spare our readers. Suffice it to say that Martin replied to the infamous creature's questions with a perfect simplicity, quite unaware of her insidious designs. When finally she asked what he had in his case he did not hesitate to open it and show her his vest and shorts and cycling shoes.

"Monsieur Martin," she said, "I would dearly love to see you dressed as a cyclist, I have never met one before."

"Oh, all right," said Martin. "I'll go and slip them on in the next room, for the sake of decency."

When he returned he found the lady even more lightly clad than himself, but we will not dwell upon the details. Martin did not turn a hair. Gravely surveying the shameless display he said with a shake of his head:

"I see that you too are thinking of taking up bicycle-racing. Let me be frank. In my opinion it is not a suitable pursuit for a woman. It is not your legs I am worrying about. I daresay that with training they would be as good as my own. But you must bear in mind that women possess bosoms, and when one has to ride a hundred and fifty miles in a day the surplus weight becomes excessive. In addition to which one must never overlook the possibility of children."

So touched was Liane by these words of wisdom and innocence that for the first time in her life she perceived the desirability of virtue. Filled with abhorrence of her many sins she burst into repentant tears and said:

"I have been mad and misguided, but now all that is over."

"Well, there's no harm done," said Martin. "Now that you've seen me in cycling-kit I'll go next door and get dressed again, for the sake of decency. You'd better be doing the same, and I hope you'll give up this idea of racing."

He left the apartment with her gratitude ringing in his ears, having restored to the wretched outcast her honour and the bliss of living at peace with her conscience. His photograph appeared that day in the evening papers. This occasioned him neither pleasure nor pride, since he had no need of advertisement to sustain his quiet confidence. The next day by the time the race left Paris he had fallen into the last place as usual, and here he remained till the end. When he reached Arles he learned that the leaders had already got to Marseilles, but he did not give up. He went on pedalling with all his might, still with a hope lurking in his heart that although the race was over he would somehow or other contrive to be first. The newspapers, furious at being deceived, assailed him with savagely sardonic comment couched in technical language unintelligible to any save the readers of sporting prints. But this did not prevent Martin from continuing to hope, or Liane from opening a *crémerie* in the Rue de la Fidelité, under the sign of "The Good Cyclist," where eggs were sold a halfpenny cheaper than elsewhere.

As he gained in age and experience so did Martin's ardour increase, and he entered nearly as many races as there were saints in the calendar. He gave himself no rest. No sooner had he finished one race than he signed on for the next. The hair began to turn white over his temples, his back was bowed and he became the doyen of racing cyclists. But he did not know this, and indeed he seemed to be unconscious of his age. He never failed to come in last, and as time went on he lagged further and further behind.

"Dear God," he murmured in his prayers, "I don't understand. I don't know what the trouble is."

One day as he was struggling up a familiar hill on the run from Paris to Orléans he found that he had a flat tyre. He stopped at the side of the road to repair it, and two women approached him. One of them, who was carrying a young child in her arms, inquired:

"Do you happen to know a racing-cyclist named Martin?"

He answered mechanically:

"I'm Martin. I'm last, but I shall do better next time."

"Martin," said the woman, "I am your wife."

He looked up without stopping work on the tyre and said tenderly:

"I'm glad to see you." And gazing at the child, which he took to be one of his own, he said: "I see the youngsters are doing well."

His wife looked embarrassed. Pointing to the young woman who was with her she said:

"This is your daughter, Martin. She's as tall as you are. She's married, and so are your sons."

"I'm glad. I had not realised they were so old. How quickly time passes. And is that my grandson you are carrying?"

The younger woman turned away her head and it was her mother who answered:

"No, Martin, this is my child, not hers. Seeing that you never came home . . ."

Martin began to pump up his tyre without saying anything. When he straightened himself he saw tears running down his wife's cheeks and he murmured:

"You know how it is if you're a racing-cyclist, you don't belong to yourself any more. I often think of you, but of course that isn't the same as being there."

The baby burst out crying and it seemed that nothing would soothe it. Martin was greatly distressed. He blew with his bicycle-pump under its nose saying in a little, squeaky voice—"Boo, boo, boo!"

The baby began to crow. Martin kissed it and took leave of his family.

"I've lost five minutes, but I don't mind, particularly as I can easily make them up. This is going to be my race, I'm sure of it."

He mounted and rode off, and the two women stood for a time watching him as he toiled painfully up the hill. He rode standing on the pedals, bringing his whole weight to bear first on one side and then on the other.

"How hard he's finding it," his wife murmured. "In the old days, even fifteen years ago, he could get up any hill simply with the strength of his legs, without moving from the saddle."

Martin reached the crest, going so slowly that it seemed as though at any moment he must stop. His figure, while he free-wheeled, appeared for an instant against the sky-line, and then his blue vest melted into the summer sky.

Martin knew the roads of France better than anyone else alive, and each of their countless milestones wore for him a familiar face. The time came when he had to walk up the hills, pushing his machine and gasping with fatigue; but still he trusted in his star.

"I'll make it up on the downward slope," he said. And when he reached the end of the stage in the evening (or sometimes it was the next day) he was always surprised to find that he was not first.

"Dear God, I don't know how it happened . . ."

Deep wrinkles furrowed his lean face which had the colour of autumn roads, and his hair was snowy white; but the spark of youth still gleamed in his weather-worn eyes. His vest flapped loosely on his bowed, skinny back, its periwinkle blue so faded that it seemed to be woven of dust and mist. He could not longer afford to travel by train to the starting point of a race, but this did not trouble him. Arriving at Bayonne three days after the riders had departed, he leapt into the saddle and set off instantly for Roubaix where another race was due to begin. He covered the length of France, walking uphill, pedalling on the flat, sleeping while he coasted downhill, and never stopping by day or by night.

"It's splendid training," he said.

But when he got to Roubaix he found that the riders had left a week before. He shook his head and murmured as he remounted:

"It's a pity. I should certainly have won. Well, there's always the Grenoble-Marseilles race. I have only to push on into the Alps."

He arrived too late at Grenoble, and at Paris, Perpignan, Brest and Cherbourg. He was always too late.

"It's a shame," he said in a small, quavering voice. "It really is a shame. But I shall catch up."

Undismayed he left Provence for Brittany, Artois for Roussilon, the Jura for the Vendée; and now and then, nodding at the milestones as he passed, he said:

"It's splendid training."

He grew so old that he could scarcely see, but his friends the milestones, even the little ones marking every hundred metres, told him when to turn left or right. His bicycle had also grown very old. It was now of an unknown make, so ancient that even historians had never heard of it. The enamel had all worn off, and the rust was only hidden by the mud and dust of the road. The wheels had lost nearly all their spokes, but Martin was now so light that the five or six that remained were enough to carry him.

"Dear God," he said, "at least I have a good bike. I have no need to worry on that score."

He was riding on the rims and the machine set up such a rattling that urchins in the streets threw stones at him crying:

"Crazy Dick, take your bit of old iron to the scrap-heap!"

"I shall catch up," said Martin, who had grown hard of hearing.

For years, he went on trying to enter a race, but he always arrived too late. Then one day he left Narbonne for Paris, where the "Tour de France" was due to begin. He arrived exactly a year late, and learned to his delight that the riders had left only an hour before.

"I'll catch them up by the evening," he said, "and I'll certainly win the second stage."

As he rode out through the Porte Maillot a lorry knocked him over. Martin staggered to his feet, still grasping the handlebars of his shattered bicycle.

"I shall catch up," he said before he died.

6

Paul Morand

The Six-Day Night

From *Open All Night*

"You ever ridden in a six-day bicycle race, Mr. Anderson?" said Bobby Walthour Jr., 70 year old former six-day bicycle racer.

"As a matter of fact, I haven't."

"Try it some time. Six days of chafing your inner thighs on a pie-shaped piece of leather. You'd be amazed at the things bike riders have used to reduce the friction. I personally have tried axle grease, Vaseline, Coconut oil, you name it. Fellow I knew even tried a preliminary heat with his shorts stuffed with Jello."

Dortha [Anderson] looked at Walthour in amazement. "Jello?"

"Strawberry, as I recall. Bad idea. Dripped down his legs, made a mess of the track. Had to halt the heat. The timer thought he'd ruptured himself." Walthour grinned. "Ah, those were the days."[1]

Those were the crazed and frenetic days when thousands cheered, applauded and screeched fanatically as their favorites undertook the ultimate endurance test—the six-day bicycle race. The howling of the mob itself became distinctive, for bicycle clubs developed their own peculiar calls. The pandemonium of the crowd at these races was so diabolically infectious that we find Eugene O'Neill drawing upon this frenzied uproar to capture the action of Yank as he sends shovel after shovel of coal into the fiery furnace in The Hairy Ape.

Yank. (chanting a count as he shovels without seeming effort) One de stuff! Let her have it! All togedder now! Sling it into her! Let her ride! Shoot de piece now! Call de toin on her! Drive her into it! Feel her move! Watch her smoke! Speed, dat's her middle name! Give her coal, youse guys! Coal, dat's her booze! Drink it up, baby!

From Paul Morand, *Open All Night* (New York: Thomas Seltzer, 1923), pp. 1027–41.

Let's see yah sprint! Dig in and gain a lap! Dere she go-o-es! [This last is the chanting formula of the gallery gods at the six-day bike race.][2]

The six-day bicycle race was, in its day, to bicycle racing what Waltham once was to watches, until Timex came on the scene. It was woven not only into the temper of the times, but it found its way also into varied literary allusions then and afterwards. Ring Lardner used the six-day bicycle race in his syndicated column as a vehicle to spoof the pretentious and grandiose living style of his showman neighbor, Gene Buck. As he put it:

Friends of the Gene Bucks report that Gene made a big mistake not leasing his living rm. for the six-day bicycle race, as the new Madison Square Garden could not begin to accomodate the devotees of this soul-stirring pastime. Gene wired that he wanted to keep the rm. neat for the Olympic Games of 1932. Gene Jr. is entered in the Marathon that yr. and is already a top heavy favorite, having circled the rm. twice in practice in 2 days, 4 hrs., 20 min., 32.5 sec. with two stops for engine trouble and milk.[3]

Ernest Hemingway, in his turn, was stimulated to begin writing A Farewell to Arms *after suffering a cut to the head from the glass from a broken skylight and then going to the bike races.[4] Indeed, Hemingway also used the six-day race to provide the backdrop for the final revisions he gave to the same novel. According to him,*

I'll never forget the time I set up operations in a box at the finish line of the six-day bike races, to work on the proof of "A Farewell to Arms." There was good inexpensive champagne and when I got hungry they sent over Crabe Mexicaine from Prunier. I had rewritten the ending thirty-nine times in manuscript and now I worked it over thirty times in proof, trying to get it right.[5]

In the early years of the six-day bike race, "Plugger Bill" Martin would cover 1,466 miles in six days. But the feat of Charlie Miller in 1897 is legendary. He raced over 2,093 miles at the popular Madison Square Garden track, winning a total cash prize of $3,550 and receiving a bonus kiss from Anna Held, beauty of the musical stage. According to one account,

Miller told newsmen that his ankles had swollen rather badly after the third day of the race, and that the cigar smoke and the dust rising from under the boards had been so bad that all he could see was the black line ahead of him and the wall around the track. He became so hypersensitive that the very nailheads in the track had jarred him "fearfully," and he thought his bones were coming apart. During the race he ate three pounds of boiled rice and a pound of oatmeal, and he drank three gallons of strong coffee and twenty quarts of milk. In six days he had been off the track a total of ten hours, of which *only four* had been spent in sleeping.[6]

The heroes of the six-day bicycle races were restrained from exceeding the six-day limit only by their compliance with English (where it is said the six-day torment originated) tradition which protected the Sabbath from despoiling by the ardors of the six-day riders. But six days was ample time for the steeply banked boards of the velodromes to resound with the crashes and the comedy of rabid riders on fixed-gear bicycles.

The Australian, Reggie McNamara, dubbed the Iron Man, was said to have fractured his left collarbone during fourteen different six-day races. The Iron Man has become the Finn McCool of six-day riders, for the troubadours who sing of their exploits now maintain that the Iron Man bicycled around the track despite having broken every bone in his body, some more than once, and having sustained a fractured skull.[7]

In the 1930s, when solo riders had become two-man teams, Madison Square Garden was the scene of a scandalously comical episode. It was early in the morning of the last day of a six-day race. Only one member of each team was on the track, bicycling in a leisurely, effortless way—as was the custom at such hours—when one of the riders, bending passion to pedal, sprang from the pack daring to "steal a lap" on the others. His partner, who had been feigning a nap by track-side, suddenly jumped on his bicycle to assist in the breakaway. The other riders were momentarily confounded. The sleeping partners were urgently summoned. Like pilots racing for their planes during a World War II air raid, the dozing teammates were jettisoned out of bed onto the track. Dress did not matter or even undress so long as they were able to pedal.

One of the untimely awakened bicyclists appeared on the tracks "in his shoes and nothing else." This attire created a unique problem. He lacked the shorts needed for his partner to "sling" him forward into the speeding fray. In the emergency of the moment, the teammates improvised as best they could. The naked bicyclist was given the heave-ho by a grab and a pull of the skin where his shorts should have been. The effort succeeded; the breakaway team was caught and the few bystanders there were went away clothed in smiles.[8]

Even though the six-day bicycle races have all but disappeared from the American racing scene, they were given a recent, nostalgic revival by journalist-author Jimmy Breslin in his movie-made book The Gang That Couldn't Shoot Straight. *The plot is a devastating lampoon of the Cosa Nostra's bungling in seeking to gangsterize the six-day bicycle race. Baccala, the don who, cautious to a fault, would never put a key into the ignition of his car in the morning until his wife had done so first, concocted a scheme to sponsor a six-day bicycle race when he recalled that*

During the Depression, when even fine gangsters were broke, Baccala went to a bike race at Madison Square Garden and quickly noticed that when everybody stood up to cheer they left their coats draped over the seats. On the second sprint of the night Baccala grabbed a great camel-hair from Row B, Section 205. A while later he took a black Chesterfield out of the last row of the end arena. He got into the side arena and came off with a terrific storm coat. He happened to look around, and he saw so many guys running around the arena and stealing coats that he thought he was having a vision of heaven.

Over the loudspeaker, later on that night, the announcer for the bike race said, "The score at this point . . ."

"Forty-nine coats!" somebody screamed from the mezzanine.[9]

Unhappily, Baccala's plans misfire when his hirelings botch the deal, causing the crowd to riot. The next morning, the 91st Precinct is a crowded place, somewhere between bedlam and babble. It all ends as it started—with a frolic and a banter.

The long-lived French novelist Paul Morand's "The Six-Day Night" is a tale whose ending must be impossible for modern man to take seriously. An affair of the heart cannot be ousted by an affair on the track. Yet, six-day bicycle races were overpowering stimulants to six-day fanaticism. All else was as nothing, even a slightly meretricious dalliance could be lapped.

She had been there for three nights running. She was always alone except for the dances, which she never missed, but which she only danced with the professional dancers or with girl friends. If anyone else asked her for a dance she refused; she refused me also, although I only went there to see her and she knew it. It was not so much her milk-white back, her jet bead dress which was a shimmering black water-fall, her excess of onyx jewellery, or her long narrow eyes meeting her side-locks and looking like onyxes themselves; it was rather her flat nose, the rise and fall of her bosom, her beautiful Jewish complexion like a sulphur-dusted vine, the odd fact of her being alone. And in addition to this her curious manoeuvrings several times each evening towards the lavatory and the telephone.

She spent her money on drinks, not in tipping the head waiter. She went on from short drinks to long ones. Between the hours of midnight and three o'clock on this third evening these consisted of two glasses of champagne, six anisettes and a small decanter of brandy, to say nothing of toothpicks and green almonds.

She went upstairs to the telephone with me behind her.

"Léa speaking. Is your milk good? Everything going on all right? . . . No stitch or anything? Has he eaten yet? Ah . . .? From the bottle?"

We seemed to know one another better in the setting of this waterless lavatory polluted by dead flowers, cigarette ends, broken dolls, cocaine, assignations and poudre rachel. She examined herself pitilessly in the mirror beneath the lamp, so closely that she kissed her own lips. On the mist of the breath she left there I inscribed my heart. She shrugged a shoulder.

She was wearing a bodice on which numerous Chinese officials in silver thread were discussing affairs of state on the threshold of numerous pagodas.

"Any of these to let?" I inquired, placing my finger on the door of the pagoda at each place where the pattern repeated it on her chest. She drew herself up with dignity.

"Are you often taken that way?"

The lavatory attendant, who was wiping her hands on an overcoat, turned round and pleaded for me.

"Yes, you look like a gentleman," said Léa, "but when I'm tight I'm always wrong."

From the balcony, above the up-coming bows of the fiddlers, one saw a picture of niggers in seaside clothes chewing at nothing and quaking with a kind of religious ague. Twisted copper irises, like offshoots of the "metro," lit up views of the Seine, no longer spoilt by factories, but steeped in romance and in which naked ladies were bathing timidly. Clasped body to body in the waltzing-trough the dancers surged along. The hall emitted an aroma of oxo, addled egg, arm-pit and of un jour viendra.

"Where do you like?" I asked her. "I love you."

"Go on! You're kidding. Or d'you mean it?"

"Both together, as usual."

She went on, inevitably.

"I seem to have seen you before somewhere."

"You are my very sister," I said, kissing her dress, "and I cannot live without you."

I must have seemed to her brazen, contemptible and utterly devoid of character. She disengaged herself.

"You seem in a desperate hurry."

"I'm not really, but I always do everything quickly and badly because I'm so afraid of ceasing to want to do it too soon."

"Well, it's nearly two o'clock. I've got to clear off now."

"Not before you've told me why you disappear every other moment. Are you selling it?"

She opened her eyes wide, like saucers.

"Not likely," she replied; "do you think I want five years?"

"Well then, what?"

"It's to get the latest news of my boy who's working."

"What does your boy do?"

"He's a long-distance cyclist, a six-day man. . . . He's in a six-day race, see? Do you mean to tell me you've never heard of Petitmathieu? Where on earth do you come from?"

With a sweep of her arm she enveloped herself in the skins of ninety-eight white rabbits.

"I told my coachman not to wait. Get me a taxi. Tell him to go towards Grenelle."

Along the banks of the winding Seine the taxi clock kept beating like a fevered pulse. Lamps like the husks of pink pearls along the Cours la Reine, phosphorescent sewer out-falls, the girl's dry cough, bursts of affection, resolutions on my part not to have any more nonsense after leaving the Champ de Mars, carts full of blue cabbages.

"I love cabs," I said. "We ought to take one of these cabs and live in it for months until we get to know its lamps, its springs, it tyres by heart. You know, for instance, that the blinds of the Urbaine cabs only pull down half-way and that it is nice to be behind a slow horse when Paris seethes beneath its cloak of mist and one does that which depopulates the world . . ."

Grenelle. The river sweeps beneath the yoke of the bridge. Red lights on the lovers' parapet, green ones on the business men's. Fourteen francs twenty-five centimes on the clock.

I inquire anxiously:

"Don't you live in Paris?"

"Idiot," she replies, "who said anything about where I live? I am going to the Winter Cycletrack for the two o'clock stakes."

*   *   *

An underground passage led to the enclosure. The cheap carpet over the door was rippled by draughts. When we were half-way through there was a terrific thundering overhead. The boards groaned. Then we came out into a wooden circus connected to its glass roof by a fog broken up into luminous conical sections. Under enamelled shades powerful electric lamps followed the track; Léa stood imperially on tiptoe.

"Look: yellow and black. . . . The Wasps . . . the team of 'aces.' That's Van den Hoven racing now. They'll wake Petitmathieu up for the two o'clock stakes."

Shrill whistles cut through the air. Then four thousand yells broke out, yells that seemed to burst straight from the throat, such as one only gets from a Parisian crowd.

The Australian tried to forge ahead. They were beginning to sprint. Above the advertisement placards I saw the drawn features and eager eyes of the populace. A band broke out. Latriche was singing. *"Hardi coco!"* was taken up in chrous. This livened matters up. The sixteen competitors passed by every twenty seconds in a compact body, keeping a watchful eye on each other.

The weighing-room occupied one end of the velodrome. At each end of the track turned, and there it gradually banked until it was as steep as a wall which the racers in their impetus climbed almost up to the words "THE MOST RELIABLE PETROL." The notice board began to show signs of life. Figures came down and others took their place.

"4th night, 85th hour. 2300 kilometres 650 metres."

"Look, there he is!" said Léa, "there's my darling getting on to his machine."

So far Petitmathieu was still swinging along easily by himself, with his curled hair, his dirty neck and his eyes as treacherous as those of a cat.

"Isn't he a lamb, considering it's his fourth night, the dear boy!"

The nickelled megaphone announced two stakes of a hundred francs each for the best time done over a given number of laps. The signal for the start of these was given with pistol shots.

"Let's go closer, things are becoming more exciting. Ah! he has seen us."

He had seen me. I was holding Léa's hand. We exchanged a look of hatred as man to man.

The noise seemed to echo in spirals through the length of the building and then gradually to die down. At the signal the sixteen men seemed to shoot round the corners and were hurled into the straight again by the steep twisted turns.

"Léa," I murmured, "I wish that, in the words of that old puritan Agrippa d'Aubigne, we were 'cradled in delights.' What do you like for breakfast?"

The mob was making an inhuman din.

"You're barmy," she replied. "Go on the spree when that darling is going round and round on the track there? Not much. A pretty sort of thing I'd be if I thought of anything but him during these six days and six nights."

At the finish they pounced on the stakes like carp on a crust of bread, the woolly Italian, the Swiss giant, the Corsican N.C.O.'s, and all the niggers amongst the fair Flemings.

"It's all over. The Australian's won. Just like our luck! Petitmathieu let himself be hemmed in," said Léa.

"He's going to get off; let's go and see him, the love!"

*   *   *

The competitors' quarters had sprung up at the small end of the track. Each man had reserved for him a wooden cubicle with a curtain in front, in which there was a bed. In a slot above one of these was written: VELOX STAND. PETITMATHIEU—VAN DEN HOVEN TEAM. A searchlight played on the innermost recesses of the cubicles so that the crowd should not miss a single action of its favourites, even during their rest. The attendants dressed in white hospital overalls bustled about with a clinking of plates amongst the petrol and grease stains, mixing embrocations with eggs and camphor on garden chairs. Dismantled machines, bicycle frames, rubber washers, pieces of black cottonwool soaking in basins. Petitmathieu was lying stretched on his back, his hands behind his head, resigning his hairy and heavily veined legs to the masseur who was patting them to make them supple.

"Do let me kiss him, Bibendum," said Léa to the manager. Petitmathieu opened an eye.

"That's all right," he said crossly, pushing her away. "Let him get on with his job."

"You haven't shaved, you ugly old thing."

"Oh! shut up!"

Silence fell. The racers passed by us, along the rails, their shadows being thrown on the awning above the cubicles. Their naked legs went round like mechanical toys. Van den Hoven called out as he passed:

"Buck up! to-morrow night's nearly here."

I made Petitmathieu's acquaintance, but he seemed to ignore my presence entirely. He was grumbling to himself. That would teach him to get up again for a bloody stake. And only a hundred franc one at that. Stingy brutes. A lot of touts who came there with their tarts, that is, if they didn't come to pinch other people's girls!

His thighs were now like wet ivory.

"Petitmathieu! Stand up there!" he mob cried relentlessly from above the Peugeot lions. But he made a sign with his hand that he was fed up with them.

The soiled mechanics in khaki shirts with their five days' beard were binding handlebars with pitched string, making bundles of wheels to be examined, tightening nuts.

Petitmathieu was feeling uncomfortable.

"My stomach, when are you going to do my stomach?"

The masseur pulled down the elastic belt of Petitmathieu's shorts. Below his navel was written *"4th Zouave Regiment. 1st Company,"* with the motto *"All I can get."* He rubbed him with the palm of his hand.

"Put some talc powder on my thighs."

Those who had just been relieved by their team mates got off their machines for two hours' sleep. Their managers stopped them by grasping their saddles and handle-bars, undid the straps fastening their feet to the pedals and carried their charges with tender care towards their beds.

Then everything settled down for the night. In spite of the noise some of the competitors were snoring. Others got up and ragged about from bed to bed like in a barrack-room. One heard the noise of bicycle pumps being used, followed by that of compressed air whistling through valves.

Petitmathieu remained on his back like a corpse, his hands with their square black nails and thick aluminum rings crossed on his chest. Lea sat herself at his feet and rouged her cheeks. I moved away.

From behind the partition I heard Petitmathieu talking:

"All the same, I told you I wouldn't have you go to Maxim's during the race."

Léa explained that she was too nervy to stay at home by herself. She couldn't sleep. She only thought of him and of his lovely thighs working away so hard, of his beloved face with his black curly hair, his Charlie Chaplin moustache, his square jaw, his eyes fixed on the back wheel of the pacer, his scarlet sweater fastened at the neck by mother-of-pearl buttons. It was not the first time he had been tested. Hadn't she simply *lived* at the end of a telegraph wire all the time he was grinding round Madison Square the year before?

Crushed beneath the weight of their 87 hours of work and 2352 kilometres 580 metres of distance, the competitors were going round in Indian file to the silvery trill of bearing balls, a negro leading the way. Some of them had put on goggles. Now and then someone had a puncture or a chain broke. Hurriedly his sleeping comrade was awakened and seated forcibly on the saddle; still asleep he attached himself to the others. The round became monotonous as always at the end of those nights which no one ever dreams of leaving except in a state of collapse. A silence weighing tons descended on the assembly.

Léa rejoined me in the enclosure.

"Hop it, or he won't be able to sleep. He's watching us all the time. It drives him mad to know I'm with someone and that he can't leave his bunk. He'll get tireder and tireder and nervier and nervier.

"It isn't that he's got it in for you, he even thinks you're rather a sport, if a little half-baked," she went on; "but he's got it in for me. He won't have me go to Maxim's or dance. He's frightfully touchy."

So I learnt that Petitmathieu only allowed her to go to the Excelsior, the racers' café, to write letters and see people. There at any rate he knew what was going on, from his pals and from the waiters.

In vain I promised her a surprise, presents, complete discretion; I could not persuade Léa to come back with me. I only got her permission to meet her next day at the apéritif hour. I needed her. She described such sweet plump curves and her harsh voice, a delight in itself, enchanted me. All that soft skin smoothed by beauty creams, washed with ointments, all those jewels, all her hidden charms, her dyes, drugs and tenderness, were all at the disposition of those strong, hairy, piston-like legs now resting, rolled so carefully in their blankets. The whole thing was an illogical and yet natural game into which I was intruding as a third party, and which amazed and

irritated me but, at the same time, was the only thing that gave me the strength to bear
that cruel moment in which the night prowler has to confess himself beaten.

*   *   *

Sunset. Grenadine. The hour flowed smoothly. A feeling of peace crept over everything in spite of the fierceness of my drink. I was waiting for Léa at the Brasserie de la
Porte-Maillot. She came down from Montmartre in a hired brougham, dressed in an
otter-skin coat, and drank long drinks.

"This reminds me of when I first knew Petitmathieu. I rented a room by the month
in the Rue des Acacias."

My first words were to ask her for news of the race.

"A little tired," she said. "Backache. And colic. But the other leading team has it
too. The Australian is done in. Water on the knee coming on. He's chucked it.
They've hardly moved all the morning; they're just crawling along."

"And Van den Hoven?"

"Pedals like a demon all the time. But he has no head, no sense of combination. It's
Bibendum and Petitmathieu who come out strong when something's got to be done."

I began to realize that my pleasure at seeing Léa again was not an unmixed one. I
loved her plebian hands, her eyelids the colour of a fifty-franc note . . . that cold heart
which warmed as if by magic to physical strength, but I could not forget the struggle
going on round and round down there.

Drawn up by the kerb the cars of the patrons exhausted the catalogue of strange
shapes. There were guns, yachts, bath-tubs, airships, whilst some of them were
merely hastily covered with a champagne case. Their owners were those highly-
polished and beautiful young men who stand for hours behind plate-glass windows in
the avenue des Champs Élysées in tiled show-rooms containing nothing but a palm, a
Persian prayer-rug and a nickelled chassis. They always remind me of the ladies
sitting in their windows in the low quarters of Amsterdam.

The waiters hurried about between the tables, holding a black-coloured apéritif
between each finger. Mechanics in overalls, cyclists with tyres wrapped round their
bodies, pugilists leaving Cuny's. Each man greeted his friends with a gesture characteristic of his occupation. Bantam weights gave each other hearty right hood in the
ribs, footballers slapped each other on the legs.

Léa was still pretty and elusive. The only thing which roused her at all was a yellow
and black scarf, the colours of the team, which I had bought specially for her. She
wore a large white felt hat trimmed with a single vulture's feather and drop ear-rings
which reminded me of the Far West and of the ladies who shoot over their shoulders,
aiming in a mirror. I told her this. I also told her that I was not a man like Petitmathieu
with *"All I can get"* for his motto, and that I had never wanted anything for six days
and six nights in my life, that the doctor forbade me cold baths, that in matters of daily
life I had always done "the correct thing" to a dreadful extent, that my heart was an
object entirely distinct from myself, and that very thin women with curly hair were not
without their charm.

On the other hand, she was enthralled when she discovered that I knew the Italian lakes and the author of "Tipperary," and that I had some autographs of Marshal Joffre. I even boasted of having in my studio an exact replica of an arab chief's tent and of being able to play her Tartini's "Devil's Sonata" on the violin.

She looked at me:

"I say, you're not a bit like other people, are you?"

"Thank you, Léa. It is only women who say things like that to one; and yet it is above all with them that one *is* like everyone else."

The school of motoring near by emitted a foetid stench. In the distance a hunt could be heard in progress just beyond the fortifications, mixed with the melancholy hooting of the siren in the shadows of the scenic railway at Luna Park, which is like the hull of a huge steamer abandoned on the stocks of a bankrupt shipbuilder.

*   *   *

I had to admit to myself with some annoyance on arriving at the race track that evening that I was going there just as much for the race as for Léa; nothing had changed on the announcements. But suddenly there was an uproar. The six racers were going round in a coloured ribbon in which were mixed green, yellow, white, scarlet and orange. By their nimble pedalling they devoured the track worn smooth by their tyres, to the clang of the bell marking their progress.

Petitmathieu was in the saddle; he saw me and gave me a smile of recognition with his left eyelid. Then, towards the 2921st kilometre in the 109th hour an effort was made to get a lead. The balconies groaned beneath the weight of the public surprised during their supper, their mouths full of food.

The negro, his nose glued to his handle-bars, went off like an arrow, and getting half a lap ahead, kept his lead. There was instant confusion. Those who were suffering from the effects of a fall or from aching backs and those whose wheels were buckled were left behind one by one and were soon caught up again. Led by Petitmathieu, the competitors threw themselves in the wake of the negro, who began to weaken and look round: his team mate was asleep and did not come; the crowd yelled to him to come to the rescue.

"Hi, cocky! Boot-face! Get mounted!"

A waiter let a glass of beer fall from the first tier. The hall shook beneath the howls, the rattles and the whistles until suddenly the negro straightened his back, brought his hands to the centre of his handle-bars and "resting on his oars," showed that he had had enough.

I made for the competitors' quarters. Petitmathieu began to dine heartily. Washed, shaved, a fine-looking lad in his cashmere dressing-gown, he was gnawing away at a cutlet he held in his hand. Seated on the edge of the bed, Léa watched him chew, her eyes moist and submissive. He offered me a bowl of champagne and some whisked eggs in a tin that had once held rubber solution.

I was proud of my acquaintance with this athlete whom the programme called "A Caruso of the pedal." I found myself admiring his supple legs, his faultless knees. I assured him of my warm support and spurred him on.

"I led the pack," he explained, simply. "When that happened it didn't take long to break the nigger's heart. All we wanted was to work together."

Petitmathieu amazed me most by his calm, dining peacefully like an ordinary citizen a few minutes after that hue and cry, surrounded now by his assiduous attendants, his adoring mate beside him, propped up by cushions, with a screen decorated with wistaria behind him which gave him the appearance of being in his home.

Léa held one of his fingers tenderly and said nothing. I loved them both equally. I told them so.

We clinked glasses. Léa proposed the following toast:

> To our health which is dear to us all
> And which is so necessary to us,
> Because with health one can earn money,
> With money one can buy sugar,
> With sugar one can catch flies.

Petitmathieu explained his happiness to me: "She's a regular scream. But a good girl for all that. And always ready with tempting dishes, bandages and anything else that's wanted. She's got a coachman by the month who plays the trumpet and knows all about mushrooms. Clever isn't the word for her, and what a talker! Makes a party go like anything. Between ourselves, a skin with veins in it like rivers on a map, a mane of hair down to her heels, none of those three blobs of hair which women wear nowadays and which don't keep a comb busy. And what breasts! cool as an icehouse; and then going about things painstakingly whilst only putting half her back into it; washes her teeth after every meal, eats asparagus with special tongs and never wears stays.

"Wait till you know her better," he said, "and you'll see what I mean."

The orchestra was playing a boston which sounded like switchbacks. From exquisite heights one was cast into the languourous valleys of the refrains. Some comedians with powdered chins came in after the theatre. They wanted to dance, but the mob treated them as good-for-nothings, braggarts, sausage-eaters.

I left Petitmathieu in high spirits, holding his audience, pretending to be in bed with Léa in his cubicle.

I had to give my promise that I would return the next day for the supreme effort and that I would stay there all night.

*   *   *

Sixth night, 138th hour, 3864 kil. 570. The same monotonous spectacle. They slept as they went round, like weary squirrels; one of them touched the wheel in front and fell, dragging the others with him. One heard shouts in English, Turkish oaths, a desultory clamour caused by someone giving up the race; then the round began again.

"Nothing," I replied, "could have afforded me greater pleasure, even as late as yesterday. And perhaps to-morrow again. But to-day my whole heart is here; I am a prey to one thought only, and that is that Petitmathieu should win. I no longer belong to myself; nor do you; we have become part of the velodrome, an incident in the race, waiting for victory. A few hours more and just think of the click of the cameras, the crowd, the special editions of the papers, the banquet with its flags and deputies. We will ourselves have contributed in our own small way to our winner getting all this."

"Dearest," said Léa, annoyed, "you're a good boy. That's nice. It's sweet of you. I love you more for that."

Disappointment turned down the corners of her mouth.

She waited. She closed her eyes. Then half dreaming she said:—

"I don't know how Petitmathieu will take this."

On our right, above the advertisement of Éternol varnish, through the glass roof the desolate dawn appeared, heralded by a pianola. I sang:

> 'Tis the hour of tumbled bedclothes and the dawning of the day,
>   And the rooster to the rooster hoarsely cries.
> 'Tis the hour of sweet denials when flowers are cast away,
>   Yet how strangely, while you sleep, my passion dies.

It was very late. The night sprints were over. The competitors circled round, their hands reversed to rest their wrists and wrapped in thick woollen shawls against the night cold.

Petitmathieu was resting in his cubicle. Van den Hoven was carrying out the humble toil of the night, leaving to his team mate the brilliant work of the last hour which was about to begin. I offered to lend a hand to Bibendum, whose face was as drawn by weariness as though distorted in a spoon. In our shirt-sleeves we put an inner tube into a bucket of water to find the leak in it. Léa found me doing this and reproached me for neglecting her. I shrugged my shoulders.

Many of the spectators were spending the night there. Children were sleeping lying on pink or yellow sporting papers. Orderlies from the École Militaire, private chauffeurs, workmen from les Moulineaux on their way to their factories, clerks on their way to their offices, provincial couples in mourning, yawned, kept themselves awake by playing cards and opened bottles with a pop.

"Ugène," said someone, "pass me the scent-sprayer."

* * *

Wrapping ourselves in blankets, our heads on sacking, we waited side by side for the dawn. Léa took my hand in hers.

"What small bones you've got! I feel I'm going to get into trouble over you," she said, like the heroine of a penny novelette. Her voice was soft and silky. "You're just the opposite to a record breaker. You're more like a priest or a comic singer. You don't say much but you're full of life. And besides, I've always longed to be interested in someone whose health wasn't very good. A young artist, for instance, with his shirt open at the neck, veins much too blue and a fine pointed beard. . . . Take me."

Part VII

No Flying Creature

Introduction

My good Hopkins, I have investigated many crimes, but I have never yet seen one which was committed by a flying creature. As long as the criminal remains upon two legs so long must there be some indentation, some abrasion, some trifling displacement which can be detected by the scientific searcher.[1]

A terse primer for the scientific sleuth, as many of Sherlock Holmes's insights were.

Edmond Locard, the French criminologist, famed for his authorship of the exchange principle, expressed the same thought but without the literary zest of A. Conan Doyle. "When two objects come into contact," he said, "there is always a transfer of material from each object to the other."[2]

A clue is nothing, however, without a suspect. The comparison of the unknown with the known is the key to the riddle of many a crime. Where the English cookbook recipe for rabbit directs, so should the investigating detective follow. "First catch a hare." But without an appreciation of the value of Locard's principle, the suspect might forever elude detection. The investigation of the murder of Maria Flosky ideally illustrates that "no flying creature" commits a crime.[3]

On September 11, 1963, the body of Maria Flosky was found in the woods near a camping area outside the industrial town of Kahl in northern Bavaria. She had been mushroom gathering, basket in hand, when she had been attacked and strangled. She was found with a scarf loosely knotted about her neck. The motive for the crime was undetermined since there was no evidence of a robbery nor had the victim been sexually molested. The police investigators surmised that she had been assaulted for the purpose of rape but that her attacker had been interrupted and fled after garroting her.

The investigation was conducted mainly by Detective Inspector Degen of the State Criminal Office. The wooded area in the vicinity of the crime was canavassed for persons who might have seen the murderer escape. It soon became apparent that only one of two parallel paths proceeding northward to a paved road could have been the killer's escape route. Laborious investigation developed a pensioner who admitted to having been seated on a bench beside one of these paths on the afternoon of the crime. He remembered a bicyclist's having passed him with a pleasant "Good day" shortly

"An invisible man?" inquired Angus, raising his red eyebrows. "A mentally invisible man," said Father Brown. (From "The Invisible Man" by G. K. Chesterton)

after the crime had been committed. Further tracking revealed that this bicyclist was, in all probability, Anton Flittner, a thirty-two-year-old, twice-married machinist who had been on sick leave from his work on the day of the murder. He had spent his free time bicycling to various places in the area, including the camping grounds in question. Flittner was an unsavory character who had been convicted of indecent behavior against his small step daughter just a few months before. His unrestrained "sexuality and brutality" had been the cause of much complaint by his second wife to the local authorities. Flittner instantly became the principal suspect.

Inspector Degen, well-schooled in the methods of obtaining trace evidence from crime scenes, used adhesive to obtain whatever minute particles might still be clinging to the hands of the murder victim. He then convinced Flittner to allow him to analyze the fibers from the outer clothes he had been wearing on the day of the crime. The results of this fiber analysis were inconclusive, providing no definite link between Flittner and the deceased.

Meanwhile, Degen had set a trap for Flittner in order to have him identified by the pensioner who had seen the conversational bicyclist on the woodland path on the day of the murder.

The pensioner, Otto Hock, was told to sit along the path precisely where he had been on that earlier, tragic day. He was instructed to be on the alert for all bicyclists.

Then Detective Sergeant Rudingsdorfer bicycled to Flittner's residence and invited him to join the sergeant on a bicycle outing. Flittner acquiesced and the two bicycled off to various places, including the camping ground near which the crime had occurred. Flittner was noted to be pedaling rather slowly.

Later the two bicyclists were joined by Degen, also on a bicycle, and the three cycled to the scene of the crime at about the same time of day that the crime was said to have been committed. They then bicycled north along the path where Otto Hock was waiting, Degen bringing up the rear. On Degen's inquiry, Hock identified Flittner as having "looked awfully like the man he had seen" on the day of the murder. Moreover, he'd also been struck by the fact that the man said "Good afternoon" to him, although they were not acquainted. The cyclist of September 11 had likewise said "Good day."

With this information, confirming his suspicions, Degen raced along the path, halted Flittner and demanded why he had said "Good afternoon" to Hock and whether he had ever seen the man before. Flittner listened in silence and then, without raising his eyes, merely admitted that his prior statements of his bicycle journeyings on September 11 had been in error.

Hock's identification, although highly incriminating, was only circumstantial evidence of Flittner's guilt, and inconclusive at that. The evidence against Flittner was still insufficient to warrant a murder charge.

The detective, methodical to a fault, now returned to the trace analysis of clothing fibers. He remembered that the deceased's fingernails had been clipped prior to her burial and that the clippings had been saved. Further, Degen surmised that the scarf found around the victim's neck had been used to line the basket she intended to fill with her mushroom pickings. Degen obtained a number of shirts from Flittner's wife, any one of which he might have been wearing on the day of the murder. Finally and most imaginatively, the detective returned to the now well-trampled crime scene.

He observed a lone fir tree near the site where the body had been discovered. In a desperate gamble that the victim and her attacker had brushed against the fir tree in struggling, he applied strips of adhesive tape about the trunk of the tree all the way up to a man's height. He carefully removed them, hoping aainst hope that they would bear traces of fibers from Flittner's clothing or that of Maria Flosky or, better yet, from both. He then assembled all of this evidence and forwarded it to the state crime lab for analysis and comparison of the fibers.

The results were two anxious days in arriving. The report was not only an immense relief. It was definitive. It read:

1. On the adhesive tape samplings taken from Maris Flosky's palms are fragments of blue and blue-violet cotton fibers. These correspond to blue and blue-violet fibers in a blue and green checked shirt belonging to the suspect Flittner, and are indistinguishable from these fibers. 2. The tapes taken from the fir tree in the immediate vicinity of the scene of the crime contain fragments of light blue cotton fibers, and a fragment of a blue-violet cotton fiber. These fibers are indistinguishable from corresponding fiber traces on the victim's palms and from the fibers of the blue and green checked shirt belonging to the suspect. 3. On the inside of the

basket are several white synthetic fibers. These fibers correspond in hue and quality to the fibers of the scarf. Furthermore, on the inner rim of the basket are a blue cotton fiber and a light ocher woolen fiber. Both fibers occur in the fabric of Flittner's sports jacket.[4]

When confronted with this scientific evidence, Flittner made a full confession, reenacted the crime, and was later sentenced to life imprisonment. Inspector Degen's ingenuity had been vindicated. And Locard's exchange principle had been reaffirmed. No flying creature had committed this crime. Just a sex-crazed bicyclist.

The bicycle itself may provide a clue to the identity of a criminal. As will be seen in "The Adventure of the Priory School," which follows, a bicycle's tires may leave their distinctive signature on permeable ground. A bent pedal and a freshly cleaned bicycle, on the other hand, put Inspector Maigret on the trail of a murderer in Georges Simenon's mystery novel *Maigret Meets a Milord*. Inspector Maigret of the Flying Squad was summoned to investigate the death of the fashionable, charming Mary Lampson, who had been found strangled in a stable next to the Café de la Marine at lock 14 of the inland canal near Dizy, France. The victim had disappeared from the yacht *Southern Cross* a few days before after a particularly rowdy party on board at the dock at Meaux. A barge, the *Providence*, was also moored at Meaux at the time of Mrs. Lampson's vanishing.

During Maigret's investigations at Dizy, the *Providence* moves away down the canal, after its husband-and-wife owners and their carter, burly Jean Liberge, are quizzed by Maigret. Shortly, Willy Marco, a ne'er-do-well crewman on the *Southern Cross*, is found floating in the canal, another victim of strangulation.

The plot comes to a boil when Madame Gloria Negretti, Colonel Lampson's lady-in-waiting, is summarily evicted from her quarters on the *Southern Cross*. In an interview with Maigret, she vengefully bares her soul including the fact that the *Southern Cross* is now hurrying, full tilt, through the canal to overtake the *Providence*—on an unexplained mission.

Maigret springs into action, borrows a bicycle, and dashes off in pursuit of the *Providence* along the towpath adjoining the canal. Along the way his inquiries are all fruitless until, after thirty-odd miles of bicycling "without drinking so much as a glass of beer," the lockkeeper at Pogny protests that someone must have borrowed his wife's bicycle the night before. The lockkeeper's suspicions have been aroused by the condition of the bicycle on the morning after. As he put it to Maigret:

> "Well, this morning the bike was perfectly clean, although it rained all night. . . . You've seen the mud on the towpath. . . .
> "But the left pedal is out of truth and the tyre looks as if it had done at least fifty miles."[5]

Maigret's instincts as a bloodhound are instantly alerted. Willy was killed last night. The *Providence* was berthed in the vicinity of Pogny at the time. And the *Southern Cross* is now chasing the barge.

He stuffs the pedals from the lockkeeper's bicycle into his pockets, mounts his bicycle, and scorches ten more miles down the towpath until he overtakes the *Providence* at Vitry-le-François. Maigret confronts the carter, Jean Liberge, whom he finds "scowling angrily." The bent left pedal is taken from Maigret's pocket while Liberge removes his boots. Then

> Standing close to the lamp, Maigret compared the pedal, some of the treads of which were broken, with the scarcely visible marks on the leather [of the carter's boot].
> "You took the lock-keeper's bicycle at Pogny last night!" he said slowly and accusingly, without taking his eyes off the two objects.[6]

The murderer is unmasked. The bent pedal has spoken. Jean Liberge, ex-convict, ex-doctor and ex-husband of Mary Lampson, had killed his former wife in a fit of jealous rage and Willy Marco too when he became suspicious of him.

A bicycle's tires can pick up as well as put down marks signifying its presence at or near a crime scene. The deductions of Lord Peter Wimsey in Dorothy Sayers's *Five Red Herrings* were suggested by "tarry marks on the cushions" of the landscape painter Campbell's car, which was found at the scene of his apparently accidental death. And a close look "at this smear of tar" under a magnifying glass showed "traces of the tread of a [bicycle] tyre." This and other clues at the lonely spot where Campbell's battered body was discovered on the rocks below the promontory where his latest, unfinished painting is propped on an easel convince Lord Peter that foul play has been done.

As he sees it, Campbell's already lifeless body was brought to this location. The killer simulated the setting of a painting in progress. Campbell's body was then thrown over the cliff and the murderer lifted a bicycle from the trunk of Campbell's car and bicycled off unconcerned and unobserved. The scene was faked to give the impression of a distracted painter's backing off a cliff while stepping back to view his painting, the paint still wet.

Lord Peter's carefully deduced conclusions are later proved to be correct, but not until he has cleared "five red herrings" of complicity in the affair. The whereabouts of bicyclist after bicyclist must be tracked including a "pinched push-bike . . . wi' new tyres on both wheels," a six-year-old Raleigh that the murderer had used to secure his escape. Throughout the tale, the bicycle clues become more and more nightmarish, for, as Lord Peter complained, "there are more bicycles per head of the population in Kirkcudbright than in any town I ever struck." Moreover, "they all look much alike— honest, hardworking bicycles, half as old as time." To Inspector Macpherson the time had come to talk of other things besides who was riding what bicycle where.

> "Bicycles?" said Inspector Macpherson. "Dinna ye talk toe me o' bicycles. I'm fair fed up wi' the name o' them. Wad ye believe that there could be sic a stour aboot twa-three bicycles?"[7]

In the end, it was not a bicycle that solved the mystery. A railway ticket, with forged punch holes, led to the identification of the murderer. But the homicide, having been provoked, was adjudged by the jury to be manslaughter, not murder. The culpable bicycle was not even brought to trial.

In other tales of crime and mystery the bicycle has played a subsidiary role. Megan Hunter, in Agatha Christie's *The Moving Finger*, had "quite a craze for bicycling." Rather than aiding in the development of the plot, the bicycle just defines Megan's character and, in doing so, excludes her as a suspect.

Bicycles, although of minor importance to the plot, do appear under rather strange circumstances in a number of John D. MacDonald's Travis McGee thrillers. Jason Breen, in *The Dreadful Lemon Sky*, was a certified bike freak. He was the proud owner of a Schwinn Sports Tourer with the most stylish and costly accoutrements. Save for that "azure blue" bicycle, Travis McGee might never have discovered the murdered Jason's body buried, bicycle and all, in an impromptu grave and partially concealed under the carcass of a horse, shot for the occasion.

In MacDonald's latest Travis McGee mystery, *The Green Ripper*, the bicycle serves to introduce the plot when forty-six-year-old Herm Ladwigg is found dead, lying in the road beside his bicycle, an apparent heart-attack victim. It later is discovered that Ladwigg was deliberately killed by a rock thrown into his face, causing him to fall from his bicycle to his death. A fanatical religious cult is behind it all, and Travis McGee must summon up untold reserves of strength and resourcefulness to deal with it.

The selections in this chapter portray the bicycle as a dynamic force, rather than a casual artifact, in fashioning the plot and in elucidating its solution.

1

Sir Arthur Conan Doyle

The Adventure of the Priory School

Contemplation bakes no loaves. Or so Sherlock Holmes might have pontificated. Like Hercule Poirot, Holmes made most effective use of his little gray cells. But he could also box the bullying red-mustached ruffian Mr. Woodley to the floor in "The Adventure of the Solitary Cyclist." Or he could mount a bicycle and track a carriage even to the point of overtaking it in his effort to unravel the mystery of the disappearance of Geoffrey Staunton, star rugby player.[1]

Holmes, like his creator, Sir Arthur Conan Doyle, was a man of energy and action. Doyle, himself a boxer, forward on the Edinburgh University football team, whaler, seal killer, horseman, cricket player, skier, fox hunter, golfer, and tricyclist, would hardly have conceived a detective of a sedentary persuasion. Indeed, Hesketh Pearson, in his biography of Doyle, mentions that "many of his [Doyle's] ideas came to him in the afternoons when walking or cricketing or tricycling or playing tennis."[2]

Doyle, according to the account of one of his contemporaries, entered

liberally into all outdoor sports—football, tennis, bowls, and cricket. . . . But in exercise he most leans toward tricycling. He is never happier than when on his tandem with his wife, and starting on a thirty-mile spin; never merrier than when he perches his little three-year-old Mary on the wheels, and runs her round the green lawn of his garden.[3]

His excursions with his first wife, Louise, were against the doctor's orders, so to speak, for she would tricycle with him "in wet weather without protective covering," she who was to die of tuberculosis.

Reprinted from *The Strand Magazine*, vol. 27 (February 1904), pp. 122–40.

Unhappily, Doyle did not mention his bicycling or tricycling in his autobiographical "Some Recollections of Sport."[4] But he does include a bicycling incident, entitled "Venit Tandem Felicitas," in his early romantic gambol Beyond the City. *In it, we find twenty-six-year-old Charles Westmacott romancing Ida Walker on a tandem tricycle as they fly "along the beautiful smooth suburban roads in the direction of Forest Hill." They must have cut quite a handsome figure together, not unlike that of Conan Doyle and his Louise, for in Doyle's description we see that*

The great limbs of the athlete made the heavy machine spring and quiver with every stroke, while the mignon grey figure with the laughing face, and the golden curls blowing from under the little pink-banded straw hat, simply held firmly to her perch, and let the treadles whirl round beneath her feet. Mile after mile they flew, the wind beating in her face, the trees dancing past in two long ranks on either side, until they had passed round Croydon, and were approaching Norwood once more from the further side.[5]

Conan Doyle considered "The Adventure of the Priory School" to be number ten among the twelve best of his Sherlock Holmes adventures. This assessment was founded on the dramatic impact of the "moment when Holmes points his finger at the Duke."[6] Dorothy Sayers also was impressed by Holmes's "grimmer vein" in the "Priory School," which had led him to rebuke "wickedness in high places." Ms. Sayers, however, demonstrated more than mild approval of the "Priory School," for it is the only selection of all the Sherlock Holmes tales that merited inclusion in her The Omnibus of Crime.

We have had some dramatic entrances and exits upon our small stage at Baker Street, but I cannot recollect anything more sudden and startling than the first appearance of Dr. Thorneycroft Huxtable, M.A., Ph.D., etc. His card, which seemed too small to carry the weight of his academic distinctions, preceded him by a few seconds, and then he entered himself—so large, so pompous, and so dignified that he was the very embodiment of self-possession and solidity. And yet his first action when the door had closed behind him was to stagger against the table whence he slipped down upon the floor, and there was that majestic figure prostrate and insensible upon our bearskin hearthrug.

We had sprung to our feet, and for a few moments we stared in silent amazement at this ponderous piece of wreckage, which told of some sudden and fatal storm far out on the ocean of life. Then Holmes hurried with a cushion for his head and I with brandy for his lips. The heavy white face was seamed with lines of trouble; the hanging pouches under the closed eyes were leaden in colour, the loose mouth drooped dolorously at the corners, the rolling chins were unshaven. Collar and shirt bore the grime of a long journey, and the hair bristled unkempt from the well-shaped head. It was a sorely stricken man who lay before us.

"What is it, Watson?" asked Holmes.

"Absolute exhaustion—possibly mere hunger and fatigue," said I, with my finger on the thready pulse, where the stream of life trickled thin and small.

"Return ticket from Mackleton, in the north of England," said Holmes, drawing it from the watch-pocket. "It is not twelve o'clock yet. He has certainly been an early starter."

The puckered eyelids had begun to quiver, and now a pair of vacant, grey eyes looked up at us. An instant later the man had scrambled on to his feet, his face crimson with shame.

"Forgive this weakness, Mr. Holmes: I have been a little overwrought. Thank you, if I might have a glass of milk and a biscuit I have no doubt that I should be better. I came personally, Mr. Holmes, in order to ensure that you would return with me. I feared that no telegram would convince you of the absolute urgency of the case."

"When you are quite restored—"

"I am quite well again. I cannot imagine how I came to be so weak. I wish you, Mr. Holmes, to come to Mackleton with me by the next train."

My friend shook his head.

"My colleague, Dr. Watson, could tell you that we are very busy at present. I am retained in this case of the Ferrers Documents, and the Abergavenny murder is coming up for trial. Only a very important issue could call me from London at present."

"Important!" Our visitor threw up his hands. "Have you heard nothing of the abduction of the only son of the Duke of Holdernesse?"

"What! the late Cabinet Minister?"

"Exactly. We had tried to keep it out of the papers, but there was some rumour in the *Globe* last night. I thought it might have reached your ears."

Holmes shot out his long, thin arm and picked out Volume "H" in his encyclopaedia of reference.

" 'Holdernesse, 6th Duke, K.G., P.C.'—half the alphabet! 'Baron Beverley, Earl of Carston'—dear me, what a list! 'Lord Lieutenant of Hallamshire since 1900. Married Edith, daughter of Sir Charles Appledore, 1888. Heir and only child, Lord Saltire. Owns about two hundred and fifty thousand acres. Minerals in Lancashire and Wales. Address: Carlton House Terrace; Holdernesse Hall, Hallamshire; Carston Castle, Bangor, Wales. Lord of the Admiralty, 1872; Chief Secretary of State for'—Well, well, this man is certainly one of the greatest subjects of the Crown!"

"The greatest and perhaps the wealthiest. I am aware, Mr. Holmes, that you take a very high line in professional matters, and that you are prepared to work for the work's sake. I may tell you, however, that his Grace has already intimated that a cheque for five thousand pounds will be handed over to the person who can tell him where his son is, and another thousand to him who can name the man, or men, who have taken him."

"It is a princely offer," said Holmes. "Watson, I think that we shall accompany Dr. Huxtable back to the North of England. And now, Dr. Huxtable, when you have consumed that milk you will kindly tell me what has happened, when it happened, how it happened, and, finally, what Dr. Thorneycroft Huxtable, of the Priory School, next Mackleton, has to do with the matter, and why he comes three days after an event—the state of your chin gives the date—to ask for my humble services."

Our visitor had consumed his milk and biscuits. The light had come back to his eyes and the colour to his cheeks as he set himself with great vigour and lucidity to explain the situation.

"I must inform you, gentlemen, that the Priory is a preparatory school, of which I am the founder and principal. 'Huxtable's Sidelights on Horace' may possibly recall my name to your memories. The Priory is, without exception, the best and most select preparatory school in England. Lord Leverstoke, the Earl of Blackwater, Sir Cathcart Soames—they all have entrusted their sons to me. But I felt that my school had reached its zenith when, three weeks ago, the Duke of Holdernesse sent Mr. James Wilder, his secretary, with the intimation that young Lord Saltire, ten years old, his only son and heir, was about to be committed to my charge. Little did I think that this would be the prelude to the most crushing misfortune of my life.

"On May 1st the boy arrived, that being the beginning of the summer term. He was a charming youth, and he soon fell into our ways. I may tell you—I trust that I am not indiscreet, but half-confidences are absurd in such a case—that he was not entirely happy at home. It is an open secret that the Duke's married life had not been a peaceful one, and the matter had ended in a separation by mutual consent, the Duchess taking up her residence in the South of France. This had occurred very shortly before, and the boy's sympathies are known to have been strongly with his mother. He moped after her departure from Holdernesse Hall, and it was for this reason that the Duke desired to send him to my establishment. In a fortnight the boy was quite at home with us, and was apparently absolutely happy.

"He was last seen on the night of May 13th—that is, the night of last Monday. His room was on the second floor, and was approached through another larger room in which two boys were sleeping. These boys saw and heard nothing, so that it is certain that young Saltire did not pass out that way. His window was open, and there is a stout ivy plant leading to the ground. We could trace no footmarks below, but it is sure that this is the only possible exit.

"His absence was discovered at seven o'clock on Tuesday morning. His bed had been slept in. He had dressed himself fully before going off in his usual school suit of black Eton jacket and dark grey trousers. There were no signs that anyone had entered the room, and it is quite certain that anything in the nature of cries, or a struggle, would have been heard, since Caunter, the elder boy in the inner room, is a very light sleeper.

"When Lord Saltire's disappearance was discovered I at once called a roll of the whole establishment, boys, masters, and servants. It was then that we ascertained that Lord Saltire had not been alone in his flight. Heidegger, the German master, was missing. His room was on the second floor, at the farther end of the building, facing the same way as Lord Saltire's. His bed had also been slept in; but he had apparently gone away partly dressed, since his shirt and socks were lying on the floor. He had undoubtedly let himself down by the ivy, for we could see the marks of his feet where he had landed on the lawn. His bicycle was kept in a small shed beside this lawn, and it also was gone.

"He had been with me for two years, and came with the best references; but he was a silent, morose man, not very popular either with masters or boys. No trace could be found of the fugitives, and now on Thursday morning we are as ignorant as we were on Tuesday. Inquiry was, of course, made at once at Holdernesse Hall. It is only a few miles away, and we imagined that in some sudden attack of home-sickness he had gone back to his father; but nothing had been heard of him. The Duke is greatly agitated—and as to me, you have seen yourselves the state of nervous prostration to which the suspense and the responsibility have reduced me. Mr. Holmes, if ever you put forward your full powers, I implore you to do so now, for never in your life could you have a case which is more worthy of them."

Sherlock Holmes had listened with the utmost intentness to the statement of the unhappy schoolmaster. His drawn brows and the deep furrow between them showed that he needed no exhortation to concentrate all his attention upon a problem which, apart from the tremendous interests involved, must appeal so directly to his love of the complex and the unusual. He now drew out his note-book and jotted down one or two memoranda.

"You have been very remiss in not coming to me sooner," said he, severely. "You start me on my investigation with a very serious handicap. It is inconceivable, for example, that this ivy and this lawn would have yielded nothing to an expert observer."

"I am not to blame, Mr. Holmes. His Grace was extremely desirous to avoid all public scandal. He was afraid of his family unhappiness being dragged before the world. He has a deep horror of anything of the kind."

"But there has been some official investigation?"

"Yes, sir, and it has proved most disappointing. An apparent clue was at once obtained, since a boy and a young man were reported to have been seen leaving a neighbouring station by an early train. Only last night we had news that the couple had been hunted down in Liverpool, and they prove to have no connection whatever with the matter in hand. Then it was that in my despair and disappointment, after a sleepless night, I came straight to you by the early train."

"I suppose the local investigation was relaxed while this false clue was being followed up?"

"It was entirely dropped."

"So that three days have been wasted. The affair has been most deplorably handled."

"I feel it, and I admit it."

"And yet the problem should be capable of ultimate solution. I shall be very happy to look into it. Have you been able to trace any connection between the missing boy and this German master?"

"None at all."

"Was he in the master's class?"

"No; he never exchanged a word with him so far as I know."

"That is certainly very singular. Had the boy a bicycle?"

"No."

"Was any other bicycle missing?"

"No."

"Is that certain?"

"Quite."

"Well, now, you do not mean to seriously suggest that this German rode off upon a bicycle in the dead of the night bearing the boy in his arms?"

"Certainly not."

"Then what is the theory in your mind?"

"The bicycle may have been a blind. It may have been hidden somewhere and the pair gone off on foot."

"Quite so; but it seems rather an absurd blind, does it not? Were there other bicycles in this shed?"

"Several."

"Would he not have hidden *a couple* had he desired to give the idea that they had gone off upon them?"

"I suppose he would."

"Of course he would. The blind theory won't do. But the incident is an admirable starting-point for an investigation. After all, a bicycle is not an easy thing to conceal or to destroy. One other question. Did anyone call to see the boy on the day before he disappeared?"

"No."

"Did he get any letters?"

"Yes; one letter."

"From whom?"

"From his father."

"Do you open the boys' letters?"

"No."

"How do you know it was from the father?"

"The coat of arms was on the envelope, and it was addressed in the Duke's peculiar stiff hand. Besides, the Duke remembers having written."

"When had he a letter before that?"

"Not for several days."

"Had he ever one from France?"

"No; never."

"You see the point of my questions, of course. Either the boy was carried off by force or he went of his own free will. In the latter case you would expect that some prompting from outside would be needed to make so young a lad do such a thing. If he has had no visitors, that prompting must have come in letters. Hence I try to find out who were his correspondents."

"I fear I cannot help you much. His only correspondent, so far as I know, was his own father."

"Who wrote to him on the very day of his disappearance. Were the relations between father and son very friendly?"

"His Grace is never very friendly with anyone. He is completely immersed in large public questions, and is rather inaccessible to all ordinary emotions. But he was always kind to the boy in his own way."

"But the sympathies of the latter were with the mother?"

"Yes."

"Did he say so?"

"No."

"The Duke, then?"

"Good heavens, no!"

"Then how could you know?"

"I have had some confidential talk with Mr. James Wilder, his Grace's secretary. It was he who gave me the information about Lord Saltire's feelings."

"I see. By the way, that last letter of the Duke's—was it found in the boy's room after he was gone?"

"No; he had taken it with him. I think, Mr. Holmes, it is time that we were leaving for Euston."

"I will order a four-wheeler. In a quarter of an hour we shall be at your service. If you are telegraphing home, Mr. Huxtable, it would be well to allow the people in your neighbourhood to imagine that the inquiry is still going on in Liverpool, or wherever else that red herring led your pack. In the meantime I will do a little quiet work at your own doors, and perhaps the scent is not so cold but that two old hounds like Watson and myself may get a sniff of it."

That evening found us in the cold, bracing atmosphere of the Peak country, in which Dr. Huxtable's famous school is situated. It was already dark when we reached it. A card was lying on the hall table, and the butler whispered something to his master, who turned to us with agitation in every heavy feature.

"The Duke is here," said he. "The Duke and Mr. Wilder are in the study. Come, gentlemen, and I will introduce you."

I was, of course, familiar with the pictures of the famous statesman, but the man himself was very different from his representation. He was a tall and stately person, scrupulously dressed, with a drawn, thin face, and a nose which was grotesquely curved and long. His complexion was of a dead pallor, which was more startling by contrast with a long, dwindling beard of vivid red, which flowed down over his white waistcoat, with his watch-chain gleaming through its fringe. Such was the stately presence who looked stonily at us from the centre of Dr. Huxtable's hearthrug. Beside him stood a very young man, whom I understood to be Wilder, the private secretary. He was small, nervous, alert, with intelligent, light-blue eyes and mobile features. It was he who at once, in an incisive and positive tone, opened the conversation.

"I called this morning, Dr. Huxtable, too late to prevent you from starting for London. I learned that your object was to invite Mr. Sherlock Holmes to undertake the conduct of this case. His Grace is surprised, Dr. Huxtable, that you should have taken such a step without consulting him."

"When I learned that the police had failed—"

"His Grace is by no means convinced that the police have failed."

"But surely, Mr. Wilder—"

"You are well aware, Dr. Huxtable, that his Grace is particularly anxious to avoid all public scandal. He prefers to take as few people as possible into his confidence."

"The matter can be easily remedied," said the brow-beaten doctor; "Mr. Sherlock Holmes can return to London by the morning train."

"Hardly that, doctor, hardly that," said Holmes, in his blandest voice. "This northern air is invigorating and pleasant, so I propose to spend a few days upon your moors, and to occupy my mind as best I may. Whether I have the shelter of your roof or of the village inn is, of course, for you to decide."

I could see that the unfortunate doctor was in the last stage of indecision, from which he was rescued by the deep, sonorous voice of the red-bearded Duke, which boomed out like a dinner-gong.

"I agree with Mr. Wilder, Dr. Huxtable, that you would have done wisely to consult me. But since Mr. Holmes has already been taken into your confidence, it would indeed be absurd that we should not avail ourselves of his services. Far from going to the inn, Mr. Holmes, I should be pleased if you would come and stay with me at Holdernesse Hall."

"I thank your Grace. For the purposes of my investigation I think that it would be wiser for me to remain at the scene of the mystery."

"Just as you like, Mr. Holmes. Any information which Mr. Wilder or I can give you is, of course, at your disposal."

"It will probably be necessary for me to see you at the Hall," said Holmes. "I would only ask you now, sir, whether you have formed any explanation in your own mind as to the mysterious disappearance of your son?"

"No, sir, I have not."

"Excuse me if I allude to that which is painful to you, but I have no alternative. Do you think that the Duchess had anything to do with the matter?"

The great Minister showed perceptible hesitation.

"I do not think so," he said, at last.

"The other most obvious explanation is that the child has been kidnapped for the purpose of levying ransom. You have not had any demand of the sort?"

"No, sir."

"One more question, your Grace. I understand that you wrote to your son upon the day when this incident occurred."

"No; I wrote upon the day before."

"Exactly. But he received it on that day?"

"Yes."

"Was there anything in your letter which might have unbalanced him or induced him to take such a step?"

"No, sir, certainly not."

"Did you post that letter yourself?"

The nobleman's reply was interrupted by his secretary, who broke in with some heat.

"His Grace is not in the habit of posting letters himself," said he. "This letter was laid with others upon the study table, and I myself put them in the post-bag."

"You are sure this one was among them?"

"Yes; I observed it."

"How many letters did your Grace write that day?"

"Twenty or thirty. I have a large correspondence. But surely this is somewhat irrelevant?"

"Not entirely," said Holmes.

"For my own part," the Duke continued, "I have advised the police to turn their attention to the South of France. I have already said that I do not believe that the Duchess would encourage so monstrous an action, but the lad had the most wrong-headed opinions, and it is possible that he may have fled to her, aided and abetted by this German. I think, Dr. Huxtable, that we will now return to the Hall."

I could see that there were other questions which Holmes would have wished to put; but the nobleman's abrupt manner showed that the interview was at an end. It was evident that to his intensely aristocratic nature this discussion of his intimate family affairs with a stranger was most abhorrent, and that he feared lest every fresh question would throw a fiercer light into the discreetly shadowed corners of his ducal history.

When the nobleman and his secretary had left, my friend flung himself at once with characteristic eagerness into the investigation.

The boy's chamber was carefully examined, and yielded nothing save the absolute conviction that it was only through the window that he could have escaped. The German master's room and effects gave no further clue. In his case a trailer of ivy had given under his weight, and we saw by the light of a lantern the mark on the lawn where his heels had come down. That one dint in the short green grass was the only material witness left of this inexplicable nocturnal flight.

Sherlock Holmes left the house alone, and only returned after eleven. He had obtained a large ordnance map of the neighbourhood, and this he brought into my room, where he laid it out on the bed, and, having balanced the lamp in the middle of it, he began to smoke over it, and occasionally to point out objects of interest with the reeking amber of his pipe.

"This case grows upon me, Watson," said he. "There are decidedly some points of interest in connection with it. In this early stage I want you to realize those geographical features which may have a good deal to do with our investigation.

"Look at this map. This dark square is the Priory School. I'll put a pin in it. Now, this line is the main road. You see that it runs east and west past the school, and you see also that there is no side road for a mile either way. If these two folk passed away by road it was *this* road."

"Exactly."

"By a singular and happy chance we are able to some extent to check what passed along this road during the night in question. At this point, where my pipe is now resting, a country constable was on duty from twelve to six. It is, as you perceive, the first cross road on the east side. This man declares that he was not absent from his post for an instant, and he is positive that neither boy nor man could have gone that way unseen. I have spoken with this policeman to-night, and he appears to me to be a perfectly reliable person. That blocks this end. We have now to deal with the other.

There is an inn here, the Red Bull, the landlady of which was ill. She had sent to Mackleton for a doctor, but he did not arrive until morning, being absent at another case. The people at the inn were alert all night, awaiting his coming, and one or other of them seems to have continually had an eye upon the road. They declare that no one passed. If their evidence is good, then we are fortunate enough to be able to block the west, and also to be able to say that the fugitives did *not* use the road at all."

"But the bicycle?" I objected.

"Quite so. We will come to the bicycle presently. To continue our reasoning: if these people did not go by the road, they must have traversed the country to the north of the house or to the south of the house. That is certain. Let us weigh the one against the other. On the south of the house is, as you perceive, a large district of arable land, cut up into small fields, with stone walls between them. There, I admit that a bicycle is impossible. We can dismiss the idea. We turn to the country on the north. Here there lies a grove of trees, marked as the 'Ragged Shaw,' and on the farther side stretches a great rolling moor, Lower Gill Moor, extending for ten miles and sloping gradually upwards. Here, at one side of this wilderness, is Holdernesse Hall, ten miles by road, but only six across the moor. It is a peculiarly desolate plain. A few moor farmers have small holdings, where they rear sheep and cattle. Except these, the plover and the curlew are the only inhabitants until you come to the Chesterfield high road. There is a church there, you see, a few cottages, and an inn. Beyond that the hills become precipitous. Surely it is here to the north that our quest must lie."

"But the bicycle?" I persisted.

"Well, well!" said Holmes, impatiently. "A good cyclist does not need a high road. The moor is intersected with paths and the moon was at the full. Halloa! what is this?"

There was an agitated knock at the door, and an instant afterwards Dr. Huxtable was in the room. In his hand he held a blue cricket-cap, with a white chevron on the peak.

"At last we have a clue!" he cried. "Thank Heaven! at last we are on the dear boy's track! It is his cap."

"Where was it found?"

"In the van of the gipsies who camped on the moor. They left on Tuesday. To-day the police traced them down and examined their caravan. This was found."

"How do they account for it?"

"They shuffled and lied—said that they found it on the moor on Tuesday morning. They know where he is, the rascals! Thank goodness, they are all safe under lock and key. Either the fear of the law or the Duke's purse will certainly get out of them all that they know."

"So far, so good," said Holmes, when the doctor had at last left the room. "It at least bears out the theory that it is on the side of the Lower Gill Moor that we must hope for results. The police have really done nothing locally, save the arrest of these gipsies. Look here, Watson! There is a watercourse across the moor. You see it marked here in the map. In some parts it widens into a morass. This is particularly so in the region between Holdernesse Hall and the school. It is vain to look elsewhere for tracks in this dry weather; but at *that* point there is certainly a chance of some record being left. I will call you early to-morrow morning, and you and I will try if we can throw some little light upon the mystery."

The day was just breaking when I woke to find the long, thin form of Holmes by my bedside. He was fully dressed, and had apparently already been out.

"I have done the lawn and the bicycle shed," said he. "I have also had a ramble through the Ragged Shaw. Now, Watson, there is cocoa ready in the next room. I must beg you to hurry, for we have a great day before us."

His eyes shone, and his cheek was flushed with the exhilaration of the master workman who sees his work lie ready before him. A very different Holmes, this active, alert man, from the introspective and pallid dreamer of Baker Street. I felt, as I looked upon that supple figure, alive with nervous energy, that it was indeed a strenuous day that awaited us.

And yet it opened in the blackest disappointment. With high hopes we struck across the peaty, russet moor, intersected with a thousand sheep paths, until we came to the broad, light-green belt which marked the morass between us and Holdernesse. Certainly, if the lad had gone homewards, he must have passed this, and he could not pass it without leaving his traces. But no sign of him or the German could be seen. With a darkening face my friend strode along the margin, eagerly observant of every muddy stain upon the mossy surface. Sheep-marks there were in profusion, and at one place, some miles down, cows had left their tracks. Nothing more.

"Check number one," said Holmes, looking gloomily over the rolling expanse of the moor. "There is another morass—down yonder and a narrow neck between. Halloa! halloa! halloa! what have we here?"

We had come on a small black ribbon of pathway. In the middle of it, clearly marked on the sodden soil, was the track of a bicycle.

"Hurrah!" I cried. "We have it."

But Holmes was shaking his head, and his face was puzzled and expectant rather than joyous.

"A bicycle certainly, but not *the* bicycle," said he. "I am familiar with forty-two different impressions left by tyres. This, as you perceive, is a Dunlop, with a patch upon the outer cover. Heidegger's tyres were Palmer's, leaving longitudinal stripes. Aveling, the mathematical master, was sure upon the point. Therefore, it is not Heidegger's track."

"The boy's, then?"

"Possibly, if we could prove a bicycle to have been in his possession. But this we have utterly failed to do. This track, as you perceive, was made by a rider who was going from the direction of the school."

"Or towards it?"

"No, no, my dear Watson. The more deeply sunk impression is, of course, the hind wheel, upon which the weight rests. You perceive several places where it has passed across and obliterated the more shallow mark of the front one. it was undoubtedly heading away from the school. It may or may not be connected with our inquiry, but we will follow it backwards before we go any farther."

We did so, and at the end of a few hundred yards lost the tracks as we emerged from the boggy portion of the moor. Following the path backwards, we picked out another spot, where a spring trickled across it. Here, once again, was the mark of the bicycle, though nearly obliterated by the hoofs of cows. After that there was no sign but the path ran right on into Ragged Shaw, the wood which backed on to the school. From this wood the cycle must have emerged. Holmes sat down on a boulder and rested his chin in his hands. I had smoked two cigarettes before he moved.

"Well, well," said he, at last. "It is, of course, possible that a cunning man might change the tyre of his bicycle in order to leave unfamiliar tracks. A criminal who was capable of such a thought is a man whom I should be proud to do business with. We will leave this question undecided and hark back to our morass again, for we have left a good deal unexplored."

We continued our systematic survey of the edge of the sodden portion of the moor, and soon our perseverance was gloriously rewarded. Right across the lower part of the bog lay a miry path. Holmes gave a cry of delight as he approached it. An impression like a fine bundle of telegraph wires ran down the centre of it. It was the Palmer tyre.

"Here is Herr Heidegger, sure enough!" cried Holmes, exultantly. "My reasoning seems to have been pretty sound, Watson."

"I congratulate you."

"But we have a long way still to go. Kindly walk clear of the path. Now let us follow the trail. I fear that it will not lead very far."

We found, however, as we advanced that this portion of the moor is intersected with soft patches, and, though we frequently lost sight of the track, we always succeeded in picking it up once more.

"Do you observe," said Holmes, "that the rider is now undoubtedly forcing the pace? There can be no doubt of it. Look at this impression, where you get both tyres clear. The one is as deep as the other. That can only mean that the rider is throwing his weight on to the handle-bar, as a man does when he is sprinting. By Jove! he has had a fall."

There was a broad, irregular smudge covering some yards of the track. Then there were a few footmarks, and the tyre reappeared once more.

"A side-slip," I suggested.

Holmes held up a crumpled branch of flowering gorse. To my horror I perceived that the yellow blossoms were all dabbled with crimson. On the path, too, and among the heather were dark stains of clotted blood.

"Bad!" said Holmes. "Bad! Stand clear, Watson! Not an unnecessary footstep! What do I read here? He fell wounded, he stood up, he remounted, he proceeded. But there is no other track. Cattle on this side path. He was surely not gored by a bull? Impossible! But I see no traces of anyone else. We must push on, Watson. Surely with stains as well as the track to guide us he cannot escape us now."

Our search was not a very long one. The tracks of the tyre began to curve fantastically upon the wet and shining path. Suddenly, as I looked ahead, the gleam of metal caught my eye from amid the thick gorse bushes. Out of them we dragged a bicycle, Palmer tyred, one pedal bent, and the whole front of it horribly smeared and slobbered with blood. On the other side of the bushes a shoe was projecting. We ran round, and there lay the unfortunate rider. He was a tall man, full bearded, with spectacles, one glass of which had been knocked out. The cause of death was a frightful blow upon the head, which had crushed in part of his skull. That he could have gone on after receiving such an injury said much for the vitality and courage of the man. He wore shoes, but no socks, and his open coat disclosed a night-shirt beneath it. It was undoubtedly the German master.

Holmes turned the body over reverently, and examined it with great attention. He then sat in deep thought for a time, and I could see by his ruffled brow that this grim discovery had not, in his opinion, advanced us much in our inquiry.

"It is a little difficult to know what to do, Watson," said he, at last. "My own inclinations are to push this inquiry on, for we have already lost so much time that we cannot afford to waste another hour. On the other hand, we are bound to inform the police of the discovery, and to see that the poor fellow's body is looked after."

"I could take a note back."

"But I need your company and assistance. Wait a bit! There is a fellow cutting peat up yonder. Bring him over here, and he will guide the police."

I brought the peasant across, and Holmes dispatched the frightened man with a note to Dr. Huxtable.

"Now, Watson," said he, "we have picked up two clues this morning. One is the bicycle with the Palmer tyre, and we see what that has led to. The other is the bicycle with the patched Dunlop. Before we start to investigate that, let us try to realize what we *do* know so as to make the most of it, and to separate the essential from the accidental.

"First of all I wish to impress upon you that the boy certainly left of his own free will. He got down from his window and he went off, either alone or with someone. That is sure."

I assented.

"Well, now, let us turn to this unfortunate German master. The boy was fully dressed when he fled. Therefore, he foresaw what he would do. But the German went without his socks. He certainly acted on very short notice."

"Undoubtedly."

"Why did he go? Because, from his bedroom window, he saw the flight of the boy. Because he wished to overtake him and bring him back. He seized his bicycle, pursued the lad, and in pursuing met his death."

"So it would seem."

"Now I come to the critical part of my argument. The natural action of a man in pursuing a little boy would be to run after him. He would know that he could overtake him. But the German does not do so. He turns to his bicycle. I am told that he was an excellent cyclist. He would not do this if he did not see that the boy had some swift means of escape."

"The other bicycle."

"Let us continue our reconstruction. He meets his death five miles from the

school—not by a bullet, mark you, which even a lad might conceivably discharge, but by a savage blow dealt by a vigorous arm. The lad, then, *had* a companion in his flight. And the flight was a swift one, since it took five miles before an expert cyclist could overtake them. Yet we survey the ground round the scene of the tragedy. What do we find? A few cattle tracks, nothing more. I took a wide sweep round, and there is no path within fifty yards. Another cyclist could have had nothing to do with the actual murder. Nor were there any human foot-marks."

"Holmes," I cried, "this is impossible."

"Admirable!" he said. "A most illuminating remark. It *is* impossible as I state it, and therefore I must in some respect have stated it wrong. Yet you saw for yourself. Can you suggest any fallacy?"

"He could not have fractured his skull in a fall?"

"In a morass, Watson?"

"I am at my wits' end."

"Tut, tut; we have solved some worse problems. At least we have plenty of material, if we can only use it. Come, then, and, having exhausted the Palmer, let us see what the Dunlop with the patched cover has to offer us."

We picked up the track and followed it onwards for some distance; but soon the moor rose into a long, heather-tufted curve, and we left the watercourse behind us. No further help from tracks could be hoped for. At the spot where we saw the last of the Dunlop tyre it might equally have led to Holdernesse Hall, the stately towers of which rose some miles to our left, or to a low, grey village which lay in front of us, and marked the position of the Chesterfield high road.

As we approached the forbidding and squalid inn, with the sign of a game-cock above the door, Holmes gave a sudden groan and clutched me by the shoulder to save himself from falling. He had had one of those violent strains of the ankle which leave a man helpless. With difficulty he limped up to the door, where a squat, dark, elderly man was smoking a black clay pipe.

"How are you, Mr. Reuben Hayes?" said Holmes.

"Who are you, and how do you get my name so pat?" the countryman answered, with a suspicious flash of a pair of cunning eyes.

"Well, it's printed on the board above your head. It's easy to see a man who is master of his own house. I suppose you haven't such a thing as a carriage in your stables?"

"No; I have not."

"I can hardly put my foot to the ground."

"Don't put it to the ground."

"But I can't walk."

"Well, then, hop."

Mr. Reuben Hayes's manner was far from gracious, but Holmes took it with admirable good-humour.

"Look here, my man," said he. "This is really rather an awkward fix for me. I don't mind how I get on."

"Neither do I," said the morose landlord.

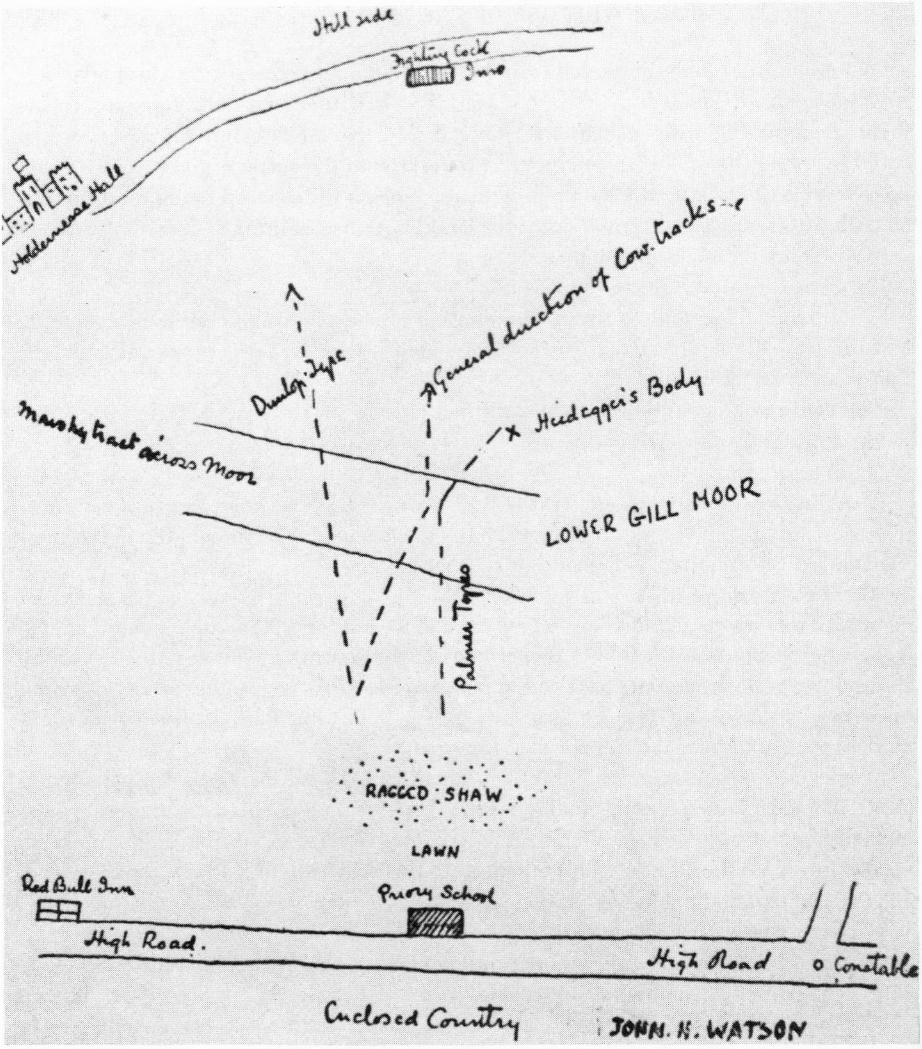

Hill side

Fighting Cock Inn

Holdernesse Hall

↑

Dunlop Type

↗ General direction of Cow. Tracks

Marshy tract across Moor

✗ Heidegger's Body

LOWER GILL MOOR

Palmer Type

RAGGED SHAW

LAWN

Red Bull Inn

Priory School

High Road.

High Road

o Constable

Enclosed Country   JOHN. H. WATSON

"The matter is very important. I would offer you a sovereign for the use of a bicycle."

The landlord pricked up his ears.

"Where do you want to go?"

"To Holdernesse Hall."

"Pals of the Dook, I supporse?" said the landlord, surveying our mud-stained garments with ironical eyes.

Holmes laughed good-naturedly.

"He'll be glad to see us, anyhow."

"Why?"

"Because we bring him news of his lost son."

The landlord gave a very visible start.

"What, your're on his track?"

"He has been heard of in Liverpool. They expect to get him every hour."

Again a swift change passed over the heavy, unshaven face. His manner was suddenly genial.

"I've less reason to wish the Dook well than most men," said he, "for I was his head coachman once, and cruel bad he treated me. It was him that sacked me without a character on the word of a lying corn-chandler. But I'm glad to hear that the young lord was heard of in Liverpool, and I'll help you to take the news to the Hall."

"Thank you," said Holmes. "We'll have some food first. Then you can bring round the bicycle."

"I haven't got a bicycle."

Holmes held up a sovereign.

"I tell you, man, that I haven't got one. I'll let you have two horses as far as the Hall."

"Well, well," said Holmes, "we'll talk about it when we've had something to eat."

When we were left alone in the stone-flagged kitchen it was astonishing how rapidly that sprained ankle recovered. It was nearly nightfall, and we had eaten nothing since early morning, so that we spent some time over our meal. Holmes was lost in thought, and once or twice he walked over to the window and stared earnestly out. It opened on to a squalid courtyard. In the far corner was a smithy, where a grimy lad was at work. On the other side were the stables. Holmes had sat down again after one of these excursions, when he suddenly sprang out of his chair with a loud exclamation.

"By Heaven, Watson, I believe that I've got it!" he cried. "Yes, yes, it must be so. Watson, do you remember seeing any cow-tracks to-day?"

"Yes, several."

"Where?"

"Well, everywhere. They were at the morass, and again on the path, and again near where poor Heidegger met his death."

"Exactly. Well, now, Watson, how many cows did you see on the moor?"

"I don't remember seeing any."

"Strange, Watson, that we should see tracks all along our line, but never a cow on the whole moor; very strange, Watson, eh?"

"Yes, it is strange."

"Now, Watson, make an effort; throw your mind back! Can you see those tracks upon the path?"

"Yes, I can."

"Can you recall that the tracks were sometimes like that, Watson"—he arranged a number of bread-crumbs in this fashion— : : : : : —"and sometimes like this"— : · : · : · : —"and occasionally like this"— . ˙ . ˙ . ˙ . "Can you remember that?"

"No, I cannot."

"But I can. I could swear to it. However, we will go back at our leisure and verify it. What a blind beetle I have been not to draw my conclusion!"

"And what is your conclusion?"

"Only that it is a remarkable cow which walks, canters, and gallops. By George, Watson, it was no brain of a country publican that thought out such a blind as that! The coast seems to be clear, save for that lad in the smithy. Let us slip out and see what we can see."

There were two rough-haired, unkempt horses in the tumbledown stable. Holmes raised the hind leg of one of them and laughed aloud.

"Old shoes, but newly shod—old shoes, but new nails. This case deserves to be a classic. Let us go across to the smithy."

The lad continued his work without regarding us. I saw Holmes's eye darting to right and left among the litter of iron and wood which was scattered about the floor. Suddenly, however, we heard a step behind us, and there was the landlord, his heavy eyebrows drawn down over his savage eyes, his swarthy features convulsed with passion. He held a short, metal-headed stick in his hand, and he advanced in so menacing a fashion that I was right glad to feel the revolver in my pocket.

"You infernal spies!" the man cried. "What are you doing here?"

"Why, Mr. Reuben Hayes," said Holmes, coolly, "one might think that you were afraid of our finding something out."

The man mastered himself with a violent effort, and his grim mouth loosened into a false laugh, which was more menacing than his frown.

"You're welcome to all you can find out in my smithy," said he. "But look here, mister, I don't care for folk poking about my place without my leave, so the sooner you pay your score and get out of this the better I shall be pleased."

"All right, Mr. Hayes—no harm meant," said Holmes. "We have been having a look at your horses, but I think I'll walk after all. It's not far, I believe."

"Not more than two miles to the Hall gates. That's the road to the left." He watched us with sullen eyes until we had left his premises.

We did not go very far along the road, for Holmes stopped the instant that the curve hid us from the landlord's view.

"We were warm, as the children say, at that inn," said he. "I seem to grow colder every step that I take away from it. No, no; I can't possibly leave it."

"I am convinced," said I, "that this Reuben Hayes knows all about it. A more self-evident villain I never saw."

"Oh! he impressed you in that way, did he? There are the horses, there is the smithy. Yes, it is an interesting place, this Fighting Cock. I think we shall have another look at it in an unobtrusive way."

A long, sloping hillside, dotted with gray limestone boulders, stretched behind us. We had turned off the road, and were making our way up the hill, when, looking in the direction of Holdernesse Hall, I saw a cyclist coming swiftly along.

"Get down, Watson!" cried Holmes, with a heavy hand upon my shoulder. We had hardly sunk from view when the man flew past us on the road. Amid a rolling cloud of dust, I caught a glimpse of a pale, agitated face—a face with horror in every lineament, the mouth open, the eyes staring wildly in front. It was like some strange caricature of the dapper James Wilder whom we had seen the night before.

"The Duke's secretary!" cried Holmes. "Come, Watson, let us see what he does."

We scrambled from rock to rock until in a few moments we had made our way to a point from which we could see the front door of the inn. Wilder's bicycle was leaning against the wall beside it. No one was moving about the house, nor could we catch a glimpse of any faces at the windows. Slowly the twilight crept down as the sun sank behind the high towers of Holdernesse Hall. Then in the gloom we saw the two side-lamps of a trap light up in the stable yard of the inn, and shortly afterwards heard the rattle of hoofs, as it wheeled out into the road and tore off at a furious pace in the direction of Chesterfield.

"What do you make of that, Watson?" Holmes whispered.

"It looks like a flight."

"A single man in a dog-cart, so far as I could see. Well, it certainly was not Mr. James Wilder, for there he is at the door."

A red square of light had sprung out of the darkness. In the middle of it was the black figure of the secretary, his head advanced, peering out into the night. It was evident that he was expecting someone. Then at last there were steps in the road, a second figure was visible for an instant against the light, the door shut, and all was black once more. Five minutes later a lamp was lit in a room upon the first floor.

"It seems to be a curious class of custom that is done by the Fighting Cock," said Holmes.

"The bar is on the other side."

"Quite so. These are what one may call the private guests. Now, what in the world is Mr. James Wilder doing in that den at this hour of night, and who is the companion who comes to meet him there? Come, Watson, we must really take a risk and try to investigate this a little more closely."

Together we stole down to the road and crept across to the door of the inn. The bicycle still leaned against the wall. Holmes struck a match and held it to the back wheel, and I heard him chuckle as the light fell upon a patched Dunlop tyre. Up above us was the lighted window.

"I must have a peep through that, Watson. If you bend your back and support yourself upon the wall, I think that I can manage."

An instant later his feet were on my shoulders. But he was hardly up before he was down again.

"Come, my friend," said he, "our day's work has been quite long enough. I think

that we have gathered all that we can. It's a long walk to the school, and the sooner we get started the better."

He hardly opened his lips during that weary trudge across the moor, nor would he enter the school when he reached it, but went on to Mackleton Station, whence he could send some telegrams. Late at night I heard him consoling Dr. Huxtable, prostrated by the tragedy of his master's death, and later still he entered my room as alert and vigorous as he had been when he started in the morning. "All goes well, my friend," said he. "I promise that before tomorrow evening we shall have reached the solution of the mystery."

At eleven o'clock next morning my friend and I were walking up the famous yew avenue of Holdernesse Hall. We were ushered through the magnificent Elizabethan doorway and into his Grace's study. There we found Mr. James Wilder, demure and courtly, but with some trace of that wild terror of the night before still lurking in his furtive eyes and in his twitching features.

"You have come to see his Grace? I am sorry, but the fact is that the Duke is far from well. He has been very much upset by the tragic news. We received a telegram from Dr. Huxtable yesterday afternoon, which told us of your discovery."

"I must see the Duke, Mr. Wilder."

"But he is in his room."

"Then I must go to his room."

"I believe he is in his bed."

"I will see him there."

Holmes's cold and inexorable manner showed the secretary that it was useless to argue with him.

"Very good, Mr. Holmes, I will tell him that you are here."

After an hour's delay, the great nobleman appeared. His face was more cadaverous than ever, his shoulders had rounded, and he seemed to me to be an altogether older man than he had been the morning before. He greeted us with a stately courtesy and seated himself at his desk, his red beard streaming down on the table.

"Well, Mr. Holmes?" said he.

But my friend's eyes were fixed upon the secretary, who stood by his master's chair.

"I think, your Grace, that I could speak more freely in Mr. Wilder's absence."

The man turned a shade paler and cast a malignant glance at Holmes.

"If your Grace wishes—"

"Yes, yes, you had better go. Now, Mr. Holmes, what have you to say?"

My friend waited until the door had closed behind the retreating secretary.

"The fact is, your Grace," said he, "that my colleague, Dr. Watson, and myself had an assurance from Dr. Huxtable that a reward had been offered in this case. I should like to have this confirmed from your own lips."

"Certainly, Mr. Holmes."

"It amounted, if I am correctly informed, to five thousand pounds to anyone who will tell you where your son is?"

"Exactly."

"And another thousand to the man who will name the person or persons who keep him in custody?"

"Exactly."

"Under the latter heading is included, no doubt, not only those who may have taken him away, but also those who conspire to keep him in his present position?"

"Yes, yes," cried the Duke, impatiently. "If you do your work well, Mr. Sherlock Holmes, you will have no reason to complain of niggardly treatment."

My friend rubbed his thin hands together with an appearance of avidity which was a surprise to me, who knew his frugal tastes.

"I fancy that I see your Grace's check-book upon the table," said he. "I should be glad if you would make me out a check for six thousand pounds. It would be as well, perhaps, for you to cross it. The Capital and Counties Bank, Oxford Street branch are my agents."

His Grace sat very stern and upright in his chair and looked stonily at my friend.

"Is this a joke, Mr. Holmes? It is hardly a subject for pleasantry."

"Not at all, your Grace. I was never more earnest in my life."

"What do you mean, then?"

"I mean that I have earned the reward. I know where your son is, and I know some, at least, of those who are holding him."

The Duke's beard had turned more aggressively red than ever against his ghastly white face.

"Where is he?" he gasped.

"He is, or was last night, at the Fighting Cock Inn, about two miles from your park gate."

The Duke fell back in his chair.

"And whom do you accuse?"

Sherlock Holmes's answer was an astounding one. He stepped swiftly forward and touched the Duke upon the shoulder.

"I accuse *you*," said he. "And now, your Grace, I'll trouble you for that check."

Never shall I forget the Duke's appearance as he sprang up and clawed with his hands, like one who is sinking into an abyss. Then, with an extraordinary effort of aristocratic self-command, he sat down and sank his face in his hands. It was some minutes before he spoke.

"How much do you know?" he asked at last, without raising his head.

"I saw you together last night."

"Does anyone else beside your friend know?"

"I have spoken to no one."

The Duke took a pen in his quivering fingers and opened his check-book.

"I shall be as good as my word, Mr. Holmes. I am about to write your check, however unwelcome the information which you have gained may be to me. When the offer was first made, I little thought the turn which events might take. But you and your friend are men of discretion, Mr. Holmes?"

"I hardly understand your Grace."

"I must put it plainly, Mr. Holmes. If only you two know of this incident, there is no reason why it should go any farther. I think twelve thousand pounds is the sum that I owe you, is it not?"

But Holmes smiled and shook his head.

"I fear, your Grace, that matters can hardly be arranged so easily. There is the death of this schoolmaster to be accounted for."

"But James knew nothing of that. You cannot hold him responsible for that. It was the work of this brutal ruffian whom he had the misfortune to employ."

"I must take the view, your Grace, that when a man embarks upon a crime, he is morally guilty of any other crime which may spring from it."

"Morally, Mr. Holmes. No doubt you are right. But surely not in the eyes of the law. A man cannot be condemned for a murder at which he was not present, and which he loathes and abhors as much as you do. The instant that he heard of it he made a complete confession to me, so filled was he with horror and remorse. He lost not an hour in breaking entirely with the murderer. Oh, Mr. Holmes, you must save him— you must save him! I tell you that you must save him!" The Duke had dropped the last attempt at self-command, and was pacing the room with a convulsed face and with his clenched hands raving in the air. At last he mastered himself and sat down once more at his desk. "I appreciate your conduct in coming here before you spoke to anyone else," said he. "At least, we may take counsel how far we can minimize this hideous scandal."

"Exactly," said Holmes. "I think, your Grace, that this can only be done by absolute frankness between us. I am disposed to help your Grace to the best of my ability, but, in order to do so, I must understand to the last detail how the matter stands. I realize that your words applied to Mr. James Wilder, and that he is not the murderer."

"No, the murderer has escaped."

Sherlock Holmes smiled demurely.

"Your Grace can hardly have heard of any small reputation which I possess, or you would not imagine that it is so easy to escape me. Mr. Reuben Hayes was arrested at Chesterfield, on my information, at eleven o'clock last night. I had a telegram from the head of the local police before I left the school this morning."

The Duke leaned back in his chair and stared with amazement at my friend.

"You seem to have powers that are hardly human," said he. "So Reuben Hayes is taken? I am right glad to hear it, if it will not react upon the fate of James."

"Your secretary?"

"No, sir, my son."

It was Holmes's turn to look astonished.

"I confess that this is entirely new to me, your Grace. I must beg you to be more explicit."

"I will conceal nothing from you. I agree with you that complete frankness, however painful it may be to me, is the best policy in this desperate situation to which James's folly and jealousy have reduced us. When I was a very young man, Mr. Holmes, I loved with such a love as comes only once in a lifetime. I offered the lady marriage, but she refused it on the grounds that such a match might mar my career. Had she lived, I would certainly never have married anyone else. She died, and left this one child, whom for her sake I have cherished and cared for. I could not acknowledge the paternity to the world, but I gave him the best of educations, and since he came to manhood I have kept him near my person. He surprised my secret, and has presumed ever since upon the claim which he has upon me, and upon his power of provoking a scandal which would be abhorrent to me. His presence had something to do with the unhappy issue of my marriage. Above all, he hated my young legitimate heir from the first with a persistent hatred. You may well ask me why, under these circumstances, I still kept James under my roof. I answer that it was because I could see his mother's face in his, and that for her dear sake there was no end to my long-suffering. All her pretty ways too—there was not one of them which he could not suggest and bring back to my memory. I *could* not send him away. But I feared so much lest he should do Arthur—that is, Lord Saltire—a mischief, that I dispatched him for safety to Dr. Huxtable's school.

"James came into contact with this fellow Hayes, because the man was a tenant of mine, and James acted as agent. The fellow was a rascal from the beginning, but, in some extraordinary way, James became intimate with him. He had always a taste for low company. When James determined to kidnap Lord Saltire, it was of this man's service that he availed himself. You remember that I wrote to Arthur upon that last day. Well, James opened the letter and inserted a note asking Arthur to meet him in a little wood called the Ragged Shaw, which is near to the school. He used the Duchess's name, and in that way got the boy to come. That evening James bicycled over—I am telling you what he has himself confessed to me—and he told Arthur, whom he met in the wood, that his mother longed to see him, that she was awaiting him on the moor, and that if he would come back into the wood at midnight he would find a man with a horse, who would take him to her. Poor Arthur fell into the trap. He came to the appointment, and found this fellow Hayes with a led pony. Arthur mounted, and they set off together. It appears—though this James only heard yesterday—that they were pursued, that Hayes struck the pursuer with his stick, and that the man died of his injuries. Hayes brought Arthur to his public-house, the Fighting Cock, where he was confined in an upper room, under the care of Mrs. Hayes, who is a kindly woman, but entirely under the control of her brutal husband.

"Well, Mr. Holmes, that was the state of affairs when I first saw you two days ago. I had no more idea of the truth than you. You will ask me what was James's motive in doing such a deed. I answer that there was a great deal which was unreasoning and fanatical in the hatred which he bore my heir. In his view he should himself have been heir of all my estates, and he deeply resented those social laws which made it impossible. At the same time, he had a definite motive also. He was eager that I should break the entail, and he was of opinion that it lay in my power to do so. He intended to make a bargain with me—to restore Arthur if I would break the entail, and so make it possible for the estate to be left to him by will. He knew well that I should never willingly invoke the aid of the police against him. I say that he would have proposed such a bargain to me; but he did not actually do so, for events moved too quickly for him, and he had not time to put his plans into practice.

"What brought all his wicked scheme to wreck was your discovery of this man Heidegger's dead body. James was seized with horror at the news. It came to us yesterday, as we sat together in this study. Dr. Huxtable had sent a telegram. James was so overwhelmed with grief and agitation that my suspicions, which had never been entirely absent, rose instantly to a certainty, and I taxed him with the deed. He made a complete voluntary confession. Then he implored me to keep his secret for three days longer, so as to give his wretched accomplice a chance of saving his guilty life. I yielded—as I have always yielded—to his prayers, and instantly James hurried off to the Fighting Cock to warn Hayes and give him the means of flight. I could not go there by daylight without provoking comment, but as soon as night fell I hurried off to see my dear Arthur. I found him safe and well, but horrified beyond expression by the dreadful deed he had witnessed. In deference to my promise, and much against my will, I consented to leave him there for three days, under the charge of Mrs. Hayes, since it was evident that it was impossible to inform the police where he was without telling them also who was the murderer, and I could not see how that murderer could be punished without ruin to my unfortunate James. You asked for frankness, Mr. Holmes, and I have taken you at your word, for I have now told you everything without an attempt at circumlocution or concealment. Do you in turn be as frank with me."

"I will," said Holmes. "In the first place, your Grace, I am bound to tell you that you have placed yourself in a most serious position in the eyes of the law. You have condoned a felony, and you have aided the escape of a murderer, for I cannot doubt that any money which was taken by James Wilder to aid his accomplice in his flight came from your Grace's purse."

The Duke bowed his assent.

"This is, indeed, a most serious matter. Even more culpable in my opinion, your Grace, is your attitude towards your younger son. You leave him in this den for three days."

"Under solemn promises—"

"What are promises to such people as these? You have no guarantee that he will not be spirited away again. To humour your guilty elder son, you have exposed your innocent younger son to imminent and unnecessary danger. It was a most unjustifiable action."

The proud lord of Holdernesse was not accustomed to be so rated in his own ducal hall. The blood flushed into his high forehead, but his conscience held him dumb.

"I will help you, but on one condition only. It is that you ring for the footman and let me give such orders as I like."

Without a word, the Duke pressed the electric bell. A servant entered.

"You will be glad to hear," said Holmes, "that your young master is found. It is the Duke's desire that the carriage shall go at once to the Fighting Cock Inn to bring Lord Saltire home.

"Now," said Holmes, when the rejoicing lackey had disappeared, "having secured the future, we can afford to be more lenient with the past. I am not in an official position, and there is no reason, so long as the ends of justice are served, why I should disclose all that I know. As to Hayes, I say nothing. The gallows awaits him, and I would do nothing to save him from it. What he will divulge I cannot tell, but I have no doubt that your Grace could make him understand that it is to his interest to be silent. From the police point of view he will have kidnapped the boy for the purpose of ransom. If they do not themselves find it out, I see no reason why I should prompt them to take a broader point of view. I would warn your Grace, however, that the continued presence of Mr. James Wilder in your household can only lead to misfortune."

"I understand that, Mr. Holmes, and it is already settled that he shall leave me forever, and go to seek his fortune in Australia."

"In that case, your Grace, since you have yourself stated that any unhappiness in your married life was caused by his presence, I would suggest that you make such amends as you can to the Duchess, and that you try to resume those relations which have been so unhappily interrupted."

"That also I have arranged, Mr. Holmes. I wrote to the Duchess this morning."

"In that case," said Holmes, rising. "I think that my friend and I can congratulate ourselves upon several most happy results from our little visit to the North. There is one other small point upon which I desire some light. This fellow Hayes had shod his horses with shoes which counterfeited the tracks of cows. Was it from Mr. Wilder that he learned so extraordinary a device?"

The Duke stood in thought for a moment, with a look of intense surprise on his face. Then he opened a door and showed us into a large room furnished as a museum. He led the way to a glass case in a corner, and pointed to the inscription.

"These shoes," it ran, "were dug up in the moat of Holdernesse Hall. They are for the use of horses, but they are shaped below with a cloven foot of iron, so as to throw pursuers off the track. They are supposed to have belonged to some of the marauding Barons of Holdernesse in the Middle Ages."

Holmes opened the case, and moistening his finger he passed it along the shoe. A thin film of recent mud was left upon his skin.

"Thank you," said he, as he replaced the glass. "It is the second most interesting object that I have seen in the North."

"And the first?"

Holmes folded up his check and placed it carefully in his notebook. "I am a poor man," said he, as he patted it affectionately, and thrust it into the depths of his inner pocket.

Afterword

In 1911, Msgr. Ronald Knox delivered a delightful spoof on the internal inconsistencies in the various adventures of Sherlock Holmes and, since then, that stone has gathered no moss. "The Adventure of the Priory School" has had its share of scholarly and not-so-scholarly analysis over the years. Most of this line searching has involved James Wilder's bicycle, with the Dunlop tire "with a patch upon the outer cover."

The three main inquiries which have thus far been probed are:

1. How could Holmes have known the tire marks were made by a Dunlop tire?

2. Since James Wilder could only have bicycled to the Ragged Shaw from Holdernesse across the moor, why was there only one track of the bicycle with the Dunlop tires, and that one going away from the School?

3. How could Holmes have so confidently ascertained the direction the bicycle was traveling from an observation of its tracks alone?

Holmes might well have been "familiar with forty-two different impressions left by tyres," as he was acquainted with the many varieties of cigar ashes, but we are not told exactly how he deduced that James Wilder's bicycle was equipped with Dunlop tires. Palmer tires, like those on poor Herr Heidegger's bicycle, were easily distinguished by their longitudinal stripes—stripes giving the appearance of "a fine bundle of telegraph wires." Dunlop tires, although first developed in 1887, were not so plainly marked until in 1901 the name Dunlop was embossed on the tread. Since the events of the Priory School occurred in May 1901, Holmes might have read the name Dunlop imprinted in the turf of the moor. But that is doubtful since, as detective fiction, it would be so utterly unimaginative.

Apparently Professor Jay Finley Christ[7] was the first person to question the lack of two sets of tracks on the moor. It may be answered that the other tracks might have taken a somewhat different route across the moor or that the direction of travel from Holdernesse Hall was sufficiently distinct from that to the Fighting Cock Inn that the tracks would not, in any event, be a source of confusion.

Finally, and most voluminously, have the commentators belabored Holmes's instant and unexplained judgment as to the direction the bicycle had taken simply from the evidence of the tracks. A Boston lawyer, Stuart C. Rand,[8] seems to be one of the first to address this dilemma. Most Holmes scholars have proposed canny solutions for this conundrum.

Some have theorized that the front and rear wheels were unlikely to have run through the same track.[9] Particularly across the uneven terrain of the moor, the tires were likely to have followed a zigzag course with the tire marks crisscrossing each other. If so, then the fact that the front wheel moves from side to side more freely than the rear would enable Holmes to have plotted the direction the bicycle was traveling by gauging the points of intersection and the amount of side-play in between them.

Another favored explanation has it that the typography of the moor country was so rolling that the depth of the impressions would be a telltale sign of the bicycle's direction. The hypothesis is that going uphill the tracks would be deeper than on the downhill runs.[10] Doyle himself gave this rationale for Holmes's observation in his autobiography Memories and Adventures:

I had so many remonstrances upon this point, varying from pity to anger, that I took out my bicycle and tried. I had imagined that the observations of the way in which the track of the hind wheel overlaid the track of the front one when the machine was not running dead straight would show the direction. I found that my correspondents were right and I was wrong, for this would be the same whichever way the cycle was moving. On the other hand the real solution was much simpler, for on an undulating moor the wheels make a much deeper impression uphill and a more shallow one downhill, so Holmes was justified of his wisdom after all.[11]

Lord Donegall, in a spirit of glib mockery, has written that

Hoping to shed new light on this controversy, I cabled to Senor Irrazaga, the Patagonian artist, whose wall-papers are the sensation of the Middle West. Senor Irrazaga creates his designs by riding bicycles fitted with porous tyres pumped up with different coloured paints.

"My paintings reveal nothing," was the artist's courteously cabled reply. While adding little to the bicycle argument, this does confirm what many less modern minded art lovers long have suspected.[12]

The explanation to end all explanations was that of the commentator who noted the "uncommonly rough" terrain on the moor which would have necessitated the bicyclist's occasionally putting his foot down into the turf to rest. The shoe print would be an arrow pointing the direction in which the bicycle was headed.[13] That supposition has the merit of putting a brake on this controversy.

2

P. D. James

For Want of a Bicycle . . .

From *Death of an Expert Witness*

Every mystery story has at least one sine qua non, without which the solution would be delayed interminably or even mucked up altogether. The better tales weave the strands of one causal element with others to keep the reader captivated and unsuspecting in the face of a plot in which "the force" is encountered here, there, and everywhere.

In 1868, Wilkie Collins masterfully executed this plan of causative action in The Moonstone, *which T. S. Eliot has feted as "the first and greatest of English detective novels." The plot focuses on the loss or theft of the fabled diamond the moonstone, which had been stolen many years before from its native Indian owners. Sergeant Cuff of the Detective Force is summoned to investigate the diamond's disappearance and notices a smudge on the newly painted door to Rachel Verinder's sitting room, from which the diamond has vanished. This lead expands the investigative possibilities and accelerates the action of the complex plot.*

But for the painting of the door just prior to the moonstone's loss and someone's brushing against it while it was still wet, Sergeant Cuff would have cut a less convincing figure as a detective and the plot would have lacked an intriguing link in the chain of circumstances which inexorably point to Godfrey Albewhite's larceny as the base deed.

Modern mystery story writers have similarly been attracted to deceptively innocuous odds and ends which give the plot momentum and add zest to the investigation. In Murder at the Savoy, *for example, Swedish police detective Martin Beck tracks the killer of an industrialist who has been gunned down while dining at a fashionable restaurant. The killing has all the indicia of a senseless murder by a deranged person until a Danish boy on vacation discovers an empty Arminius .22 gun carton while walking*

From *Death of an Expert Witness* (New York: Charles Scribner's Sons, 1977), pp. 262–68.

along the beach on the Danish coast at Dragør. Equally fortuitously, Martin Beck notices the entry of this empty box on a routine list of items turned in to the Danish police which they had supplied as a matter of course to the Swedish police. But for these circumstances the murder would have been more difficult to solve and the tale less pleasurable to read.

P. D. *James, acclaimed as "Agatha Christie's Crown Princess," has effectively utilized this same cause-and-effect device in her immensely engrossing mystery stories. In* Black Tower, *one of her most thrilling and taut yarns, her detective, Adam Dalgleish, is held captive by the murderer and is about to become one of his victims. Dalgleish, with utmost sangfroid while looking down the barrel of imminent death, recalls that Mrs. Reynolds, the widow of a police constable, will shortly bicycle along the very same road from which he is now being ordered into the trunk of the murderer's car. Slyly and unobserved, Dalgleish manages to drop his wallet onto the road where he anticipates Mrs. Reynolds will find it. His gambit succeeds when Mrs. Reynolds stops her bicycle, spies the wallet, and alerts the police, and they intercept the murderer at the Black Tower before Commander Dalgleish is killed.*

For want of a bicycling charwoman, the detective would have been lost.

Whereas the bicycle was Adam Dalgleish's saving grace in Black Tower, *it or rather the lack of it portends disaster for Brenda Pridmore in P. D. James's latest thriller,* Death of an Expert Witness.

Dr. *Lorrimer, senior biologist at Hoggatt's Forensic Science Laboratory, must be counted among the least loved of humans. Most of the white-collar staff at the laboratory, save possibly Brenda Pridmore, have formidable grounds for wishing him dead, if not also for doing the deed. Even quiet, kindly and efficient Inspector Blakelock has a motive for murder if Dr. Lorrimer is the expert witness whose blundering resulted in the acquittal of the motorist who had killed the Inspector's beloved sixteen-year-old daughter many years before.*

The issue for Adam Dalgleish, upon his arrival in the fen country of East Anglia to investigate the death by bludgeoning of Dr. Lorrimer, was the usual one, i.e., whose motive was sufficiently intense to have precipitated the murder?

Maxim Howarth, newly appointed director of the laboratory, sees Dr. Lorrimer as corrupting his stepsister and interfering with his incestuous fantasies for her. Stella Mawson, the novelist friend and roommate of Angela Foley, the lab director's private secretary, had been Dr. Lorrimer's partner in an unconsummated and annulled marriage. Paul Middlemass, document examiner at the laboratory, had bloodied Dr. Lorrimer's nose on the very day of his murder.

The list of likely suspects can be extended but it is clear that Brenda Pridmore is above suspicion as she is above approach. It was she who found Dr. Lorrimer's battered body in the lab and it is she who is the focus of the following excerpt, which recounts events occurring during the investigation of Dr. Lorrimer's murder while the lab routine is seeking to return to its own level—that of normality.

The incident related in this chapter has all the minatory impact appearing in To Kill a Mockingbird *when eight-year-old Scout Finch and her thirteen-year-old brother Jem leave the Halloween party at their school, still dressed in their costumes, and take a*

shortcut home through darkened, more than spook-lined, byways. The outcome in both
tales is spellbinding and wholly unexpected.

By seven o'clock the work was at last up to date, the last court report had been
checked, the last completed exhibit packed for the police to collect, the figures of
cases and exhibits received had been calculated and checked. Brenda thought how
tired Inspector Blakelock seemed. He had hardly spoken an unnecessary word during
the last hour. She didn't feel that he was displeased with her, merely that he hardly
knew she was there. She had talked little herself, and then in whispers, afraid to
break the silence, eerie and almost palpable, of the empty hall. To her right the great
staircase curved upward into darkness. All day it had echoed to the feet of scientists,
policemen, scene of crime officers arriving for their lecture. Now it had become as
portentous and threatening as the staircase of a haunted house. She tried not to look at
it, but it drew her eyes irresistibly. With every fleeting upward glance she half
imagined that she could see Lorrimer's white face forming out of the amorphous
shadows to hang imprinted on the still air. Lorrimer's black eyes gazing down at her in
entreaty or despair.

At seven o'clock Inspector Blakelock said:

"Well, that's about all then. Your mum won't be best pleased that you've been kept
late tonight."

Brenda said with more confidence than she felt:

"Oh, Mum won't mind. She knew I was late starting. I rang her earlier and said not
to expect me until half past."

They went their separate ways to collect their coats. Then Brenda waited by the
door until Inspector Blakelock had set and checked the internal alarm. All the doors
of the separate laboratories had been closed and checked earlier in the evening.
Lastly they went out by the front door and he turned the two final keys. Brenda's
bicycle was kept in a shed by the side of the old stables, where the cars were garaged.
Still together, they went around to the back. Inspector Blakelock waited to start his
car until she had mounted, then followed her very slowly down the drive. At the gate
he gave a valedictory hoot and turned to the left. Brenda waved and set off briskly,
pedaling in the opposite direction. She thought she knew why the Inspector had
waited so carefully until she was safely off the premises, and she felt grateful.
Perhaps, she thought, I remind him of his dead daughter and that's why he's so kind to
me.

And then, almost immediately, it happened. The sudden bump and the scrape of
metal against tarmac were unmistakable. The bicycle lurched, almost throwing her
into the ditch. Squeezing on both brakes she dismounted and examined the tires by
the light of the heavy flashlight which she always kept in her bicycle saddlebag. Both
were flat. Her immediate reaction was one of intense irritation. This would happen on
a late night! She swept the flashlight beam over the road behind her, trying to identify
the source of the mishap. There must be glass or something sharp on the road
somewhere. But she could see nothing and realized that it wouldn't help if she did.
There was no hope of repairing the punctures. The next bus home was the one due to

pass the laboratory just after nine o'clock, and there was no one left at the lab to give her a lift. She spent very little time in thinking. The best plan was obviously to return the bicycle to its rack and then make her way home through the new laboratory. It would cut off nearly a couple of miles and, if she walked fast, she could be home just after seven-thirty.

Anger, and ineffective railing against bad luck, is a powerful antidote to fear. So is hunger and the healthy tiredness that longs for its own fireside. Brenda had jerked the bicycle, now reduced to a ridiculously antiquated encumbrance, back into its stand and had walked briskly through the grounds of Hoggatt's and unbolted the wooden gate that led to the new site before she began to feel afraid. But now, alone in the darkness, the half-superstitious dread, which it had seemed safe to stimulate in the laboratory with Inspector Blakelock so reassuringly by her side, began to prick at her nerves. Before her the black bulk of the half-completed laboratory loomed like some prehistoric monument, its great slabs bloodstained with ancient sacrifices, rearing upward toward the implacable gods. The night was fitfully dark with a low ceiling of cloud obscuring the faint stars.

As she hesitated, the clouds parted like ponderous hands to unveil the full moon, frail and transparent as a Communion wafer. Gazing at it she could almost taste the remembered transitory dough, melting against the roof of her mouth. Then the clouds formed again and the darkness closed about her. And the wind was rising.

She held the flashlight more firmly. It was solidly reassuring and heavy in her hand. Resolutely she picked out her way between the tarpaulin-shrouded piles of bricks, the great girders laid in rows, the two neat huts on stilts which served as the contractor's office, toward the gap in the brickwork that marked the entrance to the main site. Then once again she hesitated. The gap seemed to narrow before her eyes, to become almost symbolically ominous and frightening, an entrance to darkness and the unknown. The fears of a childhood not so far distant reasserted themselves. She was tempted to turn back.

Then she admonished herself sternly not to be stupid. There was nothing strange or sinister about a half-completed building, an artifact of brick, concrete, and steel, holding no memories of the past, concealing no secret miseries between ancient walls. Besides, she knew the site quite well. The laboratory staff weren't supposed to take a shortcut through the new buildings—Dr. Howarth had pinned up a notice on the staff notice board pointing out the dangers—but everyone knew that it was done. Before the building had been started there had been a footpath across Hoggatt's field. It was natural for people to behave as if it were still there. And she was tired and hungry. It was ridiculous to hesitate now.

Then she remembered her parents. No one at home could know about the punctures and her mother would soon begin worrying. She or her father would ring the laboratory and, getting no reply, would know that everyone had left. They would imagine her dead or injured on the road, being lifted unconscious into an ambulance. Worse, they would see her lying crumpled on the floor of the laboratory, a second victim. It had been difficult enough to persuade her parents to let her stay on in the job, and this final anxiety, growing with every minute she was overdue and culminating in the relief and reactive anger of her late appearance, might easily tip them into an unreasoned but obstinate insistence that she should leave. It really was the worst possible time to be late home. She shone her flashlight steadily on the entrance gap and moved resolutely into the darkness.

She tried to picture the model of the new laboratory set up in the library. This large vestibule, still unroofed, must be the reception area from which the two main wings diverged. She must bear to the left through what would be the Biology Department for the quickest cut to the Guy's Marsh road. She swept the beam over the brick walls, then picked her way carefully across the uneven ground toward the left-hand aperture. The pool of light found another doorway, and then another. The darkness seemed to increase, heavy with the smell of brick dust and pressed earth. And now the pale haze of the night sky was extinguished and she was in the roofed area of the laboratory. The silence was absolute.

She found herself creeping forward, breath held, eyes fixed in a stare on the small pool of light at her feet. And suddenly there was nothing, no sky above, no doorway, nothing but black darkness. She swept the light over the walls. They were menacingly close. This room was surely far too small even for an office. She seemed to have stumbled into some kind of cupboard or storeroom. Somewhere, she knew, there must be a gap, the one by which she had entered. But, disorientated in the claustrophobic darkness, she could no longer distinguish the ceiling from the walls. With every sweep of the torch the crude bricks seemed to be closing in on her, the ceiling to descend inexorably like the slowly closing lid of a tomb. Fighting for control, she inched gradually along one wall, telling herself that, soon, she must strike the open doorway.

Suddenly the flashlight jerked in her hand and the pool of light spilled over the floor. She stopped dead, appalled at her peril. In the middle of the room was a square protected only by two planks thrown across it. One step in panic and she might have kicked them away, stumbled, and dropped into inky nothingness. In her imagination the well was fathomless; her body would never be found. She would lie there in the mud and darkness, too weak to make herself heard. And all she would hear would be the distant voices of the workmen as, brick on brick, they walled her up alive in her black tomb. And then another and more rational horror struck.

She thought about the punctured tires. Could that really have been an accident? The tires had been sound when she had parked the bicycle that morning. Perhaps it hadn't been glass on the road after all. Perhaps someone had done it purposely, someone who knew that she wquld be late leaving the lab, that there would be no one left to give her a lift, that she would be bound to walk through the new building. She pictured him in the darkness of the early evening, slipping soundlessly into the bicycle shed, knife in hand, crouching down to the tires, listening for the hiss of escaping air, calculating how big a rent would cause the tires to collapse before she had cycled too far on her journey. And now he was waiting for her, knife in hand, somewhere in the darkness. He had smiled, fingering the blade, listening for her every step, watching for the beam of her flashlight. He, too, would have a flashlight, of course. Soon it would blaze into her face, blinding her eyes, so that she couldn't see the cruel, triumphant mouth, the flashing knife. Instinctively she switched off the light and listened, her heart pounding with such a thunder of blood that she felt that even the brick walls must shake.

And then she heard the noise, gentle as a single football, soft as the brush of a coat sleeve against wood. He was coming. He was here. And now there was only panic. Sobbing, she threw herself from side to side against the walls, thudding her bruised palms against the gritty, unyielding brick. Suddenly there was a space. She fell through, tripped, and the flashlight spun out of her hand. Moaning, she lay and waited for death. Then terror swooped with a wild screech of exultation and a thrashing of wings which lifted the hair from her scalp. She screamed, a thin wail of sound that was lost in the bird's cry as the owl found the paneless window and soared into the night.

She didn't know how long she lay there, her sore hands clutching the earth, her mouth choked with dust. But after a while she controlled her sobbing and lifted her head. She saw the window plainly, an immense square of luminous light, pricked with stars. And to the right of it gleamed the doorway. She scrambled to her feet. She didn't wait to search for the flashlight but made straight for that blessed aperture of light. Beyond it was another. And, suddenly, there were no more walls, only the spangled dome of the sky swinging above her.

Still sobbing, but now with relief, she ran unthinkingly in the moonlight, her hair streaming behind her, her feet hardly seeming to touch the earth. And now there was a belt of trees before her and, gleaming through the autumn branches, the Wren chapel, lit from within, beckoning and holy, shining like a picture on a Christmas card. She ran toward it, palms outstretched, as hundreds of her forebears in the dark fens must have rushed to their altars for sanctuary. The door was ajar and a shaft of light lay like an arrow on the path. She threw herself against the oak, and the great door swung inward into a glory of light.

At first her mind, shocked into stupor, refused to recognize what her dazzled eyes so clearly saw. Uncomprehending, she put up a tentative hand and stroked the soft corduroy of the slacks, the limp, moist hand. Slowly, as if by an act of will her eyes traveled upward and she both saw and understood. Stella Mawson's face, dreadful in death, drooped above her, the eyes half open, the palms disposed outward as if in a mute appeal for pity or for help. Circling her neck was a double cord of blue silk, its tasseled end tied high to a hook on the wall. Beside it, wound on a second hook, was the single bell rope. There was a low wooden chair upended close to the dangling feet. Brenda seized it. Moaning, she grasped at the rope and swung on it three times before it slipped from her loosening hands, and she fainted.

Adam Dalgleish now has two murders to solve, but, paradoxically, the killing of Stella Mawson makes more conclusive the guilt of Dalgleish's prime suspect. The plot's denouement must await the reader's consulting the book in full. What Charles Dickens did accidentally in The Mystery of Edwin Drood, *I do intentionally here—leave the solution of the mystery to the reader's own devices.*

3

Edward Marjoribanks

The Green Bicycle Mystery

From *For the Defense*

In 1920, as his long, illustrious, and often tumultuous career as a barrister neared its close, Sir Edward Marshall Hall undertook the defense of Ronald Vivian Light for the shooting death of Bella Wright. The case was uniquely appropriate for Hall to defend, since it appeared to have elements of the occult that fitted his fervor for spiritualism and the anticipated scientific evidence of firearms identification suited his knowledge of that branch of forensic science.

Edward Marshall Hall was born in 1858 and, after a career as "one of the most prominent advocates of his day," died in 1927. Throughout his illustrious days at the bar, Hall was a forensic orator of flamboyance, impulse and distinction. He was at once both "sensitive and vain." He could quote Shakespeare in his arguments to the jury and act out his peroration with such frenzy that it would leave him bathed in sweat. His advocacy was that of the old school of lawyers in the great tradition of Clarence Darrow and Earl Rogers, men who were showmen as much as lawyers, and whose showmanship, it seemed, knew no bounds.

Although Hall was actively engaged in the conduct of civil trials, his appearances in the criminal courts seemed destined to mark those trials as celebrated ones. He defended the much-pilloried Dr. Crippin for poisoning his wife. The poisoner Seddon, as cruel and calculating a scoundrel as ever there was, was fortunate to have the services of Marshall Hall but, withal, he was convicted and executed. Hall's defense

Adapted by the editor from Edward Marjoribanks, *For the Defense: The Life of Sir Edward Marshall Hall* (New York: The Macmillan Company, 1929), pp. 384–97.

of George Joseph Smith, killer of three wives, in 1915 was equally unsuccessful although it was ardent and, at times, inspired. In 1917, his prominence at the bar was recognized by knighthood.

According to his biographer, Marshall Hall regarded the "Green Bicycle" case as "one of his two greatest triumphs in the Criminal Courts." It justified his place as an Olympian among lawyers.

Ronald Vivian Light, ex-officer of the Honourable Artillery Company and shell-shock victim of the trench warfare of World War I, had not made the charge of murder preferred against him any easier to refute. Upon his arrest for the murder of Bella Wright, he had denied his ownership of the green bicycle upon which the murderer had been seen riding. Later he had changed his story, admitting ownership but asserting that he had sold the bicycle well before the crime had been committed. When informed that a bicycle-shop owner had identified him as the man who had retrieved his bicycle, earlier left for repairs on the same day on which the murder had occurred, Light's reply did nothing to bolster his cause. He said: "My word, that man had me spotted." Not only did he have Light spotted, but the tradesman had related that Light had said, upon reclaiming his bicycle, "that he was going for a run in the country." It was in the nearby country that Bella Wright was found dead.

If all of this were not incriminating enough, Light had denied any connection with a revolver holster and the cartridges in it which had been discovered along with his green bicycle. Both bicycle and holster could easily and conclusively be established to have been either in his possession or owned by him on the day of the death. His case was bleak, indeed. A jury's finding of guilty of murder appeared to be a foregone conclusion.

Light's predicament might never have come to pass if Bella Wright, a young working girl, had not gone bicycling on Saturday, July 5, 1919. But she did, and she met Light, who was the last person who it could be said had been in her company prior to the time her body was found lying on a country road near Little Stretton in Leicestershire, her bicycle beside her.

Bella Wright's body did not evidence any signs of sexual molestation, nor were there any indications of a struggle. Her face was bloodied, and a pool of blood was found near her head. Natural causes were at first thought to have precipitated Bella's unfortunate death. But that early medical opinion was soon revised for, upon wiping the blood from her face, two holes were observed, one in the left cheek and the other, somewhat higher up, on the right side of her head. A spent bullet was also discovered in the road some seventeen feet from the girl's body. These were the signs of either murder or an accidental death. Suicide could hardly be considered a realistic possibility.

More ominous and inexplicable—save, it was thought, on supernatural terms—was the body of a dead raven lying in a field adjacent to the country lane where Bella was found. Some would afterwards say that the raven gave the appearance of having died in an orgy of blood-gorging after Bella's death. As if to cement this ghoulish view, the bloody imprint of the feet of a large bird was found on a gatepost near the scene.

The police investigators had few leads to assist in tracking the murderer, if murder it was. No gun was found at the scene, nor, for that matter, was one ever recovered. Two little girls, impressionable like all children, had remembered that a man on a green bicycle had attempted to converse with them some time before the killing at a point very near where the body of Bella Wright had later been found. The girls had felt threatened by this bicyclist's general attitude, even though he had made no menacing moves against them. the description of this stranger which these girls provided the police was widely disseminated but no new leads were developed until February 1920.

In that month, wholly by chance, the tow rope of a barge traveling near Leicester pulled the frame of a green bicycle out of the canal through which it was passing. Its long immersion in the water had effaced all signs of the manufacturer's identity, but a secret mark remained which enabled the police to trace the bicycle to Ronald Vivian Light, who had purchased it in 1910. A dredging of the canal produced a holster for a revolver that contained both live and blank ammunition. The revolver, however, was not recovered.

Ronald Light's situation was a bleak one, circumstantial though the evidence was, when Marshall Hall was called to defend him. The lines of available defense strategies were confounded by Light's pretrial statements to the police. Not only was there a defense theory to be unearthed and elaborated, but the issue of whether Light should take the witness box in his own behalf had to be resolved. It is well recognized among the defense bar that a prisoner stands to lose by remaining silent at trial. The jury expects a proclamation of innocence from the accused. They wish to be able to evaluate the prisoner's credibility for themselves on a face-to-face appraisal.

But how could Light testify to his advantage if he were to reaffirm his palpably false pretrial statements? To do so would trench on perjury. The lawyer's dilemma when confronted by a client whom the lawyer reasonably believes to be about to perjure himself is one over which much ink and some phlegm has been spilled in recent years. For Marshall Hall, these reflections posed a tactical predicament, for he was ethically determined to avoid perjury at all costs.

On the other hand, Hall felt no ethical compunction about preparing a vigorous defense to the prosecution's anticipated evidence. Toward that end, Hall sought the advice of a gunsmith and performed his own experiments to test the prosecution's theory that Light had shot Bella Wright at close range with a revolver. These experiments convinced Hall that the distance of the cartridge found in the road from the victim's body, the location of the entry and exit wounds in Bella's head, the predetermined velocity of the bullet, and its likely trajectory pointed to some other explanation for Bella's death than the sinister one attributed to Light.

In spite of this scientific evidence, Hall realized that Light's case was a desperate one. He had lied to the police, he had been seen in the vicinity at or about the time of the death, and he had disposed of the bicycle and the revolver holster in the canal for only one reason—to conceal his implication in the event. Even Lignt was morose, for during his pretrial confinement in Leicester Castle he was heard to remark as he looked from his room across the fertile countryside, "Damn and blast that canal."

In his opening statement for the prosecution, the Attorney General, with utmost reserve, detailed his view of the facts. He would prove, he said, that Ronald Light had met Bella, bicycled with her, and later murdered her with a revolver that the cartridges seized from the road and the canal would fit. Even the motive for this base deed was not troublesome to the prosecution. "Suppose that the prisoner had made certain overtures to her and been rebuffed, or suppose that in anger, or, it might be, desire of concealing that which had been attempted, it is not difficult to conceive the motive"—so the prosecutor speculated.

The prosecution's evidence proceeded smoothly enough until the two young girls who had seen Light testified to their identification of him. At that point Hall, for the first time, introduced the fact that he would not dispute either his client's ownership or the identity of the green bicycle and the holster. With that surprise announcement the prosecution was on reasonable notice that Light would testify in his own defense. In that event, Light's character, reputation, and credibility would be crucial.

It took no master advocate of Hall's abilities to scuttle the testimony of the two girls. Not only where they impressionable, but the police, in investigating the crime after the lapse of many months, had volunteered the date of July 5 as the day when they had seen Light. The jury could rightly ask: Was this the testimony of the girls or that of the police through their mouths?

The trial took a distinct and perceptible turn in Light's favor during Marshall Hall's telling cross-examination of Dr. Williams and Mr. Clarke, the gunsmith. Dr. Williams was permitted to refer to a boldly inflammatory exhibit—a well-preserved piece of skin, clearly evidencing a bullet hole, which had been taken from Bella Wright's face. Marshall Hall did his best to diminish the damaging impact of this exhibit. Inserting a thin, silver pencil into the hole in the skin, he demonstrated that the hole was very small, too small for what the good doctor had described as a bullet fired from five to seven feet away—particularly a .455 bullet fired with tremendous velocity which was just commencing its flight.

But the doctor was firm in his opinion until Marshall Hall asked, "Then how do you get out of this dilemma? A bullet going in an upward direction at high velocity found six yards away from the body?"

"My theory," responded the doctor, "is that the woman was shot whilst lying on the road, and the bullet went through her head into the ground." The fact that the bullet was actually found seventeen feet from the body could only be explained by an unconvincing rebound.

Having the doctor near, if not on, the ropes, Marshall Hall pressed home his advantage. "If a bullet," he asked, "was fired without any further resistance than the girl's head, it would be absurd to suppose that it would be found only six yards away." To which the doctor could only agree.

The gunsmith's cross-examination added further strength to Hall's defense and brought to light a new and compelling issue. A microscope was brought into the court and, unchallenged, Hall was permitted to have Mr. Clarke view the supposed murder bullet through it. In the ensuing colloquy, the gunsmith admitted that the questioned bullet could have been fired from a rifle as well as a revolver. Suddenly the possibility of a hunting accident's having caused the death was before the jury.

To fortify his hold on this new position, Hall asked: "Supposing the shot to have been fired some distance away, and that in its flight it came in contact with a fence, tree, or something else, and then struck someone in the roadway, would you expect to find that bullet within a few feet of where the person was shot?"

The gunsmith admitted the possibility.

Marshall Hall then tacked about to a question that the gunsmith was really not capable, as a firearms expert, of answering. "Have you ever seen a human being who has been shot at a distance of within five yards with a service revolver?" "No, sir," came the reply.

"I suggest that the effect of such a bullet on the skull of a human being is almost to blow the side of the head off?" Hall was allowed to testify in the form of a veiled interrogation.

"It depends on the velocity, sir," said Mr. Clarke, with the equivocation customary to expert witnesses.

"Of course it does," rebounded Marshall Hall. One can imagine a slight smile of triumph stealing across his face.

The prosecution's case was closed. It was predicated upon inference pyramided on inference with a large ingredient of speculation. Hall's cross-examination had been keen, deliberate, and to the point. If the prosecution's arguments had not been neutralized, they had been, at a minimum, weakened. The lynchpin upon which the guilt or innocence of Light would now hinge was the eagerly awaited testimony of the prisoner himself.

On the second day of the trial, without fanfare, Marshall Hall said to a hushed audience:

"I desire to call the prisoner."

Ronald Vivian Light was obviously prepared for this courtroom engagement. He may have acted precipitously and without reasoned judgment, as he explained, on the day of Bella Wright's death, but his appearance and attitude in court on this vital day was that of a man of calm judgment and controlled emotion.

Light recanted his statements to the police and admitted them to have been false. He confessed to having discarded his green bicycle, his holster, and even the clothes he wore on that fateful day. He explained that he was in terror that his involvement would become known and that his invalid mother would suffer the agonies of it. The revolver, he asserted, had been left in France when he was returned from the war disabled by shell-shock. Then he came to his bicycling and meeting with Bella Wright on July 5.

Yes, he had indeed met her at two different times on that day. He encountered her first at about 8 P.M., when he had assisted her in making an adjustment to her front wheel. They had then bicycled together to her uncle's house, where he left her, even though she indicated an interest in continuing their ride if he would but wait a short while. He demurred and left.

Later Light himself had mechanical trouble with his bicycle. He effected the necessary repairs and decided to retrace his tracks to see if he might again meet Bella, whose name he did not learn until the death was reported in the press. He returned almost to the uncle's house when she was spied wheeling along. They journeyed together a while until they parted, she going down a lane to the left and he off in the opposite direction. "I never saw her again," said Light. So ended his direct examination, an examination all observers agreed would be difficult for the prosecution to vitiate.

On the third day of the trial, Light was cross-examined, but no matter how deftly the prosecution queried, he could not be ruffled. His story, as he had told it the day before, was unshaken.

The judge concluded the examination by asking, once again, for Light to elaborate the reasons for his actions and statements after the girl's death and upon his arrest. The accused's response gave added credence to his testimony. "I did not make up my mind deliberately not to come forward," he said. "I was so astonished at the unexpected thing that I kept on hesitating, and in the end I drifted into doing nothing at all. I had drifted into the policy of concealment, and I had to go on with it."

In his summation to the jury, Marshall Hall addressed the weaknesses of the prosecution's case. There had been inadequate proof, he said, that any murder had occurred or even that the bullet recovered from the roadway had struck Bella Wright. No motive that could withstand close analysis had been shown. Hall then explained why Light had sought to find Bella after having left her at her uncle's residence. He drew the jury's attention to the power of young romance, indeed even to the sexual drive in all normal young men. To seek out an attractive young girl with whom he had been pleasantly journeying was but a harmless and understandable exercise of this sexual impulse.

Marshall Hall was beginning to reach the peaks of forensic oratory for which he was justly renowned when the mesmerism of his voice and presence was interrupted by the disturbance created by a photographer in the courtroom. After the newspaperman had been admonished by the trial judge for seeking to take pictures in the courtroom, Hall could not recapture the momentum of his peroration until, near the end, he called attention to Light's war experiences. "You must not forget that he is a man who has undergone the awful ordeal of shell-shock, an ordeal which reduces the strongest men to human wrecks, and leaves them bereft of human strength."

The trial judge's instructions to the jury were unexceptional until he directed the jury to consider whether "it is credible or possible that an innocent man should have behaved in the way he did? . . . The question you have to decide is whether that deception could have been practised by an innocent man, or whether it points the finger at the guilty man."

The jury had deliberated for more than three hours when the judge summoned them to ask if an agreement was at all possible. The foreman requested a further fifteen minutes, but in three minutes they returned to the courtroom.

Light had seen death in France and walked away, his nerves shattered. Now he was awaiting his own destiny in a court of law, boldly and bravely. With lips tight, eyes narrowed, and fists tightly clenched, Light stood to hear the verdict. Upon the foreman's announcing "Not guilty," he collapsed.

The verdict did not disappoint the populace. The thousands, both inside and outside the courtroom, who had gathered in anticipation of this moment loudly and energetically applauded the verdict. Marshall Hall, too, received praise, but from an unexpected source. The trial judge sent Hall a note stating "Your defence of Light seemed to me to be without a fault."

Light was exonerated, if an acquittal can be so interpreted. The death of Bella Wright is still, however, unexplained. The mystery remains in spite of the short story by H. Trueman Humphries in *The Strand Magazine*, which suggests that a hunter had been lying in a field adjoining the road when Bella Wright bicycled by, concealed behind the high hedges lining the road. Spying a raven on a fence gate parallel to and near the road, the marksman had fired, striking the bird, causing it to plummet from its perch to the ground. However, the bullet continued its path and struck Bella, who had emerged from the concealment of the hedges just as the hunter fired. By a bizarre coincidence and a freakish quirk of fate, the bullet struck both bird and bicyclist, instantly killing them both.

Marshall Hall never adopted Humphries's conjecture, carefully drawn though it was. In any event, the presence of the raven added to the case an occult element that would delight any devotee of the "twilight zone."

4

Alan Sillitoe

The Bike

From *The Ragman's Daughter*

Bicycle theft may not be as spectacular as "The Great Train Robbery," but it is equally catastrophic to its victims. And it is everywhere more prevalent as a theme in literature and as a practice in the streets.

Even though Chicago, Illinois, reported the theft of 11,922 bicycles in 1974,[1] bicycle theft is not limited to the cities of democratic societies. Simon Leys in his Chinese Shadows[2] has related that, in the People's Republic of China, bicycle parking lots are equipped with pay-as-you-use facilities as well as watchmen. If this were not security enough, the watchman, however, "always reminds" the bicyclist to lock his bicycle upon leaving it in the guarded bicycle lot. More recently, Chalmers M. Roberts has observed[3] that bicycles on the Chinese mainland come with innovative, built-in, chain-type bicycle locks. More security, still!

The problem of bicycle theft is one that will not solve itself. But the police are not at all energetic in ferreting out bicycle thieves. In some places (such as San Jose, California), the police statistics on stolen bicycles list only licensed bicycles. In 1974 alone this resulted in an underreporting and lack of investigation of more than 4,000 bike thefts in San Jose.[4] The insouciance of the police toward this crime is solidly entrenched in spite of an occasional police official's recognition that, in human and economic terms, bicycle theft is a serious crime.[5]

The lost-bicycle detail, according to Lieutenant Larry Byrnes of the Eighty-Seventh Precinct, is child's play, not police work. Even when a police officer's bungling results in a fellow officer's death, tracing lost bicycles is not even good enough for intradepartmental discipline. The good lieutenant, in the words of author Ed McBain in Killer's

From Alan Sillitoe, "The Bike," in *The Ragman's Daughter* (New York: Alfred A. Knopf, 1964), pp. 104–12.

"Bicycle thieves run down the back streets, old pros wheeling them three abreast at a good pace." (From *Gravity's Rainbow* by Thomas Pynchon)

Choice, *casts about for a remedy for the blundering officer. "What am I gonna do with him? Put him on tracing lost bicycles?"[6] In this same unmemorable mystery novel, we learn that the Eighty-Seventh Precinct is unlike the Thirtieth Precinct. The Thirtieth did not even keep a "file on lost bicycles."*

This police attitude of indifference or only haphazard concern for bicycle theft is fueled by a comparable popular reaction. A recent "Grin & Bear It" cartoon, in making light of the matter of bike theft, catches the public mood. It pictures the foreman of a jury addressing his brethren during their deliberations with the observation "If the kid is old-fashioned enough to steal a bike, I say give him another chance."[7]

The passive police response to bicycle theft has caught the eye and the ire of some well-known authors. Robert Graves, in his New Yorker *short story "A Bicycle on Majorca," decries the police disinterest in apprehending or in furthering the prosecution of a thief who had "abstracted" his son's bicycle.*

On the screen, too, bicycle theft has had a chilling documentary quality. Vittorio de Sica's The Bicycle Thief *has won vast acclaim for its poignant portrayal of a man, Antonio Ricci, trapped by the callous disregard of a society, police included, which will not heed his pleas for help. Ricci's bed sheets are pawned to redeem his bicycle. His bicycle enables him to secure a job as a bill poster. But in the first joyous day of work, his bicycle is stolen. Then society's jaws are snapped shut. No one will free him, least of all the police, until, in a foredoomed act of self-destruction, he steals a bicycle. He is caught after a short chase. Who can forget the agonized look of Bruno, Ricci's young son, as he gazes with pained incredulity at the caged animal which his father has become, now being debased by the police.*

The bicycle can be a potent vehicle for social commentary. The police in The Bicycle Thief *are panned as functionaries in a cruel society. In* Blue Bike Brings a Blue Day, *Chicano author Jéronimo G. Ortega portrays the police as agents of a society that discriminates against its minorities. The Chicano boy must have stolen the bicycle found in his possession. Being Chicano, the police cannot trust his explanation that he found it, dismantled it, and then refurbished it out of his own dearly earned pocket money. Alan Sillitoe, author of* The Bike, *writes with the same clenched-fist attitude toward deprivation and discrimination.*

When Sillitoe, best known as the author of The Loneliness of the Long-Distance Runner, *writes about bicycles, he knows whereof he speaks. He left school at fourteen and went to work in a bicycle factory. The incident in "The Bike" is clearly drawn from the experiences of those days. His first novel,* Saturday Night and Sunday Morning, *also involves a principal, Arthur Seaton, who is employed in a bicycle factory, on this occasion as a capstan-lathe operator as Sillitoe himself was. Seaton is depicted throughout this ribaldly riotous book as regularly straddling his bike and riding "along the canal bank into the country to fish"[8] or simply explaining his preference for this diversion from Brenda's blandishments. As he would say, "there's nowt I like better than going out into the country on my bike and fishing near Cotgrave or Trowel and sitting for hours by myself."[9]*

The Easter I was fifteen I sat at the table for supper and Mam said to me: "I'm glad you've left school. Now you can go to work."

"I don't want to go to wok," I said in a big voice.

"Well, you've got to," she said. "I can't afford to keep a pit-prop like yo' on nowt."

I sulked, pushed my toasted cheese away as if it was the worst kind of slop. "I thought I could have a break before starting."

"Well you thought wrong. You'll be out of harm's way at work." She took my plate and emptied it on John's, my younger brother's, knowing the right way to get me mad. That's the trouble with me: I'm not clever. I could have bashed our John's face in and snatched it back, except the little bastard had gobbled it up, and Dad was sitting by the fire, behind his paper with one tab lifted. "You can't get me out to wok quick enough, can you?" was all I could say at Mam.

Dad chipped in, put down his paper. "Listen: no wok, no grub. So get out and look for a job tomorrow, and don't come back till you've got one."

Going to the bike factory to ask for a job meant getting up early, just as if I was back at school; there didn't seem any point in getting older. My old man was a good worker though, and I knew in my bones and brain that I took after him. At the school garden the teacher used to say: "Colin, you're the best worker I've got, and you'll get on when you leave"—after I'd spent a couple of hours digging spuds while all the others had been larking about trying to run each other over with the lawn-rollers. Then the teacher would sell the spuds off at threepence a pound and what did I get out of it? Bogger-all. Yet I liked the work because it wore me out; and I always feel pretty good when I'm worn out.

I knew you had to go to work though, and that rough work was best. I saw a picture once about a revolution in Russia, about the workers taking over everything (like Dad wants to) and they lined everybody up and made them hold their hands out and the working blokes went up and down looking at them. Anybody whose hands was lily-white was taken away and shot. The others was O.K. Well, if ever that happened in this country, I'd be O.K., and that made be feel better when a few days later I was walking down the street in overalls at half-past seven in the morning with the rest of them. One side of my face felt lively and interested in what I was in for, but the other side was crooked and sorry for itself, so that a neighbour got a front view of my whole clock and called with a wide laugh, a gap I'd like to have seen a few inches lower down—in her neck: "Never mind. Colin, it ain't all that bad."

The man on the gate took me to the turnery. The noise hit me like a boxing-glove as I went in, but I kept on walking straight into it without flinching, feeling it reach right into my guts as if to wrench them out and use them as garters. I was handed over to the foreman; then the foreman passed me on to the toolsetter; and the toolsetter took me to another youth—so that I began to feel like a hot wallet.

The youth led me to a cupboard, opened it, and gave me a sweeping brush. "Yo' do that gangway," he said, "and I'll do this one." My gangway was wider, but I didn't bother to mention it. "Bernard," he said, holding out his hand, "that's me. I go on a machine next week, a drill."

"How long you been on this sweeping?" I wanted to know, bored with it already.

"Three months. Every lad gets put on sweeping first, just to get 'em used to the place." Bernard was small and thin, older than me. We took to each other. He had round bright eyes and dark wavy hair, and spoke in a quick way as if he'd stayed at school longer than he had. He was idle, and I thought him sharp and clever, maybe because his mam and dad died when he was three. He'd been brought up by an asthmatic auntie who'd not only spoiled him but let him run wild as well, he told me later when we sat supping from our tea mugs. He'd quietened down now though, and butter wouldn't melt in his mouth, he said with a wink. I couldn't think why this was, after all his stories about him being a mad-head—which put me off him at first, though after a bit he was my mate, and that was that.

We was talking one day, and Bernard said the thing he wanted to buy most in the world was a gram and lots of jazz records—New Orleans style. He was saving up and had already got ten quid.

"Me," I said, "I want a bike, to get out at week-ends up Trent. A shop on Arkwright Street sells good 'uns second hand."

I went back to my sweeping. It was a fact I've always wanted a bike. Speed gave me a thrill. Malcolm Campbell was my bigshot—but I'd settle for a two-wheeled push-bike. I'd once borrowed my cousin's and gone down Balloon House Hill so quick I passed a bus. I'd often thought how easy it would be to pinch a bike: look in a shop window until a bloke leaves his bike to go into the same shop, then nip in just before him and ask for something you knew they hadn't got; then walking out whistling to the bike at the kerb and ride off as if it's yours while the bloke's still in the shop. I'd brood for hours: fly home on it, enamel it, file off the numbers, turn the handlebars round, change the pedals, take lamps off or put them on . . . only, no, I thought, I'll be honest and save up for one when I get forced out to work, worse luck.

But work turned out to be a better life than school. I kept as hard at it as I could, and got on well with the blokes because I used to spout about how rotten the wages was and how hard the bosses slaved us—which made me popular you can bet. Like my old man always says, I told them: "At home, when you've got a headache, mash a pot of tea. At work, when you've got a headache, strike." Which brought a few laughs.

Bernard was put on his drill, and one Friday while he was cleaning it down I stood waiting to cart his rammel off. "Are you still saving up for that bike, then?" he asked, pushing steel dust away with a handbrush.

"Course I am. But I'm a way off getting one yet. They rush you a fiver at that shop. Guaranteed, though."

He worked on for a minute or two then, as if he'd got a birthday present or was trying to spring a good surprise on me, said without turning round: "I've made up my mind to sell my bike."

"I didn't know you'd got one."

"Well"—a look on his face as if there was a few things I didn't know—"I bus it to work: it's easier." Then in a pallier voice: "I got it last Christmas, from my auntie. But I want a record player now."

My heart was thumping. I knew I hadn't got enough, but: "How much do you want for it?"

He smiled. "It ain't how much I want for the bike, it's how much more dough I need to get the gram and a couple of discs."

I saw Trent Valley spread out below me from the top of Carlton Hill—fields and villages, and the river like a white scarf dropped from a giant's neck. "How much do you need, then?"

He took his time about it, as if still having to reckon it up. "Fifty bob." I'd only got two quid—so the giant snatched his scarf away and vanished. Then Bernard seemed in a hurry to finish the deal: "Look, I don't want to mess about, I'll let it go for two pounds five. You can borrow the other five bob."

"I'll do it then," I said, and Bernard shook my hand like he was going away in the army. "It's a deal. Bring the dough in the morning, and I'll bike it to wok."

Dad was already in when I got home, filling the kettle at the scullery tap. I don't think he felt safe without there was a kettle on the gas. "What would you do if the world suddenly ended, Dad?" I once asked when he was in a good mood. "Mash some tea and watch it," he said. He poured me a cup.

"Lend's five bob, Dad, till Friday."

He slipped the cosy on. "What do you want to borrow money for?" I told him. "Who from?" he asked.

"My mate at wok."

He passed me the money. "Is it a good 'un?"

"I ain't seen it yet. He's bringing it in the morning."

"Make sure the brakes is safe."

Bernard came in half an hour late, so I wasn't able to see the bike till dinner-time. I kept thinking he'd took bad and wouldn't come at all, but suddenly he was stooping at the door to take his clips off—so's I'd know he'd got his—my—bike. He looked paler than usual, as if he'd been up the canal-bank all night with a piece of skirt and caught a bilious-bout. I paid him at dinner-time. "Do you want a receipt for it?" he laughed. It was no time to lark about. I gave it a short test around the factory, then rode it home.

The next three evenings, for it was well in to summer, I rode a dozen miles out into the country, where fresh air smelt like cowshit and the land was coloured different, was wide open and windier than in streets. Marvellous. It was like a new life starting up, as if till then I'd been tied by a mile long rope round the ankle to home. Whistling along lanes I planned trips to Skegness, wondering how many miles I could make in a whole day. If I pedalled like mad, bursting my lungs for fifteen hours I'd reach London where I'd never been. It was like sawing through the bars in a clink. It was a good bike as well, a few years old, but a smart racer with lamps and saddlebag and a pump that went. I thought Bernard was a bit loony parting with it at that price, but I supposed that that's how blokes are when they get dead set on a gram and discs. They'd sell their own mother, I thought, enjoying a mad dash down from Canning Circus, weaving between the cars for kicks.

"What's it like, having a bike?" Bernard asked, stopping to slap me on the back—as jolly as I'd ever seen him, yet in a kind of way that don't happen between pals.

"You should know," I said. "Why? It's all right, ain't it? The wheels are good, aren't they?"

An insulted look came into his eyes. "You can give it back if you like. I'll give you your money."

"I don't want it," I said. I could no more part with it than my right arm, and he knew it. "Got the gram yet?" And he told me about it for the next half-hour. It had got so many dials for this and that he made it sound like a space ship. We were both satisfied, which was the main thing.

That same Saturday I went to the barber's for my monthly D. A. and when I came out I saw a bloke getting on my bike to ride it away. I tagged him on the shoulder, my fist flashing red for danger.

"Off," I said sharp, ready to smash the thieving bastard. He turned to me. A funny sort of thief, I couldn't help thinking, a respectable-looking bloke of about forty wearing glasses and shiny shoes, smaller than me, with a moustache. Still, the swivel-eyed sinner was taking my bike.

"I'm boggered if I will," he said, in a quiet way so that I thought he was a bit touched. "It's my bike, anyway."

"It bloody-well ain't," I swore, "and if you don't get off I'll crack you one."

A few people gawked at us. The bloke didn't mess about and I can understand it now. "Missis," he called, "just go down the road to that copperbox and ask a policeman to come up 'ere, will you? This is my bike, and this young bogger nicked it."

I was strong for my age. "You sodding fibber," I cried, pulling him clean off the bike so's it clattered to the pavement. I picked it up to ride away, but the bloke got me round the waist, and it was more than I could do to take him off up the road as well, even if I wanted to. Which I didn't.

"Fancy robbing a working-man of his bike," somebody called out from the crowd of idle bastards now collected. I could have mowed them down.

But I didn't get a chance. A copper came, and the man was soon flicking out his wallet, showing a bill with the number of the bike on it: proof right enough. But I still thought he'd made a mistake. "You can tell us all about that at the Guildhall," the copper said to me.

I don't know why—I suppose my brains testing—but I stuck to a story that I found the bike dumped at the end of the yard that morning and was on my way to give it in at a copshop, and had called for a haircut first. I think the magistrate half believed me, because the bloke knew to the minute when it was pinched, and at that time I had a perfect alibi—I was in work, proved by my clocking-in card. I knew some rat who hadn't been in work though when he should have been.

All the same, being found with a pinched bike, I got put on probation, and am still doing it. I hate old Bernard's guts for playing a trick like that on me, his mate. But it was lucky for him I hated the coppers more and wouldn't nark on anybody, not even a dog. Dad would have killed me if ever I had, though he didn't need to tell me. I could only thank God a story came to me as quick as it did, though in one way I still sometimes reckon I was barmy not to have told them how I got that bike.

There's one thing I do know. I'm waiting for Bernard to come out of borstal. He got picked up, the day after I was copped with the bike, for robbing his auntie's gas meter to buy more discs. She'd had about all she could stand from him, and thought a spell inside would do him good, if not cure him altogether. I've got a big bone to pick with him, because he owes me forty-five bob. I don't care where he gets it—even if he goes out and robs another meter—but I'll get it out of him, I swear blind I will. I'll pulverise him.

Another thing about him though that makes me laugh is that, if ever there's a revolution and everybody's lined-up with their hands out, Bernard's will still be lily-white, because he's a bone-idle thieving bastard—and then we'll see how he goes on; because mine won't be lily-white, I can tell you that now. And you never know, I might even be one of the blokes picking 'em out.

Epilogue

All bicyclists have something to learn from Jesus Christ and George Bernard Shaw. Both possessed God-ordained and (at least, one of them) godly talents. Both urged men, after their unexcelled example, to move mountains.

No, the bicycle does not appear in the Bible, nor, for that matter, does George Bernard Shaw. But the Bible and GBS have, on occasion, spoken in a kindred tongue.

After the transfiguration, according to Matthew, Christ, upon descending from the mountain, was approached by a father whose son was sorely diseased. Christ, with words expressing annoyance, cured the son. When the disciples inquired of him why they too could not heal the boy, Jesus replied: "Because you have little faith. I tell you solemnly, if your faith were the size of a mustard seed you could say to this mountain, 'Move from here to there,' and it would move; nothing would be impossible for you."[1]

Shaw, in his turn, preached the same homily. In his tedious and overlong preface to *Back to Methusaleh*, he propounds his theory of Creative Evolution or the élan vital, in contrast to Darwin's theory of circumstantial selection. His thoughts were not original for the French naturalist, Jean Baptiste Lamarck, had stated the same thesis almost two hundred years before. But Shaw's words and illustrative arguments were uniquely his own.

Shaw's view relied heavily on the power of the will. "If you have no eyes," he said, "and want to see, and keep trying to see, you will finally get eyes."[2] This principle is what operates to elevate a pedestrian to a bicyclist, so Shaw said. The skilled bicyclist "has acquired a new habit, an automatic unconscious habit, solely because he wanted to and kept trying until it was added into him."[3]

The possibilities for constructive action are limitless if the will has such power. "If," by the power of self-determination, "you can turn a pedestrian into a cyclist,"[4] then the cyclist could become a pianist or violinist. In truth, a bicyclist could become a superman if the will were trained to be dominant. And it all started with a bicycle.

Now, did you know that a bicyclist could move mountains?

Notes

Preface

1. Paul Theroux, *The Great Railway Bazaar: By Train through Asia* (Boston: Houghton Mifflin Company, 1975), p. 28.
2. Vladimir Nabokov, *The Real Life of Sebastian Knight* (New York: New Directions, 1959), p. 196.
3. Simon Leys, *Chinese Shadows* (New York: Penguin Books, 1978), p. 45.
4. Roger Vailland, *The Law* (London: Jonathan Cape, 1958), pp. 48–49.
5. Thomas Gray, "Elegy Written in a Country Churchyard" (Mount Vernon: Peter Pauper Press).
6. Robert Benchley, "The Return of the Bicycle," *Liberty*, July 19, 1930, p. 51.
7. F. R. Whitt, "What *Is* That Cherub Doing?," *Cycletouring*, April–May 1971, p. 80.
8. Augusto Marinoni, "The Bicycle," in *The Unknown Leonardo*, edited by Ladislao Reti (New York: McGraw-Hill Book Co., 1974), Appendix.
9. David Davenport, "The Richard Nixon Freischütz Rag," in *Da Vinci's Bicycles* (Baltimore: Johns Hopkins University Press, 1979), p. 4.
10. Christopher Morley, *Parnassus on Wheels* (New York: Modern Library, 1925), p. 146.
11. R. K. Narayan, *The Painter of Signs* (New York: The Viking Press, 1976), pp. 13–14.

Part I: A Bicycling Calliope

1. Iris Murdoch, *The Red and the Green* (New York: The Viking Press, 1965), p. 29.
2. Elizabeth West, *Hovel in the Hills* (London: Faber and Faber, 1977), p. 185.
3. François Mauriac, *Thérèse*, trans. Gerard Hopkins (New York: Doubleday Anchor Book, 1947), p. 69.
4. John Betjeman, "The Commander" in *Collected Poems* (Boston: Houghton Mifflin Co., 1971), pp. 330–31.
5. Heinrich Böll, *The Clown* (New York: McGraw-Hill Book Company, 1971), pp. 14–15.
6. Jack London, *Martin Eden* (New York: The Review of Reviews Company, 1915), p. 147.
7. Simone de Beauvoir, *La Force de L'age*, trans. Shauna Russell (Paris: Gallimard, 1960), pp. 505–6.
8. Samuel Beckett, *More Pricks Than Kicks* (New York: Grove Press, Inc., 1970), pp. 31–32.
9. John Wain, *Born in Captivity* (New York: Alfred A. Knopf, 1954), pp. 88–89.
10. Peter Sears, "Place for Four-Letter Words"—source unknown.
11. Henry Beetle Hough, *Singing in the Morning* (New York: Simon and Schuster, 1951), p. 75.
12. Louis J. Halle, Jr., *Spring in Washington* (New York: Atheneum, 1963), p. 16.
13. Ernest Hemingway, *By-Line* (New York: Charles Scribner's Sons, 1967), p. 364.
14. Alain Fournier, *The Wanderer*, trans. Françoise Delisle (Boston: Houghton Mifflin Co., 1928), p. 198.
15. Henri Troyat, *Tolstoy* (New York: Doubleday and Co., 1967), p. 510.

16. Henry Adams, *The Education of Henry Adams* (Boston: Houghton Mifflin Co., 1918), p. 330.

17. Edmund Wilson, *The Twenties* (New York: Farrar, Straus and Giroux, 1975), p. 455.

18. K. M. Elizabeth Murray, *Caught in the Web of Words* (New Haven: Yale University Press, 1977), p. 328.

19. Vladimir Nabokov, *Glory* (New York: McGraw-Hill Book Company, 1971), p. 61.

20. Will Carleton, "The Silent Wheel" in *City Ballads* (New York: Harper and Brothers, 1885), pp. 155–56.

21. Marcel Moré, *Nouvelles Explorations de Jules Verne. Musique, Misogamie, Machine*, trans. Shauna Russell (Paris: Gallimard, 1963), p. 213.

22. Quoted in I. A. Leonard, *When Bikehood Was in Flower* (Goldenrod, Fla: Bearcamp Press, 1969), p. 55.

23. Max Beerbohm, *More* (Freeport, N.Y.: Books for Libraries Press, 1967), p. 148, 150.

Stijn Streuvels: Memories of a Naming Day

1. Dorothy W. Baruch, "Different Bicycles," in Helen Ferris, compiler, *Favorite Poems, Old and New* (New York: Doubleday and Co., 1957).

Frederic Remington: The Bicycle Goes to War

1. Cornelius Ryan, *A Bridge Too Far* (New York: Simon and Schuster, 1974), pp. 29, 202.

2. Martin Caidin and Jay Barbree, *Bicycles in War* (New York: Hawthorn Books, 1974), p. 31.

3. J. G. Farrell, *The Siege of Krishnapur* (New York: Harcourt Brace Jovanovich, 1973), p. 218.

4. Caidin, *Bicycles in War*, p. 31.

Flann O'Brien: All Those Endearing Charms

1. Vladimir Nabokov, *Lolita* (New York: Berkley Publishing Corporation, 1969), pp. 184–85.

2. Ibid., p. 171.

John Galsworthy: Pedaling the Suffrage

1. Kelly, Fred C., "The Great Bicycle Craze," *American Heritage*, no. 8 (1956): 69.

2. *Puck* 37 (August 7, 1895): 391.

3. A. L. Anderson, *Wisconsin Then and Now* 13, no. 11 (June 1967).

4. Roger Vailland, *The Law* (London: Jonathan Cape, 1958), p. 146.

5. Stewart Parker, "Spokesong, or, The Common Wheel," *Plays and Players Magazine* (December 1976 and January 1977), p. 44 col. 3 and p. 45 col. 1.

Part II: Bicycling into the Orbicular Millennium

Introduction

1. L. Sprague de Camp, *H. P. Lovecraft: A Biography* (New York: Doubleday and Co., 1975), p. 395.

2. Richard L. Edgeworth, *Memoirs of Richard Lovell Edgeworth, Esq.* (London, 1820), vol. i, pp. 149–51.

3. Roger Shattuck, *The Banquet Years* (New York: Vintage Books, 1968), p. 12.

Alfred Jarry: Pass the E.R.G., Please!

1. Robert A. Smith, *A Social History of the Bicycle* (New York: McGraw-Hill Book Company, 1972), pp. 137–38.

Flann O'Brien: The Lilt of a Bicycle by Bogside

1. Quoted by Padraic Colum, "James Stephens as a Prose Artist," in Lloyd Frankenburg, ed., *A James Stephens Reader* (New York: The Macmillan Company, 1962), p. x.

Alain Robbe-Grillet: A Murderer to Watch

1. John McPhee, *The Crofter and the Laird* (New York: Farrar, Straus and Giroux, 1970), pp. 45–46.

Samuel Beckett: Things Are Not What They Seem

1. Samuel Beckett, "The Calmative," in *Stories and Texts for Nothing* (New York: Grove Press, 1967), p. 38.

Bruno Schulz: Signs and Wonders in the Heavens

1. Bruno Schulz, *The Street of Crocodiles* (New York: Penguin Books, 1977), p. 28.

Part III: Not in Vain the Distance Beckons!

Introduction

1. Edmund Wilson, *A Prelude* (New York: Farrar, Straus and Giroux, 1967), p. 72.
2. Kenneth Rexroth, "The Dragon and the Unicorn," in *The Collected Longer Poems* (New York: New Directions, 1968), p. 236.
3. Ibid., pp. 237, 239–40.
4. Bernard Newman, *British Journey* (London: Robert Hale and Company, 1945), p. 234.
5. Ernest Hemingway, "A Way You'll Never Be," in *The Short Stories of Ernest Hemingway* (New York: Charles Scribner's Sons, 1953), p. 413.
6. Rexroth, *The Collected Longer Poems*, p. 145.
7. Samuel Hoffenstein, "Songs to Break the Tedium of Riding a Bicycle, Seeing One's Friends, or Heartbreak," in *Poems in Praise of Practically Nothing* (New York: Garden City Publishing Co., 1939), pp. 15–17.
8. Newman, *British Journey*, p. 11.
9. Edmund Wilson, *The Twenties* (New York: Farrar, Straus and Giroux, 1975), p. 454.
10. Robert Frost, "The Wood-Pile," in Edward Connery Lathem, ed., *The Poetry of Robert Frost* (New York: Holt, Rinehart and Winston, 1972), p. 101.
11. Harold Elvin, *Elvin's Rides* (London: Longmans, Green and Co., 1963), p. 97.
12. Daniel Behrman, *The Man Who Loved Bicycles* (New York: Harper's Magazine Press, 1973), p. 63.
13. Ibid., p. 80.
14. Ibid., p. 33.
15. Sinclair Lewis, "I'm a Stranger Here Myself," in Burton Rascoe and Groff Conklin, eds., *The Bachelor's Companion* (New York: Reynal and Hitchcock, 1934), pp. 142–54.
16. Harold Elvin, *The Ride to Chandigarh* (New York: Macmillan and Co., 1957), p. 4.

17. H. G. Wells, *The Wheels of Chance: A Cycling Holiday Adventure* (London: J. M. Dent and Sons, 1896), pp. 44–45.

18. Sean O'Faolain, "Silence of the Valley," in *The Man Who Invented Sin and Other Stories* (New York: The Devin-Adair Company, 1948), p. 48.

19. Eve Curie, *Madame Curie* (New York: Doubleday and Co., 1937), p. 149.

20. Thomas Stevens, *Around the World on a Bicycle* (New York: Charles Scribner's Sons, 1887).

21. Dylan Thomas, "Who Do You Wish Was with Us," in *Portrait of the Artist as a Young Dog* (New York: New Directions, 1955), pp. 77–78.

Gavin Casey: "That Day at Brown Lakes"

1. P. D. James, *Unnatural Causes* (New York: Popular Library, 1967), p. 187.

2. Elizabeth West, *Hovel in the Hills* (London: Faber and Faber, 1977), p. 186.

Aldous Huxley: The Bard and the Bicycle

1. Ernest Hemingway, *To Have and Have Not* (London: Penguin Books, 1962), pp. 138–39.

H. G. Wells: A Bolt of Blue

1. John Gardner, *The Life and Times of Chaucer* (New York: Alfred A. Knopf, 1977), p. 59.

2. H. G. Wells, *Experiment in Autobiography* (New York: Macmillan Company, 1934), p. 458.

3. Frank O'Connor, "Masculine Protest," in *Masculine Protest and Other Stories from Collection Three* (London: Cox and Wyman, 1977), pp. 1–11.

Part IV: Head over Wheels in Love

Introduction

1. Bertrand Russell, *The Autobiography of Bertrand Russell, 1872–1914* (Boston: Little, Brown and Co., 1967), p. 222.

2. Kenneth Koch, "To You," in *Contemporary American Poetry*, ed. A. Poulin, Jr. (Boston: Houghton Mifflin, 1971), pp. 198–99.

3. Marcel Proust, *Within a Budding Grove*, trans. C. K. Scott Moncrieff (New York: Random House, Inc., 1951), p. 241.

4. F. Scott Fitzgerald, "Basil—The Scandal Detectives," in *Taps at Reveille* (New York: Charles Scribner's Sons, 1935) pp. 8–9.

5. Ibid., p. 23.

6. Stephen Crane, "Showin' Off," in *Whilomville Stories* (New York: Harper and Brothers, 1900) pp. 50–53.

Vladimir Nabokov: The Summer of '15

1. Andrew Field, *Nabokov: His Life in Part* (New York: Viking Penguin, 1977), pp. 103–4.

2. Vladimir Nabokov, *The Real Life of Sebastian Knight* (New York: New Directions, 1959), pp. 139–40.

3. Vladimir Nabokov, *Mary* (New York: McGraw-Hill Book Company, 1970), p. 34.

4. Ivan S. Turgenev, "First Love," in *The Borzoi Turgenev*, trans. Harry Stevens (New York: Alfred A. Knopf, 1955), p. 372.

Iris Murdoch: The Red and the Green

1. Iris Murdoch, *The Sandcastle* (London: Chatto and Windus, 1957), p. 73.

Part V: Not Just Ordinary Humor

Introduction

1. Mark Twain, *Pudd'n Head Wilson* (New York: Harper and Brothers, 1922), p. 6.
2. Robert Gibbings, *Lovely Is the Lee* (London: J. M. Dent and Sons, 1945), pp. 84–85.
3. Patent #650,002, patented 5/22/1900 by Adolph A. Neubauer of Camden, New Jersey.
4. "Résponses à la violence," Rapport du Comité d'Etudes Preside par Alain Peyrefitte (July 1977), pp. 365–66.
5. Norman Mailer, *Of a Fire on the Moon* (New York: New American Library, 1971), p. 384.
6. Marcel Pagnol, *La Gloire de mon père (Souvenirs d'enfance)*, vol. 1, trans. Claudine Novi. (Monte Carlo: Editions Pastorelly, 1958), p. 45.
7. Dudley Barker, *G. K. Chesterton* (New York: Stein and Day, 1975), p. 133.
8. Ibid, p. 243.
9. Julia Lamb, " 'The Commodore' Enjoyed Life but New York Society Winced," *Smithsonian*, November 1978, p. 136.
10. Richard Ellmann, ed., *Selected Joyce Letters* (New York: Viking Press, 1975), p. 308.
11. Unknown Source.
12. William Packard, ed., *The Craft of Poetry: Interviews from the New York Quarterly* (New York: Doubleday and Co., 1974), p. 124.
13. Isabel G. Homewood, *Recollections of an Octogenarian* (London: John Murray, 1932), p. 192.
14. Healy, T. M., "On Bicycles: A Speech" (July 7, 1898), in *The Portable Irish Reader*, Diarmuid Russell, ed. (New York: The Viking Press, 1966), pp. 43–44.
15. Kurt Vonnegut, Jr., *Cat's Cradle* (New York: Dell, 1971), pp. 65–66.
16. Samuel Beckett, *Mercier and Camier* (New York: Grove Press, 1974), p. 85.
17. J. P. Donleavy, *The Ginger Man* (New York: Berkeley Medallion Book, 1965), p. 98.
18. Samuel Beckett, "All That Fall," in *Krapp's Last Tape and Other Dramatic Pieces* (New York: Grove Press, 1970), pp. 38–40.

Colossal Collisions

1. James Joyce, *A Portrait of the Artist as a Young Man* (New York: The Viking Press, 1962), pp. 41–42, 57.
2. Simone de Beauvoir, *La Force de l'age* (Paris: Gallimard, 1960) trans. Gabriele Rooz, pp. 509–10.
3. Olivia Collidge, *George Bernard Shaw* (Boston: Houghton Mifflin Company, 1968), p. 75.
4. Ibid., p. 86.
5. Bertrand Russell, *Portraits from Memory* (London: George Allen and Unwin, 1956), p. 72.

Ernest Hemingway: Saddlesores for Early Birds

1. A. E. Hotchner, *Papa Hemingway* (New York: Random House, 1966), p. 50.
2. Ibid., p. 48.

Part VI: Bang of the Last Lap Bell

Introduction

1. Maurice Le Blanc, *The Extraordinary Adventures of Arsène Lupin, Gentleman-Burglar*, trans. George Morehead (New York: Dover Publications, 1977), pp. 35–36.
2. Deirdre Bair, *Samuel Beckett* (New York: Harcourt Brace Jovanovich, 1978), p. 382.
3. Ibid., p. 557.
4. James Joyce, *Ulysses* (New York: Vintage Books, 1961), p. 86.
5. Ibid., p. 237.
6. Maurice Shadbolt, "Love Story," in *The New Zealanders: A Sequence of Stories* (London: Victor Gollancz, 1960), p. 86.
7. Thomas Pynchon, *Gravity's Rainbow* (New York: Bantam Books, 1974), p. 712.
8. Daniel Behrman, *The Man Who Loved Bicycles* (New York: Harper's Magazine Press, 1973), p. 56.
9. Ibid.
10. Roger Vailland, *The Law*, trans. Peter Wiles (London: Jonathan Cape, 1958), pp. 137–38.
11. Shadbolt, *The New Zealanders*, p. 98.

Ernest Hemingway: On the Right Track!

1. Ernest Hemingway, *The Sun Also Rises* (New York: Charles Scribner's Sons, 1926), pp. 234–37.
2. Ernest Hemingway, *By-Line* (New York: Charles Scribner's Sons, 1967), p. 364.
3. Ernest Hemingway, "A Pursuit Race," in *The Short Stories of Ernest Hemingway* (New York: Charles Scribner's Sons, 1966), p. 350.

John D. MacDonald: A Century Ride Is Not a Race, Is Not a Race . . .

1. Robert A. Smith, *A Social History of the Bicycle* (New York: American Heritage Press, 1972), p. 132–34.

Marcel Aymé: "The Last"

1. Roger Vailland, *The Law* (London: Jonathan Cape, 1958), p. 155.
2. Ralph Hurne, *The Yellow Jersey* (New York: Simon and Schuster, 1973), p. 15.
3. Ibid., pp. 161–62.
4. Alastair Reid, "Whoosh Whoosh Whoosh," in *Passwords* (Boston: Little, Brown and Co., 1963), p. 215.

Paul Morand: The Six-Day Night

1. William C. Anderson, *The Great Bicycle Expedition* (New York: Crown Publishers, 1973), pp. 1–2.
2. Eugene O'Neill, "The Hairy Ape," in *The Plays of Eugene O'Neill* (New York: Random House, 1954), p. 224.
3. Jonathan Yardley, *Ring—A Biography of Ring Lardner* (New York: Random House, 1977), p. 259.
4. A. E. Hotchner, *Papa Hemingway* (New York: Random House, 1966), p. 50.
5. Ibid., p. 43.
6. Robert A. Smith, *A Social History of the Bicycle* (New York: American Heritage Press, 1972), p. 136.
7. Fred Hawthorne, "Six-Day Bicycle Racing," in Allison Danzig and Peter Brandwein, eds., *Sport's Golden Age—A Close-up of the Fabulous Twenties* (New York: Harper and Brothers, 1948), p. 295.
8. Owen Mulholland, "Six-Day Racing," *Bicycling*, March 1976, p. 27.
9. Jimmy Breslin, *The Gang That Couldn't Shoot Straight* (New York: Bantam Books, 1971), pp. 5–6.

Part VII: No Flying Creature

Introduction

1. Sir Arthur Conan Doyle, "The Adventure of Black Peter," in *The Complete Sherlock Holmes* (New York: Doubleday and Company, 1930), p. 562.

2. Edmond Locard, *Traité de criminalistique*, vol. 2 (Paris: Desvigne, 1931), pp. 832–33.

3. Adapted from Jürgen Thorwald, *Crime and Science*, trans. Richard and Clara Winston (New York: Harcourt, Brace and World, 1967), pp. 388–408.

4. Ibid., p. 406.

5. Georges Simenon, *Maigret Meets a Milord* (London: Penguin, 1974), p. 81.

6. Ibid., p. 89.

7. Dorothy L. Sayers, *Five Red Herrings* (New York: Avon Books, 1968), p. 180.

Sir Arthur Conan Doyle: "The Adventure of the Priory School"

1. Sir Arthur Conan Doyle, "The Adventure of the Missing Three-Quarter," in *The Complete Sherlock Holmes* (New York: Doubleday and Company, 1930), p. 631.

2. Hesketh Pearson, *Conan Doyle: His Life and Art* (New York: Taplinger Publishing Company, 1977), pp. 95–96.

3. Harry How, "A Day with Dr. Conan Doyle," *The Strand Magazine*, August 1892, p. 183.

4. Sir Arthur Conan Doyle, "Some Recollections of Sport," *The Strand Magazine*, September 1909, p. 271.

5. Sir Arthur Conan Doyle, *Beyond the City* (J. W. Arrowsmith, 1893), p. 216.

6. Sir Arthur Conan Doyle, "How I Made My List?," *The Strand Magazine*, January–June 1927, pp. 611–12.

7. Jay Finley Christ, "Letter," *The Baker Street Journal* 2 (October 1947): 474.

8. Stuart C. Rand, "What Sherlock Didn't Know?," *The Atlantic*, November 1945, pp. 122–25.

9. Thomas D. Stowe, "More about Tires in the Priory School," *The Baker Street Journal* 16 (December 1966): 142; James Edward Holroyd, "The Egg-Spoon," *The Sherlock Holmes Journal* 5, no. 2 (1961): 58.

10. Kohkl Naganuma, "On Tires in the Priory School," *The Baker Street Journal* 16 (June 1966): 94, 98.

11. Sir Arthur Conan Doyle, *Memories and Adventures* (Boston: Little, Brown and Co., 1924), p. 102.

12. Lord Donegall, "Kidnapping, Murder, Cycle Tracks, A Duke and His Cheque!," *The New Strand* (June 1962), p. 811.

13. Dan Morrow, "Letter," *The Holmesian Observer* 1, no. 7 (September 1971): 5.

Alan Sillitoe: "The Bike"

1. David Brickell and Lee S. Cole, *Bike Theft* (Santa Cruz, Calif.: Davis Publishing Company, 1976), p. 173.

2. Simon Leys, *Chinese Shadows* (New York: Penguin, 1978), p. 45.

3. Chalmers M. Roberts, "New Images of China in a Time of Change," *Washington Post*, December 31, 1978, B4.

4. Brickell, *Bike Theft*, p. 173.

5. Robert H. Frailing, "Bicycle Theft—A Serious Crime," *FBI Law Enforcement Bulletin* (June 1974), pp. 7–10.

6. Ed McBain, *Killer's Choice* (New York: Ballantine Books, 1958), p. 13, 83.

7. Lichty and Wagner, "Grin & Bear It," *Washington Post*, June 28, 1978, p. B9.

8. Alan Sillitoe, *Saturday Night and Sunday Morning* (New York: Alfred A. Knopf, 1958), p. 137.

9. Ibid., p. 158.

Epilogue

1. The Holy Bible, Matt. 17:19–20.

2. George Bernard Shaw, *Back to Methuselah: A Metabiological Pentateuch* (New York: Dodd, Mead and Company, 1938), p. xxiii.

3. Ibid., p. xxiv.

4. Ibid., p. xxv.

Bibliography

Adams, Henry. *The Education of Henry Adams*. Boston: Houghton Mifflin Co., 1918.

Anderson, A. L. *Wisconsin Then and Now* 13, no. 11 (June 1967).

Anderson, William C. *The Great Bicycle Expedition*. New York: Crown Publishers, 1973.

Aronson, Sidney H. "The Sociology of the Bicycle," *Social Forces* 30 (1952): 305–12.

Auden, W. H. "Miss Gee." In *Selected Poetry of W. H. Auden*. New York: Random House, 1958.

Aymé, Marcel. "The Last." In *The Proverb*. Translated by Norman Denny. New York: Atheneum, 1961.

Baden-Powell, Major-General R. S. S. *Sketches in Mafeking and East Africa*. London: Smith, Elder and Co., 1907.

Bair, Deirdre. *Samuel Beckett*. New York: Harcourt Brace Jovanovich, 1978.

Barker, Dudley. *G. K. Chesterton*. New York: Stein and Day, 1975.

Baruch, Dorothy W. "Different Bicycles." In *Favorite Poems, Old and New*, compiled by Helen Ferris. New York: Doubleday and Co., 1957.

Baum, L. Frank. *The Wizard of Oz*. Chicago: Henry Regnery Company, 1956.

Beckett, Samuel. "All That Fall." In *Krapp's Last Tape and Other Dramatic Pieces*. New York: Grove Press, 1970.

―――. *Mercier and Camier*. New York: Grove Press, 1974.

―――. *Molloy*. New York: Grove Press, 1965.

―――. *More Pricks Than Kicks*. New York: Grove Press, 1970.

―――. *Stories and Texts for Nothing*. New York: Grove Press, 1967.

Beerbohm, Max. *More*. Freeport, N.Y.: Books for Libraries Press, 1967.

Behrman, Daniel. *The Man Who Loved Bicycles*. New York: Harper's Magazine Press, 1973.

Benchley, Robert. "The Return of the Bicycle." *Liberty*, July 19, 1930, p. 51.

Betjeman, John. "The Commander." In *Collected Poems*. Boston: Houghton Mifflin Co., 1971.

―――. "The Wykehamist." In *Collected Poems*. Boston: Houghton Mifflin Company, 1971.

Böll, Heinrich. *The Clown*. New York: McGraw-Hill Book Company, 1971.

Bradbury, Ray. "The Great Collision of Monday Last." In *A Medicine for Melancholy*. New York: Bantam Books, 1960.

Breslin, Jimmy. *The Gang That Couldn't Shoot Straight*. New York: Bantam Books, 1971.

Brickell, David., and Cole, Lee S. *Bike Theft*. Santa Cruz, Calif.: Davis Publishing Company, 1976.

Carleton, Will. "The Silent Wheel." In *City Ballads*. New York: Harper and Brothers, 1885.

Casey, Gavin. "That Day at Brown Lakes." In *Short Shift Saturday and Other Stories*. Sydney, Australia: Angus and Robertson, 1973.

Christ, Jay Finley. "Letter." *The Baker Street Journal* 2 (October 1947): 474.

Christie, Agatha. *The Moving Finger*. London: Fontana Books, 1971.

Christie, Agatha. *The Murder of Roger Ackroyd*. New York: Dodd, Mead and Company, 1926.

Clarke, Arthur C. *Rendezvous with Rama*. New York: Harcourt Brace Jovanovich, 1973.

———. *2001: A Space Odyssey*. New York: New American Library, 1972.

Cockrell, Thomas M. "The Bicycle Key." In *The Best College Writing, 1961*. New York: Random House, 1962.

Collins, Wilkie. *The Moonstone*. New York: Random House, 1937.

Collidge, Olivia. *George Bernard Shaw*. Boston: Houghton Mifflin Company, 1968.

Cormier, Robert. *I Am the Cheese*. New York: Random House, 1977.

Crane, Stephen. "New York's Bicycle Speedway." In *The New York City Sketches of Stephen Crane and Related Pieces*, edited by R. W. Stallman and E. R. Hageman. New York: New York University Press, 1966.

———. "Showin' Off." In *Whilomville Stories*. New York: Harper and Brothers, 1900.

Curie, Eve. *Madame Curie*. New York: Doubleday and Co., 1937.

Davenport, David. "The Richard Nixon Freischütz Rag." In *Da Vinci's Bicycle*. Baltimore: Johns Hopkins University Press, 1979.

Davidson, Avram. "Or All the Seas with Oysters." In *The Hugo Winners*, vol. 1, edited by Isaac Asimov. Greenwich, Conn.: Fawcett Crest, 1958.

de Beauvoir, Simone. *La Force de l'age*. Paris: Gallimard, 1960.

de Camp, L. Sprague. *H. P. Lovecraft: A Biography*. New York: Doubleday and Co., 1975.

de Sica, Vittorio. *The Bicycle Thief*. Translated by Simon Hartog. New York: Simon and Schuster, 1968.

Dickens, Charles. *The Mystery of Edwin Drood*. New York: New American Library, 1961.

Divide, Steven. *Reader's Digest*, April 1977, p. 101.

Donleavy, J. P. *The Destinies of Darcy Dancer, Gentleman*. New York: Delacorte Press, 1977.

———. *The Ginger Man*. New York: Berkley Medallion Book, 1965.

Doyle, Sir Arthur Conan. "The Adventure of Black Peter." In *The Complete Sherlock Holmes*. New York: Doubleday and Company, 1930.

———. "The Adventure of the Missing Three-Quarter." In *The Complete Sherlock Holmes*. New York: Doubleday and Company, 1930.

———. "The Adventure of the Priory School." *The Strand Magazine* 27 (February 1904), 122–40.

———. *Beyond the City*. J. W. Arrowsmith, 1893.

———. "How I Made My List?" *The Strand Magazine*, January–June 1927, pp. 611–12.

———. *Memories and Adventures*. Boston: Little, Brown and Co., 1924.

———. "Some Recollections of Sport." *The Strand Magazine*, September 1909, p. 271.

Dunegall, Lord. "Kidnapping, Murder, Cycle Tracks, A Duke and his Cheque!" *The New Strand*, June 1962, p. 811.

Durant, Will. *Transition*. New York: Simon and Schuster, 1927.

———, and Durant, Ariel. *A Dual Autobiography*. New York: Simon and Schuster, 1977.

Edgeworth, Richard L., *Memoirs of Richard Lovell Edgeworth, Esq*. London, 1820.

Editorial, "Easy Radar," in *New York Times*, November 1, 1977.

Ellmann, Richard, ed. *Selected Joyce Letters*. New York: The Viking Press, 1975.

Elvin, Harold. *The Ride to Chandigarh*. New York: Macmillan and Co., 1957.

———. *Elvin's Rides*. London: Longmans, Green and Co., 1963.

Empson, William. "Invitation to Juno." In *Collected Poems of William Empson*. New York: Harcourt, Brace and Co., 1949.

Farrell, J. G. *The Siege of Krishnapur*. New York: Hawthorn Books, 1974.

———. *Troubles*. New York: Alfred A. Knopf, 1970.

Field, Andrew. *Nabokov: His Life in Part*. New York: Viking Penguin, 1977.

Fitzgerald, F. Scott. "Basil—The Scandal Detectives." In *Taps at Reveille*. New York: Charles Scribner's Sons, 1935.

Fournier, Alain. *The Wanderer*. Translated by Françoise Delisle. Boston: Houghton Mifflin Co., 1928.

Frailing, Robert H. "Bicycle Theft—A Serious Crime." *FBI Law Enforcement Bulletin*, June 1974.

Frankenburg, Lloyd, ed. *A James Stephens Reader*. New York: The Macmillan Company, 1962.

Frost, Robert. "The Wood-Pile." In *The Poetry of Robert Frost*, edited by Edward Connery Lathem. New York: Holt, Rinehart and Winston, 1972.

Galsworthy, John. "Four-in-Hand Forsyte." In *On Forsyte 'Change*. New York: Charles Scribner's Sons, 1930.

Gardner, John. *The Life and Times of Chaucer*. New York: Alfred A. Knopf, 1977.

Gibbings, Robert. *Lovely Is the Lee*. London: J. M. Dent and Sons, 1945.

Grotta-Kurska, Daniel. *J. R. R. Tolkien—Architect of Middle Earth*. New York: Warner Books, 1977.

Guareschi, Giovanni. *The Little World of Don Camillo*. Translated by Una Vincenzo Troubridge. London: Victor Gollancz, 1951.

Halle, Louis, J., Jr. *Spring in Washington*. New York: Atheneum, 1963.

Harasymowicz, Jerzy. "The Bicycle." In *Some Haystacks Don't Even Have Any Needles*, edited by Stephen Dunning, Edward Lueders, and Hugh Smith. Glenview, Ill.: Scott, Foresman and Company, 1969.

Hawthorne, Fred. "Six-Day Bicycle Racing." In *Sport's Golden Age—A Close-up of the Fabulous Twenties*, edited by Allison Danzig and Peter Brandwein. New York: Harper and Brothers, 1948.

Healy, T. M. "On Bicycles: A Speech" (July 7, 1898). In *The Portable Irish Reader*, edited by Diarmuid Russell. New York: The Viking Press, 1966.

Hemingway, Ernest. *By-Line*. New York: Charles Scribner's Sons, 1967.

———. *To Have And Have Not*. London: Penguin Books, 1962.

———. *A Moveable Feast*. New York: Charles Scribner's Sons, 1964.

———. "A Pursuit Race." In *The Short Stories of Ernest Hemingway*. New York: Charles Scribner's Sons, 1966.

———. *The Sun Also Rises*. New York: Charles Scribner's Sons, 1926.

———. "A Way You'll Never Be." In *The Short Stories of Ernest Hemingway*. New York: Charles Scribner's Sons, 1953.

Hoffenstein, Samuel. "Songs to Break the Tedium of Riding a Bicycle, Seeing One's Friends, or Heartbreak." In *Poems in Praise of Practically Nothing*. New York: Garden City Publishing Co., 1939.

Hofstadter, Richard. *The American Political Tradition*. New York: Alfred A. Knopf, 1949.

Holroyd, James Edward. "The Egg-Spoon." *The Sherlock Holmes Journal* 5, no. 2 (1961): 58.

The Holy Bible, Matt. 17: 19–20.

Homewood, Isabel G. *Recollections of an Octogenarian*. London: John Murray, 1934.

Hotchner, A. E. *Papa Hemingway*. New York: Random House, 1966.

Hough, Henry Beetle. *Singing in the Morning*. New York: Simon and Schuster, 1951.

How, Harry. "A Day with Dr. Conan Doyle." *The Strand Magazine*, August 1892, p. 183.

Humphries, H. Trueman. "The Green Bicycle Case." *The Strand Magazine* 63 (February 1922): 136–45.

Hurne, Ralph. *The Yellow Jersey*. New York: Simon and Schuster, 1973.

Huxley, Aldous. *Crome Yellow*. New York: Perennial Library, 1974.

James, P. D. *Black Tower*. New York: Popular Library, 1976.

———. *Death of an Expert Witness*. New York: Charles Scribner's Sons, 1977.

———. *Unnatural Causes*. New York: Popular Library, 1967.

Jarry, Alfred. *The Supermale*. Translated by Ralph Gladstone and Barbara Wright. New York: New Directions Publishing Corp., 1977.

Jerome, Jerome K. *Three Men on the Bummel*. New York: Dodd, Mead and Company, 1900.

Johnson, Uwe. *The Third Book about Achim*. New York: Harcourt Brace Jovanovich, 1967.

Jones, Stephen, ed. *A Flann O'Brien Reader*. New York: The Viking Press, 1978.

Joyce, James. "Grace." In *Dubliners*. New York: The Viking Press, 1972.

———. *A Portrait of the Artist as a Young Man*. New York: The Viking Press, 1962.

———. *Ulysses*. New York: Vintage Books, 1961.

Keefe, Frederick L. *The Bicycle Rider and Six Short Stories*. New York: Delacorte Press, 1970.

Kelly, Fred C. "The Great Bicycle Craze." *American Heritage* 8, no. 1 (1956): 69.

Kendrick, George. *Bicycle Tyre in a Tall Tree*. Cheshire, England: Carcanet Press, 1974.

Knox, Msgr. Ronald. "Studies in the Literature of Sherlock Holmes." In *Essays in Satire*. Fort Washington, N.Y.: Kennikat Press, 1968.

Koch, Kenneth. "To You." In *Contemporary American Poetry*, edited by A. Poulin, Jr. Boston: Houghton Mifflin, 1971.

Lamb, Julia. " 'The Commodore' Enjoyed Life—But New York Society Winced." *Smithsonian*, November 1978, p. 136.

Lardner, Ring. " 'My Kingdom for a Horse,' But Ring Prefers a Bicycle." *San Francisco Examiner*, August 2, 1925, E4.

Lawrence, D. H. *The Fox*. New York: The Viking Press, 1923.

———. *Sons and Lovers*. New York: Michael Kennerley, 1913.

Leblanc, Maurice. *The Extraordinary Adventures of Arsène Lupin, Gentleman-Burglar*. Translated by George Morehead. New York: Dover Publications, 1977.

Lee, Harper. *To Kill a Mockingbird*. New York: J. B. Lippincott Company, 1960.

Leek, Sybil, and Leek, Stephen. *The Bicycle—That Curious Invention*. Nashville, Tenn.: Thomas Nelson, 1973.

Leonard, I. A. *When Bikehood Was in Flower*. Goldenrod, Fla.: Bearcamp Press, 1969.

Lewis, Sinclair. "I'm a Stranger Here Myself." In *The Bachelor's Companion*, edited by Burton Rascoe and Groff Conklin. New York: Reynal and Hitchcock, 1934.

Leys, Simon. *Chinese Shadows*. New York: Penguin Books, 1978.

Lichty and Wagner, "Grin & Bear It." *Washington Post*, June 28, 1978.

Locard, Edmond. *Traité de criminalistique*, vol. 2. Paris: Desvigne, 1931.

London, Jack. *Martin Eden*. New York: The Review of Reviews Company, 1915.

McBain, Ed. *Killer's Choice*. New York: Ballantine Books, 1958.

MacDonald, John D. *Condominium*. Philadelphia: J. B. Lippincott Company, 1977.

———. *The Dreadful Lemon Sky*. New York: J. B. Lippincott Company, 1974.

———. *The Green Ripper*. New York: J. B. Lippincott Company, 1979.

Mace, Bob. "By Enemy Action." *Cycle Touring*, June–July 1978, pp. 121–22.

McGonagle, Seamus. *The Bicycle in Life, Love, War and Literature*. Cranbury, N.J.: A. S. Barnes and Co., 1969.

Mack, John E. *A Prince of Our Disorder: The Life of T. E. Lawrence*. Boston: Little, Brown and Co., 1976.

McPhee, John E. *The Crofter and the Laird*. New York: Farrar, Straus and Giroux, 1970.

Mailer, Norman. *Of a Fire on the Moon*. New York: New American Library, 1971.

Marinoni, Augusto. "The Bicycle." In *The Unknown Leonardo*, edited by Ladislao Reti. New York: McGraw-Hill Book Company, 1974.

Maugham, W. Somerset. *Cakes and Ale*. New York: Random House, 1950.

————. *Of Human Bondage*. New York: Modern Library, 1942.

Mauriac, Francois. *Thérèse*. New York: Doubleday Anchor Book, 1947.

Miller, Henry. "My Best Friend." In *My Bike & Other Friends*. Santa Barbara, Calif.: Capra Press, 1978.

Morand, Paul. "The Six-Day Night." In *Open All Night*. Translated by H. B. V. New York: Thomas Seltzer, 1923.

Moré, Marcel. *Nouvelles Explorations de Jules Verne. Musique, Misogamie, Machine*. Translated by Shauna Russell. Paris: Gallimard, 1963.

Morrow, Dan. "Letter." *The Holmesian Observer* 1, no. 7 (September 1971): 5.

Mulholland, Owen. "Six-Day Racing." *Bicycling*, March 1976, p. 27.

Murdoch, Iris. *The Red and the Green*. New York: The Viking Press, 1965.

————. *The Sandcastle*. London: Chatto and Windus, 1957.

Murray, K. M. Elisabeth. *Caught in the Web of Words*. New Haven: Yale University Press, 1977.

Nabokov, Vladimir. *Glory*. New York: McGraw-Hill Book Company, 1971.

————. *Lolita*. New York: Berkeley Publishing Corporation, 1969.

————. *Mary*. New York: McGraw-Hill Book Company, 1959.

————. *The Real Life of Sebastian Knight*. New York: New Directions, 1959.

————. *Speak, Memory*. Rev. ed. New York: Putnam, 1966.

Naganuma, Kohkl. "On Tires in the Priory School." *The Baker Street Journal* 16 (June 1966): 94, 98.

Narayan, R. K. *The Painter of Signs*. New York: The Viking Press, 1976.

Newman, Bernard. *British Journey*. London: Robert Hale and Company, 1945.

Niven, Larry. *Ringworld*. New York: Ballantine Books, 1975.

O'Brien, Flann. *The Dalkey Archive*. New York: Viking Penguin, 1977.

————. *The Third Policeman*. New York: Walker and Company, 1967.

O'Connor, Frank. "Masculine Protest." In *Masculine Protest and Other Stories from Collection Three*. London: Cox and Wyman, 1977.

O'Faolain, Sean. "Silence of the Valley." In *The Man Who Invented Sin and Other Stories*. New York: The Devin-Adair Company, 1948.

Olyesha, Yuri. "The Bicycle Chain." In *Love and Other Stories*. Translated by Robert Payne. New York: Washington Square Press, 1967.

O'Neill, Eugene. "The Hairy Ape." In *The Plays of Eugene O'Neill*. New York: Random House, 1954.

Oppen, George. "The Bicycles and the Apex." In *Collected Poems*. New York: New Directions, 1975.

Ortega, Jéronimo G. "Blue Bike Brings a Blue Day." In *Voices of Aztlan: Chicano Literature of Today*. New York: New American Library, 1974.

Packard, William, ed. *The Craft of Poetry: Interviews from the New York Quarterly*. New York: Doubleday and Co., 1974.

Pagnol, Marcel. *La Gloire de mon père (Souvenirs d'enfance)*, vol. 1. Monte Carlo: Editions Pastorelly, 1958.

Parker, Stewart. "Spokesong or, the Common Wheel." *Plays and Players Magazine*, December 1976 and January 1977.

Pearson, Hesketh. *Conan Doyle: His Life and Art*. New York: Taplinger Publishing Company, 1977.

Proust, Marcel. *Within a Budding Grove*. Translated by C. K. Scott Moncrieff. New York: Random House, 1951.

Puck 37 (August 7, 1895): 391.

Pynchon, Thomas. *Gravity's Rainbow*. New York: Bantam Books, 1974.

Rand, Stuart C. "What Sherlock Didn't Know?" *The Atlantic*, November 1945, pp. 122–45.

Rapport du Comité d'Etudes Preside par Alain Peyrefitte. "Résponses à la violence." July 1977.

Reid, Alastair. "Whoosh Whoosh Whoosh." In *Passwords*. Boston: Little, Brown and Co., 1963.

Remington, Frederic. "The Colonel of the First Cycle Infantry." *Harper's Weekly*, May 18, 1945.

Rexroth, Kenneth. "The Dragon and the Unicorn." In *The Collected Longer Poems*. New York: New Directions, 1968.

Robbe-Grillet, Alain. *The Voyeur*. New York: Grove Press, 1958.

Robbins, Tom. *Even Cowgirls Get the Blues*. Boston: Houghton Mifflin, 1976.

Roberts, Chalmers M. "New Images of China in a Time of Change." *Washington Post*, December 31, 1978.

Rooney, Frank. "Cyclists' Raid." In *How We Live*, edited by Penney C. Hills and L. Rust Hills. New York: Macmillan Company, 1968.

Russell, Bertrand. *The Autobiography of Bertrand Russell, 1872–1914*. Boston: Little, Brown and Company, 1967.

———. *Portraits from Memory*. London: George Allen and Unwin, 1956.

Ryan, Cornelius. *A Bridge Too Far*. New York: Simon and Schuster, 1974.

Saroyan, William. *The Bicycle Rider in Beverly Hills*. New York: Ballantine Books, 1952.

———. "The Bike." *Good Housekeeping*, February 1952, pp. 652–53.

———. "The Coldest Winter since 1854." In *Little Children*. New York: Harcourt, Brace and Company, 1937.

———. *The Human Comedy*. New York: Harcourt, Brace and Company, 1943.

———. "What a World, Said the Bicycle Rider." *Saturday Evening Post*, November 3, 1962, pp. 42–47.

Sayers, Dorothy L. *Five Red Herrings*. New York: Avon Books, 1968.

———, ed. *The Omnibus of Crime*. New York: Garden City Publishing Co., 1937.

Schulz, Bruno. *The Street of Crocodiles*. Translated by Celina Wieniewska. New York: Penguin Books, 1977.

Sears, Peter. "Place for Four-Letter Words." Source unknown.

Severin, Tim. *The Brendan Voyage*. New York: McGraw-Hill Book Company, 1978.

Shadbolt, Maurice. "Love Story." In *The New Zealanders: A Sequence of Stories*. London: Victor Gollancz, 1960.

Shapiro, David. "The Bicycle Rider." In *An Anthology of New York Poets*. New York: Random House, 1970.

Shattuck, Roger, and Taylor, Simon Watson. "The Passion Considered as an Uphill Bicycle Race." In *Selected Works of Alfred Jarry*. New York: Grove Press, 1965.

Shaw, George Bernard. *Back to Methuselah: A Metabiological Pentateuch*. New York: Dodd, Mead and Company, 1938.

Sillitoe, Alan. "The Bike." In *The Ragman's Daughter*. New York: Alfred A. Knopf, 1964.

———. *The Loneliness of the Long-Distance Runner*. New York: Alfred A. Knopf, 1959.

———. *Saturday Night and Sunday Morning*. New York: Alfred A. Knopf, 1958.

Simenon, Georges. *Maigret Meets a Milord*. London: Penguin Books, 1974.

Sjöwall, Maj, and Wahlöö, Per. *Murder at the Savoy*. New York: Pantheon Books, 1971.

Sloane, Eugene. *The Complete Book of Bicycling*. New York: Trident Press, 1970.

Smith, Robert A. *A Social History of the Bicycle*. New York: American Heritage Press, 1972.

Solzhenitsyn, Aleksandr I. *The Gulag Archipelago, 1918–1956: An Experiment in Literary Investigation*. Translated by Thomas P. Whitney. New York: Harper and Row, 1974.

Stevens, Thomas. *Around the World on a Bicycle*. New York: Charles Scribner's Sons, 1887.

Stowe, Thomas D. "More about Tires in the Priory School." *The Baker Street Journal* 16 (December 1966): 142.

Streuvels, Stijn. *Volledige Werken, Deel 9: Herinneringen*. 't Leieschip Kortryk.

Thomas, Dylan. *Me and My Bike*. New York: McGraw-Hill Book Co., 1965.

———. "Who Do You Wish Was with Us." In *Portrait of the Artist as a Young Dog*. New York: New Directions, 1955.

Thorwald, Jürgen. *Crime and Science*. New York: Harcourt, Brace and World, 1967.

Troyat, Henri. *Tolstoy*. New York: Doubleday and Co., 1967.

Turgenev, Ivan S. "First Love." In *The Borzoi Turgenev*. Translated by Harry Stevens. New York: Alfred A. Knopf, 1955.

Twain, Mark. *A Connecticut Yankee in King Arthur's Court*. New York: Charles L. Webster, 1889.

———. *Pudd'n Head Wilson*. New York: Harper and Brothers, 1922.

Vailland, Roger. *The Law*. Translated by Peter Wiles. London: Jonathan Cape, 1958.

Vining, Ergot. "The Taming of a Medieval Pestilence." *Technology Review* 81 (December 1978–January 1979): 69.

Vonnegut, Kurt, Jr. *Cat's Cradle*. New York: Dell, 1971.

Wain, John. *Born in Captivity*. New York: Alfred A. Knopf, 1954.

Wallechinsky, David; Wallace, Irving; and Wallace, Amy. *The Book of Lists*. New York: Bantam Books, 1978.

Wells, H. G. *Experiment in Autobiography*. New York: Macmillan Company, 1934.

———. *The Wheels of Chance: A Cycling Holiday Adventure*. London: J. M. Dent and Sons, 1896.

West, Elizabeth. *Hovel in the Hills*. London: Faber and Faber, 1977.

White, E. B. *Quo Vadimus? Or the Case for the Bicycle*. New York: Grosset and Dunlap, 1938.

Whitt, F. R. "What Is That Cherub Doing?" *Cycletouring*, April–May 1971, p. 80.

Wilson, David Gordon, and Whitt, Frank R. *Bicycling Science: Ergonomics and Mechanics*. Cambridge, Mass.: M.I.T. Press, 1975.

Wilson, Edmund. *A Piece of My Mind*. New York: Farrar, Straus and Cudahy, 1956.

———. *A Prelude*. New York: Farrar, Straus and Giroux, 1967.

———. *The Twenties*. New York: Farrar, Straus and Giroux 1975.

Yardley, Jonathan. *Ring—A Biography of Ring Lardner*. New York: Random House, 1977.

Young, Jim, and Young, Elizabeth. *Bicycle Built for Two*. Portland, Oregon: Binfords and Mort, 1940.

Index